W9-BFZ-872

Instruction

FOURTH EDITION

Instruction

A Models Approach

Mary Alice Gunter

The University of Virginia

Thomas H. Estes

The University of Virginia

Jan Schwab

Charlottesville Public Schools
Charlottesville, Virginia

Boston   New York   San Francisco
Mexico City   Montreal   Toronto   London   Madrid   Munich   Paris
Hong Kong   Singapore   Tokyo   Cape Town   Sydney

Editor: *Traci Mueller*
Editorial Assistant: *Erica Tromblay*
Marketing Manager: *Amy Cronin*
Editorial Production Administrator: *Deborah Brown*
Composition and Prepress Buyer: *Linda Cox*
Editorial Production Coordinator: *P. M. Gordon Associates*
Electronic Composition: *Peggy Cabot, Cabot Computer Services*
Manufacturing Manager: *JoAnne Sweeney*
Cover Coordinator: *Kristina Mose-Libon*

For related titles and support materials, visit our online catalog at www.ablongman.com.

Between the time Website information is gathered and then published, it is not unusual for some sites to have closed. Also, the transcription of URLs can result in unintended typographical errors. The publisher would appreciate notification where these occur so that they may be corrected in subsequent editions.

To obtain permission(s) to use material from this work, please submit a written request to Allyn and Bacon, Permissions Department, 75 Arlington Street, Boston, MA 02116 or fax your request to 617-848-7320.

Library of Congress Cataloging-in-Publication Data

Gunter, Mary Alice.
      Instruction : a models approach / Mary Alice Gunter, Thomas H. Estes, Jan Schwab.—4th ed.
          p.   cm.
      Includes bibliographical references and index.
      ISBN 0-205-36775-5 (alk. paper)
          1. Teaching. 2. Curriculum planning. 3. Classroom environment. 4. Group work in education. 5. Teachers—In-service training. I. Estes, Thomas H. II. Schwab, Jan Hasbrouck. III. Title.
      LB1025.3 G86 2003
      371.1021—dc21   2002026142

Printed in the United States of America

10 9 8 7 6 5 4 3 2 1   07 06 05 04 03 02

Credits: Pages xxvi, 9, 34, 43, 56, 70, 83, 122, 213, 223, 239, 273, 279, 304, and 345: Shoe cartoons © Tribune Media Services, Inc. All rights reserved. Reprinted with permission. Page 135: "Fog" from *Chicago Poems* by Carl Sandburg, copyright 1916 by Holt, Rinehart and Winston, Inc., renewed 1944 by Carl Sandburg, reprinted by permission of Harcourt Brace & Company.

CONTENTS

14   Cooperative Learning Models: Improving Student Achievement Using Small Groups   256

PREFACE

Teachers today are under unprecedented pressure from all sides. Everyone, it seems, is an expert on teaching. Newspapers and magazines are full of advice about what teachers should do in classrooms, and still more advice comes from sources as varied as legislators and preachers, parents and students, members of school boards, and university professors. Who isn't qualified to speak with authority about schools and teaching? After all, didn't everyone go to school for many years and leave with the full knowledge of how school should have been?

More to the point, perhaps, there is a sense in which everyone *is* a teacher. The root meaning of the word *teach* is "to show, to tell, to point out." Parents *tell* their children what to do; doctors *point out* proper procedures to their patients; auto mechanics may *show* how to make minor adjustments to a car. Everyone teaches others to do things, and so everyone is a teacher, at least in an amateur sense.

Before mistakenly jumping to the conclusion that there is really nothing special or unique about being a teacher, consider the word *teach* in its professional sense, in relation to the word *instruction*. The meaning of the word *instruct* derives from the root "to build" or "to structure." Professional teachers not only *teach* in the usual sense of the word, they also *instruct*. They *structure* classroom environments and *build* series of experiences for students who have wide ranges of abilities, interests, and learning needs. Whereas parents, doctors, and auto mechanics usually teach spontaneously by telling, pointing out, or showing, professional educators must carefully design and plan for their teaching. There is a natural analogy between instruction and building based on the process of structuring environments. The teacher, as an instructor, is comparable to the builder in three ways:

1. *Planning for a specific audience.* The builder and the teacher alike must first determine the needs of their clients. The house required for a family of six with four dogs, three hamsters, and a rabbit will be very different from that for an elderly couple with a parakeet. Similarly, the instructional design for an advanced-placement class in physics will be different from the design for a fifth-grade math class. Both the builder and the teacher must consider their clients, and they need to know how to formulate a plan that will be sound, original, and functional.

A good design for teaching grows out of a clear understanding of the needs of learners and the goals of education. Each design that a professional teacher creates is unique because different groups of learners have individual needs and different types of learning require specific instructional approaches.

2. *Formulating objectives and evaluation procedures.* The needs of their clients will help both the builder and the teacher specify the intended outcome of their work as clearly as possible. No builder would think of starting a construction project without having a clear picture of how the final product should look. To get halfway through the project only to realize that what was emerging was not what the client wanted or needed would be professionally embarrassing and expensive to correct. The teacher who works without a careful design also leaves too much to chance. As a professional, the teacher must plan how to achieve specific, intended learning outcomes. Otherwise, valuable instructional time can go to waste, and neither the teacher nor the students will find satisfaction.

An essential part of setting objectives is determining effective evaluation procedures to make certain that what was intended is taking place. Like the builder who must constantly check on the construction, the teacher must determine whether the instruction is producing the desired results. It would be foolish to wait until a building has been completed to check on the quality of the work and to determine if all is proceeding as planned. Likewise, a teacher must use effective evaluation procedures throughout the teaching process.

Evaluation is continual, forming the basis of all decisions at every step: determining needs, formulating objectives, and selecting materials and methods. Evaluation is the process of continually asking questions such as: Where are we going? How do we get there? How far along are we? The teacher can never stop asking whether the instruction is appropriate and effective. Thus, evaluation showing the intermediate and ultimate results of teaching must be used to reform the process of teaching. Continual evaluation makes this possible.

3. *Selecting materials and procedures.* The builder has available a variety of materials and techniques from which to choose and must decide which combination will produce the structure most nearly like the one intended. Each project must be analyzed to determine the appropriate combinations; for instance, not every house is built only of brick or wood. Likewise, each student is an individual with his or her needs, strengths, and interests. Moreover, each class is unique in terms of the dynamics of a particular group. Therefore, the teacher needs to have at hand a variety of approaches and techniques to accomplish specific instructional objectives and to manage problems as they arise.

Unfortunately, classroom environments are sometimes boring and monotonous, for the teacher and for the students, because there is so little variety in instruction. The teacher who repeatedly uses the same instructional technique is like the builder who can build only one type of house. A repertoire of instructional and management strategies is necessary to meet the varied needs of learners.

Plan for the Text

Since the first edition was published nearly 13 years ago, many experienced teachers and teachers in training have found this text useful. In fact, many teachers have told us that this book has become part of their permanent professional collections. Whenever possible, we have incorporated into this edition the excellent ideas and valuable corrections we have received from classroom teachers who use the models daily.

The philosophy behind this book is that the process of instruction unites all teachers as professional educators. Our intended audience is teachers of any subject who teach or plan to teach learners of any age. We have tried to address teaching as a challenging, exciting, and demanding profession with great rewards for all who follow it.

This text was written not as a rule book but as an invitation to consider the opportunities for professional decision making that constitute instruction. Our goal was to present a variety of intriguing possibilities available to professional educators as they attempt to identify procedures appropriate to situations that arise in the classroom.

Progress toward mastery teaching is a continuous process of learning and adapting, modifying, and changing. The differences between last year's class and this year's, between third period and fourth, between one reading group and another, between the child in the front seat in the second row and the child in the last seat in the corner are the challenges that make instruction a process of seeking solutions and making choices.

We have divided this text into three parts. Part One, Planning for Instruction, centers on a description of the process of setting goals, writing objectives, and designing units. The teacher must decide *what* is to be learned in the classroom before considering *how* to present the material through instruction. A variety of options may be considered in the instructional plan.

Part Two, Matching Objectives to Instruction: A Models Approach, presents a selected group of instructional models along with illustrations of how they can be used in the design process. We are indebted to the many individuals whose research formed the basis for these models. We also relied on our own experience and the experience of many classroom teachers in determining what steps make these models most effective.

Part Three, Putting It All Together: Matching Objectives to Instructional Models, contains four chapters. Three of them are case studies that describe how teachers match objectives to instruction in the design process. We have based these case studies on real experiences and have deliberately structured each to reflect the individuality of those who were a part of the process. Effective teachers do not think and plan in the same way, but they all *do* plan and attend to certain basic requirements. Part Three concludes with a chapter that suggests ways of creating a positive environment for learning in the classroom.

We have included scenarios and case studies in the text to assist instructors in presenting the material. In addition, both exercises and activities appear throughout the book. The exercises are specific, focusing on the particular subject under discussion, and can be completed as the text is read. Answers are provided immediately following each exercise so that the reader may react to suggestions for how the questions could be answered. Activities, in contrast, are more general and usually require that the reader complete them outside the classroom. No answers are provided for the activities, as they require the evaluation of a teacher or a participating group.

Included in this edition are listings of web resources that should prove useful with these models. We also discuss how teachers and students can understand and effectively use these resources. Web resources developed for this text include sample lesson and unit plans together with practical suggestions for using the models. We anticipate that these resources will serve as a valuable aid to both teachers and students who use this text. These resources may be found on the Allyn and Bacon Curriculum and Instruction Supersite (www.ablongman.com/C&I). Talk to your local sales representative to gain access to the site.

Because of the nature of the content of this book, readers can learn only by doing. Thus, ample opportunity must be provided for practice and feedback. Ideally, this would include feedback from peers together with a review of videotaped sequences. No one can learn these models simply from reading about them or memorizing the steps, just as no one can learn to drive a car by reading an owner's manual. An individual must practice a model many times before he or she can be said to "own" the procedure, and it is essential that students be able to prepare lesson plans and units incorporating the models into an instructional design.

We have each had the opportunity to interact daily with both preservice and experienced teachers who are discovering the possibilities of growing professionally through the use of instructional models. We affirm that the models approach provides the tools that enable teachers to make professional decisions about instruction and share these decisions with other professional instructors through a common body of knowledge.

Acknowledgments

Appearing by special invitation in the text is Skyler, a character in the cartoon creation "Shoe" by Jeff McNelly, reprinted by permission of Tribune Media Services. Skyler reminds us that one of the most important characteristics of a successful teacher is a good sense of humor.

We wish to thank all the teachers and students who have used the first three editions of this text and shared their experiences and love of teaching and learning with us.

We would also like to acknowledge those individuals who reviewed this text at various stages. The first edition reviewers are Kent Davis, Purdue University; F. Elizabeth Fridt, Metropolitan State College; Meredith Gall, University of Oregon; Tom Gregory, Indiana University; Howie Jones, University of Houston; Larry Kennedy, Illinois State University; Wayne Mahood, State University of New York at Geneseo; Dennie Smith, Memphis State University; and Patty Wiley, University of Tennessee. The second edition reviewers are Kay Alderman, University of Akron; Thomas Lasley, University of Dayton; and Laurie Pariseau, University of Texas–San Antonio. The third edition reviewers are Mary V. Bicouvaris, Christopher Newport University; Jewell Linville Cress, Northeastern Oklahoma State University; and Ronald C. McClendon, University of Akron. The fourth edition reviewers are Marilyn S. Howe, Clarion University of Pennsylvania, and Patricia Moseley, University of Northern Texas.

Instruction

PART ONE

Planning for Instruction

An old farmer was asked how his family happened to settle in a remote section of Arkansas. He replied, "Well, we were heading for California when Pap took a wrong turn at the Mississippi River."

Pity these travelers, crossing a continent with no map and only a vague notion of their destination. Likewise, for many students and teachers traveling across unfamiliar intellectual terrain, there are wrong turns in the classroom. Too often, students and teachers work without a map in the form of specific plans and without clearly defined objectives for their travels. At the end of a poorly planned lesson or unit, teachers are often let down, not having reached their intended destination. In the classroom, careful planning is essential if students are to enjoy a successful journey toward knowledge and understanding.

The planning process we describe in the following chapters is an interdependent process with overlapping steps. These steps are not a formula to be followed rigidly or even a series to be completed one step after another. In fact, no exact formula or recipe for good instruction exists, although good instruction is founded in good planning. With these caveats in mind, we have listed, in the most general terms, the steps of instructional planning:

1. Set goals and develop a rationale for instruction.
2. Define objectives.
3. Construct a means of evaluation.
4. Create units of study that encompass the content of the course of study.
5. Design lessons for instruction using a variety of instructional models.

These steps are the major topics of the three chapters in Part One of this text. Step 1 is discussed in Chapter 1, "Describing Educational Goals." Steps 2 and 3 are discussed in Chapter 2, "Determining Educational and Instructional Objectives." Steps 4 and 5 are discussed in Chapter 3, "Organizing Content."

Planning for instruction is a continual process, and the steps of planning overlap. Some procedures for instructional design that can help in this process are covered in Part One. It is each reader's responsibility to determine the ways in which he or she will implement these procedures. What is not optional is the incorporation of a serious planning process into every teacher's approach to instruction.

1 Describing Educational Goals

The Learner, Society, and the Subject Matter

Overhead in the teacher's lounge was this comment: "I have two goals in teaching. My short-term goal is Friday and my long-term goal is June." Busy teachers may feel that they have no time to think about the goals of education. Often, the pressure of just "getting the job done" seems overwhelming. Teachers and prospective teachers usually ask for techniques or rules on *how* to teach before determining *what* students need to be taught. Effective teaching, however, must begin with a determination of appropriate educational goals. Some goals are predetermined, and some are left to the teacher to decide.

Setting Goals

Goals provide an essential vision for the future of the educational process. They set the standards by which to measure our success as educators. Lorin Anderson and David Krathwohl define educational goals or global objectives as "complex, multifaceted learning outcomes that require substantial time and instruction to accomplish."[1]

Educational goals are general statements of intent that reflect (1) the needs of the learner, (2) the societal purpose of schooling, and (3) the subject matter to be learned. The ability to consider, express, and incorporate these various goals in planning for teaching is one of the defining qualities of a professional educator.

The Needs of Learners

Concern for students must be the foundation of all instructional planning. No matter how interesting or relevant information may be or how enthusiastic the teacher is about the subject, learners must be willing and able to learn. If teaching does not result in learning, then it fails. If, however, teaching has the effect of engaging learners in the process of understanding, of bringing learners into close contact with what the teacher wants them to learn, and of giving learners an opportunity to explain what they understand, then learning is likely to occur. These are the needs of the learner:

1. Meaningful engagement in the process of learning
2. Direct contact with what is to be learned (to the greatest possible extent)
3. Opportunity to explain his or her understandings
4. Creative evaluation that tests what was taught

Background Knowledge.   There is probably nothing more important to new learning than prior knowledge. An informal assessment of the prior knowledge of students in relation to what they are expected to learn is essential to good planning and teaching. Successful learning often depends on making a connection between what the learner already knows and what he or she is trying to understand, regardless of innate ability or past performance.

Teachers can use many methods to determine what students know. A simple way is to ask the class, "If you were going to write a book (or book chapter) on this topic, what ideas and information would you be sure to include?" A group of students who are brainstorming ideas will often reveal an impressive array of understandings, expectations, and background knowledge. Another way to probe for background knowledge is to ask students to write a key word in the center of a sheet of paper and then surround that key word with all of the ideas that come to mind when they think of this word. This technique, called *clustering*, is often used by teachers of writing because of its effectiveness in drawing out ideas in preparation for writing. In the same manner, it can serve to draw out ideas in preparation for learning and to establish a base onto which new learning can be built.

Regardless of the technique used, describing their prior knowledge serves to give learners a part in the preparation for what they are about to undertake. The sense of ownership that results will go a long way toward ensuring the success of teaching and learning.

Learning Styles.   Research on learning styles[2] has verified that people learn differently. Even though most people can learn in various ways, they have preferences for how they like to learn and perhaps how they learn best. For instance, some people are reflective and intuitive; others are more impulsive and spontaneous. Some respond to material presented in a logical order; others learn better through unstructured problem solving. Some students learn better through listening; others learn better by reading or viewing films. Some prefer to learn alone; others learn better in groups. Some students prefer to be given the rule and then examples; others prefer to formulate the rule for themselves after a presentation of examples.

There are at least four different learning style preferences,[3] including the following:

- The Myers-Briggs Type Indicator, which classifies learners on dimensions of extrovert/introvert, sensor/intuitor, thinker/feeler, and judger/perceiver
- The Kolb learning style model, which distinguishes concrete/reflective, abstract/reflective, abstract/active, and concrete/active learning

- The Hermann Brain Dominance Instrument, which classifies learners along preferences for thinking in four different modes, based on the task-specialized functioning of the physical brain
- The Felder-Silverman learning style model, which categorizes learners along dimensions of sensing/intuiting, visual/verbal, inductive/deductive, active/reflective, and sequential/global

Regardless of the system chosen for looking at the issue of learning styles, the following is true: Teachers who teach in ways that allow for the same subject matter to be learned in different ways help to balance students' achievement across different learning preferences.

Multiple Intelligences.   Early research on intelligence established a paradigm that limited the concept of intelligence to an IQ score expressed as dual ratios of verbal test and quantitative test scores to age. This narrow view of intelligence has led to mistaken and pervasive judgments of people and a theory of hereditary limits that Stephen Gould[4] has called "the mismeasure of man." Not only do learners have preferences for how they learn, but research conducted over the past 15 years has affirmed that there are more kinds of intelligences than was previously thought, with more being added as this line of research continues.

Howard Gardner[5] is the researcher most responsible for this paradigm shift to multiple intelligences. Rather than limiting the concept of intelligence to a singular, heritable entity expressed as an IQ score, Gardner and his associates in a Harvard University project called Project Zero have described at least nine categories of intelligences:

1. *Linguistic intelligence:* Ability to use words effectively both orally and in writing
2. *Logical-mathematical intelligence:* Ability to use numbers effectively
3. *Spatial intelligence:* Ability to perceive and to graphically represent the visual-spatial world
4. *Bodily kinesthetic intelligence:* Ability to use one's whole body to express ideas and feelings
5. *Musical intelligence:* Ability to discriminate, transform, and express musical forms
6. *Interpersonal intelligence:* Ability to perceive the moods, intentions, and feelings of others
7. *Intrapersonal intelligence:* Ability to act on the basis of accurate self-knowledge
8. *Naturalistic intelligence:* Ability to appreciate the subtle distinctions of nature and the outdoors
9. *Existentialist intelligence:* Ability to see humankind in relation to the big picture of all existence[6]

The implication of the research on multiple intelligences is that what matters most is "not how smart you are, but how you are smart."[7] Dr. Gardner affirms that most people have several of these intelligences in which they are strongest and others in which they may be only marginally strong, but he also contends that all intelligences can be developed in most individuals to a relatively high degree. Teachers can use the concept of multiple intelligences to enhance students' understandings in three important ways:

- By providing multiple points of entry to every topic
- By offering multiple analogies to every topic
- By providing multiple representations of the central or core ideas of every topic in the curriculum[8]

The Learning Styles–Multiple Intelligences Connections.   In relating learning-styles research with the intelligences, Thomas Armstrong asserts that "a person's learning style is *the intelligences put to work.*"[9] For example, a child who learns best through drawing pictures or working with computer programs containing graphics may have a highly developed spatial intelligence.

Students with different learning-style preferences and different strengths in the intelligences require different instructional approaches. All students need to learn in more than one way to develop their potential. The more the teacher knows about the learning styles and the intelligences of the students, the more he or she is able to plan a variety of instructional approaches. If a teacher cannot vary instruction to meet this variety of needs, many students will be left out of the instructional process. The models presented in Part Two provide this essential variety.

The Brain and Learning.   Some needs of learners are predetermined by the nature of the organ of learning, the human brain. Caine and Caine[10] describe 12 principles of brain-based learning, facts about the human brain, with implications for teaching and learning. We summarize those principles, borrowed from Chapter 7 of Caine and Caine's book, as part of our statement on the needs of learners. The principles are theirs; the comments following each principle are ours.

1. *The brain is a parallel processor.* The brain is always performing many tasks at once, such as regulating bodily functions, allocating attention, and processing information from multiple sources. The implication for instruction is that good teaching "orchestrates" the learner's experience of many things—what the learner sees, what the learner hears, and so on—simultaneously.

2. *Learning engages the entire physiology.* Whatever affects the physical well-being of the learner, from lighting and temperature to the feelings of safety and cheer, affects learning. The implication for instruction is that teachers must take "creature comfort" into account when planning and orchestrating learning, must control those factors that can be controlled, and must do whatever possible to take advantage of, or alleviate, other factors.

3. *The search for meaning is innate.* Learning is necessarily an active brain process, and the activity can be called "meaning-making." The ingredients of meaning are prior knowledge and new information, which combine to create new understandings meaningful to the learner. The implication for teaching is *not* to transmit knowledge directly to the learner, but to engage with the learner in an active, collaborative construction of meaning, much like that which occurs in everyday conversation.[11]

4. *The search for meaning occurs through patterning.* Information to be learned becomes meaningful when the learner is able to perceive or impose a pattern upon it. When the learner finds connections between what is being learned and what is already known or when the learner can categorize information into previously existing "slots," then that information becomes meaningful. The implication for teaching is that the teacher may facilitate learning by exploring connections and categorizations with learners through a process of sorting and classifying. For example, an effective instructional conversation about the topic *mammals* would include questions such as "What sort of animal is a mammal?" and "What sorts of mammals are there?"

5. *Emotions are crucial to patterning.* It might be said that caring drives cognition; that is, learners think most deeply about and learn more easily those things they care about. The implication for teaching is that the teacher must take students' attitudes and dispositions into account in planning instruction.

6. *The brain processes parts and wholes simultaneously.* Right brain/left brain thinking is merely a metaphor, a way of thinking about the way the brain learns. According to this metaphor, the left half of the brain understands information in parts, or by taking information apart, whereas the right half of the brain understands information in wholes, or by putting information together. The left half knows the words of the song, and the right half knows the tune. Because singing requires both the words and tune, the music is incomplete when one of these components is missing. Fortunately, the human brain is inclined to grasp parts and wholes simultaneously. The implication for teaching is that the teacher must help learners keep perspective: Teach the big picture and the parts that make it up, both at the same time.

7. *Learning involves both focused attention and peripheral perception.* The brain processes information straight on and from the side. Part of this process is what learners think they see, and part is what they see without thinking. If this were not so, an activity such as driving a car would be much more dangerous than it is. The implication for teaching is that the teacher must pay almost as much attention to what students will experience indirectly as to what they will experience directly. The design of the classroom, the "music" (literally and figuratively) that pervades the atmosphere of learning, either contributes to learning or impedes it.

8. *Learning always involves conscious and unconscious processes.* The expression "to sleep on it" reflects folk wisdom, insinuating that information needs to percolate before it can be understood. Do you notice that trying hard to remember something may actually keep you from remembering and that as soon as you stop trying so hard, you remember? This occurs because much of what the brain does is completely unconscious and unknown to us. The implication for teaching is that because understanding takes time (by some estimates, up to 3 weeks for some learning), time for reflection and contemplation should be built into instructional plans.

9. *We have at least two different types of memory: a spatial memory system and a set of systems for rote learning.* What did you have for breakfast this morning? The answer to that question requires no rehearsal and relies on no conscious learning. Even if your answer is "I didn't have breakfast," you know the answer without having learned it. It is part of your spatial learning, so-called because it occurs in three-dimensional space—in this case, where you eat breakfast every morning.

What is the square root of 25? This question probably requires at least 1 or 2 seconds longer to answer than the breakfast question, if indeed you remember the meaning of a square root. This time, the question calls for information from rote memory, memories formed deliberately through rehearsal. (We are not using the word *rote* pejoratively, but merely to describe one kind of memory and learning.) The human brain is capable of both spatial learning and rote learning, the major difference being that one kind of learning requires more effort than the other. The implication for teaching is that where rote knowledge is required, the teacher will want to provide plenty of time for rehearsal and application so that information will be firmly remembered.

10. *We understand and remember best when facts and skills are embedded in natural, spatial memory.* Increased emphasis on spatial learning is one important way in which education can be improved. Imagine a life science class that focuses on the world in which the child lives—the neighborhood, the backyard, and the stream that runs behind the school playground. Imagine that all reading, writing, and discussion about living things stemmed from the questions that arose from observations that learners made of the world around them. This exists in many classrooms today, where teachers have grasped the implication that what a learner can experience spatially, in three dimensions, can be understood in the abstract much more readily than rote learning can be understood in the abstract.

11. *Learning is enhanced by challenge and inhibited by threat.* There is perhaps a subtle distinction to be drawn here; what is a challenge to one learner may be a threat to another. The difference results from how the brain responds, not from what actually occurs. The brain responds to threat with a "fight or flight" reaction—resist or remove oneself from the threatening circumstance. Although challenge is always accompanied by risk to one's self-esteem or success, the learner will thrive in what Caine and Caine call "relaxed alertness." The implication for teaching is that students should perceive no risk in what they are asked to learn. Yet, mistakes are natural in the early stages of learning, and learners need to feel comfortable about making such mistakes. Grades, for example, should be based on the final results of learning, not on intermediate attempts.

12. *Each brain is unique.* As Robert Fulghum, the popular essayist, put it: "The single most powerful statement to come out of brain research in the last twenty-five years is this: *We are as different from one another on the inside of our heads as we appear to be from one another on the outside of our heads.*"[12] The implication for teaching is that teachers need to be completely open to infinite possibilities in learners; that is, they should expect that there will be great diversity in understandings of what they teach. Perhaps we will all have to give up the notion that everyone will have the same answer or that there is any one answer worth having.

Special Needs. In every classroom there are children with special needs. With the advent of inclusion and growing emphasis on the least-restrictive environment, children with many different kinds of disabilities have entered the general education classroom. Some disabilities are easily identified by observation; others are less obvious. For instance, some children are extremely gifted, a condition that is often disabling because these children may feel left out and different from the group. Thus every teacher needs to be something of a special education teacher to meet the needs of all children scheduled into the standard curriculum.

Even among children who are not identified as having special needs, there are many factors that cause a wide disparity of development in children of the same age. Although there are predictable stages of children's growth and development—physically, intellectually, socially, and morally—one child may be intellectually advanced and physically slow in development whereas another may have well-developed social skills and yet have problems with physical coordination.

In addition, boys and girls of the same age obviously have different patterns of development. In a sixth-grade classroom, most males still look like little boys, while about half of the females look like young women. Girls are usually taller, stronger, and more verbal than boys. As teachers set goals for the curriculum, they need to be conscious of the many ways that children differ from one another.

Societal Needs

State and federal agencies, local school boards, and individual schools often set broad educational goals applicable to all courses and toward which all teachers are expected to direct their instruction. These might be called the *macro goals* of education. These statements were once a very general and noncontroversial outlining of the purposes of schooling to which a majority of people would presumably agree. In earlier editions of this text, for instance, we listed the following examples of seven goals:

1. Develop competence in the basic learning skills.
2. Learn to cherish the foundations of a free society.
3. Develop ethical standards of behavior.
4. Develop skills necessary to obtain productive employment or to continue higher education.

5. Gain respect for one's body and value good health habits.
6. Come to value beauty and learn to participate in some form of aesthetic expression.
7. Achieve progress commensurate with his or her ability.

Today, goals such as these, which once seemed "general and noncontroversial," are the source of controversy in many states. If computer literacy is now a basic skill, what about the children who attend schools that have no computers? Can we any longer agree on the foundations of our free society? For instance, is the separation of church and state one of those foundations? Where does the extremely volatile issue of sex education fit into ethical standards of behavior, respecting one's body, and valuing good health habits? Increasingly, we seem to be uncertain about our goals as a society and thus divided about educational goals for our children.

This situation creates unprecedented problems for local schools and for individual teachers. A change of administration at the state or local level may dramatically alter the directions set by a previous administration. The trend toward using the public schools for ideological ends has become more pronounced. For instance, guidance counselors may be deemed unnecessary or sex education eliminated as the result of an election. In many situations, teachers find themselves limited by an increasing reliance on standardized test scores as the sole measure of instructional success.

In a time when societal goals regarding education are confused, it is essential that every teacher understand the limitations imposed by this situation and consider carefully the possibilities open to the individual. It is important to remember that the decisions one makes as a teacher on how best to teach students and what subject matter and concepts they can best learn will be made within certain imposed limitations. State legislatures, superintendents of public instruction, parents, school boards, and courts can and do say much about what will and will not be taught in schools.

Subject Matter Content

Subject matter content is increasingly dominated by the standards movement. Although it is still possible in some subject areas and in some locales for the teacher to make major decisions regarding the subject matter to be taught, testing programs aligned with national, state, and local standards make it imperative to teach to the tests.

The history of the current standards movement in American schools begins with the 1983 publication of *A Nation at Risk* by the National Commission on Excellence in Education. This short book, like nothing that had come before it, excited both the lay public and professionals in education. Few sentences in the canon of educational literature have been as often repeated as the dire warning it posited with the following words:

> The educational foundations of our society are presently being eroded by a rising tide of mediocrity that threatens our very future as a nation and a people. . . . We have, in effect, been committing an act of unthinking, unilateral educational disarmament.[13]

The nation rallied in the cause of excellence to mount a war on mediocrity. States and professional education organizations began immediately to develop new content standards and curriculum frameworks. In 1989, 1996, and 1999, major education summits were held at which most state governors, educators, and business leaders came together. At each of these meetings, the major accomplishment was to identify academic standards to combat specific educational problems, including underachievement, the teacher shortage, and the question of accountability for all parties in the educational system. Although some of the reaction to *A Nation at Risk* was more reactionary than reasonable, for the most part the sustained attention to standards has had several good effects. Among these positive effects are the following:

- Every state but one, Iowa, has adopted standards for its schools.
- Most schools in our nation now operate with a more clearly defined mission.
- Children who need special attention to help them reach specific goals are more likely to get that attention.
- A heightened expectation of success has bred success in many schools, where the expectation of failure previously bred failure.
- The collection of longitudinal data on students, using a consistent and repeatable assessment, has helped states and local schools to improve their efficiency and effectiveness.[14]
- A common set of standards provides the basis for everyone's understanding of what is to be taught and what kind of performance is to be expected.[15]

Now that we have entered a new millennium, the news to report regarding improvements in the accomplishments of the nation's schools is mixed. The publication *The State of State Standards*[16] offers a state-by-state report card. It must be read with care, however: Because no consensus exists as to what form standards should take or how they should be used, cross-state comparisons will always put apples and oranges in the same basket. Whatever judgment one might make of the results presented, it cannot be disputed that many people are engaged in the effort to improve the nation's schools, with the best of intentions and often-positive effects. Many of these effects are documented in the September 2001 issue of *Educational Leadership*, which is wholly devoted to the theme "Making Standards Work." Readers are encouraged to view the contents of this issue and take advantage of a fee-based download of each of the articles at http://www.ascd.org/infocon/, the Association for Supervision and Curriculum Development's web portal to all of its publications.

The Mid-continent Research for Education and Learning (McREL) has now published the third edition of *Content Knowledge: A Compendium of Standards and Benchmarks for K–12 Education*,[17] perhaps the best single source of information on the standards movement. By reviewing 137 national- and state-level documents addressing standards and benchmarks across 14 areas of study, the authors of this indispensable resource, John Kendall and Robert Marzano, have identified more than 250 standards and 3,900 benchmarks. These are organized by type of standard, grade level, and subject area. As a resource for creating new standards or for validating existing standards, *Content Knowledge* is the most appropriate beginning point.

A second indispensable reference can be found on the web site of Putnam Valley Central Schools.[18] The site provides a continually updated index to information about educational standards and curriculum frameworks from national, state, and local sources. This is the primary resource for an exhaustive listing of information on standards-based education.

A third set of resources that are invaluable for anyone developing standards includes the national standards documents provided by subject area organizations. Many of these are now available on line. Where that is the case, we have provided the URL for the document listed:

- National Council of Teachers of English and the International Reading Association. *Standards for the English Language Arts*. Urbana, IL: National Council of Teachers of English, 1996. Ordering information available at: http://www.ncte. org/standards/
- National Council for the Social Studies. *Expectations of Excellence: Curriculum Standards for Social Studies*. National Council for the Social Studies, 1994. Ordering information available at: http://www.socialstudies.org/standards/
- National Council for History Education. *Reinvigorating History in U.S. Schools: Reform Recommendations for the States*. Westlake, OH: National Council for History Education, 1996. Available at: http://www.history.org/nche/
- National Council of Teachers of Mathematics. *Principles and Standards for School Mathematics*. Reston, VA: National Council of Teachers of Mathematics, 2000. Available at: http://standards.nctm.org/document/prepost/cover.htm
- American Association for the Advancement of Science (AAAS). *Science for All Americans*. American Association for the Advancement of Science, 1990. Available at: http://www.project2061.org/tools/sfaaol/sfaatoc.htm (See also AAAS's *Benchmarks for Science Literacy*, available at: http://www.project2061.org/tools/benchol/bolframe.htm)
- National Research Council. *National Science Education Standards*. National Academy Press, 1996. Available at either: http://www.nap.edu/readingroom/books/nses/html/ or in PDF format at: http://www.nap.edu/readingroom/books/nses/html/acrobat.html

Not surprisingly, as we near the twentieth anniversary of the National Commission on Excellence in Education's warning of the rising tide of mediocrity, the heralded standards movement has proven more glacial than revolutionary. It has been aptly said that "Good ideas and strong public support do not guarantee successful and widespread improvement [of education]. The key is in the execution—the translation of the broad goals upon which we agree into policies and practices that play out in the classroom."[19] There are many obstacles to rapid reform of a system as diverse as American education. Although the citizens of our country, on the whole, want schools to adhere to standards, troubling questions will always surround the effort to set those standards: Who shall set the standards? Shall standards be for all students alike, despite differences in cultural and linguistic backgrounds? Shall the accountability for these standards be rigidly applied, or should schools provide alternative educational channels for students with different life goals and academic gifts? These kinds of questions are not easy to answer, but through asking them, educators must at least confront anew the problems and challenges of their profession.

EXERCISE 1.1

Label each of the following goal statements with an *L* if the focus is *predominantly* on the learner, an *SO* if the focus is on a societal need, or an *SU* if the focus is on the subject matter.

1. Students will practice sound habits of personal health.
2. Students will recognize major American writers.
3. Students will acquire lifetime learning skills.
4. Students will practice principles of good citizenship.
5. Students will appreciate beauty and participate in aesthetic activities.
6. Students will acquire the basic skills of reading, writing, and computer literacy.
7. Students will increase their sense of personal integrity and self-worth.
8. Students will respect the rights of others.

Answers to Exercise 1.1
Some of the goal statements seem to have more than one focus. For instance, basic skills of reading, writing, and computer literacy are certainly essential as societal goals as well as for the learner. Goal statements 1, 3, 5, and 7, however, seem to focus primarily on the learners; statements 4 and 8 are essentially societal goals; and statements 2 and 6 are oriented more toward subject matter. ■

ACTIVITY 1.1

To avoid the possibility of setting student goals that are unrealistic or reflect unexamined values, consider the following: (1) the society in which your students live and will live in the future, (2) the conceptual and factual framework of the subject matter you are prepared to teach, and (3) the aspirations you have for the students you will teach.

- If you are in secondary or middle school education, describe a course you would like to teach or one that you are currently teaching. Try to word your course description to account for the interaction of society, the subject matter, and learner needs.
- If you are in elementary education, focus on one of the subjects you teach. Explain why you believe this subject is worth knowing. Is it useful to your students? How will it make their lives better, make them more productive, and enhance their future? Can all your students benefit from this knowledge?
- As a student preparing to teach, think of the age and ability of the students you are most interested in teaching. What do you believe the world will be like

when your students are mature adults? Will the subject matter that you teach be important in the future, or will it be obsolete? ▪

Developing a Rationale

Activity 1.1, which asked you to consider the fundamental reasons for teaching what you want to teach, should help you formulate a statement of justification for any course or subject you want to teach. Such an exposition of the logical basis behind setting particular objectives and teaching specific content is a *rationale*. One method of clarifying teaching goals is to expand the goals into the form of a rationale, usually a three- to five-paragraph statement of reasons for the choice of goals, objectives, and subject matter. The rationale incorporates the goals and refines them into a description of the subject or course (see Figure 1.1).

Examples of Course Rationales

The following example, entitled "Our Window on the World," is an appropriate course rationale written by a teacher for a sixth-grade science class:

> The focus of the science program this year will be on the wonderful world outside our window. From our classroom we can see a field, a stream, and a small stand of trees. Weekly field trips to this area will focus on the study of ecosystems.

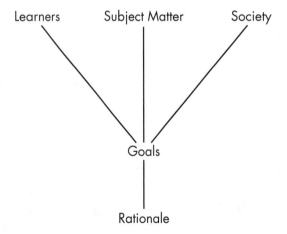

FIGURE 1.1   Sources for a Rationale

Sixth-graders are just beginning to deal with abstractions; concepts such as interdependence and community can best be understood by actually experiencing and observing situations in which they exist. This study will allow the students to spend more time moving about and being outdoors—activities important to these young adolescents.

The skills of data gathering and analysis will be emphasized throughout this course. Each child will maintain a record of the experiments and observations that are conducted. In cooperation with the language arts teacher, the children will be writing about their experiences, drawing from this record of their observations.

Other teachers will also play a part in this instruction. The art teacher has agreed to teach several lessons in sketching natural observations so that artwork can be a part of students' records. Graphs and charts, which they are learning in math, will be incorporated into this study, and the social studies teacher has agreed to utilize this experience in discussing the effects of environment on various parts of our history.

Understanding the world in which we live is essential to our survival, and the world outside our window is the world we can influence the most. Helping the children view that world with wonder, enthusiasm, and concern will be a major goal of this course.

This rationale displays an awareness of the physical, social, and cognitive needs of the learners. It also includes a statement of the manner in which interdisciplinary studies will be brought into the course. The importance of learning this material is explained, and the essential concepts and skills are described. As the teacher selects and develops the units of this course and designs the instructional plan, this rationale will be a guide.

A similar plan might be written for a seventh-grade social studies class in an urban environment. Consider a unit with the title "Our Window on the World" in the context of a school located in a metropolitan area.

The students will use our city as a resource for their social studies this year. Every city is rich in stories about people and events with which students can identify. Walking trips with a camera will enable students to photograph people and places, which will provide rich resource material for reading and writing activities in class.

For instance, near the school is a public park named for a famous Civil War general. This park should provide many opportunities for historical research. Many buildings and parks in the city are named for outstanding local and national historical figures who will have prominent places in our studies. Interviews with family members who have lived in the city for many years will provide a basis for historical biographies that will be assembled as part of a class history project. For those students who do not have family members who have lived in the city for a long time, interviews with long-term residents will be arranged. Ethnic differences will be explored, and the students will be encouraged to discover how their families came to the United States. Research and reporting techniques will be stressed as a part of this experience.

By concentrating on the world outside the windows of the school building, we will emphasize that history is a real experience that affects the lives of us all, not something that exists only in books. Urban young people often hear only of the problems of their environment rather than of the rich legacy of people and events that make up their world.

Writing a convincing and appropriate rationale is not easy. The following excerpts from three sample rationales contain some potential problems. As you read them, think what each reveals about the values and the beliefs of the writers regarding the learners, the subject, and society. What problems with instruction do you anticipate for each writer? Each excerpt has some positive aspects, but you should spot some problems.

Rationale for a Ninth-Grade General English Class in an Urban Area

I plan to transmit my love for Shakespeare to the students in my class. The Bard continues to gain in significance, and these young people can feel themselves in touch with generations past as they read the immortal words of Hamlet and quake at the evil deeds of Lady Macbeth. Some believe that Shakespeare is too difficult and too demanding for young people, but I can transcend their reluctance and win the students over to the magnificent stories and the fascinating characters. The students will be immersed in the language and in the times of the Elizabethans. What better way to improve the quality and the fluency of today's culturally illiterate young people?

In this first example, the teacher's love for her subject, particularly Shakespeare, is evident, and such enthusiasm will probably be evident to the students. The question is, can ninth-graders identify as quickly with Hamlet and Macbeth as can a person who has spent years studying literature? It is easy to forget that novices to a subject need to be introduced gradually to its finer points. Students asked to plunge in too deeply at first may develop a distaste for the subject that can never be altered. If love for a subject or a particular part of that subject overshadows consideration of the learner, the teacher may be asking for trouble. One way the teacher might have considered introducing Shakespeare is by starting with plays such as *Romeo and Juliet*, with its obvious parallels in *West Side Story* and contemporary news of gang violence in U.S. cities, or *A Midsummer Night's Dream*, with its playful fantasy. Both of these plays would be better suited to young adolescents, but they will still need to be taught with care and consideration to learners who will find Shakespeare's language anachronistic.

Rationale for a Fifth-Grade Math Program in a Farming Community

The purpose of math instruction for this year will center on understanding mathematical principles and concepts. Math is the key to understanding the universe, and the children will develop an appreciation for the subtleties and excitement of the wonderful world of mathematics. Once the principles have been mastered, the children can apply these to problems encountered in the world around them. Because space exploration is such an interesting topic today, problems will be drawn from the space program. Math can be learned and loved by all students; it is simply a matter of dedication and perseverance.

In this second selection, the teacher assumes that fifth-graders are extremely interested in the space program and that the quality of their lives depends on knowing about the program. Fifth-graders in a farming community may be more interested in problems close at hand than in adventures in outer space. What is interesting and fascinating to adults may be less interesting to children. In addition, an approach to mathematics that is completely oriented toward an understanding of principles may be inappropriate in a community that demands practical application of those principles.

Rationale for a Science Class in a University Community

This course will focus on a balanced presentation regarding the creation of life on this planet, including both the theories of evolution and the biblical theory of creation. It is shockingly anti-intellectual to accept only the theory of evolution and reject a viable alternative.

This teacher would certainly be safe in this approach if teaching in a private religious school that espoused this conviction or even in a public school where community goals on this issue were consistent with those of the teacher. In many circumstances, however, the presentation of biblical accounts belongs in a literature class or a religious studies class.

ACTIVITY 1.2

Consider a course you would like to teach or are currently teaching, and write a rationale incorporating your goals. Make clear your beliefs about the learners in the class, the importance of this subject to the students' lives, the emphasis and focus of the subject matter, and the skills most needed by these students. Do not try to describe specific instructional techniques or units, but define your overall goals for the course. When you have finished, share your rationale with the class or with a colleague. Analyze the content to see that your goals are compatible with the needs of the learners, the expectations of society, and the demands of subject matter. ■

Matching Rationales to Learning Environments

The following descriptions cover a variety of learning environments. As you read, analyze each situation described and consider the unique needs of the students—academic, career, and personal. Also consider the community in which the school is located and how the social forces within the community affect education. Assess how your own subject matter specialty could be used best to meet the varying needs in each situation.

I. Hancock is an inner-city middle school (grades 6–8). Located in a once-affluent neighborhood, the school building is a heavy, gray pile of stone surrounded by decrepit Victorian houses. Half the students are bused in from a large public housing project; many others walk from an old Italian American neighborhood. The building, once a high school, contains a massive auditorium and gymnasium, both of which have been closed to conserve heat. Vandalism in the building is a problem. The rate of teacher turnover is high, but some dedicated staff members have been at the school for years. Drug use in the school is a problem, and gang fights are frequent. Many families of students at Hancock, however, strongly support the school and their children's education.

II. Baylor is a small farming community in New Hampshire. Most of the families have lived in New England for generations. There is no movie theater or shopping center in the village. The general store and a local lake are the gathering places for the young. The teenagers often drive to a larger city 30 miles away in search of entertainment.

There is a small college in the area, and many faculty members send their children to the local school. In addition, the town's economy depends on a local lumber company, farms, and several small businesses. The white frame school buildings are overcrowded, and several bond issues to build new ones have failed. Despite the beauty of the village, most of the young people choose to leave; opportunities for careers in the community are limited. In general, children of the college professors go to college and the others go to work in factories.

III. Valdez Unified School System is on a remote desert Indian reservation. The pay scale for teachers is well below average for the county. Ninety-six percent of the children are eligible for free breakfast and lunch, meaning that the income of their families is below poverty level. In fact, 60 percent of the adult male population of Valdez is unemployed, and those who are employed commute 65 miles to relatively low-paying jobs. Alcoholism is the major social problem. Most homes have electricity and running water, but few have indoor toilet facilities. The average life span of the people on the reservation is 30 percent lower than that of the general population.

English is the first language of the children and most of their parents; most grandparents speak only their native language. Few children attend school beyond high school, and only two-thirds graduate from high school. Eighth-grade graduation is a very big social event.

The purpose of school in this setting is a point of debate. Preparing children to leave the reservation and take a place in the major (white) culture is tantamount to cultural genocide. Yet, staying on the reservation, for most people, is a dead-end choice because there is little upward mobility possible there.

IV. Jefferson School District is an affluent suburb near a large city. The median family income is high, but many non–English speaking children have entered the school district in the last 10 years. The school division's interpretation of federal laws is to provide programs to include children in general education classroom settings as rapidly as possible. Some parents of these children believe that their cultural heritage should be preserved; others feel that their children should be absorbed into the majority culture quickly.

Language barriers hinder many of the parents in their search for employment, and the crime rate in the community is rising. Some affluent families have moved their children to private schools.

ACTIVITY 1.3

Now, imagine that you are in each of these school environments. Bear in mind that the macro goals of any state department of education could easily be the same for each school district, but specific instructional goals will differ at the school district, building, and classroom levels.

Select two districts and write goal statements for your subject or main area of teaching, based on the information given for each school district. Remember that goals are general statements expressing your philosophical beliefs and values; they also reflect the needs of the students you will be teaching, the society in which you will teach, and the application of the subject matter. Consider the need for an examination of your personal values in light of each school's environment and the particular needs of the students. Finally, look at the rationale you wrote for Activity 1.2. Would you make any changes or adjustments if you were a teacher in any one of these school districts? ■

Summary

In determining instructional goals, the teacher should consider (1) the needs of the learners, (2) the nature and needs of the society in which the students are presently living and the one(s) in which they will live as adults, and (3) the requirements of the subject matter to be taught. Goals stated in the form of a rationale help teachers clarify this process and focus on the essential components of the curriculum. This examination must be ongoing, because society, the learners, and the subject matter are continually changing, as are the needs and the interests of the teacher.

WEB RESOURCES

1. http://www.surfaquarium.com/im.htm

This site is maintained by Walter McKenzie of Surfaquarium Consulting. It provides a link to a National Education Association interview with Howard Gardner, a ready-to-use multiple intelligences inventory, Gardner's criteria for identifying an intelligence, and dozens of useful links, many of them teaching ideas related to the nine intelligences.

2. http://www.multi-intell.com/

Use this site to explore multiple intelligences from the vantage of four questions: *What is multiple intelligence? Where is it being implemented? What resources are available?* and *What training opportunities exist?* This site provides a portal to everything you want to know about multiple intelligences but may not know how to ask.

3. http://www.newhorizons.org/bibmishelf.html

This site provides up-to-date information on the seminal research on multiple intelligences, Project Zero at the Harvard University Graduate School of Education. In addition to offering many useful weblinks, the site contains a comprehensive bibliography of multiple intelligences resources.

4. http://www.cainelearning.com/

At this site you will find detailed explanations of brain/mind learning principles from the people who "invented" the idea that how the brain works should inform how teaching works.

5. http://www.kovalik.com/

Quoting from the top of this web page, "The mission of Susan Kovalik & Associates is to participate in the creation of learning communities that are dedicated to growing responsible, caring citizens using the best we know about the biology of learning, effective teaching strategies, and meaningful curriculum development." This is the site to visit for ideas on how to implement, in teaching, what is known about how the brain functions.

6. http://www.funderstanding.com/about_learning.cfm

Twelve different theories of how people learn are defined and discussed, with brief and understandable explanations of how each theory bears on the teaching/learning process.

7. http://www.ncate.org/resources/factsheettq.htm

In case you were wondering whether teacher training makes a difference in student achievement, the question is answered at the site of the National Council for Accreditation of Teacher Education.

8. http://www.ets.org/research/pic/teamat.pdf

Adobe Acrobat is needed to read this article: "How Teaching Matters: Bringing the Classroom Back into Discussions of Teacher Quality," by Howard Wenglinsky, Educational Testing Service, 2000.

NOTES

1. Lorin W. Anderson and David Krathwohl, eds., *A Taxonomy for Learning, Teaching, and Assessing: A Revision of Bloom's Taxonomy of Educational Objectives* (New York: Longman, 2001), 15.

2. John O'Neal, "Making Sense of Style," *Educational Leadership* 48, no. 2 (1990): 4–9.

3. Richard M. Felder, "Matters of Style," *ASEE Prism* 6, no. 4 (1996): 18–23.

4. Stephen Jay Gould, *The Mismeasure of Man* (New York: W. W. Norton, 1981).

5. Howard Gardner, *Multiple Intelligences: The Theory in Practice* (New York: Basic Books, 1993).

6. Howard Gardner, *Frames of Mind* (New York: Basic Books, 1987).

7. Walter McKenzie, *It's Not How Smart Your Are, It's How You Are Smart*. Available: http://www.surfaquarium.com/mi.htm, 1999.

8. Howard Gardner, *The Disciplined Mind: What All Students Should Know* (New York: Simon and Schuster, 1999).

9. Thomas Armstrong, *Multiple Intelligences* (Alexandria, VA: Association for Curriculum Development, 1994), 13.

10. R. N. Caine and G. Caine, *Making Connections: Teaching and the Human Brain* (Menlo Park, CA: Addison Wesley, 1994), 88–95.

11. Gordon Wells, *The Meaning Makers* (Portsmouth, NH: Heinemann Educational Books, 1986).

12. Robert Fulghum, *It Was on Fire When I Lay Down on It* (New York: Villard Books, 1989), 42.

13. National Commission on Excellence in Education, *A Nation at Risk* (Washington, DC: Government Printing Office, 1983), 5.

14. Chris Dougherty, "More Than a Snapshot," *Education Week* 20, no. 33 (2001): 39, 42.

15. Diane Ravitch, *National Standards in American Education* (Washington, DC: The Brookings Institution, 1995), 8–9.

16. The Thomas B. Fordham Foundation, *The State of State Standards 2000*. Available: http://www.edexcellence.net/library/soss2000/2000soss.html.

17. John Kendall and Robert Marzano, Mid-continent Research for Education and Learning, *Content Knowledge: A Compendium of Standards and Benchmarks for K–12 Education*, 3rd Edition. Available: http://www.mcrel.org/standards-benchmarks.

18. Putnam Valley Central Schools, *Developing Educational Standards: An Annotated List of Internet Sites with K–12 Educational Standards and Curriculum Frameworks Documents*. Available: http://putnamvalleyschools.org/Standards.html.

19. Matthew Gandel and Jennifer Vranek, "Standards: Here Today and Here Tomorrow," *Educational Leadership* 59, no. 1 (2001): 9.

2 Determining Educational and Instructional Objectives

A few years ago we visited a third-grade classroom in Appalachia. Of the 33 children in the crowded classroom, many had come to school hungry and without adequate clothing. The room was poorly heated, and materials were scarce. An elaborate chart of educational objectives, printed on expensive, shiny paper, covered part of one wall. Every skill conceivable (so it seemed) was broken into minuscule parts. The chart's presence in the room had been mandated by the school district. When asked how the chart could be useful to her, the weary teacher smiled and said, "At least it adds a little color to the walls."

Many teachers have been disillusioned with educational objectives that seem to have little or nothing to do with the reality of their classrooms. They have been asked to spend precious time mechanically developing objectives to fit a prescribed formula that has little connection to what they really teach. Despite mindless abuses, however, the writing of objectives can be an exciting and rewarding professional experience.

Defining Objectives

The goals stated in a rationale are essential to the planning process, but they are too general to serve as organizers for specific lessons or as a basis for evaluation. The next step in the process is to state the intended learning outcomes as objectives that can be measured.

Learning objectives are written at different levels of specificity. Objectives for a course are stated in more general terms than objectives for a unit of study, which are more general than objectives for a lesson to be completed in a class period (see Figure 2.1). But whatever the level of generality, objectives provide a framework and guide for the specific instructional decisions that follow.

Objectives may be defined and written in various ways. For our purposes, *a learning objective is a statement of the measurable learning that is intended to take place as a result of instruction.* The following are examples of learning objectives:

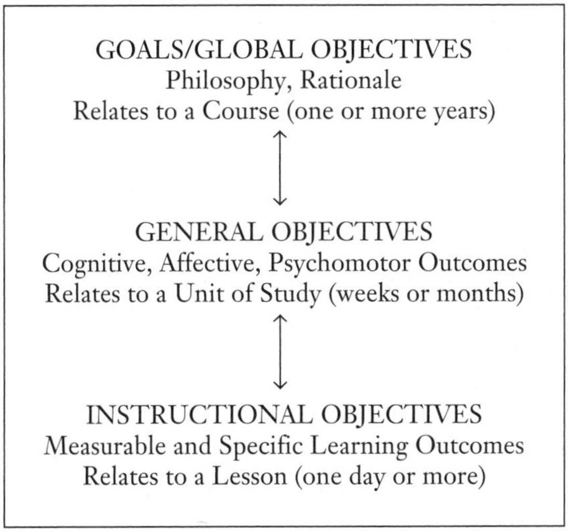

```
┌─────────────────────────────────────────────────┐
│            GOALS/GLOBAL OBJECTIVES               │
│              Philosophy, Rationale               │
│       Relates to a Course (one or more years)    │
│                       ↑                          │
│                       ↓                          │
│             GENERAL OBJECTIVES                   │
│   Cognitive, Affective, Psychomotor Outcomes     │
│     Relates to a Unit of Study (weeks or months) │
│                       ↑                          │
│                       ↓                          │
│            INSTRUCTIONAL OBJECTIVES              │
│     Measurable and Specific Learning Outcomes    │
│       Relates to a Lesson (one day or more)      │
└─────────────────────────────────────────────────┘
```

FIGURE 2.1   Levels of Objectives

As a result of instruction, the students will be able to do the following:

- *Apply* the principles of standard deviation in the solution of word problems.
- *Compare* and *contrast* the causes of the French and American Revolutions.
- *Discriminate* among vowel sounds.
- *Apply* the principles of design in the construction of a birdhouse.
- *Appreciate* the humor in the writings of Mark Twain.

Look carefully at the verbs in these examples. Notice that the objectives are statements of anticipated effects of instruction, not merely statements of activities. They describe what the students will be able to do, feel, or think as a result of instruction. Furthermore, they can be *measured* in some manner.

The following statements are *not* learning objectives. Do you see why?

- The students will go on a field trip to the zoo.
- The students will read the novel *A Tale of Two Cities.*
- The students will keep journals.
- The students will use learning centers.

These are *activities* in which the students will engage, not descriptions of what students will *learn* as a result of the instruction. In the first example, "The students will go on a field trip to the zoo," no evaluation is possible other than counting heads to see who showed up and who got left behind. Learning objectives for this activity could be expressed as follows:

As a result of their field trip to the zoo, the students will be able to do the following:

- Name four classes of mammals and compare their living environments.
- Collaborate in gathering data.

One must not take statements of objectives to such extreme specificity as to lose sight of the learners. Many times the opportunity to teach an important lesson is unexpected and unintended. We recall a story about a teacher who was escorting her students on a field trip through a zoo. She was overheard saying to her students, who were staring in rapt amazement at the towering necks of the giraffes, "Now remember, children, we're here to look at feet." It is equally ridiculous, however, to send children on a field trip to the zoo and have them learn only the location of the refreshment stand.

Stating objectives for learning causes teachers and students to focus on what is important in a learning experience. In addition, it helps the teachers to identify clearly the type of instruction needed to achieve the objectives and to evaluate the success of the instruction.

E X E R C I S E   2 . 1

In the following exercise, mark each activity with an *A* and each objective with an *O*.

1. The students will be able to print the letters of the alphabet legibly.
2. The students will assemble a small motor and use it to operate a simple machine.
3. The students will view a filmstrip.
4. The students will be able to identify three causes of World War I.
5. The students will read *Huckleberry Finn*.
6. The students will be able to describe the character of Huck in *Huckleberry Finn*.
7. The students will do the exercises in the workbook.
8. The students will participate in a volleyball game, displaying enthusiasm and confidence, as evidenced by periodical videotaped records of the games.
9. The students will be able to float on their backs for at least 2 minutes.

Answers to Exercise 2.1
Numbers 3, 5, and 7 are activities; the rest are learning objectives. In number 3, we assume that viewing the filmstrip is a means to some end, not an end in itself. In number 5, the ability to read *Huckleberry Finn* may be the objective, but it is probably an activity required for other learning related to character and plot. Doing the exercises in the workbook in number 7 may be an activity to reinforce learning, but it is not an end of learning. ■

Drafting Objectives

There is no magic formula for writing objectives. When instructional objectives are clear, however, it is possible to select effective strategies to bring about the learning desired. In addition, clear objectives make the evaluation process much easier.

Objectives should be written at every level of the planning process. Course-level objectives are more general than unit objectives, and unit-level objectives are more general than lesson objectives. Course objectives should guide the decisions made at each succeeding level.

A rule of thumb for writing a good objective is that students must act on the material they are learning and, in so doing, connect that material in some way to something else. In this process of connecting, students go beyond mere memorization. Objectives, then, should enable students to learn by acting on and manipulating ideas.

ACTIVITY 2.1

Consider the following objectives. Discuss the different classroom activities that would result from each.

1. The students will be able to recite from memory a poem by Wordsworth.

   or

   The students will interpret through music and dance a poem of their own choosing.

2. The students will be able to label the parts of a flower.

   or

   The students will analyze the effects of different environmental factors on plants grown in the laboratory.

3. The students will be able to identify the parts of speech.

   or

   The students will increase their ability to express themselves effectively by editing their own writing in groups and by evaluating their progress toward a final draft. ■

Types of Objectives

Three basic types of learning objectives should be written during the planning process: (1) cognitive, (2) affective, and (3) psychomotor. Cognitive objectives describe the knowledge that learners are to acquire. Affective objectives describe the attitudes, feelings, and dispositions that learners are expected to develop. Psychomotor objectives relate to the manipulative and motor skills that learners are to master.

Every instructional design needs to include both cognitive and affective objectives. Psychomotor objectives are most prevalent in those classes involving the mastery of physical skills, such as orchestra, shop, handwriting, computer or typewriter keyboarding, and physical education. Psychomotor skills, however, should not be overlooked as a basic skill for performing other activities. For instance, manual dexterity is essential for working with laboratory equipment or with a compass and protractor in math class.

Cognitive Objectives

Cognitive objectives relate to the processing of information by the learner. They specify what students will *be able to do* intellectually as a result of instruction; such instructional results range from the memorization of facts to the most complex processes of evaluation and assessment.

Over 45 years ago, a committee of college and university examiners, headed by Benjamin S. Bloom of the University of Chicago, placed the cognitive behaviors related to the acquisition of knowledge within a taxonomy.[1] The taxonomy was published in 1956 in the book *Taxonomy of Educational Objectives* and was revised in 2001 by Lorin W. Anderson and David Krathwohl.[2] The taxonomy is not a statement of educational objectives, but rather it is a system for classifying learning objectives with respect to cognitive categories.

Higher-Order Thinking Skills.   Within the cognitive domain, it is important that not all the objectives of instruction are at the lower levels of the taxonomy. There is an interesting relationship between memory and understanding and between understanding and thinking. Generally, students will best remember those things that they best understand, and they will best understand those things that they think about. (We elaborate on these relationships of memory and understanding in Chapter 15, "Models for Memory," particularly the section entitled Basis for the Memory Models.) Objectives of instruction should capitalize on the necessity of higher-order thinking skills. Table 2.1 shows a sample of verbs in the cognitive domain described in the taxonomy.

To be able to process information at higher levels, students must be taught *how* to think, not merely *what* to think. Giving out information is not the most important instructional process, although perhaps it is the most common. The models presented in Part Two describe a variety of instructional approaches that facilitate thinking in the classroom.

Four Types of Knowledge.   Cognitive objectives specify the knowledge that students will retain as a result of instruction. Anderson and Krathwohl identify four general types of knowledge: *factual, conceptual, procedural,* and *metacognitive.*[3]

Factual knowledge consists of knowing the details and elements related to the specific facts and terminology of a discipline. It is defined by Gilbert Ryle as "knowledge that."[4] Factual knowledge can be expressed in true statements. Examples are

TABLE 2.1 Sample of Verbs in the Cognitive Domain

Remembering	to recognize, to recall, to repeat, to list
Understanding	to interpret, to exemplify, to classify, to compare, to summarize, to match, to infer, to explain, to contrast, to illustrate
Applying	to execute, to implement, to use, to solve, to carry out, to draw
Analyzing	to differentiate, to organize, to attribute, to describe, to investigate, to distinguish, to discriminate, to focus, to select, to verify
Evaluating	to check, to assess, to critique, to judge, to appraise, to detect, to monitor, to defend
Creating	to generate, to plan, to produce, to formulate, to design, to construct

"Columbus sailed in 1492" and "Water is composed of two molecules of hydrogen and one molecule of oxygen."

Conceptual knowledge requires a deeper understanding of content and an ability to fit the bits and pieces of factual knowledge into a more cohesive whole. This process includes forming categories, testing theories, and constructing models.

Procedural knowledge is defined by Ryle as "knowledge how." It is knowledge of the reasoning process. Each discipline of study in school encompasses a way of thinking. Thus there is a mathematical way of thinking, a scientific way of thinking, a historical way of thinking, an artistic way of thinking, and so on. Virtually every course of study, from auto mechanics to integral calculus, is characterized by a manner of thinking that is in some ways peculiar to that discipline.

Consider the verb *to draw* in relation to the various disciplines. One may draw conclusions, be drawn toward a work of literature, draw a circle, draw a rose, draw out a liquid, end a game in a draw, draw up a proposal, draw out a speech, or draw the curtain. In each instance, the meaning depends on the context in which the action is to take place. Likewise, each discipline defines the thought processes that occur within that discipline.

Metacognitive knowledge refers to the knowledge students gain about their own thinking. This involves self-regulation and an understanding of how to rethink directions and procedures to learn more effectively. This knowledge goes beyond cognition to an ability to regulate, control, and monitor one's own cognitive processes.

A teaching demonstration was taking place in a classroom when a 16-year-old student exclaimed aloud, "Oh, wow!" She had just drawn the connection between the Renaissance and the journey of Columbus, which led to an expansion of her understanding of that historical period. Although she knew that Columbus sailed to America, she had never made a connection to the frame of reference in which that discovery took place. What was once singular, isolated information was now set in a meaningful context, and she was excited. If this student continues to make such connections and begins to examine pre-conceptions in light of this process, then she will master the art of metacognition.

EXERCISE 2.2

The following verbs are often used to describe cognitive learning in the classroom. Consider these in relation to the categories listed in Table 2.1 and included here in parentheses. Write an objective using each of these verbs.

design (create)	*formulate* (create)
solve (apply)	*match* (understand)
draw (apply)	*list* (remember)
verify (analyze)	*defend* (evaluate)

Possible Answers to Exercise 2.2
- The students will be able to *design* an electrical circuit (create).
- The students will be able to *solve* problems using square roots (apply).
- The students will be able to *draw* a circle (apply).
- The students will be able to *verify* data (evaluate).
- The students will be able to *formulate* a hypothesis (create).
- The students will be able to *match* words with definitions (comprehend).
- The students will be able to *give examples of* (or *list*) proper nouns (remember).
- The students will be able to *defend* an ethical position (evaluate).

These words may be placed in more than one category, depending on interpretation. A *design* may be a creative process of many different procedures in which the designer originates a unique procedure, or it may be merely an application of material that has been previously presented. A drawing by a great artist is certainly a creation, whereas the drawing of a line between two given points is the application of a skill. (As mentioned before, the context of the discipline usually determines the level of the thought process.) Choosing between alternatives may be comprehension (or understanding) if it requires reiterating what has been taught; the process of choice in a situation requiring the assessment of values, however, calls for evaluation. ■

The taxonomic placement of cognitive behaviors depends on what the teacher intends the outcome of instruction to be. Will the learner be expected to give reasons for a new situation based on previous experience, or will the learner have to repeat the reasons given by the teacher? In the first case, the learning will be at the evaluation level; in the second, it will be at the level of understanding.

When writing objectives, avoid using vague descriptors such as *learn* or *know* for describing the cognitive learning that is to take place; precise descriptions will increase the effectiveness of instruction. Ivor Davies, author of *Objectives in Curriculum Design*, stresses the importance of the action verb in writing objectives, with the emphasis on what the learner is to *do*. "This is the reason for rejecting verbs like 'to understand' and accepting verbs like 'to identify.'"[5]

EXERCISE 2.3

What verbs could be used in the following examples to make the objectives more descriptive of a desired instructional outcome? Assume for the moment that these are *cognitive* objectives for specific lessons.

1. The students will *know* the causes of the Civil War.
2. The students will *study* the Declaration of Independence.
3. The students will *solve* word problems.

Possible Answers to Exercise 2.3

1. The verb *to know* is perhaps the most general of all possible descriptors of cognitive behavior. Knowing transcends all the levels of the cognitive domain, and thus there are many different ways in which an objective containing this verb could be rewritten. For example:

   - "Students will *list* the causes of the Civil War" puts the objective at the level of remembering.
   - "Students will *appraise* the causes of the Civil War as to their relative order of importance" puts the same objective at the level of evaluation.

2. The verb *to study* does not refer to cognitive behavior. Studying takes many forms and is generally the activity of students trying to learn independently by outlining, taking notes, memorizing, gathering information from a variety of sources, and so forth. One might *study* the Declaration of Independence in any number of ways, each of which might involve different levels of cognition. For example:

   - "Students will *state* the major issues in the Declaration of Independence and *describe the relationship* between these issues and the major events leading to the Revolutionary War." This puts the objective at two related levels of cognition: remembering and analysis.

3. Every mathematics teacher wants students to be able *to solve* word problems; the error in the objective relates to the generality of the statement. As stated, the objective is appropriate as a course or unit objective, but not as a specific instructional objective. *To solve* is an appropriate verb at the cognitive level of application, but *to solve word problems* subsumes many more specific objectives. For example:

   - "Students will *solve* word problems that involve time, distance, and speed of travel" specifies the kind of word problems students will solve.
   - "Students will *formulate* word problems in answering questions that involve rates of interest and amortization of loans" puts the objective at the creation level. ■

TABLE 2.2   Sample of Verbs in the Affective Domain

Receiving	to take in, to listen, to encounter, to be aware
Responding	to react, to reply, to answer, to comply
Valuing	to accept, to reject, to esteem, to regard, to desire
Organization	to compare, to order, to prioritize
Characterization	to internalize, to personalize, to demonstrate

Affective Objectives

Following the development of the cognitive taxonomy of objectives by Benjamin Bloom and his committee in 1956, an affective taxonomy of objectives was developed by Krathwohl, Bloom, and Masia.[6] Objectives in this domain concern feelings and attitudes that students are expected to develop as a result of instruction (see Table 2.2). Krathwohl classified these objectives in five parts on a continuum, ranging from willingness to receive to an internalization of the beliefs or values presented. Because teachers believe that affective objectives are difficult to measure, they frequently omit the affective from lists of objectives. Much teaching is directed toward the development of beliefs, attitudes, and values, however; and it is important to describe these objectives.

Affective learning is not completely separable from cognitive learning: Students often think about their attitudes and feelings, and they will have attitudes and feelings about what they think. Teachers should write objectives that describe attitudes and feelings because they want students to care about the subject being taught and to grow from the experience. If the subject is worth learning, it should have some impact on the life of the learner; it should *affect* learners in other than intellectual ways. It should make them more understanding, more caring, more tolerant, more effective, more communicative, and so on. As one teacher friend of ours said, "I think the future will say of us that we did a good job of teaching if in the manner of our teaching we reveal to students connections between what they learn and how they live. Perhaps from time to time, we might ask ourselves and our students whether what they are learning is making them not only smarter, but also better."[7] Unless a conscious effort is made to describe the kind of affective learning outcomes that should result from instruction, it is possible to overlook or take for granted this important aspect of learning.

EXERCISE 2.4

Consult Table 2.2 and decide which category applies to each of the following verbs. Then, write an objective for each of these verbs. Be prepared to justify your decisions in discussion with a colleague or classmate.

to appreciate
to advocate
to participate
to prefer
to attend

Possible Answers to Exercise 2.4

- *To appreciate*—valuing. Students will appreciate the importance of good nutritional habits as evidenced by their keeping food diaries throughout the semester.
- *To advocate*—characterization. Students will advocate the preservation of natural resources as evidenced by their participation in a clean water campaign.
- *To participate*—responding. Students will participate in classroom discussions as evidenced by data taken periodically by an observer.
- *To prefer*—organization. Students will prefer to read books by authors recommended in class as opposed to making random choices, as evidenced by a survey of the books checked out of the library voluntarily.
- *To attend*—receiving. Students will attend to their work as evidenced by completion of assignments. ■

Psychomotor Objectives

In the domain of psychomotor objectives, learning depends on mastery of a physical skill. Learning to hold a pencil, to play the piano, to throw a baseball, and to operate a machine all depend at least in part on manipulative and motor skills. This domain has not, however, received the attention and development that the cognitive and affective domains have received. Table 2.3 describes one possible taxonomy in the psychomotor domain.

Too often, psychomotor objectives are considered to be the domain of the physical education teacher or the teacher of the very young. Many learning difficulties in students of all ages are associated with an inability to use some part of the body effectively. A person who has difficulty with handwriting may have great difficulty completing essay exams; a person with speech problems will seldom volunteer answers in class.

TABLE 2.3   Sample of Verbs in the Psychomotor Domain

Readiness	willing, prepared, watches
Observation	attends, is interested
Perception	senses, has a feel for, is able
Response	practices, imitates, replicates
Adaptation	masters, develops, changes

E X E R C I S E   2 . 5

Place each phrase below into one of the categories described in Table 2.3.

Get in the water   Pronounce clearly
Type by touch   Show an aptitude for
Position fingers as instructed   Cut on the dotted line
Correct the stance   Come to practice
Copy the numbers

Answers to Exercise 2.5
    Get in the water—readiness
    Type by touch—adaptation
    Position the fingers—response
    Correct the stance—adaptation
    Copy the numbers—response
    Pronounce clearly—adaptation
    Show an aptitude for—perception
    Cut on the dotted line—response
    Come to practice—observation ■

You will notice that the three categories of objectives—cognitive, affective, and psychomotor—are interrelated. One cannot play basketball (psychomotor) without knowing the rules (cognitive) and having the desire (affective) to be a player. The categories primarily serve to assure that a variety of learnings and a range of outcomes are considered in deciding what students will learn from instruction.

A C T I V I T Y   2 . 2

At this point, write 10 objectives for the course rationale you wrote in Chapter 1. Remember that these objectives are the major learnings you want students to acquire by the end of the course. Make sure that you have used a range of verbs from the charts and have included affective and skill objectives as well as cognitive objectives. Be sure to check these with a colleague or a class to confirm that your objectives clearly state intended learning. ■

Determining Evaluation Strategies

An important test for any objective is to ask the question "Is there implied in the objective a reasonable means of evaluating whether students learned what was taught?" One way to do this is to write evaluation methods into the objective. For instance:

- The students will be able to apply the principles of long division to the solution of word problems *as evidenced by their ability to solve three out of five word problems correctly.*
- The students will analyze the causes of the Civil War *as evidenced by their solution to problems in a simulated activity.*
- Given a series of musical scales, *90 percent of the students will perform the exercise on the piano with 100 percent accuracy.*

Not all evaluation needs to or should be conducted by paper and pencil tests. Oral questioning, classroom interviews, student journals and logs, and participation in activities and projects are alternative methods of evaluating learning. Grant Wiggins, director of the Center on Learning, Assessment, and School Structure, writes, "We cannot be said to understand something unless we can employ our knowledge wisely, fluently, flexibly and aptly in particular and diverse contexts."[8]

Wiggins describes two types of tests designed for use in a middle school general science program. The first test requires students to choose the correct answer on a 90-minute multiple-choice test. The second test, called the Sludge, takes 2 weeks. Students are presented with a sludgelike mixture of unknown solids and liquids that they must analyze. "This is an ill-structured and authentic task par excellence," writes Wiggins. "Though the methods and criteria are quite clear to all students in the course, there are no pat routines, procedures, or recipes for solving the problem. Thus the test faithfully simulates a wide range of real-world 'tests' of chemical analysis."[9] Although the first test may provide an indication of superficial content knowledge, the second test replicates the actual practice of science.

Another important consideration for evaluation is to use, as Joan Baron discusses, both "a wide-angle and a telephoto lens" in evaluation.[10] The wide-angle lens allows the teacher to evaluate the class as a whole. Through this evaluation, the teacher determines the dynamics of the classroom, assessing how well the students are interacting with one another and the level of excitement and enthusiasm in the room.

Shifting to the telephoto lens, the teacher determines how well each student is doing. In a group activity, for instance, the classroom may seem to be very enthusiastic and involved. On closer inspection, some students may not be participating or may be using inappropriate thinking strategies. "Although being busy, being excited, being well behaved, and answering questions are generally desirable characteristics of effective classrooms, they do not guarantee that effective thinking is occurring."[11]

Objectives in the three domains—cognitive, affective, and psychomotor—require different types of evaluation processes. In the following sections, evaluation strategies for each domain are discussed.

Evaluating Cognitive Objectives

Always keep in mind that evaluation procedures must match learning objectives. For instance, if one's objective is to have students be able to apply the Pythagorean theorem in solving practical problems, then a test of memory of the formula $A^2 + B^2 = C^2$ is

inappropriate. Evaluation of the objective should require that the students *apply* the theorem to a new problem, such as calculating the diagonal of a soccer field given the length and width of the field.

If the instructional objective is that students *compare* the causes of the Civil War with the causes of the American Revolution, then asking students to list the causes of the Civil War will not test that objective. The evaluation question needs to test the students' understanding of causes of the conflicts, not simply the facts related to the events. Either the objective or the criterion must be adjusted into closer congruence with the other.

Written examinations are only one of the many possible ways to evaluate cognitive learning. Projects, class discussions, and simulated situations in which students are required to utilize their learning are equally effective means. Many students who do not write well are able to speak their thoughts very effectively. Tape and video recorders are useful tools in maintaining a before-and-after record of students' comprehension of a subject.

Evaluating Affective Objectives

Affective objectives are frequently neglected in the design of instruction, probably because, as noted earlier, teachers believe that these objectives cannot be measured. Measuring attitudes, feelings, and beliefs is not easy, but such measures *are* possible. Affective measures differ significantly from other kinds of measures in that they are most valid when they are least obtrusive or overt.

If the teacher wants a true measure of students' enthusiasm for a subject, an evaluation system must be designed that allows students to express their feelings anonymously or that allows the teacher to make systematic observations without the students' knowledge. Young children may be forthright about their opinions, but as individuals grow older they become more guarded in expressing their real thoughts or beliefs about a situation. Thus an unobtrusive checklist of student reactions completed by the teacher may be the best evaluation tool.

Anonymously completed pre- and postunit questionnaires can serve as part of the teacher's evaluation of a unit of study. Tallies of books checked out of the library or records of the behavior of students on those days when free reading time is provided in the classroom will serve as measures of interest in reading. If one's objective is to improve the social interactions of the students, then monitoring behavior on the playground when students believe themselves to be unobserved is an appropriate technique for evaluation. Tape recording discussions in the classroom over a period of time to see whether students' interactions have improved can also be effective.

If it is important that students care about and feel positively about experiences in the classroom and the subjects taught, then evaluating their attitudes and feelings is necessary. We once taught a seventh-grade language arts unit on poetry. One objective of the unit was that the students learn to enjoy reading poetry and choose to read it on their own. Pre- and postunit tests were developed that asked the students to check a number of responses regarding their enthusiasm for poetry. After the unit was taught, the students were tested first on their attainment of the cognitive objectives, and most of the students did very well. Regarding attitudes toward poetry, however, the students liked it less after the unit than they had before.

This unintended outcome was a shock, but it caused a significant change in the design and delivery of the poetry unit. Inasmuch as the students' feelings about poetry were deemed just as important as what they understood intellectually, instruction that caused them to like it less was unacceptable.

Evaluating Psychomotor Objectives

Writing objectives in the psychomotor domain requires a considerable amount of specificity. The psychomotor skill must be broken down into measurable parts, and the degree of acceptable performance must be stated. For instance:

- Students will be able to throw a ball with 80 percent accuracy from a distance of 3 feet into a 1-foot-diameter circle.
- Given two points on a page, students will be able to draw a straight line, using a ruler and pencil, between the two points with 100 percent accuracy.
- While listening to a paragraph read aloud, students will be able to type the paragraph with 60 percent accuracy.

Evaluating psychomotor objectives requires a careful record of each student's progress. Psychomotor skills can be broken into steps on a continuum moving from the simplest step to the most complex. Usually, it is not possible to skip a step in moving to higher steps, for each higher step depends on accomplishment of the preceding step.

In many cases, learners can keep a record of their own progress on a skill chart regularly monitored by the teacher. Seldom will all students in a group be at the same level of skill development. Thus it is necessary to pretest the students and start developing each skill at the point at which they are proficient. Progress sheets and skill charts can be useful for students learning any type of skill. For example, progress in reading and math skills can also be recorded on skill development charts.

It is relatively simple to write lists of objectives regarding what students are to learn and how they will respond to the learning experience; it is much more difficult to confirm that the desired learning has actually occurred. In addition, it is important to retest periodically to ensure that the learning has been retained and integrated into the students' knowledge base.

EXERCISE 2.6

Describe one evaluation technique for each of the following objectives. (Select a written test as a means of evaluation for no more than two of the objectives.)

1. Students will be able to apply three basic principles of paragraph development in their compositions: topic sentence, supporting detail, and concluding statement.
2. Students will appreciate impressionist art.
3. Students will individually improve their ability to throw a softball by 30 percent.
4. Students will be able to contrast realism and naturalism in literature.
5. Students will be able to locate the seven continents on a globe.
6. Students will be able to identify the primary colors.
7. Students will be able to place data into categories.
8. Students will be able to locate library materials using the computer on-line catalog.
9. Students will be able to write their names in cursive.
10. Students will be able to use effective problem-solving techniques in resolving disputes.

Possible Answers to Exercise 2.6
1. Use a periodic evaluation through writing samples. Have the students write for 5 minutes on a particular subject each month and keep these samples in an individual folder for each student. These writing folders become a record of the students' progress.
2. A questionnaire that ensures anonymity would be one technique. Another might be to invite a guidance counselor or another teacher to the class to discuss with the students how they really feel about the subject.
3. Videotaped records of student achievement can be invaluable. If this process is too expensive, use written records of a student's progress taken periodically during the course of study and recorded on a skill chart.
4. A written examination could be used effectively here. Another technique would be to have the students role play the response of characters in first a realistic and then a naturalistic manner.
5. Have each student come to the teacher's desk during a reading period and point out the continents. This should be done several weeks after the unit of study to be certain that long-term retention of the information has taken place.
6. and **7.** A learning center to which each student can go and complete assigned tasks can be valuable. The center can be designed so that different students are assigned different levels of difficulty.

8. A task that requires students to *use* the computer as a search tool for library holdings—in the library or at a remote terminal—is essential.
9. A writing sample kept periodically to track each child's progress is effective here.
10. Observation on the playground, audio- or videotapes of class discussions, role playing, and simulation activities can all measure this objective. ■

Summary

Learning objectives describe the learning that is intended to take place as a result of instruction. In developing cognitive, affective, and psychomotor objectives, the teacher determines what should be included in the instructional design. Only when objectives are clearly defined can the teacher select appropriate instructional approaches. Evaluation procedures written when objectives are developed enable the teacher to determine if those objectives have been achieved. The goal of evaluation should be effective testing of desired learning outcomes. If creativity and variety are not present in the design of evaluation, they probably are not present in the design of instruction.

Evaluation is a continuing process that allows the teacher to make corrections to achieve success. Feedback from evaluation allows the teacher to reteach, to supplement, to revise, to individualize, basically to be in control of classroom learning. The crucial feature of all evaluation is validity: The evaluation tool must accurately portray the intended learning outcome.

WEB RESOURCES

1. **http://ericae.net/**
   Begin here to search for up-to-date information on assessment and evaluation. This popular site each day hosts over 10,000 visitors. The site now includes links to full-text versions of books and articles in an assessment library. A free on-line journal, *Practical Assessment, Research and Evaluation*, is accessible from this page, with articles of special interest to teachers. "Education in the News" provides daily updated links to education-related news articles from major magazines and newspapers across the country.

2. **http://plaza.v-wave.com/kegj/mar.html**
   Entitled "A Checklist for Designing Instruction in the Affective Domain," this article provides a simple systems model for developing instruction in the affective domain. In addition to discussing the various components and providing a few examples, the article includes a checklist to guide the design process for affective instruction.

3. **http://www.uwsp.edu/education/lwilson/lessons/intro.htm**
   This site offers a wide selection of prototype lesson plans framed on different models of learning, including lesson plans that incorporate cognitive, affective, and psychomotor objectives.

4. http://www.eperc.mcw.edu/educate/flash/edmats/222.htm

This brief overview of types of educational objectives can serve as a supplement to the examples given in this chapter.

5. http://www.ce3000.com/AuthorsHelper.asp

Objectives must be clear, concise, and measurable. This "author's guide" provides a thumbnail sketch of how a teacher or instructor can create objectives that satisfy these criteria.

6. http://www.ulm.edu/~rakes/555/objectives/ and **Designing Effective Instruction** http://reach.ucf. edu/~eme6613/class/powerpoint/isd5-v3.ppt

These are two Power Point slide shows on the topic of how and why to develop instructional objectives. The first should open as a web page, the second should download directly onto your hard drive in Power Point.

7. http://www.oucom.ohiou.edu/fd/writingobjectives.pdf

This is another excellent introduction to instructional objectives—in PDF format and very easy to read.

8. http://www.scs.unr.edu/~dpg/develop.html

This is a basic tutorial in writing instructional objectives. The page includes several useful related weblinks.

9. http://www.okstate.edu/ag/agedcm4h/academic/aged6220/6220class/6220class/objectiv.htm

This site provides concise objectives-oriented evaluation.

10. http://www.askeric.org/Virtual/Lessons/Interdisciplinary/INT0132.html

At this web site, you will find an interesting lesson plan on nutrition based on the children's picture book *The Very Hungry Caterpillar* by Eric Carle. Also provided is a range of objectives to guide the reading of the story.

N O T E S

1. Benjamin S. Bloom, ed., *Taxonomy of Educational Objectives: The Classification of Educational Goals, Handbook I: Cognitive Domain* (New York: David McKay, 1956).

2. Lorin W. Anderson and David R. Krathwohl, eds., *A Taxonomy for Learning, Teaching, and Assessing: A Revision of Bloom's Taxonomy of Educational Objectives* (New York: Longman, 2001).

3. Anderson and Krathwohl, 27–29.

4. Gilbert Ryle, *The Concept of Mind* (New York: Barnes and Noble, 1949), 25–61.

5. Ivor Davies, *Objectives in Curriculum Design* (Maidenhead, Berkshire, England: McGraw-Hill, U.K., 1976), 125–126.

6. D. R. Krathwohl, B. S. Bloom, and B. B. Masia, *Taxonomy of Educational Objectives: The Classification of Educational Goals. Handbook II: Affective Domain* (New York: David McKay, 1964).

7. Quoted by Denny Burnette, teacher of Latin, St. Anne's School, Charlottesville, VA.

8. Grant Wiggins, "Assessment: Authenticity, Context and Validity," *Phi Delta Kappan* 75 (1993): 200.

9. Wiggins, 205.

10. Joan Boykoff Baron, "Evaluating Thinking Skills in the Classroom," in *Teaching Thinking Skills Theory and Practice*, ed. Joan Boykoff Baron and Robert J. Sternberg (New York: W. H. Freeman, 1957), 226–227.

11. Baron, 227.

3 Organizing Content

Course, Unit, and Lesson Design

Mrs. Jones's classroom is always fun to visit. The children seem happy and are always busy with interesting projects. Can one conclude that Mrs. Jones is a successful teacher? Perhaps, but it is possible that the children are experiencing a series of interesting and entertaining episodes that have little relationship to one another. It is essential to determine if Tuesday's instruction, for example, relates to what was taught Monday and what will be taught Wednesday, next week, and next month. Is there a plan for how content is introduced to the learners, and are the connections between the lessons clear?

When students are taught without a careful plan for the presentation of content, their experience may be akin to doing a jigsaw puzzle with some missing pieces. Although the act of putting it together is fun, when all the pieces have been assembled, it is impossible to tell what the picture was intended to be.

Subject areas of study in U.S. schools are generally organized into sequentially related courses, which are subdivided into units and lessons. A good design depends on the teacher's ability to organize course, unit, and lesson content in a systematic and interesting manner. The main concepts to be considered in the course must be identified and arranged in order of importance. Obviously, an effective process is needed to plan a unit, to organize a lesson, and to prepare a lecture.

In a well-structured course design, the learner will be able to recognize the order behind the plan, to determine how the parts fit into the whole, and to see how each part is related to other parts. Only when teachers consider the organization of content carefully and can explain why the material is presented in a particular order is it possible for students to have an overall understanding of what they are learning.

Frequently, the organization of material for a course is determined by textbooks or a curriculum guide. Although both textbooks and guides can be important tools in the organization of content, the teacher needs to consider all factors related to the learner, the society, and the subject matter (discussed in Chapter 1). Each class presents a challenge to the teacher: how best to organize the content to fit the needs of this class and *these* individual students.

Analyzing Content

We can divide most of the data processed in the classroom into three categories: facts, concepts, and generalizations. These broad categories are discussed in more detail in Chapters 5 and 6 but are dealt with briefly here.

Facts

Paul D. Eggen, a specialist in information-processing models of instruction, and colleagues have defined *facts* as the types of content, "which are singular in occurrence, which have occurred in the past or exist in the present, which have no predictive value, and which are acquired solely through the process of observation."[1] Facts may be gathered through the direct observation of an event, such as an experiment in a laboratory, or through the retrieval of information from reliable sources, such as from dictionaries or encyclopedias.

Concepts

Concepts are the names given to the categories formed as a result of classifying factual data. To make sense of all the various stimuli in the world, learners of all ages form concepts and give them names. Imagine the cognitive overload if all things in the world were seen as separate and unrelated entities. To form concepts, learners pay attention to likenesses, ignore differences, and place similar objects in the same category. A pussycat asleep by the fire and a tiger in the jungle have many differences, but by attending to similarities and ignoring differences, we form the concept of *cat*.

Generalizations

Statements that link two or more concepts are generalizations. Unlike facts, generalizations contain more than one element and are predictive.

Consider the following:

> Ten of the 15 students in Ms. McIntyre's fourth-grade class brought peanut butter sandwiches for lunch today. Nine students brought peanut butter sandwiches yesterday. Eleven students brought peanut butter sandwiches the day before.

These are factual statements formed on the basis of observation. They do not tell us if the sandwiches were eaten by the students or who made the sandwiches but are simply statements of what was observed.

A majority of the students in Ms. McIntyre's class prefer peanut butter sandwiches for lunch. This is a generalization based on the data from observation and from our understanding of concepts such as peanut butter and sandwich. We have inferred from our observation that the students prefer peanut butter sandwiches, and we may predict that a majority of the students will bring peanut butter sandwiches tomorrow.

None of these statements is necessarily true. The students may not prefer the sandwiches; they may simply have no choice in the matter. Peanut butter may have been on sale in the local market this week, and next week cheese may be the main ingredient. From the observed fact of peanut butter sandwiches being brought to school over a period of time, however, we formed a generalization that allowed us to draw inferences and to make predictions. Only data from additional observations would prove the accuracy of the generalization.

Because facts, concepts, and generalizations make up a large part of the instructional content, the teacher must select the most important combinations of these in the design process. Which facts are most important, and which facts seem most accurate and relevant? Which concepts are familiar to the students, and which ones need to be explained before students can understand the content? How do the students learn to infer and predict through forming generalizations, and how do they learn to test the reliability of data? Teachers must ask these questions as they select and organize the content of instruction.

Ordering Content

A good system for ordering and presenting content is based on the work of David Ausubel,[2] a founder of cognitive psychology, to whom all educators owe a great debt. Ausubel's approach is rooted in principles of the psychology of learning: (1) The single most important factor influencing new learning is what the learner already knows, and (2) any concept is explainable at many different levels of generality, with the highest or most general level most easily understood and the lowest or most specialized level the most difficult.

Principle One

New learnings are built on prior learnings. The very young child develops a concept of locomotion by observing the world in motion. He or she then tries to move, at first in a clumsy way, until the idea of full-fledged crawling is mastered. On that foundation walking begins, although for a while crawling is easier. From walking comes running, skipping, dancing, ballet, a limitless repertoire. Notice, though, that each stage of locomotion is a specialized refinement of the one that preceded it.

Concepts develop in the same way. At first, to the very young child, people are faces. Later, the child distinguishes mother from not mother, then moves to the stage that all men are daddy, and so on. Anyone familiar with very young children knows that almost all their learning begins with the simplest idea and develops greater and greater specificity. The student's understanding of complex mathematical puzzles began many years before with the idea of combining parts into wholes; studying forms of government traces to the learner's first ideas of fair play and equity in human relations; arranging things into successively inclusive groups (species, genera, families, orders, classes, phyla, and kingdoms) follows at least indirectly from the child's earliest notion that like objects can be grouped on the basis of their likenesses.

Principle Two

Any stage of learning and understanding builds on previous, more general levels. Every concept imaginable subsumes other more complex concepts and is at the same time subsumed by more general concepts. Imagine an analogy here between concepts and the nested boxes young children play with where each box fits exactly into the next larger one. Think of the boxes as successively inclusive concepts. Each larger concept has the same structure as all the related concepts, whether more or less inclusive, so that if a person understands the structure underlying any one of the concepts, he or she can potentially understand any of the other concepts. Here is where the second principle of learning comes into play: The easiest concept to learn will always be the one at the next level of generality from a concept already understood. In deciding what to teach, find the "box" that contains the concept you wish to teach, and ask yourself whether the learners already understand the next most inclusive concept.

Unit Design

Courses and textbooks are often organized into manageable parts that span an instructional period of up to several weeks. These parts are called units of study. Units are usually centered around a broad concept or a cluster of related concepts. For example, a unit in earth science might be entitled "Seeds and Plants" or "Ecological Systems," a unit in U.S. history might be entitled "The Colonial Period: Plymouth Rock to Revolution," and a unit in English literature might be entitled "The Short Story" or "Stories and Poems of the African American Experience." Units provide a structure or framework for the design of a course or interdisciplinary program. The plan for a series of units helps to define a course of study.

There are three essential aspects to unit design. *Scope* defines the breadth and range of content to be covered, *focus* determines what will be emphasized in the content, and *sequence* specifies the order in which the content will be arranged.

Scope

Every teacher is faced with the frustration of having too much to cover in too little time. There is an ever-present danger that in the hope of teaching much, the teacher may fail to take the time to teach well. Because all the conceivable content and information related to a course cannot be covered within the time frame of a course, choices about the actual breadth and depth of the content have to be made.

These choices will rest on two considerations: (1) the relative importance of facts, concepts, and generalizations that might be taught in terms of the continuum of the overall curriculum; and (2) the relative importance of the content to be taught with respect to the needs of society and the age, interests, and abilities of the learners. Given the choice, one would always want to teach comparatively more important rather than less important content. Likewise, one would want always to make the choice of content most appropriate to the learners, relative to their prior knowledge, abilities, and needs.

In general, learners will retain more of what they understand than of what they simply memorize. It is less important for students to remember all the facts of a topic than it is for them to understand the main ideas and concepts.

Teachers learn one lesson early: If you try to teach everything possible, nothing may be learned well. If whatever is taught is taught well, however, it is nearly impossible to keep learners from learning everything they possibly can. Beginning teachers generally believe that they have to pack as much information as possible into every lesson. Such an approach overlooks that learners learn by practicing new skills and by having material presented in a variety of ways. By giving students more than they can learn, a teacher misses the opportunity to have students learn the content well through a variety of instructional approaches.

Focus

A good way to bring focus to the planning process is to title the units within a course. Titling and organizing units around particular themes or ideas adds interest and helps learners understand the purpose of the study. For instance, the sixth-grade science teacher described in Chapter 1 titled her rationale "Our Window on the World." Next, she listed the major concepts that might be included in the course: communities, terrain, resources, habitat, environment, animals and plants, erosion, water sources, climate, and ecosystems. Each of these major concepts could potentially form the basis or serve as a major part of a unit of study within the course. The teacher decided that *environment* would serve as the basis of one unit. The next step was to put the components of the unit into a framework that accommodated the general and specific content. Thus the unit on environment took the following form:

Organizing Idea. The *environment* consists of a number of carefully balanced ecosystems that are all interrelated.

The pond		The field			The woods	
Aquatic animals	Aquatic plants	Insects	Small mammals	Grasses	Large mammals	Trees

Constructing a diagram like this helps the teacher clarify the focus of the work to be done in the unit. The foci of this unit will be the pond, the field, and the woods. Furthermore, the foci for studying the pond will be aquatic animals and plants; the foci for studying the field will be insects, small mammals, and grasses; and the foci for studying the woods will be large mammals and trees.

The organization of the main concepts in the structure of a unit may take many forms, but organization is essential if the learners are to understand how the unit's parts relate to one another and the focus of their study at any given time. Each unit's planning chart can be an excellent organizer for the students. Putting such a chart on the board at the beginning of the unit allows teacher and students to track their progress through the concepts and activities on which the unit is built. Decisions regarding the focus of a unit will lead directly to forming unit objectives.

For the unit on the woods, the objectives might be as follows:

- Students will identify three large mammals that live in the woods and list their distinguishing characteristics.
- Students will compare the habitats of woodland animals with those of field animals.
- Students will analyze the impact of environmental changes on the eating habits of woodland animals and evaluate the effectiveness of three different conservation plans.
- Students will develop a concern for limiting the use of pesticides.

Within any subject are many interesting possibilities for study; however, it is impossible to include everything in a single course or unit. As Figure 3.1 illustrates, a useful strategy is for the teacher to first survey the content in the field to be studied, considering all possible material. Then, from this survey the teacher draws together various strands of the material and determines a focus for the study. This focus enables the teacher to select related content and to develop the learning objectives, thus completing the design process. Without a focus, the selection of material may be random and disconnected.

Sequence

A third set of decisions to be made concerns the order in which to place subject matter. Subjects may be ordered chronologically or thematically. There is an obvious logic to ordering historical events chronologically, but they might also be ordered thematically, by bringing together topics in areas such as civil unrest, wars, or migrations. The resulting comparisons and contrasts can enrich students' grasp of the material.

Basic skills, such as the fundamentals of reading or arithmetic, usually require that the sequence of skills proceed from the simpler to the more complex. Even in such areas as math and reading, however, it is sometimes appropriate to sequence learning according to interest and variety. For instance, a unit on percent, in which

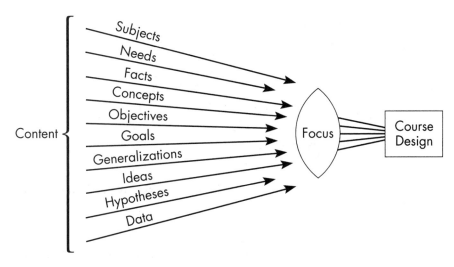

FIGURE 3.1   Bringing Focus to the Planning Process

winning percentages of the basketball team are studied, might be undertaken during basketball season, and a unit on consumer spending might be timed to coincide with the December holiday season.

New learning should be based on previous learning. Even when that is done, it is important to provide connections to help the learner identify how the new learning fits into what is already known. In short, there should be a logical order for the sequence and obvious connections between the parts to be learned and those already known.

EXERCISE 3.1

Describe the scope, focus, and sequence of the following courses, as indicated by the unit titles.

1. Secondary Science: The Earth
    Structure and History
    Atmosphere and Weather
    Continents and Oceans

2. Elementary Social Studies
    Our Neighborhood
    Our City
    Our State
    Our Nation

3. Secondary English

The Short Story
Poetry
The Novel
The Play

4. Consumer Math

Math in the Marketplace
Math in the Home
Math in the Factory

For each of these courses develop another set of unit titles using a different organization.

Possible Answers to Exercise 3.1
The focus for the secondary science class in this example is earth science. The scope includes the earth, the atmosphere, the oceans, and the continents. The sequence is from a general description of the earth to a more specific description of air, climate, oceans, and continents.

Another more general approach might be as follows:

The Earth and the Solar System
Life from the Sea to the Land
Humans Settle the Continents ■

The first step in unit design is to decide how many units are needed in a course. The content must be examined to determine how much actually to undertake, what order to place it in, and what focus to use. In working through this process, the goals and objectives need to be reviewed and revised. Perhaps the time allowed is too short to cover all the goals, or perhaps the content mandated for the course by state or local requirements does not fit the rationale. In any case, decision making is circular, with each decision requiring a review of prior decisions.

A C T I V I T Y   3 . 1

Diagram the content for a course you teach or would like to teach. Title the main units and write unit objectives. Before sharing your organization with your class or a colleague, think about whether you have considered the scope, focus, and sequence of your design. Be prepared to explain your reasons for the way you organized the content and then select one alternative approach. ■

Developing Lesson Plans

Lesson plans are the component parts of the unit design. Just as a course is divided into units, units are divided into lessons. A lesson may span several days or it may take only one day. In deciding how many lessons are necessary to accomplish the unit objectives, it may be necessary to rethink and modify the unit objectives because they may prove too ambitious or too limited. The design process is always circular in that prior decisions may be modified as the teaching progresses. Each lesson should be a logical part of the unit plan. With a clear chart of the main concepts to be studied, lesson planning flows more easily.

Four guidelines to the development of effective lessons are as follows:

1. Limit the concepts and content to be covered in a lesson to allow time for the students to review, practice, and get feedback on what they have learned.
2. Be sure that new material is connected to what has been learned previously and that the connections are clear.
3. Check frequently to ensure that the students are acquiring the intended knowledge, attitudes, and skills; be prepared to alter your plans or to reteach if the learning is not taking place or if the students seem to be disengaged.
4. Never accept students' failure to learn as inevitable or unavoidable.

Deductive and Inductive Organization

In a deductive model of instruction, the lesson usually begins with the presentation of a generalization, a rule, or a concept definition. Students are then given specific examples along with facts associated with the generalization, concept, or rule. In moving from the general to the specific, students are encouraged to draw inferences and make predictions based on the examples.

In inductive lesson designs, students are first presented with specific data and facts, and gradually, through the process of investigation and reasoning, they form the generalization, rule, or concept definition. Most of the models presented in Part Two are inductive, because induction is more conducive to stimulating students' thinking. Deductive models, particularly the lecture, however, can be very effective when used judiciously and sparingly to deliver information.

Advance Organizers

The term *advance organizer* was developed by Ausubel for what he described as "anchoring foci for the reception of new material."[3] An advance organizer is presented at the beginning of the lesson. It is usually a general statement or analogy that helps the learner place in context the material to be learned. About organizers, Ausubel wrote:

> First they provide advance ideational scaffolding. Second, they provide the learner with a generalized overview of all of the major similarities and

differences between the two bodies of ideas before he encounters the new concepts individually in more detailed and particularized form. Finally, they create an advance set in the learner to perceive similarities and differences, and by avoiding overly explicit specification, encourage him actively to make his own differentiations.[4]

In one of the earliest experiments relating to the use of advance organizers, Ausubel introduced learners to the topic of alloys before introducing material relating to the Bessemer process of making steel. Knowing something about the more general idea, alloys, facilitated an understanding of the more specific idea, steel production, because knowledge of alloys provides a context for new information about steel, a specific alloy.

Organizing concepts may be presented in statements made by the teacher or through experiences such as viewing materials or reading assignments. Depending on the instructional design and the type of organizer, its presentation might take a few minutes or an extensive amount of time. Organizers can be either *expository* or *comparative*.

Expository Organizers. Expository organizers begin at a higher level of generality than the concept to be presented in the lesson. Alloys, for instance, are more general than steel and thus set a general context for more specific understandings.

The concept of *independence* could serve as an organizer for a lesson on the Revolutionary War, *nutrition* for a lesson on the basic food groups, and *punctuation* for a lesson on the comma. As another example, a teacher might begin a lesson on insects using this expository organizer:

> Before we begin our study of insects, it is important for us to remember that both insects and humans belong to larger families. The honeybee, the bear, the fish, and all human beings are part of the animal kingdom. Let us think of all the things that we share as animals and then we will talk specifically about what makes the insect special and different from other animals.

The discussion of the more general concept, animals—all require oxygen, reproduce their own kind, take in water and food, and so forth—sets the stage for learning about a particular type of animals, insects. The focus of the study can then be on how insects in particular perform the functions common to all animals.

Comparative Organizers. Comparative organizers connect new learning to previously learned material or to experiences that are familiar to students through analogy and comparisons. For instance, a lesson on the Industrial Revolution could begin with a discussion of the word *revolution*.

> We may think of the word *revolution* as a turning around in a complete circle, like the revolution of a wheel or the revolution of Earth around the

Sun. Another way we use the word is to describe a complete change or turning around of a government, often by violent means, such as our own American Revolution.

When we speak of the Industrial Revolution, we are also talking of a complete change or turnaround from the way things had been. This change occurred, however, not as a result of war but as a result of technology, of machines.

In this example, the teacher compares a familiar meaning of the word *revolution* with a new meaning being introduced to the students. The students thus have a framework or a context within which to place the new learning.

Advance organizers are generally considered part of a deductive lesson plan. An organizer that sets the stage for the learning to take place, however, can be equally effective in an inductive lesson plan. For instance, following the organizer for the lesson on insects, the teacher could present the students with a series of examples from which they are asked to observe similarities and differences and to draw conclusions.

Like the statement of objectives, advance organizers help students comprehend the purpose of the lesson more clearly. The intent is to involve the students in the process as participants; the more they understand what is to take place, the better.

EXERCISE 3.2

Determine which of the following examples is an expository organizer and which is comparative. Also, what is the topic of each organizer and to what is the idea being compared?

1. It would be hard for us to dance without the rhythm of music to follow. The music determines how fast we will move and what kind of dance we will do. The rhythm of the music makes us feel like dancing. There is also rhythm in the way in which words are used in poetry. This rhythm determines how fast the poem will move and how we feel about the poem.

2. Imagine a shepherd in the fields long, long ago who was to take care that not a single sheep was lost. But there were very many sheep. How could he possibly keep track of them all? He had an idea. What if he picked up many little twigs and tied them in a bundle each morning when the sheep were put out to pasture? Each stick would represent one of the sheep. At night, he could check to see if there was one sheep for each twig in the bundle. His system worked well, except that he had many sticks and the bundle was heavy. He thought and thought and then he said to himself,

> I will divide this large bundle into smaller bundles, each containing as many sticks as fingers on one hand and representing that number of sheep. Then I will take a large stick and put one notch for each bundle. If any

sheep are not included in the bundles, I will make one extra bundle with as many sticks as there are sheep left over. Now I will not have to carry around so many sticks. I will have to carry only the large stick with the notches and the small bundle representing the remaining sheep.

For a long time people have been trying to devise systems for keeping records of the number of things in the world. Today, we will learn about sets and how they help to keep track of the number of things we have.

Answers to Exercise 3.2
The first example is a comparative organizer in which the rhythm of music is being compared with the rhythm of poetry. The second is an expository organizer with the broader generality of counting introducing the idea of sets. ■

ACTIVITY 3.2

Write lesson organizers for three of the following subjects. Have a colleague of your classmates determine if you have written expository or comparative organizers.

The Gettysburg Address
Administering CPR
The multiplication tables
Pronouns
The basketball dribble
The metric system ■

Objectives for Lessons

When a lesson is not a part of a unit's instructional design, there often seems to be no logical reason for its delivery. The parts of a lesson are related to one another, and lessons are related to the integrity of the unit design. Each lesson should clearly be a part of a whole.

The objectives for each lesson should be related to the objectives of the unit and of the course. As they progress through an instructional design, students should be able to trace the purposes of their lessons. The objectives for each lesson will determine the instructional strategies. To choose an appropriate instructional option, the teacher must first clearly define the objectives of every lesson.

Consider this unit-level objective for a study of the Civil War: *Students will analyze the major events leading to the Civil War.* The objectives for one lesson in the unit could be as follows:

- Students will describe the operation of the Underground Railroad.
- Students will analyze the effect of the development of the cotton gin on the economy of the South.

From the following diagram, one can determine that the objective for the Underground Railroad lesson relates to the larger issue of the morality of slavery, which is one of the issues being studied in this unit, "Causes of the Civil War." The invention of the cotton gin is one factor related to the demand for cotton that, in turn, increased the demand for slaves.

Causes of the Civil War

Morality/ economics	Expansion of the United States	Invention of the cotton gin
■ ■	■ ■	■ ■
Slavery	Tradition of state's rights	Demand for cotton
■	■	■
Underground Railroad/ abolitionists	Missouri Compromise	Increase in the number of slaves
■		
Slave trade in New England		

Diagramming the main ideas to be considered in the unit from the most general to the most specific and relating the information across categories helps the teacher organize the material and determine what to include. In addition, such a diagram can be presented to the students as a part of the advance organizer for the unit or lesson to be studied.

ACTIVITY 3.3

Write lesson objectives for a unit in the course you are planning. Determine if the objectives for the lessons fulfill the objectives for the course. You may find that either the unit objectives or the lesson objectives will need to be revised for them to be congruent. ■

Sample Outline for Lesson Planning

The following outline exemplifies one type of lesson plan:

1. Unit title:
2. Date(s) to be taught:
3. Title of lesson:
4. Lesson objectives:
5. Advance organizer:
6. Relevant textbook pages, supplementary reading materials, and demonstration materials needed:

7. Instructional design (this step includes the instructional models to be incorporated into the plan from Part Two and the examples and illustrations to accompany the lesson):
8. Questions for classroom discussion:
9. Guided and independent practice:
10. Feedback and evaluation strategies:

At this point, you should be able to complete the first four steps of this lesson plan. You should also have some ideas about how to evaluate the objectives. Before you decide on the instructional design, however, you need to consider the instructional options described in Part Two.

Summary

The design of a course consisting of units and lessons is one of the most rewarding professional experiences for an instructor. Because so much content in every subject could be included, the instructor must decide what to retain, what to omit, what to emphasize, the order in which to present the material, and whether to begin with the general and work to the specific or vice versa. Effective examples must be selected and an organizing statement determined that will help the students fit the new learning into what they know already. Similar to the design of a building or an automobile, the design for instruction determines the quality of the finished product.

WEB RESOURCES

1. **http://ericir.syr.edu**
   Ask ERIC is the premier web site for educators with information for teachers, librarians, counselors, administrators, parents, and anyone else with questions related to teaching. Visitors to the site can ask a question related to instruction and receive an answer within 48 hours. The AskERIC virtual library is an on-line repository of immediately available lesson plans, teaching tools, projects, and more.

2. **http://school.discovery.com/schrockguide/**
   Kathleen Beck Schrock is best known, beyond her job as administrator for technology for Nauset Public Schools, Cape Cod, Massachusetts, as the webmaster of Kathy Schrock's Guide for Educators. Since 1995, this page has been the first stop for the Web-savvy teacher in search of help and information. It is mainly a web page of links to educational topics used for developing lessons.

3. **http://edweb.sdsu.edu/webquest/webquest.html**
   WebQuests are designs for instruction based on open-ended problems and access to multiple sources of information, mostly drawn from the Web. Designed by Bernie Dodge in 1995, WebQuests are units of study centered on open-ended problems that students "solve" in unique ways. Hundreds of examples of WebQuests are available for browsing and use, organized by grade level and subject under the heading "Examples" on the main WebQuest page. If you are simply curious about the Web and the instructional potential of WebQuests, pay a visit to http://www.ozline.com/webquests/intro.html, which dispels some myths about the Web and provides information showing why the Web may be your best resource for instructional improvements.

4. http://encarta.msn.com/schoolhouse/default.asp

This is the home of the Encarta Lesson Collection, which includes lessons on almost every topic in the curriculum organized by grade level and searchable by keyword. The page also features an index of some of the best on-line resources for educators seeking innovative Internet projects, lesson plan ideas, source materials, and opportunities to collaborate with other schools and teachers.

5. http://www.graphic.org/goindex.html

Graphic organizers are some of the most helpful tools for students and teachers to use for organizing learning and teaching. This site displays a table of organizers arranged by type and use. Each organizer title is linked to illustrations, examples, and directions for use of that organizer.

6. http://www.engagingminds.com/inspiration/index.html

Teachers interested in excellent tools for constructing their own customized graphic organizers should visit this Web site. Inspiration® for teachers and Kidspiration® for students are popular for good reason—they are so easy to use. To test drive these software programs, download the free 30-day trial full-featured copies.

7. http://questioning.org/NC/nc4.html

"Building Standards-Based Curriculum Units with New Technologies" is the name of this site. The lessons illustrated and explained here emphasize the design approach of "scaffolding," which involves providing "very clear directions, lots of structure and good resources to optimize learning." A review of the resources given at this site is almost certain to improve anyone's lesson and unit design skills.

8. http://www.rmcdenver.com/useguide/lessons/design.htm

Two Web pages can be accessed here—one entitled "Designing a Lesson," the other entitled "Implementing a Lesson." Both pages are full of guidelines and resources for designing and teaching lessons on a great variety of topics. The archives of lessons accessible from both pages are very complete and offer excellent starting points for lessons at all grade levels. The site is billed with no exaggeration as "ideas, activities, and promising practices that address your standards." The standards are Texas State Standards, but that does not diminish the general usefulness of the ideas and links available.

9. http://www.kn.pacbell.com/wired/fil/

If you want to construct a web site to enhance your instruction but do not know the difference between .html and .htm, you are encouraged to visit the Web site "Filamentality." This fill-in-the-blank interactive site will guide you through selecting a topic, searching the Web, gathering good Internet sites, and turning Web resources into learning activities. The site will help you combine the "filaments" of the Web with a learner's "mentality."

NOTES

1. Paul D. Eggen, Donald P. Kauchak, and Robert J. Harder, *Strategies for Teachers* (Englewood Cliffs, NJ: Prentice Hall, 1979), 36–37.

2. David Ausubel, *The Psychology of Meaningful Verbal Learning* (New York: Grune and Stratton, 1963).

3. David Ausubel, "The Use of Advance Organizers in the Learning and Retention of Meaningful Verbal Material," *Journal of Educational Psychology* 51 (1960): 267–272.

4. Ausubel, *Psychology of Meaningful Verbal Learning*, 90.

Planning for Instruction

In Part One we discussed the planning phase of instruction. Goals and objectives were defined, and a technique for writing rationales was described based on the needs of learners, societal need, and subject matter content. In addition, evaluation strategies for different types of objectives were suggested together with an organizational strategy for unit and lesson planning.

In the following chapters we describe a series of instructional models that can be incorporated into the design process. A repertoire of instructional models allows the teacher to select the appropriate teaching strategies for each instructional design. We have selected models in a variety of categories that we believe form a solid base of instructional approaches.

PART TWO

Matching Objectives to Instruction

A Models Approach

Remember what it was like to make something from a pattern for the first time, such as a dress, a model airplane, a birdhouse, or a cake? The task seemed very difficult if not impossible, in the beginning. You made many mistakes and needed advice and coaching from more experienced hands. Gradually, you acquired the skills and techniques; and when many dresses or birdhouses or loaves of bread had been made, you could work without following a pattern and could even design patterns of your own that others could follow.

Instructional models, like patterns or blueprints or recipes, present the steps necessary for a desired outcome. The selection of a particular model to use in an instructional design depends on the desired outcome or objective of the instruction. The methods selected for teaching a lesson should depend on what the students are expected to learn as a result of the instruction.

When planning to build a birdhouse, it is necessary to select a pattern for a birdhouse, not a pattern for a garage or a picket fence. A recipe for a meatloaf will not produce a loaf of bread; a pattern for an evening gown will not result in a pair of blue jeans. Likewise, a model of teaching designed to bring about the recall of facts will not produce creative thinking or develop problem-solving skills. A model for teaching generalizations is not effective in teaching the skills necessary for learning to swim. An instructional model is a step-by-step procedure that leads to specific learning outcomes. The best models have been used extensively and have been found to be effective in achieving specific objectives of instruction. Effective instructional models do the following:

- They allow students to become active participants in the learning process.
- They take students through specific sequential steps.
- They reflect research about thinking, learning, and behavior.

Instructional models can be gathered from a variety of sources including classrooms, psychology labs, and training institutions, as well as from the techniques and ideas of teachers, therapists, military personnel, educators, and philosophers. The models-of-teaching approach emphasizes the need for variety in the classroom, which can only be accomplished by developing the teacher's repertoire of instructional approaches to meet a range of objectives.

Earlier in this text we discussed the varied needs of learners in the classroom. Some students learn better in a highly structured environment; some do better in a more open and student-centered atmosphere. Some students want to solve problems for themselves; others feel more comfortable if solutions are presented to them. Some learners think deductively; some are more comfortable with inductive thinking. Some students learn better by themselves; some work better in groups.

If a teacher creates a single environment in the classroom or repeatedly uses the same instructional approach, only those students who learn well in that environment or with that approach will succeed. The teacher who utilizes a variety of instructional approaches is more likely to reach all students in the classroom; moreover, students are encouraged to learn in a variety of ways.

Ironically, professional educators have frequently divided into camps, asserting that one approach is infinitely more desirable than another. Those who believe in behavioral psychology, for instance, scoff at those who insist on problem solving and inquiry. A renewed emphasis on the teaching of thinking skills rekindled the controversy between those who insist that thinking is a product of behavioral conditioning and those who believe that thinking is related to perception and psychodynamic forces.

It is our belief that such controversy is wasteful, because there is no one correct manner in which to instruct all the students all the time. Even special populations, such as those learners with mental or physical disabilities, can benefit from a variety of instructional approaches. No group or stratum of society needs to be relegated to one type of approach, although it may be reasonable to use certain approaches more often than others.

In Part One, we discussed instructional planning and identified the range of objectives that teachers can design into an instructional plan. Some objectives focus on cognitive learning, some on attitudes, some on the acquisition of skills. It is only logical that instruction to bring about this variety of learning in the classroom needs to be varied.

In addition, we stressed designing instruction so that a variety of approaches is used in each unit. A careful instructional design takes into account the age and interests of the learners, the knowledge that they bring with them to instruction, and the conditions under which instruction will occur.

In Part Two, we present instructional models, selected from a variety of sources, that provide a solid repertoire for the beginning teacher. We describe the steps for each model, provide a theoretical base for the approach, and discuss instructional situations in which the model might be used. It is important to practice these models in situations in which coaching from an expert can take place and periodic peer review can occur. Our experience in promoting models of instruction warns us that teachers may have difficulty relating instructional models to appropriate objectives, emphasizing the learning of concepts rather than activities, and finding the time to learn to properly use these models in the classroom. "Most teachers use a very narrow range of instructional practices [and] will expand that repertoire only when they are provided substantial and carefully designed training."[1]

Following the steps in the instructional models is essential in the beginning, but as the teacher gains experience and confidence, the possibilities for designing new approaches and for personalizing the models are endless. When teachers have multiple instructional procedures available, they no longer have to rely on one technique to gain the interest of the class and to teach the material. When one process is ineffective they can switch to others. The teacher becomes a professional problem solver and decision maker.

The models presented here meet a wide range of instructional objectives. Each can be used to teach individual objectives, and when combined in an instructional design, they can meet a variety of student needs and interests. Most of the models are directed toward the acquisition of cognitive objectives, as these are the ones that are most emphasized in our schools. And they are designed to include all learners; no student, even the nonreader, is excluded from the process. Thus many affective objectives related to participation and feelings of achievement are met through the use of these models.

Chapter 4. Direct instruction: Direct instruction is a highly structured model used most effectively in teaching basic skills such as reading and mathematics when the tasks to be learned can be broken down into small, discrete segments. This model is also effective in teaching cognitive objectives related to recall and recognition of facts and data. In addition, psychomotor skills, such as holding a pencil, playing the violin, and throwing a baseball, are effectively taught through this model. This model is presented first because its steps provide a basic foundation for good instruction.

Chapter 5. Concept attainment: By teaching the thinking skill of categorizing, this model helps students comprehend and analyze the meaning of a particular concept. Through a series of positive and negative examples, students define the concept and determine its essential attributes. The concept attainment model is particularly effective in meeting objectives related to comprehension, comparison, discrimination, and recall.

Chapter 6. Concept development: Originated by Hilda Taba, the concept development model teaches students to group data based on perceived similarities and then to form categories and labels for the data, effectively producing a conceptual system. In the process, students learn to think about their own thinking and to understand how concepts originate. This model is effective with objectives related to contrasting, applying, categorizing, and analyzing data.

Chapter 7. Inquiry: In the inquiry model, learners take a puzzling situation and follow a scientific process that leads to the generation of a hypothesis. The emphasis here is on the need for careful, logical procedures in problem solving, on understanding the tentative nature of knowledge, and on the need for group endeavor in solving problems. Learners are encouraged to seek more than one answer to a question. The inquiry model is effective in meeting objectives related to problem solving, analysis, hypothesizing, and evaluation. Group process, cooperation, and communication are also emphasized.

Chapter 8.   Synectics: The three versions of the synectics model presented here use group interaction to stimulate creative thought through metaphorical analogies. Far from being lonely, isolated processes, creative thinking and expression become group activities in which each individual can participate. The synectics model is particularly effective for those objectives related to exploration, comparison, identification, insight, and analogy.

Chapter 9.   Cause and effect: This model leads students through an investigation of a significant action, situation, condition, or conflict. Through inference, students hypothesize about causes and effects, consider prior causes and subsequent effects, and generalize about human behavior in similar situations.

Chapter 10.   Classroom discussion: Based on the Great Books approach, this model guides the planning and selection of questions to be used in classroom discussions. Both students and teachers learn to identify different levels and types of questions. This model also helps the teacher direct the process of classroom interactions for effective discussions.

Chapter 11.   Vocabulary acquisition: The vocabulary model was developed for this text by one of the authors, Tom Estes, a recognized expert in the teaching of reading and vocabulary acquisition. This model presents the exciting possibility of teaching vocabulary through the history of language and word derivation rather than through the memorization of lists.

Chapter 12.   Resolution of conflict: This model provides precise questioning techniques for the exploration and study of feelings as students explore the thoughts and behaviors of individuals involved in conflict situations. Students discover that an event may be interpreted in a variety of ways and that point of view may be relative.

Chapter 13.   Values development: This model stresses the use of the regular school curriculum to identify the important themes and questions that are embedded in all subject areas. These values are a part of the cultural understandings and mores that guide ordinary civility and good citizenship.

Chapter 14.   Cooperative learning: Cooperative learning models describe ways in which the teacher can encourage students to work with and help other students in the classroom. The use of these models is effective for creating a positive environment in the classroom and for meeting affective objectives related to cooperation and understanding as well as cognitive and psychomotor objectives.

Chapter 15. Memory: Memory models, which include link, loci, memory through motion, and names and faces, provide techniques through which both teachers and students can improve their memory skills. This chapter is based on the premise that a good memory can be developed and that all learners should have access to this process.

Each model is presented with a brief introduction, a description of the steps in the model, a theoretical explanation of the model, and then a scenario in which the model is used. We present the steps for each model before discussing the theoretical base because many teachers become mired in the theory of an approach before seeing how it works in the classroom.

These models are appropriate for any age, with all abilities, and with any subject matter. It is up to the teacher to apply the appropriate subject matter for the age and interests of the learners. We have used these models with learners from kindergarten to postgraduate, with special education students, with classes for the gifted, and with teachers and school administrators. The more we use these models for instruction, the more convinced we are of their effectiveness.

WEB RESOURCES

1. http://ivc.uidaho.edu/mod
This excellent site contains descriptions and activities for many of the models included in this text and background information on some of the individuals whose research formed the basis for the models approach.

NOTE

1. Bruce Joyce, Beverly Showers, and Carol Rolheiser-Bennett, "Staff Development and Student Learning: A Synthesis of Research on Models of Teaching," *Educational Leadership* 45 (October 1987): 22.

CHAPTER

4

The Direct Instruction Model

Teaching Basic Skills, Facts, and Knowledge

To understand how students feel in the classroom when they are introduced to the new and the unfamiliar, every teacher should periodically learn a new skill. If you had to learn to ski, make buttonholes, read Hebrew, arrange flowers, or program a computer tomorrow, the experience would be humbling. Yet children in school constantly encounter such experiences as they confront new tasks and strange material that must be mastered. Those experiences are made easier by carefully planned direct instruction.

Surely much in the school curriculum, such as literary appreciation and inferencing skills, cannot be taught directly. Most attempts at direct instruction of composition and rhetoric fail to have any effect on language use. Models other than direct instruction are appropriate here. By contrast, consider how very many objectives do lend themselves to direct instruction, such as those concerning mathematical procedures, grammatical rules, the states of New England, alphabetizing, carburetor overhaul, scientific equations, and the periodic table of the elements, to name a few. Every teacher, in every subject, at every level of schooling, has developed some learning objectives related to basic skills that must be mastered before the learner can move to other levels of thinking and learning.

The model is based in part on behavioral research about how effective training occurs. It is most useful in teaching skills that can be broken down into small, discrete segments, with each segment building on the prior one. Direct instruction is characterized by relatively short instructional periods followed by practice until mastery learning is achieved.

A very structured form of direct instruction known as DISTAR (Direct Instruction System for Teaching and Remediation) developed in 1968 by Siegfried Engelmann, has recently received renewed attention primarily as a result of the standards and back-to-basics movements. Robert Slavin reports that studies of the highly programmed DISTAR approach "have found strong positive effects in elementary schools, particularly with low achievers and at-risk students."[1] Although DISTAR is not the form of direct instruction described in this text, many references to this approach can be found on line or in the literature.

Teachers are frequently criticized for the predominance of rote learning in the classroom. The direct instruction model, which depends in part on rote learning, is a necessary but not a sufficient instructional tool. Many steps in this model are useful in all the other models, and to be without this effective tool is a disadvantage; to use this model exclusively, however, is deadening. Direct instruction should be used whenever the objectives of instruction and the needs of the learners indicate that such an approach will be effective.

Steps in the Direct Instruction Model

A number of excellent studies of effective teaching relate to the direct instruction model, including the research of Anderson, Evertson, and Brophy,[2] Rosenshine,[3] and Good and Grouws.[4] Many classroom teachers have been introduced to direct instruction through the work of Madeline Hunter, who describes seven steps in the process: (1) presentation of an anticipatory set, which causes the learners to focus on what they are about to learn; (2) a description of objectives and purpose, in which the teacher makes clear what is to be learned; (3) an input stage, in which a new knowledge, process, or skill is presented to the students; (4) modeling, in which the new learning is demonstrated; (5) checking for understanding to determine if students have grasped the new material; (6) guided practice under the careful supervision of the teacher; and (7) independent practice that encourages learners to perform or utilize the new learning on their own.[5]

Closely related to these steps are the six steps identified by Barak Rosenshine,[6] which are described in detail in this chapter.

1. Review previously learned material.
2. State objectives for the lesson.
3. Present new material.
4. Guide practice, assess performance, and provide corrective feedback.
5. Assign independent practice, assess performance, and provide corrective feedback.
6. Review periodically with corrective feedback if necessary.

Step 1—Review Previously Learned Material

In direct instruction, the students must clearly understand what they are expected to learn, the steps they will follow in that learning, and how the new learning connects to what has been learned previously. Read how the following teachers conduct a review.

I. Mrs. Benito is preparing to teach a lesson on alphabetizing. She begins by reviewing with the class what they learned the day before: "Yesterday we grouped words according to the first letter. On the table are the word stacks we made, each beginning with the same letter. Today, we are going to order these stacks by the first letter's place in the alphabet, starting with the A stack. First, let us review the names of the first letters in each of the stacks we made yesterday."

II. In the gym, Mr. Terry instructs his swimming class: "Last week you learned how to float. First, get in the water and practice floating for about 5 minutes, so I can see if everyone remembers that skill. Then, you will learn how to move your hands to propel yourself in the water."

III. In math class, Miss Tomlin says, "Yesterday, we learned about using X to represent an unknown. Sara, will you please put the first homework problem on the board; Jesse, will you put up the second; and, Frank, will you please put up the third? When we are sure that we understand how to use the unknown X, which you practiced for homework, we will learn how to use the X in an equation."

Each of these teachers is practicing an essential technique of the direct instruction model as described by Rosenshine: Begin with a short review of the previous learning, which is necessary for the new learning. Homework assigned for the previous lesson should be checked before proceeding. It is important to put problems on the board or examine the material learned the day before through questioning or testing before proceeding to a new skill level. If necessary, the previous lesson should be retaught before going on, particularly when the new skill is dependent on mastery of the preceding one.

Pretesting the class to determine skill levels is essential before teaching a new skill. Analyzing students' abilities to learn the skill helps the teacher determine the pace at which to proceed and allows the teacher to prepare for individual differences in the class.

Step 2—State Objectives for the Lesson

Lesson objectives should be stated clearly and written on the board in language the students can understand. We visited one second-grade classroom during a writing lesson and saw this objective written on the board: *The students will practice holding the pencil in the proper position to form the letters for cursive writing.*

Do you see the problem here? The language is not appropriate for the age of the students or even for the instructional objective, that is, practice in forming cursive letters. The purpose of stating objectives is to tell the learners clearly and simply what the purpose of the instruction is and what outcomes they should expect. Lesson objectives should be connected to previous learning and within the reach of all the students.

Step 3—Present New Material

Whether a new skill is to be learned or information is to be presented, the teacher's analysis and preparation of content are essential in this step. It is not sufficient to know the content or the procedure; you must also be able to teach it. Many experts in a subject are unable to convey their expertise to others. Preparation for this step involves ensuring that what is known by the teacher can be learned by the student. The effective teacher spends preparation time analyzing the steps needed to learn a new skill and the order in which the steps will be presented. For example, one does not introduce multiplication before addition, semicolons before commas, or the swan dive before floating.

In each step of the presentation, clear and detailed instructions and explanations must be given. Frequent and varied examples, punctuated with ample questions and corrective feedback, serve to focus learners on the material and avoid digressions. At every point, it is important to be sure that instructions and explanations are understood by the class.

The classroom teacher should combine effective verbal presentation with audiovisuals, questions, demonstration, and student participation. Information should be interesting, highly structured, well organized, and limited in scope.

Content should be similarly analyzed. If the learners do not know the meaning of basic concepts in a definition, they will not comprehend the definition. For instance, a lesson on building a table will have little meaning to learners if they cannot identify certain basic tools, such as the level, the plane, and the square. One must know the parts of speech before diagramming sentences and the parts of a right triangle before learning the Pythagorean theorem.

Organizing Content.   The process of organizing new material for presentation is similar to the process of organizing content for a unit of study, as described in Chapter 3. The content to be learned must be selected and then analyzed according to the learners' needs. Presenting material that is too difficult or presenting too much material at one time hinders learning and defeats the purpose of the presentation. Presenting a few significant points accompanied by many illustrations and questions is generally more effective than covering many points. When introducing a new skill, the procedures should be broken into small segments that can be introduced in a sequence.

Based on the age of the learners and their abilities, the teacher must determine how much content can be offered in one presentation. The less experienced the learners are, the more they need to have each step carefully explained and the more the teacher needs to limit the content in each presentation. Content should be organized so that the most general information is presented first, followed by more detailed and specific data; at each step in the process, new material should be related to material previously learned.

Some Methods for Presenting Material

Lectures.   Lectures are often an essential part of classroom instruction and one way in which new material is delivered to students. From the study of homiletics, or the art of preaching, and other public speaking models, we have selected some essential steps to follow in what might be termed a lecture model.

Steps in the Lecture Model
1. Identify the main points to be covered.
2. Select an advance organizer.
3. Use examples to illustrate each point.
4. Use repetition to reinforce the main points.
5. Summarize the points and refer back to the organizer.

One: Identify the Main Points to Be Covered.   After the material for the lesson has been carefully organized, the main points to be covered in a lecture should be selected. One temptation of any speaker is to attempt to cover too much material in too short an amount of time. Most adults can listen to a lecture for only about 20 minutes without becoming inattentive. Children have an even shorter attention span. Many speakers adhere to a rule of no more than five and no fewer than three points to be covered in a single lecture. For younger children, three points may be too many. Depending on the amount of material to be covered in the lesson, several lectures over a period of days may be desirable.

Two: Select an Advance Organizer.   After the content of the lesson has been carefully diagrammed and the main points to be covered identified, an advance organizer should be selected. Advance organizers are discussed in Chapter 3. Keep in mind the importance of selecting an idea that is more general than the new material and that can provide the learner with a context within which to relate the new learning. For instance, a lecture on baking a cake might begin with an advance organizer tracing the development of cakes from simple patties prepared by native tribes to the complex confections available in bakeries.

Three: Use Examples to Illustrate Each Point.   Examples serve as memory hooks for the listener. Because many speakers do not use visual aids, they rely on stories and anecdotes to illustrate the main points. The same technique is effective in the classroom in helping the students remember the main points. Anecdotes, such as the following, remain in memory and assist in the recall of the points made in the lecture:

> When I was a child, we made ice cream on Sundays in a freezer with a hand crank.
>
> During the war, many things were rationed. You needed stamps to buy gasoline.
>
> When the apple bopped Newton, he got more than a lump on the brow.

In the classroom, the teacher can also use many audiovisual materials to illustrate the points made in the lecture.

Four: Use Repetition to Reinforce the Main Points.   Repeat all the points made previously when each new point is introduced. And ask questions when appropriate to determine the level of interest and understanding.

Five: Summarize the Points and Refer Back to the Organizer.   At the end of the lecture, summarize the main points and conclude with a reference to the organizer. This helps to "wrap up" the presentation for the students.

Demonstrations.   If the lesson is to include a demonstration, the teacher prepares the material to be learned in small segments and checks for understanding at the end of each segment. One of the most difficult tasks of the expert is to anticipate the learning steps of the beginner, particularly one who may not have the same aptitude or enthusiasm for the skill that the teacher has.

Visual examples work particularly well in the presentation stage of this model. Too often, teachers depend on telling when showing, through either pictures or live demonstration, can be more effective and can provide learners with a memory hook for new information. Imagine a lesson on baking a cake without a demonstration phase; yet many teachers forget that one picture (activity, experiment, or demonstration) can be worth a thousand words.

In summary, the steps of presenting information are as follows:

1. Analyze the content to be presented according to the needs of the learners.
2. Chart the content from the most general to the most specific material to be presented.
3. Break all skills into small segments to be presented in a logical order.
4. Develop an advance organizer for the lesson that will provide a reference point for the new material.
5. Select the main points or steps to be presented and limit these to a reasonable number, depending on the learners.
6. Select examples to illustrate each main point and connect each point or step to the one preceding and to the advance organizer.
7. Ask questions to check for understanding and watch for signals from the class that indicate lack of attention.
8. Summarize the main points and connect them to the next phase of the lesson.

Step 4—Guide Practice, Assess Performance, and Provide Corrective Feedback

Practice, both guided and independent, is an essential part of direct instruction. New material is presented in small steps, with ample opportunity for practice following each step of the process. In the following examples, the teacher controls the process and monitors the practice of both the group and individuals within the group.

I. To tie our shoes we start with holding a lace in each hand. Now take the lace on the model shoe in front of you and hold a lace in each hand. Good. The next step is to cross the lace in the right hand over the one in the left hand (be sure to plan for children who are left-handed). Let us all practice putting the right lace over the left lace like this. Tommy, hold up your right hand. Good.

Now cross the lace in that hand over the one in your left hand, like this. Very good.

II. To operate a computer we must first turn it on. Please locate the switch in the left-hand corner and switch it to the on position.

III. We have just seen a filmstrip on the four chambers of the heart. Let us review each of these four chambers as we fill in this diagram on the board together. Who can name one of the chambers?

Questioning. The most common form of guided practice is questioning by the teacher to check for understanding. A number of questions—more than enough for the lesson—should be prepared ahead of time. Teachers frequently err in feeling that the class will become bored if too many questions are asked during instruction; in learning new material, however, repetition and review are essential. There is a greater risk that too few questions will be asked to only a small number of students than that there will be too many questions.

Wait time, the time a teacher allows for a student to answer a question, is also an essential component of the process. As Robert Slavin reports, research indicates that teachers give up too quickly when questioning students, particularly low-achieving students. A wait of approximately 3 seconds seems to produce the best results along with following up with students who do not respond.[7]

Because few students want to announce their ignorance to the world, the request "Raise your hand if you don't understand" is usually an ineffective diagnostic. Questions such as "Are there any questions?" are hardly better. Nor should the teacher call on those students who always raise their hands. A better technique is to say "In a minute I will ask someone to do this problem on the board, so be prepared" or "After we view the filmstrip, I will ask the following questions."

To monitor participation, the teacher can maintain a checklist of students responding to questions. If the same students answer most of the questions, the teacher should evaluate the questions asked and determine if the rest of the class is comprehending the material.

If a few students never raise their hands, a conference can be planned to discuss their class participation. For some students, speaking out in class is frightening even when they know the answer. One technique is to ask students to write a short answer to each question on a sheet of paper and pass it to the front of the row. If the answers given by the students who never speak out in class are correct, the teacher can ask them to read their answers aloud. Gradually, this may help them to gain the confidence needed for class participation.

There is a story about a teacher whose principal praised her at her retirement dinner by saying how impressed he had always been in observing her classroom, that whenever she asked questions all hands went up, and whoever was called on knew the answer. The teacher confessed that she had told her students to raise their hands when a guest was present: "Raise your right hand if you know the answer, your left hand if you don't know the answer." Actually, that is not a bad technique—it would at least give the teacher a way to know how many students claim to understand the

material and thus some way to adjust the pace of instruction to accommodate the learners' needs.

Effective teachers set up situations in which those who need further explanation or help can get it. They ask students to repeat the directions or the information. They ask students to summarize for each other and share those summaries. They call on students for additional examples and applications of information.

Rosenshine identifies four types of student responses to questions:[8]

1. **Correct, quick, and firm:** The teacher's response to this type of answer is to ask a new question to keep the pace of the lesson moving, avoiding overemphasis on success.
2. **Correct but hesitant:** This type of response usually occurs during the initial stages of learning, and the teacher should provide some encouragement such as saying "That's good" or "Keep up the good work."
3. **Incorrect but careless:** Simply correct and move on. The student knows the process but made a careless mistake.
4. **Incorrect and lacking knowledge of facts or process:** The teacher may provide hints, ask a simpler question, or reteach.

Correcting Error.   Rosenshine emphasizes that "errors should not go uncorrected. . . . Students learn better with feedback—as immediate as possible; and errors should be corrected before they become habitual."[9]

If the students have not learned the material, don't blame them and don't go on. A swimming coach does not allow students to drown if they are in the deep end of the pool and cannot tread water. He or she goes back to a more basic step. The same approach is needed in learning any skill or new content. If students do not meet the instructional objectives, the teacher should evaluate and analyze the original presentation, determine the problem, and then find a way to reach the entire class. The success rate for the learning of directly taught skills should be as close to 100 percent as possible. Students who understand the first presentation will benefit from any reteaching, particularly if the later presentation is different from the first. Better yet is to have early learners help others by putting their understandings into their own words for others to follow.

There are as many potential teachers in a classroom as there are people who understand what is to be taught. In addition, individualized materials, programmed learning materials, and computer-assisted instruction are potential resources for students who need additional learning time.

Effective teachers watch for signals from the class. Confused learners will usually act out in some manner. They will turn to a neighbor, put their heads on the desk, tap their pencils, grimace, or yawn. If the class has not understood, instead of reacting with anger, try again. Perhaps the skill level at which you began the instruction was too high for most of the class and you need to start at a lower level. Expect an 85 percent or higher success rate by the students before proceeding to the next level. In some cases, 100 percent is the only acceptable success rate. (For the math teacher, a 100 percent, high-speed mastery of the multiplication tables through 10 may be the goal.)

Jere Brophy's report on the behavior of effective teachers in inner-city schools pertains to instruction at all levels. Brophy writes: "If the curricula, instructional methods, or evaluation devices that [effective teachers] intended to use do not work, they find others that will work. If something is not learned the first time through, they teach it again. In general, these teachers treat student failure as a challenge."[10]

Step 5—Assign Independent Practice, Assess Performance, and Provide Corrective Feedback

Independent practice requires careful monitoring of students practicing a new skill on their own or in small groups. Before students are assigned independent work, however, sufficient time must be spent in guided practice to ensure that they are prepared to work on their own.

The teacher should circulate during independent practice, checking that no student is repeating a mistake or is actually *practicing error*. In addition, there should be some way for students to check their results as they proceed independently. Sometimes, the answers in the back of the textbook are an excellent resource. Some teachers provide checkpoints, or stations, in the classroom where students can go periodically to check their work.

Worksheets.   If worksheets are used for independent practice, they should be introduced in a setting of guided practice. As the teacher demonstrates the process, the class completes the first problem together. The next problem is done individually, and the entire class examines the problem and its solution together as the process is explained for all to see. If necessary, have the class complete several problems as a group or have small groups or pairs of students work on the problems before individuals attempt to work on their own.

The problem with many worksheet assignments given for independent practice is that students may repeatedly make the same error, and that error then becomes fixed in their learning. Often, worksheets come to dominate instruction in inappropriate ways as time fillers and busywork. Consider the following situation: A consultant hired to evaluate a reading program was visiting a classroom, just walking around to get a feel for the place, when a child looked up from his hunched-over position to ask, "Can you tell me what I'm supposed to be doing?" On the dimly printed sheet before the lad was the following: "Each of the following words has a blank space where a letter has been left out. Place a vowel that says its name in each blank space to make a word."

>   c_me   m_ne   r_in

With prompting, the child tried *a* in the first blank and successfully made *came*. Then he announced, "I get it. The next one is 'mone.'"

This child was *required* to practice a behavior that he had not been taught and that, furthermore, was abstracted from any context in which it could have meaning. The task is an abstract exercise, all too typical of worksheets.

Unitization and Automaticity.   The terms *unitization* and *automaticity* have been used to describe the two stages through which students pass in independent practice.[11] In the unitization phase, students are carefully attending to each component or unit of the skill. They are working with few errors but are working slowly and with considerable effort. As they reach automaticity, they are able to work more quickly and to respond automatically without having to think through each step in the process. To reach automaticity, students need to overlearn the skill through practice and repetition at the unitization stage.

Homework is most effective when students have reached unitization of learning but have not yet reached automaticity. As the most frequently used form of independent practice, homework is often abused when students are sent home to practice material before they understand it clearly and before there has been ample guided practice in the classroom. Much of the frustration with homework assignments occurs because students are asked to work independently with material before they are ready.

Step 6—Review Periodically, Offering Corrective Feedback If Necessary

Periodic review of the material should be built into every instructional plan. Over-learning is essential to mastering a new skill, particularly when each skill is necessary to learning the next. While students are in the process of learning a new skill, review of skills learned before is essential for automaticity. (Many English teachers say that they never learned as much grammar as when they taught it five times a day!)

Homework should be checked as a part of the review before proceeding. If homework is worth assigning, it is worth checking, yet research indicates that many teachers neglect this important part of the review process.[12] If the students have not understood the assignment, do not go on to the next step. Reteach the material and analyze the reasons for failure to learn.

If a weekly review indicates that a skill has not been retained, then reteaching is necessary. Students often forget skills and information during the summer, so it is particularly important to test for retention at the beginning of a new school year or semester.

Teachers should demand a high success rate for their students. If students are not learning, there must be a reason. Some questions to be asked are:

- Did the students have the required background to learn the new set of skills or material?
- Were the steps in the learning process broken into sufficiently small steps?
- Was each step learned before a new step was introduced?
- Were the learning objectives and the directions stated clearly?
- Was the content organized logically, and were the examples, lectures, and demonstrations effective?
- Were sufficient questions asked to determine if the class understood what was being taught?
- Was there enough guided practice? Were all the students involved in the practice, and were errors corrected quickly?
- Was there independent practice of the skill or learning? Was this independent practice checked carefully to determine if the students were performing without error?
- Were there periodic review and opportunities for practice of the new learning?

Summary of Steps in the Direct Instruction Model

1. *Review previously learned material:* Make certain that students have mastered the material taught previously and that they understand the connections to the new learning.
2. *State objectives for the lesson:* The objectives should be presented to the students at the beginning of the lesson in language they can comprehend.
3. *Present new material:* New material should be well organized and presented in an interesting manner. Frequent checks should be used to determine if the students are comprehending the information.
4. *Guide practice, assess performance, and provide corrective feedback:* Guide the students through practice sessions, making certain that they are performing correctly.
5. *Assign independent practice, assess performance, and provide corrective feedback:* Continue to supervise the students as they work independently, checking for error. Homework should be assigned for independent practice only when the teacher feels certain that the students can perform the work correctly.
6. *Review periodically, offering corrective feedback if necessary:* Homework is checked before new instruction is given, and reteaching is conducted if necessary. The

teacher conducts periodic checks to make certain that the new learning has been retained.

EXERCISE 4.1

Evaluate the effectiveness of the following remarks according to the steps in the direct instruction model.

1. Who wants to put the homework problems on the board?
2. Because you all failed the quiz this morning, there will be no recess today.
3. Today we will learn about mitosis. Listen carefully because you don't know anything about this and there will be a quiz tomorrow.
4. As you watch the filmstrip, pay attention to the names of the oceans and rivers. I will ask you questions about these later.
5. Because you were not paying attention during the lecture, I am assigning three pages of problems for homework tonight.
6. While the class is reading quietly, I will ask some individuals to come to my desk and review the reading skills that we learned last week.

Possible Answers to Exercise 4.1
1. In the first example, the teacher would gain better information in the review process by designating specific students to go to the board: Sonja, Joe, and Tomas, please put the first steps of the problem on the board. Watch carefully, class, because I will ask three other people to complete the problem.

2. The failure of the class to learn should be countered by a different instructional approach, not punishment. Teachers who consistently blame students for a failure to learn do not grow professionally. Repeatedly blaming students prevents teachers from analyzing what needs to be done differently.

3. Students are more likely to learn new material if it is presented in an interesting manner and connected to something with which they are familiar than if they are threatened by an exam.

4. The teacher is preparing the students for guided practice by instructing them to focus on the important material to be learned. Giving students a study guide to fill in as they view the filmstrip, and periodically pausing the film during the presentation to make certain that everyone is keeping up, is an even more effective procedure.

5. The students are probably going to practice error. The independent practice of homework should be based on successful guided practice in the classroom. If the class was inattentive and did not learn the material, it would be futile to assign homework that requires applying that material. At this point, the teacher needs to determine what prevented learning from taking place and then plan to reteach the material.

6. This is a good technique for evaluating individual students to determine if retention has occurred. It is also an excellent way to establish independent contact with children in the classroom. ▪

Basis for the Direct Instruction Model

Although the direct instruction model is based in part on behavioral psychology, which originated with the work of Ivan Pavlov in the early 1900s,[13] it is more directly linked to the work of B. F. Skinner[14] and to training psychology and cybernetics techniques developed primarily for the military. In the behavioral approach, the emphasis is on controlling those behaviors of the learner that can be measured and observed rather than focusing on inner psychodynamic forces such as thinking and feeling.

By providing food each time a rat exhibited the desired behavior, Skinner was able to train it to push a lever only when a light was turned on. Conversely, the rat was given no food if it pushed the lever when the light was not on. The rat was conditioned to perform the desired behavior through selective reinforcement, a process called operant conditioning. Operants are behaviors that are voluntarily performed by the learner. Because the reinforcement was contingent on the performance of the desired behavior, the process of conditioning is called contingency management. To be effective, the reinforcement following the desired behavior must be immediate, consistent, and regular.

Many educators are repelled by the idea of teaching people by methods related, even remotely, to the way in which rats are trained to push a lever. But for certain types of learning, training through contingency management has proven to be highly effective. By breaking the learning task into small steps and by reinforcing the learning at each step in the process, the teacher conditions the desired behavior and increases the probability that it will occur again. Each step in the process is followed by feedback, and the learner is rewarded for correct performance. Behaviorists point out that the instructor, by carefully determining the steps necessary to learn the desired skill and conditioning the correct response, provides the conditions for learners to gain control of their environment. Critics of this approach point out that conditioned behavior may not be of long-term duration. Once again, the reader is cautioned that this model should be used with others in a total design.

Concepts of Training Behavior

Some of the important concepts of training behavior are shaping, modeling, practice, feedback, and reinforcement.

Shaping. Once the teacher determines the desired outcome of student learning, the task is broken into the steps, or successive approximations, necessary to acquire the new learning or skill. As students progress through the steps necessary for mastery of the desired skill, their behavior is gradually shaped through reinforcement.

Modeling.   Learners acquire knowledge and skills by witnessing and imitating the teacher, who acts as a model. In some situations, a student can learn segments of information or steps in a skill much more efficiently by copying the behavior of another than by working independently.

Models can also be procedures that have been developed for the learner to follow (such as the models of teaching in this text) or carefully designed self-teaching materials that guide a learner through each step in the process. For instance, in China drawing is taught by having very young students repeatedly copy the works of masters. Originality is not valued until years later. Through this process, these young students become proficient at reproducing very sophisticated work.

Practice.   In the early stages of practice, the teacher leads learners through each step in a regimented and structured manner. It is essential in this phase that errors be corrected and that correct behaviors be reinforced. After students are able to perform a skill with 85 to 90 percent accuracy, they then practice independently with periodic supervision until they can perform the task accurately and totally independently.

Beginning practice should occur in frequent, intense, and highly structured segments. Depending on the learners' ages, these segments may vary in length of time, but the students should always be motivated and involved during these sessions. Monitoring by the teacher to ensure accuracy in performance is essential.

As learning approaches mastery, practice sessions should be gradually spaced farther apart. New learning can be introduced at this time, while the previous learning is still being practiced. For instance, a student learning scales on the piano may begin to practice the G scale but should periodically return to the C scale to reinforce the learning.

Feedback.   Feedback should be as specific as possible. It is most effective when the reinforcement given is positive and frequent. Negative statements ("That was a stupid thing to do" or "Why can't you keep up with the rest of the class?") generally discourage performance. Corrective feedback should describe the behavior and specify the way to correct it.

As practice proceeds, students need to receive feedback, either verbally, through grades, or by alternative evaluation devices (smiley faces) regarding their performances. In the beginning, the teacher provides continual feedback through reinforcement of correct behavior or through correction and reteaching. As the learning progresses, feedback can become less frequent.

Reinforcement.   Reinforcement can be continuous or intermittent; that is, the teacher can reinforce behavior each time it occurs or follow a periodic schedule of reinforcement. In the early stages of learning, behavior should be reinforced after every correct response and after responses in the right direction. Few learners can do everything right the very first time, but they need encouragement as they proceed.

As learning progresses, reinforcement should be provided at intervals determined by the teacher. These intervals may be based on a certain number of correct responses, such as after four correct responses or after a certain amount of time, by checking for retention on a schedule and reinforcing the correct response.

Basic Principles of Conditioning Behavior

The following are some basic principles related to conditioning behavior.

1. Identify the specific goals or target behaviors that you want the learner to achieve. Be specific in describing these behaviors and the success rate you will accept. For example:

- Students will be able to list with 85 percent accuracy the 12 major battles of the Civil War.
- Given 10 problems in long division, students will solve the problems with at least 85 percent accuracy.
- Students will be able to recite the multiplication tables from the 2 times to the 6 times table with 100 percent accuracy in two and a half minutes or less.

2. Pretest to determine how much of the target behavior the learner already possesses. Keep accurate data on the skill development of learners. Provide accurate feedback to students about both their current level of performance or knowledge and their progress toward mastery.

3. Set realistic goals for learners. Consider the age of the learners, their interest in the learning, and their present level of knowledge. Here, transfer of learning is an important consideration because skills related to interest and prior knowledge are more easily acquired than other skills. For instance, if a person can tune the motor of a lawn mower, he or she can probably learn to tune the engine of an automobile.

4. Break the task to be learned into small, interrelated segments and introduce a single step at a time.

5. Use positive reinforcement to change behavior whenever possible and reinforce a behavior immediately after it occurs.

6. Reinforce continually when first introducing a new learning, but then gradually schedule reinforcement at periodic intervals.

7. Keep careful records of the learners' progress, and encourage students to monitor their own progress in achieving their learning goals.

One author says of the direct instruction process:

> The teacher, in a face-to-face, reasonably formal manner, tells, shows, models, demonstrates, *teaches* the skill to be learned. The key word here is *teacher*, for it is the teacher who is in command of the learning situation and leads the lesson, as opposed to having instruction "directed" by a worksheet, kit, learning center, or workbook.[15]

EXERCISE 4.2

Indicate which of the following objectives could be effectively taught using the direct instruction model. Explain the reasons for your decisions.

1. Students will be able to diagram sentences indicating subject, verb, and direct object.
2. Students will be able to utilize metaphorical language in describing situations.
3. Students will perform the swan dive.
4. Students will be able to follow directions in cutting out a shirt.
5. Students will be able to utilize effective group problem-solving skills.

Answer to Exercise 4.2
Objectives 1, 3, and 4 are appropriate because a very specific sequence of behaviors can be identified and practiced. In 2 and 5, some aspects of these objectives can be learned through direct instruction, but other models would be more appropriate. ■

Scenario

A science class is studying a unit on chemical changes that necessitates the use of the Bunsen burner, which has not yet been used in the class. Mr. Shuman begins by determining how many people have used the burners before. Two students raise their hands, and he asks them to come to his table and serve as assistants.

Mr. Shuman begins by reviewing briefly the preceding lesson: "Yesterday, we discussed safety in the laboratory and established some basic safety rules. Let's go over those together. Latoya, please state the first rule."

Then Mr. Shuman describes the objectives of the lesson for the day: "Today, we will learn to use the Bunsen burner, an important piece of laboratory equipment. By the end of this lesson you will be able to identify the parts of the burner, and you will be able to use it with a group to perform a simple activity."

As an organizer, Mr. Shuman uses an analogy familiar to the students. He asks the students if they have ever watched a welder using a blowtorch.

TOMMY: Sure, it turned the pipe red hot when they were fixing our sink.

MR. SHUMAN: What was the plumber able to do with the pipe when it was hot?

TOMMY: I think that it could be bent.

MR. SHUMAN: Right. Heat can change the way a substance behaves, especially when the heat is intense and can be directed to a particular area; therefore, we frequently need such heat in the laboratory. A safe and convenient source of such heat is the Bunsen burner.

For the next 15 minutes, the teacher presents information on the Bunsen burner, using pictures to illustrate the parts and their function. He frequently asks questions to determine if the students are understanding the material.

After the presentation, he uses an overhead projector to show the class the steps for using the burner. Mr. Shuman demonstrates each step and then asks the assistants to demonstrate them as well. After each step the class discusses the procedure. For the guided practice step, the teacher assigns pairs of students to work together to use the burners, and he moves about the classroom, checking on the progress of each pair. When there is an error, he corrects it immediately.

At the end of the period, Mr. Shuman distributes a worksheet for a homework assignment on which the steps for using the burner are out of order and directs the students to place the steps in the proper order and then to label the parts of the burner. He tells the class that they will review the steps the following day and then each student will use the burner to complete a simple experiment.

If Mr. Shuman discovers the following day that one or two students are still having difficulty with the lesson, he may decide to assign them some additional practice, work with them individually, or ask them to work with one of the students who has mastered the procedures. If the burners are not used for a while, he will review their use carefully to be sure that the students have retained the necessary information.

ACTIVITY 4.1

Considering the lessons you plan to teach, develop a lesson plan that uses the direct instruction model to present new material or to teach a new skill. ■

Summary

It is important to repeat a statement made in the beginning of this chapter: The direct instruction model is a necessary but not a sufficient instructional tool. To be without this effective tool is a handicap because the steps in this model provide a framework for instructional design; but to use this model exclusively is deadening.

In a general sense, the other models presented in this text can be incorporated into the presentation of material phase of the direct instruction model. More specifically, this model can also be used to teach many knowledge-level objectives and skills.

A cautionary word is appropriate, however. Robert Slavin reports that "the research on direct instruction has focused mostly on basic reading and mathematics, mostly in the elementary grades. For other subjects, and at other grade levels, we have less of a basis for believing that direct instruction methods will improve student learning."[16]

WEB RESOURCES

1. **http://curry.edschool.virginia.edu/curry/class/edis/511/DI**
   Resources About Direct Instruction—John Wills Lloyd
   Direct Instruction: This site is a portal to research and resources relating to Direct Instruction.

2. http://www.adprima.com/direct.htm
Included in this site are direct teaching guidelines and information regarding links to other sites.

3. http://www-instruct.nmu.edu/education/rhrecz/IndirectDirectTeach.html
An excellent chart is included, describing the procedures of major direct instruction theorists.

4. http://chiron.valdosta.edu/whuitt/col/instruct/dirinst.html
A succinct outline of Rober Slavin's model of direct instruction is provided.

5. http://www.abacon.com/slavin/notes7.html
This is a practical guide to how a direct instruction lesson is taught.

6. http://www.humboldt.edu-tha1/hunter-eei.html decontex
Barak Rosenshine describes how effective teachers teach less structured skills: how to summarize, how to take notes, how to ask appropriate questions, etc.

7. http://www.teachreach.org/barb.htm
Two spelling study strategies on the spelling performance of second-grade students are compared and evaluated.

8. http://www.humboldt.edu/~tha1/hunter-eei.html
This site includes an outline and description of Madeline Hunter's lesson design with an explanation of each of the seven steps.

N O T E S

   1. Robert E. Slavin, *Educational Psychology: Theory and Practice*, 6th ed. (Boston: Allyn and Bacon, 2000), 235–236.
   2. L. M. Anderson, C. M. Evertson, and J. E. Brophy, "An Experimental Study of Effective Teaching in First-Grade Reading Groups," *Elementary School Journal* 79 (1979): 193–223; J. E. Brophy, "Successful Teaching Strategies for the Inner-City Child," *Phi Delta Kappan* 63 (1982): 527–532; and J. E. Brophy and T. L. Good, "Teacher Behavior and Student Achievement," in *Handbook of Research on Teaching*, 3rd ed., ed. Merlin C. Wittrock (New York: Macmillan, 1986), 328–375.
   3. B. Rosenshine, "Teaching Functions in Instructional Programs," *Elementary School Journal* 83 (1983): 335–350.
   4. T. L. Good and D. A. Grouws, "The Missouri Mathematics Effectiveness Project: An Experimental Study in Fourth-Grade Classrooms," *Journal of Educational Psychology* 71 (1979): 355–362.
   5. Madeline Hunter, "Knowing, Teaching and Supervising," in *Using What We Know about Teaching*, ed. Philip L. Hosford (Alexandria, VA: Association for Supervision and Curriculum Development, 1984), 175–176.
   6. Rosenshine, 338.
   7. Slavin, 231.
   8. Rosenshine, 344, 345.
   9. Rosenshine, 345.
   10. Brophy, 527–532.
   11. S. J. Samuels, "Some Essentials of Decoding," *Exceptional Education Quarterly* 2 (1981): 11–25.
   12. Good and Grouws, 335–362.
   13. I. Pavlov, *Conditioned Reflexes: An Investigation of Physiological Activity of the Cerebral Cortex*, trans. G. V. Anrep (London: Oxford University Press, 1927).
   14. B. F. Skinner, *Science and Human Behavior* (New York: Macmillan, 1963).
   15. J. F. Baumann, "Direct Instruction Reconsidered," *Journal of Reading Behavior* 31 (1988): 714.
   16. Slavin, 236.

5 The Concept Attainment Model

Defining Concepts Inductively

One of the great paradoxes of language is that even though the world is full of a practically infinite number of objects and ideas, humans somehow manage to talk about them all with a few thousand words. In part this is possible through the dual processes of concept development and concept attainment. Concept development, the topic of Chapter 6, is the process of creating categories by grouping similar objects and ideas; this greatly eases the burden of having so many different things to recall or understand. Concept attainment is the process of defining concepts by finding those attributes that are absolutely essential to the meaning and disregarding those that are not; it also involves learning to discriminate between what is and is not an example of the concept.

The natural tendency toward concept attainment is illustrated by every child. If a child spends her first year in the presence of a house pet, that is, a cat, she will certainly make the generalization that small furry animals with four legs are cats. This tendency to overgeneralize a concept, for example, by calling the neighbor's dog a cat, frequently surprises adults. How does that happen? In the process of attaining the concept of cat, the child encounters multiple examples of cat (shorthaired and longhaired, adult and kitten, and so forth) and examples of animals that are not cats (the canary in a cage, the neighbor's German shepherd, grasshoppers in the yard). All these examples of cats and not-cats allow the child (1) to intuit a set of attributes for cat, characteristics that define and distinguish a cat as a cat, and (2) to test her hypothesis of what a cat is and is not by trying the label *cat* on animals that might be what a cat is. The adult's role in the child's concept attainment process is to provide an enriched, idea-filled environment so that many examples of many concepts are encountered, and information and feedback regarding the accuracy of the concept definitions are given.

Teaching concept attainment is in many ways a formal enactment of the natural process of concept attainment just described. It is easy to take for granted that children possess certain concepts that in truth they do not possess and thus to base instruction on false and instructionally harmful assumptions. Adults find much humor in the misconceptions children often develop for what they are taught in school. For instance, Art Linkletter, who interviewed thousands of youngsters on his radio and television programs, recounted the following in his book *Kids Say the Darndest Things:*

> Half-heard and half-understood, words and phrases project a kaleidoscopic pattern of life on the nerve endings of a growing child. . . . One of my all-time favorites is the boy who said: "My favorite song is 'I'm going to Alabama with a band-aid on my knee.'"
>
> A little girl came to a costume party at the Linkletter house one day wearing a fancy colonial costume. "Who are you supposed to be?" I wondered.
>
> "I'm George Washington's wife. She saved her father's life by jumping on a horse and riding through the town yelling 'The British are coming.'"
>
> . . . A small friend of ours when singing "God Bless America" comes out with the logical lyrics: "Stand beside her, and guide her, with the light through the night from a bulb."[1]

Cute as these anecdotes are, one has to wonder how many concepts taught to children in school are misunderstood or misinterpreted. Too often, teachers delude themselves and students into thinking that memorization is the same as understanding. This leaves many questions: What's the use of teaching if what is taught has no meaning for the learners? Isn't conceptualization more important than memorization? Why is it so easy to assume that learners understand the meaning of the concepts used in the classroom?

The concept attainment process in the classroom helps learners attain the meaning of concepts through the inductive process of comparing examples and nonexamples of the concept until a definition is derived. In taking ownership of concepts that they have a part in developing, students can become "authorities" in what they are taught.

What Is a Concept?

Concepts are defined by the attributes we give them. Attributes are the distinguishing features of an object or an idea. There are two kinds of attributes: essential and nonessential. Even though a table is an object that we can see and touch and smell, we have a concept in our heads of what a table is, or "tableness" as the philosopher Plato expressed it. A table is often defined as a flat surface supported by legs on which we place objects. Is a board supported by two unattached cinder blocks on which we place our lunch a table? Is a board lying on the ground on which we place our lunch a table? The attributes of table that you have "taken to yourself"—the attributes that you have put in your conceptual file marked *table*—will determine your answers to these questions. Certain attributes are essential or necessary to the concept; others are nonessential or variable.

Two attributes most often associated with the concept *apple* are "red" and "round." If, however, a youngster grew up where Granny Smith apples are grown, he might consider the most common attributes to be "green" and "round," so red is actually a variable attribute. The conceptual file into which we place our apple attributes should contain information on size, shape, color, taste, texture, skin, seeds, stem, and so on. In addition to factual information, our individual files contain impressions, knowledge, opinions, memories, assumptions, inferences, generalizations, and associations such as "An apple a day keeps the doctor away" or "An apple for the teacher."

The word *concept*, therefore, refers not only to the object in itself, which many think is unknowable because one can never step out of one's own understanding, but also to those attributes that make up one's notion of that object.

Steps in the Concept Attainment Model

Steps 1 through 3 are completed by the teacher prior to instruction.

1. Select and define a concept.
2. Select the attributes.
3. Develop positive and negative examples.
4. Introduce the process to the students.
5. Present the examples and list the attributes.
6. Develop a concept definition.
7. Give additional examples.
8. Discuss the process with the class.
9. Evaluate.

Step 1—Select and Define a Concept

The concept attainment process is most appropriate for teaching concepts that have clear criterial attributes. For example, the parts of speech can be taught as concepts with clear attributes. The classification system in biology is very suitable for concept attainment, as are concepts of freedom and slavery in the Civil War, triangles and other shapes in geometry, different artistic styles in fine arts, and each of the types of sentences (simple, compound, and so forth). Select concepts for teaching with this

model that can be defined by features that clearly distinguish them from other similar concepts.

In selecting a concept to teach, think about related concepts, as well. It is important that students be able to recognize the relationships among various concepts. For instance, in teaching the concept of *apple*, the teacher must consider concepts that are coordinate to apple, subordinate to apple, and superordinate to apple. Apples, pears, and oranges (coordinate) are all fruits (superordinate). Mackintosh, Stayman, and Winesap (subordinate) are all types of apples. Although all apples are fruits, not all fruits are apples, and a Winesap is both a type of apple and a fruit.

Fruit	(Superordinate)		
Apple	(Coordinate)	Pear	Orange
Mackintosh	(Subordinate)		
Stayman			
Winesap			

Once you have identified a concept that is teachable by the concept attainment process, write a definition that is satisfactory to you and comprehensible to the learners. Concept definitions in many textbooks are confusing, so do not rely solely on the text or on the dictionary. It may take time to find a definition that will serve as an adequate base for the lesson; because a concept usually has multiple meanings, it is necessary to limit the definition to the one most appropriate for the lesson. At the close of the concept attainment process, you may discuss with the students other meanings of the concept.

The point is not merely to find a definition that will, in turn, be given to the students. Instead, it is important that the teacher formulate the definition to be used in the design of the concept attainment lesson and select the appropriate examples. The major purpose of the lesson is to allow students the chance to author their own definition; for many reasons, student-generated definitions are often superior to the initial definition created by the teacher. In any event, the outstanding function of the concept attainment model is to provide an alternative to telling learners *what* to understand and instead allowing them, literally, to participate in their understandings.

Step 2—Select the Attributes

Once the first step of selecting and defining a concept is completed, selecting the attributes essential to a definition of the concept—those that determine an object's placement into the conceptual category—is next. For example, the concept rectangle is a four-sided geometric figure containing all right angles in which the opposite sides are both parallel and equal. The essential, defining attributes are:

Geometric figure
Four-sided
Containing all right angles
Opposite sides parallel and equal

Step 3—Develop Positive and Negative Examples

Create as many examples of the concept as possible. Each positive example must contain *all* the essential attributes. For the rectangle, some examples can be drawn on the chalkboard, some can be made of cardboard, some can be projected with an overhead projector, and others can be cut out of construction paper, but each example must contain all the essential attributes: four sides that meet at four right angles, each pair of sides parallel and of equal length (see Figure 5.1).

Prepare some negative examples that do not contain all the attributes. For instance, a triangle is a geometric figure, but it does not contain all the attributes of a rectangle. These negative examples will help students focus on the essential attributes.

Step 4—Introduce the Process to the Students

Explain carefully to the students that the goal of the activity is to define the concept by identifying what is essential to the meaning. You may talk of this as a game, and you may keep the concept a secret until the end of the activity. The purpose is that the students gradually arrive at an understanding and define the concept in their own words.

Place two column headings on the chalkboard, one for positive features, one for negative features. Tell the students that you will show them positive and negative examples of the concept you want them to learn. Their job is to formulate a list of features that distinguish the positive examples, which will then lead to a clear definition of the concept.

Explain that an attribute in the positive column will be crossed out when a new positive example does not contain that attribute. It is essential that the attributes be crossed out rather than erased so that the process can be reviewed at the end to see how the essential attributes were identified.

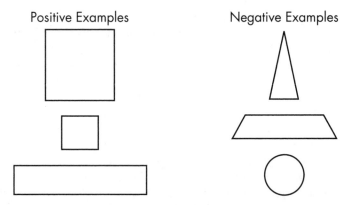

Positive Examples   Negative Examples

FIGURE 5.1   Positive and Negative Examples of Rectangles for a Concept Attainment Lesson

Step 5—Present the Examples and List the Attributes

Start with a positive example. Allow students to mention any attributes they note. There are no wrong answers. If a student says that the figure is *made of paper*, write made of paper on the chalkboard under the heading *Positive*. (*Paper* will be eliminated when there is another positive example of a rectangle made of another substance.) Stress that every positive example needs to contain all the features, attributes, and qualities of the concept. Nonessential, or "noisy," attributes, such as color or texture, can be pointed out in the discussion. For instance, imagine that a teacher has fashioned the first positive example of a rectangle from green construction paper. When they see it, the students volunteer the following list of attributes:

> Green
> Four sides
> Made of paper
> A shape
> Opposite sides are alike

The second positive example is a rectangle drawn on the chalkboard. The teacher reminds the class that every positive example must contain all the attributes of the concept. This time the class eliminates two attributes from the original list. (The teacher crosses out the eliminated words but does not erase; the students need to see how they arrived at their definition.) Now the list looks like this:

> ~~Green~~
> Four sides
> ~~Made of paper~~
> A shape
> Opposite sides are alike
> Contains all right angles

As a result of looking at the new example and comparing it with the first, they add to the list *contains all right angles*. Now the teacher tells the class that this is a negative example:

The teacher reminds the class that the negative example may contain some but not all of the attributes and that it will help them focus on the differences. The students note that this figure also has four sides but that the opposite sides are not equal and the angles are not right angles. Then one student notices that in the positive examples, all the opposite sides are parallel to each other. This fact is now added to the positive list of attributes. The negative example helped the students to note a positive attribute that they had missed. The list now looks like this:

~~Green~~
Four sides
~~Made of paper~~
A shape
Opposite sides are alike
Contains all right angles
Opposite sides are parallel

At this stage, the teacher asks the students to clarify some of their terms: "What is another name for alike?" (Equal.) "Is there another word that we could use with *shape* to make it more descriptive?" (Geometric shape.)

Negative examples serve to emphasize the positive attributes, as the trapezoid did in the rectangle example. Attributes of the negative examples listed on the board can be used for emphasis and comparison. Some negative examples will have some of, but not all, the qualities of the concept. Make it clear to the students that negative examples do not eliminate any attributes from the positive list; only positive examples that do not contain an attribute on the list allow elimination of an attribute.

This process teaches learners to attend to likenesses and differences and to understand a concept's essential attributes. Giving examples that illustrate the attributes is insufficient. For instance, if the concept is fruit, just having different fruit listed on the board will not bring about a definition. To form a definition, students must first identify the essential attributes, and the examples must give learners a clear indication of these attributes. In this case, the examples could be pictures showing different fruit cut open or actual fruit in different stages of development.

Attributes can be demonstrated in many ways. For instance, if the teacher is introducing the concept *romanticism* to a literature class, pictures from the romantic period in art provide excellent positive examples; negative examples could be drawn from art that represents other styles.

Select appropriate media; pictures, vignettes, three-dimensional objects, and verbal examples are all effective. Guard against reading long passages aloud to the students, as they will not be able to remember the information. Instead, on a sheet of paper give clear and interesting examples that they can read.

Step 6—Develop a Concept Definition

Now that a reasonably complete list of significant attributes is on the board, the teacher can ask the students to try to develop a definition for their new concept that incorporates all the essential attributes remaining on the board. Often, definitions in students' own words will be surprisingly more comprehensible than the textbook definition. The teacher may choose to give the concept name to the class before or after the definition has been developed.

Be patient with this part of the process; students are not accustomed to stating definitions in their own words. Encourage one student to make the initial effort so that others can add to or change the definition. With experience, the class will gradually become more adept at this part of the process.

Keep in mind that the objective of a concept attainment lesson is not *only* that the students derive the definition. The major objective is to engage students in the process of defining and forming concepts.

Step 7—Give Additional Examples

Once students have developed an initial definition of the concept they are learning, show them a few more positive and negative examples to test whether they can identify examples of the concept. Ask the students to provide their own examples, and then to explain why their examples fit the concept definition.

Step 8—Discuss the Process with the Class

The discussion step is essential to ensure that the students understand how they reached the definition and are able to link this process to the natural process of their own thinking. "As students learn how to categorize more effectively and as they learn how they arrived at their categories, their ability to attain concepts increases."[2] Attention to likenesses and differences is essential in any type of research or analysis, in both formal and informal thinking; the more conscious a learner is of his or her own thinking process, the sharper that thinking will be. Therefore, as you use concept attainment in teaching, have students identify the point at which they understood the essential attributes and tell which examples were the most helpful.

Step 9—Evaluate

To determine if students understand the process, ask them to develop additional examples of the essential attributes on their own or to develop positive and negative examples of the essential attributes of a new concept definition. You might also challenge the students to expand the definition of the concept and then to provide positive and negative examples that would lead to an expanded definition.

Review the concept periodically to determine if the students have retained the definition. Test to determine if this process is more effective than other techniques in learning and retaining concept definitions.

Summary of Steps in the Concept Attainment Model

Steps 1 through 3 are done prior to instruction.

1. *Select and define a concept:* Determine if the concept is appropriate and teachable according to this model. The definition should be clear and the attributes should be identifiable.

2. *Select the attributes:* Determine those qualities that are essential to the concept.

3. *Develop positive and negative examples:* This is the key step because the positive examples must contain all the essential attributes, yet they may contain some nonessential attributes that are gradually eliminated. Negative examples may have some of, but not all, the essential attributes.

4. *Introduce the process to the students:* It is important to take the time to explain clearly what you will be doing and what each step will entail.

5. *Present the examples and list the attributes:* List positive and negative attributes separately. Cross out items in the positive list when a new positive example does not contain the attribute. Remember, only positive examples can delete attributes from the positive list. Items on the negative list are there to emphasize qualities.

6. *Develop a concept definition:* Using the positive attributes, the students write a concept definition. Be patient. It takes time to work through the ideas.

7. *Give additional examples:* Determine if the class understands the concept. One advantage of this model is that all the students can participate even though some get the meaning more quickly than others. There may be some students who do not comprehend the concept until this step; meanwhile, the other students gain reinforcement of the concept.

8. *Discuss the process with the class:* Be sure that the students understand how they arrived at the definition. This helps them to see how concepts are formed. It may be helpful to remind students how often they engage in the concept attainment process daily: in their interactions with and reactions to one another, to objects in their surroundings, and to ideas they encounter in all their classes in school.

9. *Evaluate:* To determine if the concept has been retained by the students, evaluate periodically.

Variations on the Concept Attainment Model

After the class is familiar with the process, present all the positive and negative examples, labeled accordingly, to them at once and have the students determine from the examples the essential attributes of the concept. For instance, when teaching the concept of *action verb*, present a passage of text with action verbs underlined. Ask the class to identify the essential attributes from the functions of the action verbs within the context of the written material. Negative examples such as nouns and adjectives can be circled within the text for contrast.

Another approach is to present all the examples without labeling any as either positive or negative. The students must group the examples into the positive and negative categories and then determine the essential attributes of those they determine to be positive.

With young children, present a series of pictures of positive examples, such as pictures of animals that live on a farm. The negative examples, such as wild animals, would be presented only after a concept definition has been derived.

Another variation on this model is for students to develop positive and negative examples for a concept already studied in class. The object of the lesson would be to define the concept succinctly, to identify the essential attributes, and then to choose the positive and negative examples. This could be done by individuals or by groups and could serve as an excellent means of evaluating the students' understanding of the concept and the process.

The concept attainment process may also be used as an effective group activity. Divide the class into small groups using the techniques suggested in Chapter 14. Present each group with a set of positive and negative examples of a concept. The first time this activity is used, label each example as positive or negative. As the class becomes more experienced with the process, present the examples without labels. Instruct groups to determine the essential attributes of the concept and to write a definition. You may choose whether to give them the concept name or to withhold the name until after the definitions are developed.

Figure 5.2 shows pictures given to groups with the instructions to determine the essential attributes and then to define the concept *chair*.

E X E R C I S E   5 . 1

Look at Figure 5.2 and determine the concept definition for *chair* intended to be derived from these examples. Remember that *chair* might have other definitions, but these examples contain attributes for a particular definition.

Possible Answer to Exercise 5.1
The basis for these examples—the concept definition—is "a seat designed to hold one person." ■

In each of the positive examples in Figure 5.2—A, B, C, and D—all three essential attributes are present.

1. They are seats.
2. They were designed by someone.
3. They hold one person.

In the negative examples, a person could sit on E, F, and H, but those were not *designed* for seating. Example G was designed for seating but for more than one person. Other negative examples are a bed and a low table; those were not designed for our specific purpose. A negative example from nature, such as a flat rock or a log on which a person might sit, emphasizes that chairs are intentionally designed.

When these examples have been presented to a class, a variety of definitions have come from the students. For example:

■ An object that is manufactured for the purpose of providing a seat for one person

Positive Examples   Negative Examples

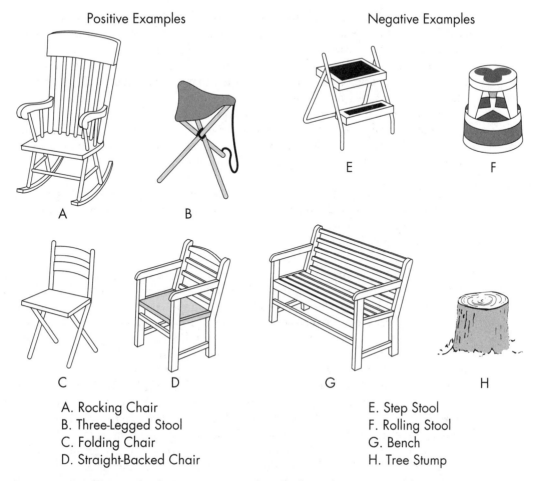

A. Rocking Chair
B. Three-Legged Stool
C. Folding Chair
D. Straight-Backed Chair

E. Step Stool
F. Rolling Stool
G. Bench
H. Tree Stump

FIGURE 5.2   Positive and Negative Examples of Chairs for a Group Concept Attainment Lesson

- A piece of furniture intended for the seating of one person
- A seat designed to hold one person in an upright position

All three of these definitions contain the essential attributes even though they are stated in slightly different terms. The class may decide to vote on the definition that most clearly states the essential attributes.

Basis for the Concept Attainment Model

The concept attainment model is based on the research of Jerome Bruner, Jacqueline Goodnow, and George Austin, which was reported in the landmark work, *A Study of Thinking*.[3] Bruner and associates were concerned primarily with the process through which individuals categorize data and attain concepts. Educators have been particularly interested in the use of this research in teaching concepts to learners. Bruner et al. wrote, "To categorize is to render discriminately different things equivalent, to group the objects and events and people around us into classes, and to respond to them in terms of their class membership rather than their uniqueness."[4] It is this process of categorizing that allows learners to simplify their complex environment through the development and attainment of concepts.

The particular aspect of the Bruner research used in the concept attainment model in this text is based on what Bruner et al. called reception strategies in concept attainment. They described three basic rules for this approach:[5]

1. Take the first positive instance and make it into your initial hypothesis.
2. Consider what is common to your hypothesis and any positive-infirming instance you may encounter.
3. Ignore everything else.

In school, students are constantly bombarded with propositions (statements of which truth or falsehood can be asserted), both in what they are told and in what they are asked to read. Always these propositions are composed of discrete concepts; often, the truth or falsity of a concept embedded in a proposition will determine how the proposition is understood. For example, every schoolchild knows the proposition "Columbus discovered America." The truth of that assertion depends, however, on how one defines the concept *discover*. It is estimated that 10 million people were living on the North American continent when Columbus stumbled onto the islands he misnamed the West Indies, in his mistaken assumption that he must be somewhere near India. Critical thinkers—schoolchildren and adults—who understand the process of thinking in terms of concept attainment will be wary of such simplistic propositions.

To summarize, concepts are the ideas or abstractions that are formed as a result of categorizing data from a number of observations. To make sense of all the various stimuli in the world, learners of all ages form concepts and give them names. Imagine the cognitive overload if every single thing in the world was seen as a separate and unrelated entity. To form concepts, learners pay attention to likenesses rather than differences and place similar objects in the same category. Apples come in many sizes, shapes, and colors, but by attending to their similarities and ignoring their differences, we form an initial concept of apple.

Many concepts used in the classroom are abstract and have many interpretations; they frequently are used, however, as though every student shared the same definition. Consider the concept *democracy*. If you asked a class of university students to write their own definition of the term, you would get many different answers. Yet we often expect that learners in elementary school have a shared definition of concepts just like this one in their vocabulary.

Teaching students to understand the meaning of the concepts taught in the classroom is one of the most important challenges of teaching. Concepts have names as well as definitions that contain essential attributes that place them in a particular category. For instance, for the concept *table*, one definition is "a piece of furniture consisting of a smooth, flat slab fixed on legs." The essential attributes of *table* are (1) piece of furniture; (2) smooth, flat slab; and (3) fixed on legs. The students are more apt to understand the meaning of the concept and be able to recognize the essential attributes if they arrive at a definition through numerous examples instead of through memorizing the concept name and definition.

In the concept attainment model, the emphasis is on the learner determining the essential attributes of the concept that have been preselected by the teacher. The final step of this model encourages learners to explore how concepts are formed through a process of attending to similarities and ignoring differences. The model serves both to teach a meaning of a particular concept and to teach students how the thinking process occurs.

In preparing to use the concept attainment model, one must determine ahead of time the following basic elements of the concept to be learned:

1. The name of the concept
2. The concept definition or rule
3. Conceptual attributes
4. Examples of the concept
5. Relationship of the concept to other concepts

ACTIVITY 5.1

In using this model, the teacher often learns as much as the students regarding the definition of concepts. Test yourself and see if you can write a definition of such concepts as freedom, law, family, line, area, or liquid without looking in a text. Now look up the concept in a dictionary and decide which of the definitions are attainable in a lesson. ■

Scenario

Mrs. Gonzales is teaching the concept of metaphor to her eighth-grade class. She explains that they are going to learn the meaning of a new concept and that the word will be a secret until they have all the essential parts of the definition on the board and the class is able to derive the meaning. She adds, "We will find the meaning of the concept by searching for the essential qualities that define it. I will give you positive examples that illustrate this word and some negative examples that may contain some of, but not all, the essential qualities of this concept."

The first example is "The moon is a silver ship sailing in the night sky." The students came up with the following possibilities, which the teacher writes on the board:

ships
night
comparison
poetry
sentence
quotation

The next example is also positive: "Superman—The Man of Steel." The students are able to eliminate all but the word *comparison* with this example. Now the list looks like this:

~~ships~~
~~night~~
comparison of different things
~~poetry~~
~~sentence~~
~~quotation~~

Next the students are given a negative example: "He had a heart like a lion."

TEACHER: What about this example is different from the ones you have seen before?

STUDENT: It is still a comparison, but this time there is *like* in there.

Under the negative examples column, the teacher writes *uses like*. Another negative example, "Frightened as a mouse," is given, and the word *as* is added to the negative list.

STUDENT: If the negative examples contain *like* or *as*, then not containing *like* or *as* should be on the positive side.

TEACHER: Here is an example. Tell me if you think that it should be a negative or a positive example: "The father was a tower of strength."

STUDENT: That is positive because it is a comparison without using *like* or *as*.

TEACHER: Is there anything you can add about the things that are compared?

STUDENT: Well, they are very different—ships and moons, people and towers, people and steel.

TEACHER: How about this example, which is also positive: "The ship plows the sea."

STUDENT: The ship is being compared to a plow that is used in the earth.

STUDENT: The ship has really become the plow in this example.

TEACHER: Are you ready to state the definition of this concept?

STUDENT: A comparison of things that are very different.

STUDENT: Don't forget that you don't use *like* or *as*.

STUDENT: One object actually becomes another, like the moon plowing the ocean of the night.

STUDENT: How about a joining of things that are very different to make a new image without using the word *like* or *as*.

TEACHER: That is an excellent definition and better than the one that I had written. We call this concept of using language *metaphor*. Notice how you arrived at this definition. How did you determine the main attributes?

STUDENT: By picking out what was similar in the different examples and what was different.

TEACHER: Here is a selection of quotations. See if you can identify the metaphors.

The teacher need not use this teaching strategy every day, but it makes for an interesting and effective variation. By forming the rule after the examples have been given, students who learn best through inductive reasoning have had their needs met. In addition, the students are more likely to remember the meaning of *metaphor* as a result of attaching it to the examples than if the meaning were learned in isolation.

A final step in the concept attainment model is to discuss with the students the process they just experienced. Ask the students questions such as "When did you realize that a particular characteristic was essential to the meaning of this concept?" or "How did we eliminate a particular characteristic?" Help the students to understand how concepts are formed and to think about their thoughts.

ACTIVITY 5.2

Select a concept from a lesson you plan to teach or would like to teach. Determine if it can be taught effectively by using this model; if so, then design a concept attainment lesson. ■

Summary

The concept attainment model describes the steps in teaching the meaning of a concept by presenting positive and negative examples of the concept to the class until the students can identify the essential attributes and state a concept definition. In addition, this model helps students understand the process through which concepts are defined. The teacher may present a new concept to the class or focus on one particular aspect of a familiar concept. Because the understanding of concepts is so essential to learning in the classroom, the time taken to identify and clarify these concepts is time well spent. In addition, teachers find that in preparing to teach this model, they clarify their own understanding of essential concepts.

WEB RESOURCES

1. http://eduation.boisestate.edu/LROGIEN/Models%20of%20teaching/ConcptAtt.htm

Here is an additional scenario to consider in coming to understand the concept attainment model.

2. http://education.nebrwesleyan.edu/mcdonald/235website/Model_Evals/CA.html

This checklist for evaluating a concept attainment lesson can be downloaded for individual use. By answering the 18 questions using a rating scale, a teacher can easily see where a concept attainment lesson is strongest and where it might need improvement.

3. http://www.jpl.nasa.gov/ice_fire/outreach/Pluto2.htm

This excellent example of an application of the concept attainment model can be used to help students sort out the swirl of controversy surrounding the status of Pluto as a full-fledged planet.

4. http://home.apu.edu/~marvidson/science2%20concept%20attain.htm

This site provides a concept attainment lesson plan for a seventh-grade life science class that focuses on the question "What qualifies as an insect?"

5. http://curry.edschool.virginia.edu/curry/class/edlf/589_004/Penelope_Miller/portfolio/envconcp. htm

This site presents a concept attainment lesson plan used in an environmental education unit. The lesson centers on the topic of waste products and helps students distinguish recyclable and nonrecyclable products.

NOTES

1. Art Linkletter, *Kids Say the Darndest Things!* (Englewood Cliffs, NJ: Prentice Hall, 1957), 109.

2. A. M. Kilgore, "Models of Teaching and Teacher Education," in *Using Research to Improve Teacher Education: Teacher Education Monograph No. 1*, ed. R. L. Egbert and M. M. Kluender (Lincoln, NE: The Nebraska Consortium, 1984), 108–126.

3. J. S. Bruner, J. J. Goodnow, and G. A. Austin, *A Study of Thinking* (New York: John Wiley and Sons, 1959; Huntington, NY: Robert E. Krieger, 1977).

4. Bruner, Goodnow, and Austin, 1.

5. Bruner, Goodnow, and Austin, 131.

6 The Concept Development Model

Analyzing the Relationships between Parts of a Concept

In one passage of *Centennial*, James Michener described Potato Brumbaugh's acquisition of two words important to him:

> He was only a peasant, but like all men with seminal ideas, he found the words he needed to express himself. He had heard a professor use the words *imprison* and *replenishment* and he understood immediately what the man had meant, for he, Brumbaugh, had discovered the concept before he heard the word, but when he did hear it, the word was automatically his, for he had already absorbed the idea *which entitled him to the symbol* [italics added].[1]

Understanding Concepts

Michener was making the point that individuals acquire vocabulary in direct relation to the acquisition of concepts. When a concept is understood, when the object or idea has become a part of our experience, a new word takes on meaning because it is useful in communicating that concept. The concept and its label become a permanent part of the individual's mental framework. However, when a new tag is given and then a definition follows before the idea has been experienced or conceptualization has occurred, the tag seldom becomes a part of the individual's mental framework for more than a few days.

What Is Concept Development?

Concept development is often thought of in relation to abstract concepts like beauty and truth. But Hilda Taba, who created the concept development strategy, used it to develop students' knowledge of concrete objects such as apples or baseballs. Let us examine the word *concept*.

The *American Heritage Dictionary of the English Language* defines a concept as:

1. A general idea or understanding, esp. one derived from specific instances or occurrences.
2. A thought or notion. . . . Late Latin *conceptus*, a thing conceived, thought, from past participle of *concipere*, to take to oneself, conceive.[2]

The first definition of the word *concept* is used more frequently than the second. It applies to highly abstract ideas such as beauty or truth or freedom or democracy, as opposed to concrete objects such as apples or baseballs or tables or trees. Why did Taba use the model on concrete objects? It is because she was using it in terms of the second definition.

Remember the words in the second definition, "to take to oneself." Imagine that our brains are rooms filled with file cabinets containing hundreds of thousands of individual files. Actually, we have files on every significant person, place, object, or idea that we have ever encountered. The information in each individual file makes up our personal "concept" of that particular person, place, object, and so on. Anything that has attributes or distinctive features—even a concrete object—projects an idea of itself, an idea in our heads that we take to ourselves (*concipere*). That is why Potato Brumbaugh learned the words *imprison* and *replenishment* so quickly. He already had the files; he simply had no labels. It is this idea or concept of something that we build in our heads that is emphasized in this chapter.

Jerome Bruner asserts that when "we see an object that is red, shiny, and roundish and infer that it is an apple, we are then enabled to infer further that 'if it is an apple, it is also edible, juicy, will rot if left unrefrigerated, etc.' The working definition of a concept is the network of inferences that are or may be set into play by an act of categorization."[3] Bruner further asserts "that virtually all cognitive activity involves and is dependent on the process of categorizing."[4] This statement points out the importance of the mental processes introduced in this chapter.

Concept development is, therefore, a strategy that extends and refines the information in our individual files; it extends and refines each of our concepts, whether it is our concept of an object such as a table or our concept of an idea such as truth.

Concept Development Mirrors Our Natural Thought Processes

The concept development model gives students practice in categorizing as well as in performing the other mental processes involved in developing concepts. By beginning with concrete objects and progressing to more complex ideas, students learn to articulate their thoughts and to compare them with the ideas of other students. Taba emphasizes that the mental processes a person employs to select attributes and arrive at his or her impression of what a concrete object is are identical to the processes involved in arriving at the meaning of more abstract ideas.[5] Whether we study an object such as a table, an idea such as democracy, or a person such as George Washington, we are using the same processes. Furthermore, Taba asserts that the more practice we have in extending, developing, and refining our concepts of simpler objects, the more efficient we will be at extending, developing, and refining our concepts of more abstract ideas.[6]

A former comedy series, "Not Necessarily the News," had a segment on *sniglets*, defined as "words that don't appear in the dictionary, but should." These words are usually nouns that refer to objects everyone knows but no one has a name for. These sniglets illustrate how names can be given to an object already familiar to us; thus the concept name follows the concept definition. Examples of sniglets, given in a book by that name, are:

- Per'-cu-burp: The final gasp a coffee percolator makes to alert you it is ready
- May'-pahp: A bald automobile or bicycle tire
- Spork: The combination spoon/fork popular in fast-food restaurants[7]

In Chapter 5, our instructional focus, concept attainment, was directed at how concepts are learned. The teacher has control over the students' initial grasp of the concept because he or she chooses the examples from which the concept emerges. In the concept development model, however, the items in the database, as well as the categories and the reasons for the categories, come from the students. In this chapter, the emphasis is on how concepts are extended and refined. Instruction is built on baseline concepts established from the learners' prior understanding. Through exploration of these prior understandings, and as conceptual interrelationships emerge, a framework for new understandings is established. Thus instruction builds on what is known, with the effect of adding to and modifying the information and understandings that learners bring to that instruction. The important principle underlying this model is that *understandings are built, not acquired.* For example, our concept of what a table may be will change and grow more sophisticated as we become interested in our own furniture and learn that there are bedside tables, coffee tables, dining room tables, formal card tables, lowboys, and so forth.

Performing this model helps students to think more effectively in several ways. The quality of an individual's understanding depends in large part on the flexibility of his or her thought processes. Is the person open to new information, willing to share and compare the contents of his or her files with others, willing to change the content of those files? Or does the person tend to reject information that may question or contradict the information now in his or her files? Does the person question or examine even information that confirms the contents of his or her files?

Practice in performing this model in a group helps individuals think more flexibly. In addition to refining and extending students' understandings of the topic under scrutiny, practice in a group situation also increases the student's ability to perform the steps alone. By calling attention to a process we normally perform subconsciously, the approach helps students become more capable thinkers. In addition, students may use these steps to generate original ideas.

Steps in the Concept Development Model

1. List as many items as possible that are associated with the subject.
2. Group the items because they are alike in some way.

3. Label the groups by defining the reasons for grouping.
4. Regroup or subsume individual items or whole groups under other groups.
5. Synthesize the information by summarizing the data and forming generalizations.[8]
6. Evaluate students' progress by assessing their ability to generate a wide variety of items and to group those items flexibly.

When performed consecutively, the first five steps mirror a process humans employ individually as they marshal their thoughts on a particular subject, as they organize and reorganize these thoughts, as they seek out new relationships and new meanings, and as they make their way through the uncharted terrains of cognition. This model may be used in kindergarten through grade 12 and beyond to explore basic concepts in different disciplines. In social studies, it may be used to explore concepts such as *capitalism*, *imperialism*, and *expansionism*; in mathematics, to explore concepts such as *velocity*, *expansion*, and *relativity*; in science, to explore concepts such as *adaptation*, *evolution*, and *interdependence*; in English, to explore concepts such as *character*, *theme*, and *point of view*. These same concepts may be expressed in simpler terms for younger students.

Using this model to explore a central idea from any discipline allows teachers to assess students' prior understandings, enables students to broaden and enrich their previous understandings, and serves as an excellent review. Students enjoy the process, because the ingredients are their contributions and the product is their product.

Step 1—List as Many Items as Possible That Are Associated with the Subject

In the first step, students are asked to enumerate items related to a subject. The data may be drawn from their own experience or from material that has been studied in the classroom. Before the class begins a study of space, a teacher might say, "Tell me everything you know about astronauts." Or after viewing a movie on space, the teacher might say, "Let's name everything that you just learned about existing in outer space."

Taba was very precise in the way she worded the questions in the steps. Table 6.1 provides an overview of the question–response–follow-through sequence that Taba established in this model.

The items in step 1 should be written on a chalkboard or somewhere visibly accessible to all participants. *Items listed must be specific or else the next step, grouping, will be confusing.* If you are asking the class to enumerate items about Halloween, for example, and a student says "scary things," ask the student to be more specific. If he has trouble you might ask "What sort of things are scary?" You hope that he will name some scary things, such as a beckoning finger or a rattling skeleton. The problem with writing down *scary things* is that it does not name, it groups, and that gets you one step ahead in the process.

It is important to have a comprehensive list from which student generalizations can emerge, because generalizations have far more validity when they are based on a

TABLE 6.1 **Developing Concepts**

Step	Teacher	Student	Teacher Follow-Through
1.	What do you see (notice, find) here?	Gives items.	Makes sure items are accessible to each student. For example: Chalkboard Transparency Individual list Pictures Item card
2.	Do any of these items seem to belong together?	Finds some similarity as a basis for grouping items.	Communicates grouping. For example: Underlines in colored chalk. Marks with symbols. Arranges pictures or cards.
3.	Why would you group them together?*a* What would you call these groups you have formed?	Identifies and verbalizes the common characteristics of items in a group. Verbalizes a label (perhaps more than one word) that appropriately encompasses all items.	Seeks clarification of responses when necessary. Records.
4.	Could some of these belong in more than one group? Can we put these same items in different groups?*b* Why would you group them that way?	States different relationships. States additional different relationships.	Records. Communicates grouping.
5.	Can someone say in one sentence something about all these groups?	Offers a suitable summary sentence.	Reminds them, if necessary, to take into consideration all the groups before them.

*a*Sometimes you ask the same child "why" when he offers the grouping, and other times you may wish to get many groups before considering "why" things are grouped together.

*b*Although this step is important because it encourages flexibility, it will not be appropriate on all occasions.

Source: Adapted from *A Teacher's Handbook to Elementary Social Studies*, Second Edition, by Hilda Taba, Mary C. Durkin, Jack R. Fraenkel, and Anthony H. McNaughton. © 1971 by Addison-Wesley Publishing Company. Used by permission of Pearson Education, Inc.

variety of data. Encourage students to continue listing, even after they appear to have run out of information. The ideas that follow the first pause are the less obvious ones, frequently derived from greater insight and more thought.

When the subject under scrutiny is already familiar to the participants, such as *football* or *grudge* or *school*, step 1 is similar to brainstorming. Brainstorming is the rapid, noncritical, noncensored listing of any and all ideas or associations on a given topic. The term is actually a misnomer. We do not "storm" with just our brains; we storm with our emotions, imaginations, memories, in short with our whole creative selves. Students list everything they can think of that is connected with the particular subject. What they list may consist of one word or it may be a phrase. Its connection may be generally recognized or it may be meaningful only to them. In this step, students share the contents of their individual files with others.

We emphasize the importance of participation by all students. To encourage the fullest possible participation, call on the more reticent students during this first step; they will find it easier to respond at this stage.

Here are a few items generated by a high school class that had performed the model several times. They were exploring the topic *football:*

school colors, jostling, ball, pom-poms, muscle, strutting, blitz, striped shirts, hot dogs, whistles

They generated more than 140 items in 5 minutes.

Step 2—Group the Items
Because They Are Alike in Some Way

When the teacher believes that sufficient items have been listed, it is time to move to the other half of the chalkboard and ask, "Which of the items we have listed go together because they are alike in some way?" In this step, students begin to examine the relationships among items. Try to elicit several groups. The first groups may be put together for the most obvious reasons. The groups mentioned after some thought are usually put together for more unusual reasons.

An example of one group is *helmets cracking, flying tackles, collisions, bone crunching,* and *injuries.* The teacher had assumed that all the items related to injuries, until a student added injuries to the group. The students later labeled the group the *might makes right* aspect of football.

Step 3—Label the Groups by
Defining the Reasons for Grouping

In this step, students give labels to the newly formed groups. In a discussion of Halloween, for example, the items *beckoning fingers* and *rattling skeletons* and *leering pumpkins* might be labeled *scary things.* The sophistication of the labels depends on the age and background of the group. Older students, for instance, might use a label such as *habitat,* whereas younger students might label the group *places where animals live.*

It is important in this step to ask students to explain the reasons for their choices. Their explanations are often surprising! Even if the reasons for grouping seem obvious, ask students to articulate their reasons. Having to explain the label they gave a particular group of items forces them to articulate and defend their reasoning processes. Frequently, they express connections they have sensed but have not precisely verbalized. Student thinking must be understood by everyone at this stage, as Taba's amusing story illustrates:

> Dr. Karplus at the University of California . . . tells about some seven-year-olds who were grouping and labeling some rocks on their desks. Dr. Karplus was interested in how the children were doing and so as he walked around the room he asked one little boy, "How are you grouping your rocks?" and the reply was, "by age."
> This was really impressive. So Dr. Karplus said, "Tell me more about that."
> And the little boy replied, "You know, big rocks and little rocks."[9]

The teacher's role in this model is basically that of recorder. The teacher may ask what other students think, but the students need to feel that their judgments are valued by the teacher and the rest of the class. It is less important to teach particular inferences or generalizations than it is to develop the students' skills in drawing inferences and in making generalizations. The students should question one another and decide among themselves.

Examples of labels from the high school group analyzing football were *stadium, parking lot, commercialism, rules, might makes right, emotions, microcosm, costumes, food,* and *atmosphere.* This step helps students learn to generalize.

Step 4—Regroup or Subsume Individual Items or Whole Groups under Other Groups

Step 4 centers on the questions "Are there items now in one group that you could put in another group?" and later "Are there whole groups that could be placed under one of the other labels?" Again, ask for the learner's reasoning here: "Why do you think _____ belongs under _____ ?"

For example, when regrouping on the topic *Halloween,* a student might want to add *witches on broomsticks,* which had been under *decorations,* to the group of scary things. If you believe the groupings were done for rather shallow or superficial reasons and that the students can go further, erase the second half of the board, leaving the initial items clearly visible, and ask the students if they can generate some new groups. Obvious groups such as *treats* or *decorations* are fine, but perhaps students will begin to see more obscure connections such as *feelings* or *masks* or *facades.* Also, no list of items is final; new items may be added at any time.

In Step 3, the more obvious items come first; with grouping, the more obvious relationships are pointed out first. Also, the connections seen when the model is first used are much less complex than those recognized after practice. As time goes on, students will find out for themselves that every person, object, or idea has many characteristics and may be grouped in many different ways. For example, when a ninth-grade student observed that the item *leering pumpkin* could be labeled *decorations* or *food* or *scary things*, depending on how you thought about it, she showed her understanding that the same object may be viewed from different perspectives. We all tend to put constraints on our thinking. If A is B, it cannot be C. In this model, students discover that one item can be viewed from several vantage points and can, therefore, appear in several groups.

Whole groups may be included with other groups. One group under *football* had been *strutting, pushing, shoving, beefy, cocky,* and *butting heads.* One student had commented that these types of behaviors reminded him of bulls, so they had labeled the group *bulls.* In step 4, the students put this entire group under another group labeled *macho.*

EXERCISE 6.1

Group the following items and then label each of the groups. Then regroup the items and relabel. Remember, be flexible. You may use an item more than once, or you may omit items.

rocks	tigers	kittens
stars	cars	the sea
ponies	cakes	roses
cookies	sausage	grass
motorcycles	roller skates	flowers

Possible Answers to Exercise 6.1

Group A

Parts of Nature	*Means of Transportation*	*Foods*
rocks	cars	cookies
stars	motorcycles	sausage
flowers	roller skates	cakes
roses	ponies	
grass		
the sea		
tigers		
kittens		
ponies		

Group B

Nonliving Parts of Nature	*Cats*	*Plants*	*Foods High in Cholesterol*
rocks	tigers	flowers	cakes
stars	kittens	roses	cookies
the sea		grass	sausages

Step 5—Synthesize the Information by Summarizing the Data and Forming Generalizations

In step 5, the teacher asks the class to look over the entire chalkboard, consider all the groups and labels, and try to make a general statement about the topic in one sentence. Students must try to pick out trends. Young children tend to think in terms of either/or. Either Halloween is a "good" holiday or a "bad" one. They do not see that Halloween can have two faces. Scary situations need not be dangerous if controlled, and they can even be fun. A private Halloween party can offer some thrilling and terrifying moments that pose no danger. If not supervised, however, trick-or-treaters can be in danger from traffic, overzealous pranksters, or the occasional sick mind. By looking at all the conflicting data at once, students begin to realize that Halloween is complex, fraught with pleasures and dangers. Even older students tend to think in terms of either/or. Football is either "good" or "bad," usually depending on whether they enjoy playing or watching it. They need to realize that football is an exciting and popular sport that can also be dangerous. This step offers an opportunity for students to begin to appreciate the richness and complexity of ideas.

Teachers will need to give students several examples of generalizations the first few times this model is used. Examples of generalizations from the analysis of football are as follows:

1. The game of football is fun but dangerous.
2. Many boys/men define themselves by their degree of success in football, which can be both helpful and harmful to their self-images.
3. A football game is a microcosm of the major elements in our society, both good and bad.

Step 6—Evaluate Students' Progress by Assessing Their Ability to Generate a Wide Variety of Items and to Group Those Items Flexibly

We do not suggest encouraging students to be conscious of grades when performing this model; the teacher, however, may believe that gauging progress is necessary. There are many ways of assessing students' progress, and several are suggested here. Later, in the section entitled Benefits of Using the Concept Development Model, other ways the model may be used are presented. These may also be used to assess students' progress.

In step 1, the sheer number of items counts. This model is a fundamental tool in helping students generate original ideas. Practice helps students become more creative and uninhibited. One student went from listing 7 items on the topic of *Columbus* to listing 70 items in 5 minutes after using the model four times.

Using a timer that students can hear ticking helps generate excitement when groups or individuals list or brainstorm items. Competition for generating the most items in a certain time limit seems to increase excitement and to help students overcome a natural tendency to put constraints on their thinking.

In step 2, growth in both the number and originality of the groups may be evaluated. Students usually begin with more obvious groups, such as *treats, costumes,* and *scary things* under Halloween. Students who have practiced the model should be able to begin to generate more creative groups. Examples are *masks, facades, stepping out of oneself,* or *commercialism.*

In step 3, a variation that provides excellent practice in flexibility in thinking happened in a class one day. The students were performing concept development as a group on the topic *school.* While performing step 3, labeling groups on the board, one student asked if she could go to the board; she said she thought that she could stump the class. She wrote down the items in a group she had generated herself. She challenged the class to come up with her label. Her items were *sand, circles, giraffes' necks, wheels,* and *the ocean.* The class was not able to identify her label, which turned out to be *things that go on forever.* She said that people always say that we should enjoy school, that we will be out before we know it, but it does not feel that way when you are there; it feels as if it goes on forever.

Generalizing and particularizing are fundamental thought processes. Generalizing is crucial in finding themes, in generating theses, in thinking critically or creatively. Asking each student to come up with one original group and having some students write their groups on the board is an effective way to evaluate student skill in these thought processes.

In step 4, it is possible to evaluate for flexibility. Occasionally, after students perform the entire model, ask pairs or small groups to put additional items that are in one group into another group or to think of other whole groups that may be put under an existing label. Here the class is repeating the step in small groups. These individual or small-group efforts may be evaluated.

In step 5, ask pairs or small groups to see if they can generate one or two more "complex" generalizations. Complex means that the generalization contains contradictory aspects of the topic.

Finally, growth in the students' mental processes is usually reflected in the performance of the class as a whole and may be judged as the model is executed. If the breadth and variety of the items in step 1, the originality of the groups in steps 2 and 4, the variety of the labels in step 3, and the sophistication of the generalizations in step 5 reflect thought and innovation, the process has been successful.

Summary of Steps in the Concept Development Model

1. *List as many items as possible that are associated with the subject:* Ask the students to name as many ideas, objects, associations, memories, concepts, or attributes related to the subject under scrutiny as possible. Thus what the learners already know is identified. The information may be based on general knowledge that students have of a subject or on what they know or think they know already. It may come from a personal experience they have had, such as school-related field trips, a preparatory reading, or a film.

2. *Group the items because they are alike in some way:* Ask the students to group the items by finding ways in which they are similar or related. Thus what learners know is qualified. Similar ideas, or ideas related to a common concept, bear similar qualities. An important part of learning consists of identifying these qualities.

3. *Label the groups by defining the reasons for grouping:* Ask the students to articulate the relationships between the items. Thus what learners know is defined. Qualities that are borne in common by ideas form the basis of the categories into which those ideas fit. Often, different labels are possible.

4. *Regroup or subsume individual items or whole groups under other groups:* Ask the students to look at the board and see if they can find items or whole groups that they could put somewhere else. This step involves looking at a single item from different perspectives. It also involves analyzing through regrouping and subsuming additional items under already established labels or subsuming labels under other labels according to relative inclusiveness. For example, under the heading *democracy*, the category *campaign* containing items such as *shaking hands* and *making speeches* might be subsumed under another category, *elections.* The most creative connections occur in this step.

5. *Synthesize the information by summarizing the data and forming generalizations:* Ask the students to look over the board and see if they can make a general statement or generalization about the subject under scrutiny that summarizes the information in the briefest terms possible. To generalize, the students must put the parts together or synthesize the information. For example, if they were studying Halloween, they might say that Halloween is both fun and dangerous.

6. *Evaluate students' progress by assessing their ability to generate a wide variety of items and to group those items flexibly:* Judge the students' progress in performing important mental processes such as analyzing, synthesizing, generalizing, and particularizing.

Basis for the Concept Development Model

Listing, grouping, labeling, regrouping, and synthesizing are all descriptions of the essential components of higher-order thinking, the thinking that makes the concept development model so powerful for teachers and students alike. From the early weeks of life to old age, all humans learn in a manner similar to what we describe as concept development.

The philosopher of language Ludwig Wittgenstein said that to know a language is to participate in a form of life.[10] Likewise, to know a subject, a discipline, is to participate in a way of thinking, to become disciplined in thought with other thinkers, other human beings whose thought processes are no different from your own. And what exactly is the process of disciplined knowing? Every field of inquiry—whether biology, algebra, literature, physics, geometry, history, geography, or any other of an almost limitless list—represents a way of thinking. Each field of human inquiry centers on different kinds of phenomena, names those phenomena, examines their various qualities, establishes categories for them, analyzes them, and synthesizes them. Ruth Benedict, in discussing scientific study in *Patterns of Culture*, writes:

> In all the less controversial fields like the study of cacti or termites or the nature of nebulae, the necessary method of study is to group the relevant material and to take note of all possible variant forms and conditions. In this way we have learned all that we know of the laws of astronomy, or of the habits of social insects, let us say.[11]

The expert and the novice, the teacher and the pupil, are different in *what* they think but similar in *how* they think. To teach, especially to teach conceptually, is to invite learners to exercise their thinking processes on new phenomena in familiar ways or familiar phenomena in new ways. The essential purpose of using concept development is that such teaching gives practice in a fundamental process of thinking. Listing, grouping, labeling, regrouping, and synthesizing are performed aloud in a group so that learning becomes actual growth in understanding of the subject under scrutiny and growth in learning how others think.

Conceptual Thinking Is Learned

A child will not approach his or her intellectual potential without guidance and practice in the process of thinking. And much possible critical thinking will never take place if a curriculum is so strongly content oriented that processes of learning and thinking are left to chance. To awaken, to encourage, and to stretch children's abilities to think for themselves is the highest goal of education. To develop thinking skills is to develop an increasingly complex mental organization with which to view the world and to solve problems. Cognitive skills are seen as products of a dynamic interaction between the individual and the stimulation he or she receives.

Learning is not merely the passive absorption of information but is rooted in perceived experience. Understandings are based on the interpretation of data available through the senses, and there is an immediate and subconscious attempt to reconcile new information with previously observed information.

Our senses are constantly transmitting signals to our brains, which our brains are constantly screening. Even at a sensory level, individual perception does not record literal descriptions of the environment. Each perception is a result of the incoming stimuli combined with overlays of past experience with similar stimuli and the object situated in the environment. Humans see, qualify, and categorize in order to understand. What we see may be completely new, but each learner brings the basis of qualification and the criteria for classification to any experience. Concerning the subject matter of education, John Dewey concluded "that education must be conceived as a continuing reconstruction of experience; that the process and goal of education are one and the same thing."[12]

Lev Vygotsky, founder of modern constructivist theories of development psychology, Bruner, and others assert that concept development and deep understanding are the essential goals of instruction.[13] The students are learning to integrate new ideas and approaches to learning with prior views and experience, thus constructing new knowledge from within. The teacher acts as a guide and facilitator who provides the opportunity for students to link main concepts throughout the learning process.

Concepts Are Creative Ways of Structuring Reality

Let us return to the image of concepts stored as files in a storage cabinet. Concepts provide easy access as we classify and thus simplify incoming information in a meaningful and retrievable form. Concepts make it possible for us to process data mentally. Take, for instance, the concept *color;* in fact, there may be more than a million discernible colors. No one, however, can manage that many colors in a concept of color. As a result, the National Bureau of Standards has developed a means of describing and naming 28 hues arranged into 267 colors. (This is an example of an institutionalized conceptualization.)

Scientists tell us that our senses are constantly being bombarded by thousands of stimuli simultaneously. Our ability to simplify, as much as our ability to absorb complexity, allows us to act upon our environment. Driving is an activity that would be impossible if we were attuned to every sign, tree, house, vehicle, or person we passed. Safety and the dictates of driving demand that we screen data and assimilate only certain relevant noises, landmarks, and conditions. Subconsciously, as we drive, we put incoming data into categories marked relevant or irrelevant.

As young children we learn to pick and choose, to assimilate only stimuli that we determine have meaning or, more accurately, to which we can assign meaning. When children come to school, the process does not change; what they can learn is what they can accommodate. Teaching is literally helping children in their natural process of learning new information and assigning meaning to that information. Taba and colleagues make the point that facts are important, but only as they relate to a theory. They felt that the teacher who said her students needed to learn facts first, before they could do any thinking in the area, may not have understood the nature of thought.[14] Facts—disparate items of information—have meaning only in relation to something more inclusive. They have meaning only in relation to the conceptual framework stored in our files.

Concepts Are the Building Blocks of Patterns

The process of creating conceptual frameworks is quite natural and forms the basis of our understanding of the world. Touching a hot stove leads to an understanding of heat. *Hot* becomes a category into which we place many things (see Figure 6.1), including the idea of caution. Experiments with falling objects (including one's own self) lead to an understanding of gravity. We impose order in our world by observing and creating patterns. We divide time into hours, minutes, and seconds. We divide space into miles, feet, inches, all manageable, bite-sized pieces. We attempt to predict the future by observing patterns in the present and recalling patterns from the past.

Taba and colleagues point out that "generalizations are . . . taken as representing a higher level of thinking than concepts in that they are a statement of relationships among two or more of these concepts."[15] Concepts are, therefore, the building

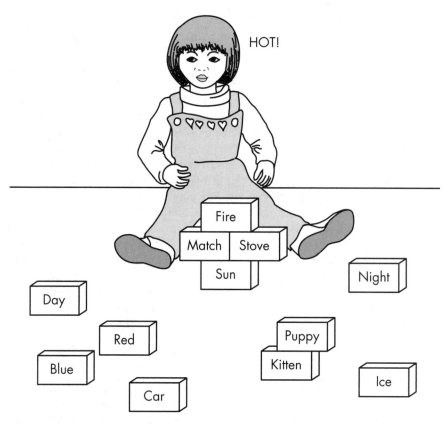

FIGURE 6.1   Building a Concept

blocks from which generalizations spring. By opening the contents of our personal mental files to others and by hearing about the contents of theirs, we refine and extend our understanding of concepts, and we refine and extend the precision of our generalizations about life. In the concept development model, a ministructure that mirrors how the human mind works is created. The focusing question produces data, not miscellaneous, indiscriminate data but data relevant to an idea contained in the focusing question. From the data come comparisons, contrasts, and finally a theory that makes sense of the myriad data. This theory constitutes our present view of the concept under scrutiny.

Scenario

The following is a description of the concept development process as a ninth-grade class explores the concept *grudge*. The class is about to read a story in which a grudge is the cause of the conflict.

Step 1

Listing results in a large number of items on the chalkboard following the question "What sort of things does the word *grudge* bring to mind?" The following is the list the class produces:

hurt	binge	friends
mean	evil eye	enemies
fight	stare	stiff
cruel	hold	hard
fudge	hate	cold
Cindy	yell	deep
whisper	stomach	dark
secrets	empty	wrinkled
not talking	argue	nose
silent	talk behind back	brown
faces	silly	trench
eyes	children	ground
cloud	childish	school
mist	people	heavy
fog	feelings	cut off
embarrassed	fat	burden

Steps 2 and 3

Grouping and labeling follow the questions "Which of these items are alike in some way? Which of these items do you think belong together?" and "Why do you think _____ and _____ go together?" Here are two examples:

Feelings Caused by a Grudge

hurt	hate	hard	brown
mean	empty	cold	heavy
cruel	silly	cut off	burden

Things Done while Holding a Grudge

whisper	not talking	embarrassed	nose in air
secrets	fight	hold	cut off
evil eye	yell	hate	hurt
stare	argue	childish	mean
talking	talk behind back	cold	binge

Step 4

Regrouping by subsuming produces additional groups when the students are told to look at the list again and are asked "Are there other groups that could be made?"

Things Associated with Food	*Things That Cause a Grudge*
binge	anger
people	friends
fudge	gossip
stomach	enemies
heavy	fights
silly	misunderstandings

Step 5

Synthesizing culminates the activity when students try to summarize all their information into one sentence, forming a generalization about the concept. Here are some examples of the students' statements about grudges:

> "Holding a grudge is not good for you."
>
> "Holding a grudge can make you do things you will be sorry for later."
>
> "A grudge can grow from something little to something very destructive."
>
> "Fighting is just another way of acting when you feel bad because someone has hurt you. You hold a grudge. I eat. Some people fight. None of these reactions really solves the problem."

Step 6

One benefit of using this model is the growing trust among class members as they share the contents of their "mental files." As this trust grows, their constraints about revealing thoughts and feelings diminish. These seventh-grade students were more frank and open in this discussion of grudges than they had been in the past. As one student's idea triggered another student's idea, they became excited. They showed a growth in creativity that they had not exhibited before. As a group, they received high marks.

The discussion was followed by an optional writing assignment, for which the students received individual grades. This is explained in the next section.

Benefits of Using the Concept Development Model

1. *Extending and refining knowledge:* The original purpose of the model is to extend and refine students' understanding of the external world. Because we all look at that world through the lens of our own personal experiences, recognizing our limitations and sharing our knowledge increase our grasp of the complexities of perception and open us to additional points of view.

2. *Generating original ideas:* Once the students have performed the model four or five times in a group, they are able to perform it on their own. It is a superb tool for generating original ideas. Whatever subject one must analyze may be approached by listing or brainstorming, grouping, labeling, and generalizing. One shortcut, called mapping, involves writing the topic in the center of a page and grouping the items as they are written.

3. *Reading and extracting meaning:* Examining a crucial concept in any discipline before studying it further brings increased understanding. Examining the concept *grudge* increased the seventh-grade students' grasp of a short story that was centered around a grudge.

4. *Problem solving:* By performing this strategy on the word *sales*, real estate agents shared their techniques, generated new ideas, and increased their number of sales. Students looking for ways to raise funds for a band trip generated several new ideas and were excited to learn a technique they felt would help them in the business world.

5. *Writing unified paragraphs and papers:* The concept development model is a superb tool for teaching paragraph unity. Grammar texts say that a paragraph is a series of sentences developing one topic. Although this definition seems reasonably straightforward, students frequently have trouble with this conceptual division. Many students simply begin a new paragraph without any reason or write a paper as one long paragraph.

When students have finished listing, grouping, and labeling a concept or a topic, ask them how they would write about the topic if they had to write a paper. Could the items on the board be useful? If so, how? Try to let them see the connection between groups and paragraphs, between labels and topic sentences. Let them pick a group and write a paragraph. The label becomes the topic sentence and the items in the group are ways of developing the idea in the label. Tell the students that they may add more items to the group and that they do not have to use all the items. When they have practiced writing coherent paragraphs, structured around one thought (the thought contained in the label), they can use this technique to write whole papers on a main topic. They can develop a central theme, idea, or generalization and support that idea with three or four paragraphs derived from different groups.

Here is a paragraph written by a ninth-grade student in the class described in the scenario, who had just finished exploring the concept *grudge*. She had picked the group *things done while holding a grudge*. She wrote the following:

Have you ever held a grudge? A grudge is a cold, mean, nasty little animal that bites and causes you to do strange things. After you touch the grudge, it might make you start to be mean to a friend because of something that friend did to you, even though it might not have been that big a deal. Soon, you and that friend have become enemies, all because of the mean little grudge. Oh, the grudge loves it, too! It will get you talking about the person behind her back, whispering about her to her friends, and causing everyone else to choose sides between you and her. The grudge is a mean, nasty little animal. Don't ever hold one![16]

Building on ideas contributed by everyone, the students and the teacher in the girl's class obtained an expanded idea of the concept *grudge* and of the consequences of holding one (see Figure 6.2). The model had led two students to use personification and analogy in their paragraphs. Because the students already had an example and a context, introducing these two new vocabulary words had additional meaning. During the discussion of grudge, the teacher had been puzzled by the item *fudge* and assumed it was a rhyming response. When she asked for clarification, the student said, "Because grudges make me unhappy, and when I'm unhappy I eat junk, like fudge." Frequently a student's reason for suggesting an item or for grouping items is quite different from what the teacher or other students may assume, so clarification is important.

ACTIVITY 6.1

Teaching is, by its nature, related to concept development. Think of a unit of study you might teach in your intended subject area or one that you already do teach. Try to name a crucial concept that might occur in this unit. (You may wish to check through a curriculum guide or typical textbook for help in identifying a concept.) Next, think of at least one question you might ask or an activity you might assign at each of these steps of the concept development process: listing, grouping, labeling, analyzing, and synthesizing.

If you have a copy (preferably a teacher's edition) of a textbook appropriate to your subject area specialty, compare your questions and activities with those suggested in the text. Do the authors assist students in the concept development process? ■

Summary

There are several benefits to using the concept development model approach regularly (once a month or more frequently). From this model, students learn much from one another about the concept, object, event, or person studied. They absorb a great deal of the accumulated knowledge and ideas of the whole group. They expand and refine their own concepts of the topic being studied; concomitantly, they expand and refine their ability to perform these mental processes.

Concepts are the building blocks of our intellectual activity. Knowledge is not static. Knowledge of even a simple object can grow and take on new dimensions, or it can recede and grow hazy with lack of exposure. It might be helpful to think of growth in knowledge as a series of overlays on an overhead projector. We add to and change an already existing impression, much as one makes an addition to a basic drawing. The concept development model is helpful to teachers, because it not only

FIGURE 6.2 "Holding a Grudge"

Source: Drawing by ninth-grade students Julia Sapir and Ted Mawyer.

allows them to enrich the original impression but also affords a glimpse of that original impression on which to build.

WEB RESOURCES

1. **http://fac-staff.seattleu.edu/kschlnoe/conceptdevelex.html**

This web site offers a summary of the steps in the concept development model together with three examples (for fourth, fifth, and middle school grades) of the use of the model for developing students' concept of theme.

2. **http:/fac-staff.seattleu.edu/kschlnoe/process.html**

How do we develop students' abilities to grasp basic concepts and themes? By visiting this web site you can read some interesting approaches put forth by Dr. Katherine L. Schlick Noe at Seattle University.

3. **http://ivc.uidaho.edu/mod/models/taba/practice.html**
This site contains an inductive thinking activity in which students are asked to form categories from a long list of teaching strategies. The activity is useful for teacher education classes.

4. **http://users.edte.utwente.nl/lanzing/cm_home.htm**
This site discusses concept mapping and provides an example of this process as a technique for representing knowledge in graphs that are networks of concepts.

5. **http://www.mcps.k12.md.us/departments/oipd/mspap/reading/LookingAtConRCL.pdf**
This site contains information on concept formation adapted from Hilda Taba, *The Three Thinking Strategies*. Included are three excellent charts detailing all steps in the process.

6. **http://www.csus.edu/indiv/m/mcvickerb/sj_hildataba.htm**
Describing inductive reasoning, this site quotes Hilda Taba as she differentiates between concepts and generalizations.

7. **http://www.utc.edu/Teaching-Resource-Center/concepts.html**
What is a concept map, and how can it facilitate curriculum design? As discussed in this site, a concept map is a device for organizing a body of knowledge. In addition, it can reveal the relationships among concepts. The site also provides a good explanation of constructivism.

8. **http://www.madison.k12.wi.us/tnl/langarts/vocabcondev.htm**
Educators in the Madison Metropolitan School District offer suggestions for teaching vocabulary based on knowledge of word meanings and the concepts they represent.

N O T E S

1. J. A. Michener, *Centennial* (New York: Random House, 1974), 678.
2. William Morris, ed., *American Heritage Dictionary of the English Language*, 4th ed. (Boston: Houghton Mifflin, 2000).
3. J. S. Bruner, J. J. Goodnow, and G. A. Austin, *A Study of Thinking* (New Brunswick, NJ: Transaction Books, 1986), 244.
4. Bruner, Goodnow, and Austin, 246.
5. Hilda Taba, *Hilda Taba Teaching Strategies Program*, Unit I, Elementary Edition (Miami: Institute for Staff Development, 1971), 176.
6. Hilda Taba, *Hilda Taba Teaching Strategies Program*, Unit I, Secondary Edition (Miami: Institute for Staff Development, 1971), 165.
7. Rich Hall and friends, *Sniglets* (New York: Collier Books, 1984).
8. Taba, *Hilda Taba Teaching Strategies Program*, Unit I, Secondary Edition, xv.
9. Taba, *Hilda Taba Teaching Strategies Program*, Unit I, Secondary Edition, 165.
10. L. Wittgenstein, *Philosophical Investigations* (New York: Macmillan, 1953).
11. Ruth Benedict, *Patterns of Culture* (Boston: Houghton Mifflin, 1934), 3.
12. John Dewey, *How We Think*, rev. ed. (Boston: D. C. Heath, 1933), 27.
13. C. T. Fosnot, ed., *Constructivism: Theory, Perspectives and Practice* (New York: Teachers College Press, 1996).
14. Hilda Taba, Mary C. Durkin, Jack R. Fraenkel, and Anthony H. McNaughton, *A Teacher's Handbook to Elementary Social Studies*, 2nd ed. (Reading, MA: Addison-Wesley, 1971), 10.
15. Taba, Durkin, Fraenkel, and McNaughton, 72–73.
16. This paragraph was submitted by Beth Brown, a ninth-grade student at Charlottesville High School.

CHAPTER

7

Inquiry Models

Teaching Problem Solving
through Discovery and Questioning

Why are caterpillars fuzzy? What causes snakes to slither and bears to growl? Why do cats always land right side up? What happens to the lightning bug's light during the day? Is a baby fish afraid of the water? Did something take a bite out of the moon? Who ever thought up the name *brussels sprouts,* and why does ketchup stick in the bottle? Was the red color in the leaves hiding under the green? Is my skin brown because I was toasted? Will the rain melt the flowers?

Remember when the world was full of questions to ask rather than answers to learn? Somewhere on the way to adulthood, children inevitably get the idea that becoming a grown-up means leaving the world of questioning for the world of knowing. Schools institutionalize the departure from questions to answers as success becomes measured by putting the right answer into the blank or circling the correct response, knowing positively what is true and what is false. Almost all questions in school have one right answer, and questions for which there are no answers do not often arise.

True wisdom, however, might better be defined as the realization of how little one knows in contrast to how much one knows. The real excitement of learning is daring to challenge ignorance with unbridled curiosity. *Homo sapiens,* meaning quite literally "humankind who taste of knowledge," have aptly named themselves. If knowing how to learn is more important than knowing all the answers, then the greatest realization of a person's intellectual life must be that good questions are more important than right answers. Thus the quality of the questions one can ask, rather than the correctness of the answers one can give, shows one's wisdom. Scientist and philosopher Lewis Thomas has described this intellectual journey:

Science, especially twentieth-century science, has provided us with a glimpse of something we never really knew before, the revelation of human ignorance. We have been accustomed to the belief, from one century to another, that except for one or two mysteries, we more or less comprehend everything on earth. Every age, not just the eighteenth century, regarded itself as the Age of Reason, and we have never lacked for explanations of the world and its ways. Now, we are being brought up short. We do

117

not understand much of anything, from the episode we rather dismissively (and, I think, defensively) choose to call the "big bang," all the way down to the particles in the atoms of a bacterial cell. We have a wilderness of mystery to make our way through in the centuries ahead.[1]

The idea of inquiry learning is based on the premise that there is indeed a "wilderness of mystery" to be explored in all fields and that every school subject represents a discipline of inquiry in which all students can participate.

Model One: The Suchman Inquiry Model

Richard Suchman,[2] who believed that the intellectual strategies used by scientists could be taught to young learners, developed one widely accepted approach to inquiry-based instruction. The natural curiosity of children and adolescents can be trained and disciplined in procedures of inquiry. When students ask *why* out of genuine interest, they are likely to grasp the information and to retain it as their own understanding. They will also come to understand the value of working within a discipline—that is, of participating in the way of knowing and thinking that is at the core of every discipline.

Steps in the Suchman Inquiry Model

1. Select a problem and conduct research.
2. Introduce the process and present the problem.
3. Gather data.
4. Develop a theory and verify.
5. Explain the theory and state the rules associated with it.
6. Analyze the process.
7. Evaluate.

Step 1—Select a Problem and Conduct Research

The Suchman model begins with the teacher selecting a puzzling situation or problem that is genuinely interesting and stimulating to the learner. It may be a scientific problem, such as why moisture sometimes accumulates on the outside of a glass or why sugar disappears in water. It may be a puzzling event, such as the mystery of the Lost Colony or of the Bermuda Triangle. It may be a scene from a play or a story that requires the students to formulate an outcome. It may be a problem requiring mathematical skills, a problem in health, or a situation to be resolved in the athletic program. Here are some examples of potential problems for students to begin the inquiry process. The answers are not provided. Most of the problems have several possible answers.

I. In 1692, there was a surge in the number of witches put to death, marking the worst outbreak of the persecution of witches in America. Strangely, this outbreak occurred 47 years after the previous epidemic of witch persecution. No one has been able to prove why this happened in 1692 in Essex County, Massachusetts, and Fairfield County, Connecticut, and not in other counties; however, there are several theories regarding this phenomenon, and one in particular that seems very plausible.

II. Jefferson Davis, the president of the Confederacy, was considered to be an outstanding leader and more capable than Abraham Lincoln at the beginning of the Civil War. Yet, by the end of the war, Davis was totally ineffectual. What might account for a leader becoming ineffectual?

III. Two plants growing in the classroom receive the same amount of water and are planted in the same soil, yet one of the plants is much larger than the other. The plants were replanted from seedlings that were exactly the same size. What might cause this difference in plant growth?

IV. Rock strata in the eastern United States are very similar. In Florida, however, the rock strata are entirely different from any other area. What might account for this dramatic difference?

Any subject lends itself to inquiry. All that is required is a puzzling situation for which the students can find a logical and reasonable solution. For many students, especially those accustomed to the process of inquiry, the best and most realistic problem situations are those for which there may be more than one answer or for which no final answers have been determined.

Once a problem has been selected, the teacher completes the necessary research on the problem and prepares a data sheet for quick reference during the questioning periods. The teacher also determines how much information should be provided to the students at the beginning of the inquiry process and what additional information could be supplied if the class has difficulty.

Step 2—Introduce the Process and Present the Problem

Before beginning the inquiry lesson, the teacher explains the process to the class; in this model, the entire class can participate. The teacher is the main source of data and will respond only to questions that can be answered with a *yes* or a *no*, thus placing the burden of framing the question on the learner. The teacher may choose to add additional information or guide the questioning, but the responsibility for hypothesizing must remain with the students; the teacher is in control of the process but not in control of the outcome. The students are presented with the following rules:

1. A student may ask a question only when called upon.
2. Students may talk with one another only during caucus periods, times given to group discussion and cooperative work among students.

3. Questions must be phrased so that the teacher can answer with a yes or no response. (The teacher may choose to give additional information if needed.)
4. A student may continue to ask questions as long as the questions are receiving a positive response from the teacher.

The teacher reads the problem aloud or distributes problem statement sheets to the class. If the students are nonreaders, the teacher provides them with the problem orally and uses pictures to illustrate the problem if possible. Students are encouraged to ask for explanations if a term is unclear.

Step 3—Gather Data

In most classrooms, students ask questions that require the teacher to do the thinking. In this model, each question must be asked as a tentative hypothesis. The student cannot ask "What makes the plant lean toward the sun?" because that would require the teacher to give the information. Rather, the question must be phrased so that the teacher can respond with a yes or no answer: "Does the plant lean toward the sun because of a magnetic force?"

The teacher may decide to add information or expand on the problem at any time; it is important, however, to let the students experience some frustration as they question. There is a temptation for the teacher to rephrase the question and say "Is this what you mean?" It is better to say "Can you restate that question?" or "Can you state the question more clearly?" or "Can you state the question so that I can answer it either yes or no?" A teacher might also say "Yes, that is a part of the answer, but why don't you consider this additional piece of information in light of what you already have discovered." The data gathered through the questioning process should be recorded on the board or on data sheets kept by each student.

Step 4—Develop a Theory and Verify

When a student poses a theoretical question that seems to be an answer to the problem, the question is stated as a theory and written on the board in a special area reserved for this purpose. Now, all data gathering relates directly to proving or disproving this one theory. In the problem regarding the different rates of plant growth, once the students have posed a theory that the amount of light received by plants affected the rate of growth, all questions are now focused on either accepting or rejecting this theory.

Students may ask to caucus to discuss the information and frame hypothetical questions they will ask the teacher. (Some teachers assign caucus groups and leaders prior to instruction, thus saving time and reducing confusion.) Depending on the nature of the problem, the teacher directs the students to other sources of information or to actual laboratory experiments. Students are encouraged to ask hypothetical questions at this point, such as "If both plants are positioned in the same part of the room, will their growth be the same?" As before, the teacher's response is either yes or no.

If the students reach a point where the theory they have posed seems to be verified, then the class accepts the theory as a solution and moves to the next step of the model. If the theory is not acceptable and does not satisfy the class as plausible, it is rejected and the general data gathering begins again. The class may be allowed to caucus at any point but only with the teacher's permission.

Step 5—Explain the Theory and State the Rules Associated with It

In this step, students are asked to explain the theory accepted as a tentative solution and state the rules associated with that theory. In addition, they must determine how the theory could be tested to see if the rules can be generalized to other situations. Students will sometimes discover essential flaws in their theory at this stage, forcing them to return to data gathering and experimentation.

In terms of the problem of plant growth and sunlight, for instance, the teacher would have the students, in their own words, state the rule based on their theory that the sun was the factor, such as "Plants need sunlight to grow strong and healthy." The class would then discuss whether all plants need the same amount of sun and decide how to test for that generalization.

Step 6—Analyze the Process

Students are asked to review the process they have just used to arrive at acceptance of the theory. At this step, it is important that the students consider how they could have expedited the process. Students should analyze the types of questions they asked to see how they could have formed more effective questioning techniques. As students become more efficient in using the steps of inquiry, the teacher may relinquish some control and allow the students to set up their own inquiry processes.

Step 7—Evaluate

Ask the students to locate and research their own puzzling situations. Conduct a contest in the class to select the most interesting problems.

Test to determine if the students understand the theory and if they can generalize the rules related to the theory to other situations.

For a theory that has no "right" answer, ask the students to identify another probable theory. The two theories could then be the basis for a debate in the class.

Summary of Steps in the Suchman Inquiry Model

1. *Select a problem and conduct research:* Choose a puzzling situation or an event that will entice the students to discover the answer and then research the problem for possible solutions.

2. *Introduce the process and present the problem:* Carefully explain and post the rules that the students will follow for the inquiry. Present the puzzling situation to the students in writing and provide them with a means for recording data.

3. *Gather data:* Respond to questions posed by the students for the purpose of gathering and verifying data. Guide the students to ask questions more clearly or more completely but avoid restating the questions for them. Encourage the students to call for a caucus when they need to talk with one another, but do not permit students to talk to each other during the questioning periods. Reinforce the idea that this is a group process; the attention and participation of the entire class are needed.

4. *Develop a theory and verify:* When a student poses a theory, stop the questioning and write the theory on the chalkboard. The class decides to accept or reject it. Emphasize that at this stage the questioning is directed toward experimenting with one particular theory. If other theories are posed, write them on the board and tell the class that they will be explored later if the theory under examination does not prove adequate. Encourage the students to consider all possible types of questions. For example, if they are focusing on an event, encourage them to consider conditions that might cause it. Questions are valuable tools at this point in the model. Students may be encouraged to do further research or to experiment in the laboratory as they try to verify a particular theory.

5. *Explain the theory and state the rules associated with it:* Once a theory or a theoretical answer has been verified by the students, lead them into an explanation and application of the theory. Discuss the rules or effects of the theory as well as the predictive value the theory may have for other events.

6. *Analyze the process:* Finally, discuss the inquiry process with the class. Examine how they arrived at an acceptable theory to explain the problem and determine how the process could be improved. As the class gains confidence in the inquiry process, they may assume more responsibility for the process.

7. *Evaluate:* Test to determine if the students have understood the theory derived from the process and determine if they are able to generalize the rules to other situations. Also, encourage the students to look for other puzzling situations and to

develop a habit of asking questions and looking for answers. Because this model is based on a scientific method, determine if the students are solving problems more effectively with this technique.

Model Two: The WebQuest Model of Inquiry

Once students are familiar with the basic steps of the inquiry model, they may be ready for a more adventurous, less teacher-directed experience. The WebQuest model is a special form of inquiry teaching that takes advantage of the Web as a primary source of information. Originated by Bernie Dodge of San Diego State University, WebQuests are thematic units that incorporate information available on the Web with a variety of other resources. Though a WebQuest is presented to students as a web page, sources of study include much more than the Web. Students also conduct textbook reading, supplemental reading and study in other sources, and independent activities related to the topic of the unit. In addition, the resources and activities embedded in a WebQuest include interviewing and reporting, observation and note taking, survey research, and many other "real-life" experiences that students write about.

The major difference between standard thematic units and WebQuests is that the former are focused on topics that students are to learn about and the latter are focused on problems that students are to solve. The "problem" is generated from the topic under study in the classroom. The distinguishing feature of a WebQuest lies in the instructional approach it requires. Is the students' learning to be guided by the topic and related materials, or by their own investigation and inquiry? WebQuests create open-ended learning opportunities for students and teachers. The underlying purpose of a WebQuest is to pose a problem for students to solve with the resources put at their disposal to help them learn the content required in the curriculum. WebQuests provide an organizational scheme for student-centered, teacher-facilitated learning.

Before deciding you could not possibly create a unit of study based on Web resources because you "don't know a thing about the Internet or even what the letters *http* or *www* stand for," suspend your disbelief for a moment and think this through, step-by-step. You already know the basic steps of inquiry. With a little tweaking of those steps, a WebQuest will take no longer to build than any other well-thought-out unit of study. In fact, the steps for the teacher are reduced in preparing a WebQuest, because much of the responsibility for the learning that occurs in the context of a WebQuest falls on the shoulders of the students.

Steps in the WebQuest Model of Inquiry

1. Select a problem and conduct research.
2. Present the problem in the WebQuest template.
3. Students gather data and information to solve the problem.
4. Students develop and verify their evaluation.

Step 1—The Teacher Selects a Problem and Conducts Preliminary Research

The WebQuest model begins with an open-ended problem or a puzzling situation that the students are going to explore with Web and text resources put at their disposal. The problem is based in the content of the curriculum, but its solution is based in the quest that the students will undertake. For example, if the curricular area is ecology, the problem might concern the reintroduction of wolves into Yellowstone Park. If the curricular area centers on the basic operations in mathematics, the problem might concern when, where, how, and why humans invented numbers, including the question of whether the base ten system is ideal. If the curricular area is Columbus's "discovery" of America, the issue of the WebQuest might be whether Europeans were justified in claiming the Western Hemisphere as their own.

The first step in creating the quest is for the teacher to search for appropriate web pages and other sources that address the issue or problem. Much of what is on the Web is too difficult for younger students to read, so the bulk of the work for the teacher will be to find links that will be the most helpful to the students for whom the WebQuest is being created.

The easiest way to illustrate this is by an example. For the purpose of illustrating how a WebQuest is built, consider the topic *weather*. Weather is in the curriculum at several grades, and it certainly encompasses many open-ended problems. We will look at the question "What causes the weather to change, and would we want to change it if we could?"

The teacher's research is straightforward, and the resources are clear. Can the local meteorologist come talk to the class? Does the school library have books on the topic of weather? What does the students' science textbook have to say on the topic? Is there mention of weather in the students' other textbooks, such as the geography text? And, of course, what web sites contain helpful information related to weather?

Answering the last question requires the use of a good search engine—an Internet tool that will automatically list all the web sites it can find related to the topic of your search. The trick is to word the search topic in a way that keeps the number of "hits" reasonable. Because even the narrowest search may yield a thousand or more sites, your job is to sift and sort them, saving only those that will be the most useful to your students. Most search engines use ranking criteria that cause the most relevant sites to appear at the top of the list, typically based on the number of times the words in the search topic match words on a web page.

The current favorite search tool, or engine, among Web enthusiasts is Google, because it is fast and accurate. There are many other choices available, however, and most searchers will use more than one tool. Because the engines differ somewhat in the criteria they use to choose and list their findings, using at least two search engines is usually worth the time and effort.

To make our weather example come to life, log on to the Web, open up Google at the address www.google.com, and conduct a search for the following: weather + change + snow + rain + wind. (The plus signs will restrict the findings to sites that contain all of these words.) Review the Google search tips and try out the various options to narrow the search. One of the values of a thorough search of the Web is that the sites you find will suggest ideas you might never have thought of otherwise. For example, the web site http://www.meds-sdmm.dfo-mpo.gc.ca/cmos/weatherlore.html contains a very readable discussion of the expressions and sayings related to the weather, such as "Red sky at night, sailor's delight; Red sky in morning, sailor take warning." Students could be asked to find the source of all these weather expressions and how many have any basis in fact. The WebQuest would involve students in studying the scientific basis of many things "everyone knows" about the weather.

It is important to save the most relevant Web addresses that appear on the search results page. Most Web browsers make this very easy. You can simply put any address that seems particularly promising into the "Favorites" or "Bookmarks" folder, or you can create a subfolder called "Weather Sites" in your "Favorites" or "Bookmarks" folder and put the addresses there. Saving these files will make subsequent steps in constructing the WebQuest very easy.

Step 2—Present the Problem in the WebQuest Template

A convenient template is available that can be used to create and present a WebQuest to students. Go to the address http://edweb.sdsu.edu/webquest/LessonTemplate.html and download "traditional no-frame version" of the template for the PC or Mac. If you opt for the PC version, you will need to have WinZip installed to open the file once it is downloaded. If this program is not on your computer already, go to www.winzip.com and get a copy of the trial version. Then note where the template file is located on the hard drive of your computer and (1) open it with a web editing tool such as Composer in Netscape Communicator or one of the many commercial tools such as Claris Home Page or Microsoft Front Page; (2) save it to a disk under a new name, such as "<your name>'s WebQuest"; and (3) replace the text you see in the template, which is actually the directions for what to include, with text of your own. You will find a good introductory tutorial on building web pages at http://archive.nesa.uiuc.edu/General/Internet/www/HTML/PrimerPrintable.html. It contains the basics of Web design and directions for saving your WebQuest to a place on the Web that anyone can get to. Those who want to know more about the Web and want to become an expert in a short time should consult *The Non-Designer's Web Book*, 2nd Edition.[3]

Any computer server in your school would be a good place to store and access your web page, and any school technical resources person can help you with this. Storing your web page on such a server will make your web page available to students from any computer at school or at home. Creating a web page is no more complicated than the steps followed in word processing on a computer, but it is a new process, and thus an intimidating one for many people. If you are among this group, be patient and take your time. A whole world will be opened to you!

The WebQuest template is practically a fill-in-the-blank recipe that is organized into the following sections, which you merely elaborate to suit the context of instruction.

1. *Introduction.* A short paragraph is written to introduce the activity or lesson to the students. The introduction sets the stage and offers a teaser to grab the students' attention. For a WebQuest on the question "Why can't we do anything about the weather?" the introduction might begin, "No newscaster gets more criticism than the meteorologists. Why are meteorologists so often wrong? What's so hard about predicting the weather? And for that matter, have you ever wondered why we really can't do anything about the weather?"

2. *The Task.* The task section provides a crisp and clear description of what the end result of the learners' activities will be. Learners should see that they will need to gather information and then transform that information into something novel. The end point, for example, may be writing and sending a letter to the editor of the local newspaper or to the National Weather Service, or it might be creating a display illustrating the forces that cause weather to change.

3. *The Process.* This section enumerates the steps the learners should go through to accomplish the task. If possible, these steps should be enumerated as a numbered list. This section of the WebQuest contains the Web links and names of other resources the students will need to complete the task. It also discusses how the students will organize and use the information they gather and how they will organize themselves. In the inquiry on weather, for example, students might work in groups to explore different aspects of weather such as precipitation, wind, heat and cold, hurricanes and tornadoes, or weather lore.

4. *Evaluation.* This section describes how the students' performance will be evaluated. Include the characteristics of the product you expect and what different levels of quality would look like.

5. *Conclusion.* Briefly summarize what students will have accomplished or learned by completing this inquiry activity or lesson.

6. *Credits and References.* This section lists the sources of any images, music, or text used in creating the WebQuest.

Step 3—Students Gather Data and Information to Solve the Problem

In the WebQuest form of inquiry, the students, not the teacher, gather the information and solve the problem. It is the students' inquiry that drives the learning. Through the structure of the WebQuest, all the resources, Web and other, are listed in the context of an open-ended problem that the students must solve by working alone or in groups. The teacher's role is to answer technical and other questions and to guide the students to the tools they will need to create a unique and reasonable product. The variety of these products is practically limitless, as a quick survey of WebQuest examples will demonstrate. (See the Web Resources section at the end of this chapter.)

Step 4—Students Develop and Verify Their Solution

Responsibility for developing, testing, and verifying solutions to the problem rests with the students. As they present the products of their work to the rest of the class or to other groups, they will "test" their findings. Because a problem posed by a WebQuest is open-ended, there is not a single solution, and every solution is subject to revision. The greatest value of WebQuests and other forms of inquiry rests in their potential for teaching students that the nature of true scholarship lies in the search for plausible answers to the complex questions that humankind faces. WebQuests help students realize that researchers often do not understand much that must be learned, but they have the courage to face the "wilderness of mystery" that constitutes every discipline. Inquiry learning invites students to participate in this great adventure.

EXERCISE 7.1

Which of the following would be appropriate problems for an inquiry model?

1. What is the answer to 3×8?
2. Who was president of the United States during the Civil War?
3. The changes of the tides on Earth seem to be related to Earth's position relative to the moon. What factors might explain this relationship?
4. We have learned how plants make food through photosynthesis. Here are pictures of certain plants that can grow in the dark. How are these plants able to survive?
5. Shakespeare did not leave a shred of paper that can be verified as his own writing, aside from a possible signature. Did he himself write all those plays and sonnets, or is it possible that someone else did the work and put Shakespeare's name on it to preserve his or her anonymity? Explore the Shakespeare mystery and find an answer to one of literature's most enduring mysteries.

Answers to Exercise 7.1
The first two questions require one right answer. Such problems are taught more effectively by means other than an inquiry model. The third problem describes a scientific conundrum for which there is no definitive answer. The fourth presents a situation that requires students to reexamine a hypothesis when presented with new data. The fifth problem is typical of the kind of question posed for a WebQuest inquiry—the answer has vexed scholars on both sides of the Atlantic, and conflicting information is abundant. Any of the last three problems could be effectively used for inquiry-based instruction. ■

Basis for the Inquiry Approach to Instruction

Too often children are taught in school as though the answers to all the important questions were in their textbooks. In reality, most of the problems faced by individuals have no easy answers. There are no reference books in which one can find the solution to life's perplexing problems. Although it is true that those who succeed in school are often those who can remember the "correct" answer, those who succeed in life are usually those who are willing to ask questions and search for solutions.

Robert Sternberg has made a persuasive argument that the problems presented by real life and those that children are taught to deal with in school are alarmingly different, so different that the training for thinking one receives in schools may be irrelevant to the thinking required in life. Sternberg's discussion of the differences between problems posed in school and the problems posed by life helps us to understand the importance of inquiry models of instruction. The following summary (with parenthetical statements inserted for transition) is meant to convey the essence of Sternberg's argument:

> In the everyday world, the first and sometimes most difficult step in problem solving is the recognition that a problem exists. . . . [Especially as] in everyday problem solving, it is often harder to figure out just what the problem is than to figure out how to solve it. . . . [Often the difficulty in solving everyday problems is that] everyday problems tend to be ill-structured. . . . In everyday problem solving, it is not usually clear just what information will be needed to solve a given problem, nor is it always clear where the requisite information can be found. . . . The solutions to everyday problems depend on and interact with the contexts in which the problems are presented. . . . Everyday problems generally have no one right solution, and even the criteria for what constitutes a test solution are often not clear. . . . [To further aggravate the matter] the solutions to everyday problems depend at least as much on informal knowledge as on formal knowledge. . . . [One of the biggest differences between problems encountered in school and those encountered in real life is that] solutions to important everyday problems have consequences that matter. . . . [Unlike in school where individuality is prized and competition rewarded] everyday problem solving often occurs in groups. . . . Everyday problems can be complicated, messy, and stubbornly persistent.[4]

In a subsequent article, Sternberg points out that one might take a number of approaches in trying to create a more satisfactory congruence between problems children learn to solve in school and those they must solve in real life.[5] He notes that the basis of inquiry teaching is derived from fundamentals of problem solving.

The inquiry model is grounded in the theory of problem-based learning, which has been described as "a pedagogical strategy for posing significant, contextualized, real world situations, and providing resources, guidance, and instruction to learners as they develop content knowledge and problem-solving skills."[6] In problem-based learning, the teacher serves as subject matter expert, resource guide, and task group consultant, but not as information transmitter or sole source. The major role of the teacher is to encourage student participation, provide appropriate information to keep students on track, avoid negative feedback, and assume the role of fellow learner.[7]

The idea of anchoring instruction in authentic problems is not especially new. It formed the basis of much of what Dewey advocated. It has been used in medical education for many years. The constructivist movement in education derives from a problem-centered perspective.

Jerome Bruner described four benefits to be gained from the experience of learning through the process of discovering answers to problems:[8]

1. *An increase in intellectual potency.* Bruner hypothesizes that in the process of discovery, the learner learns how to problem solve and learns the fundamentals of "the task of learning." He suggests that learners who engage in discovering possible answers for themselves learn to recognize constraints in hypothesizing solutions, which reduces what he calls potshotting or stringing out random hypotheses one after the other. These learners also learn to connect previously obtained information to new information and to develop persistence in sticking to a problem until it is satisfactorily resolved.

2. *The shift from extrinsic to intrinsic rewards.* Rather than striving for rewards gained primarily from giving back the right answer, students achieve rewards from the satisfaction of manipulating the environment and from solving problems. The learner develops an ability to delay gratification in seeking the solution to a problem rather than depending on the immediate reward of giving back to the teacher what was expected.

3. *Learning the heuristics of discovery.* Bruner points out that the process of inquiry involves learning how to pose a problem in such a form that it can be worked on and solved. He believes that only by practice and by being involved in the process of inquiry can one learn how best to go about solving problems. The more experienced the learner, the more the inquiry process can be generalized to other tasks and problems to be solved.

4. *Aid to memory processing.* The primary problem in the memory process is the retrieval of what is to be remembered, according to Bruner. He believes that material that is figured out by the learner is more readily available to memory than that stored on demand. In addition, the learner who is a good problem solver also discovers techniques for remembering information.

In the inquiry model, strategies used by scientists for solving problems are presented as a systematic mode for processing data and learning to approach puzzling situations in all fields of study. In teaching with any variety of the inquiry model, be aware that there are both convergent and divergent ways of conducting the process. If the teacher already knows the answer to a problem and wants the students to discover it, then the process is convergent. If the information presented to the students might lead to a number of legitimate responses, then the process is more divergent. The initial problems one chooses may be primarily convergent in that the answer is known and the teacher leads the students toward the right answer through the information given. But students should gradually be introduced to more divergent situations in which one right answer is not known or agreed to. Confronted with ill-structured and open-ended problems, students practice a heuristic process in learning to solve problems and deal with ambiguity such as that presented in the "everyday world" problems that Sternberg distinguishes.

Scenario

In her environmental science class, Ms. Whitaker introduces the unit on toxins using the inquiry process. She begins by asking the students if they have heard the expression "mad as a hatter." One girl raises her hand and says that she remembers a character called the Mad Hatter in the movie *Alice in Wonderland*. Another says that the movie was made from a book by Lewis Carroll in which the Mad Hatter had a tea party. Another student recalls having read a book in which someone was described as being mad as a hatter. "I thought it meant the character was really angry about his hat," the student says.

Ms. Whitaker tells the class that she is going to present them with a problem for which they will try to find an acceptable solution. They will ask her questions that can be answered yes or no. She explains the rules for the inquiry procedure, which she has posted at the front of the room, and then assigns the students to their caucus groups. She encourages the students to ask questions as though they were actually doing research. She also gives them some examples of the type of questions they might ask her, ranging from simple fact questions to those that are more complex, such as "If I did ____, could I expect ____ to happen?" Because she will be the source of the information, she has prepared a fact sheet for her own use. (See Figure 7.1.)

Ms. Whitaker reads aloud the following problem statement:

> In England during the 18th and 19th centuries, a very large number of workers who made men's hats went "mad" and behaved as though they were insane. In fact, many of them were committed to the lunatic asylums of that time. Why did this group of people have such a high incidence of insanity, thus giving rise to the saying "mad as a hatter"?

She then asks the students to begin the questioning process.

STUDENT: What about the people who made women's hats—did a lot of them go mad too?

TEACHER: No.

STUDENT: Did men wear some particular kind of hat in those days?

TEACHER: Yes. Ask another question.

STUDENT: Was it those stovepipe-looking hats like Abe Lincoln wore?

FIGURE 7.1   Fact Sheet Used by Teacher in Responding to Questions

---

Fact Sheet

---

1. Working conditions in England were bad, and many people developed work-related illnesses without realizing the cause.
2. Workplaces were not well ventilated, and few safety precautions were taken. Workers did not wear protective clothing.
3. Most men's hats were made from felt, which was processed from the under-hair of beavers imported from Canada.
4. Mercury was one of the chemicals used in the manufacture of felt hats.
5. As we now know, mercury is highly poisonous and, if allowed to build up in a person's body, can cause an illness resembling insanity.
6. Today, this illness is named Minamata disease after a small factory town in Japan where thousands of people were poisoned after eating fish taken from a bay into which tons of mercury had been dumped by a local industry from 1932 to 1968.

TEACHER: Be more specific.

STUDENT: Those black hats with the high tops—oh, they called them top hats, I think.

TEACHER: Yes, most were like that.

STUDENT: Did it have something to do with what the hats were made of?

TEACHER: Yes.

STUDENT: Can we caucus?

TEACHER: Yes.

STUDENT: (After the caucus) Didn't they also call those hats "beavers"?

TEACHER: Yes.

STUDENT: Were they made out of beaver pelts?

TEACHER: Yes. Ask another question. You may keep asking questions as long as you get a positive response.

STUDENT: If we went into one of those factories, could we see what was making the people go mad?

TEACHER: Be more specific, please.

STUDENT: Well, could we see the workers being beaten, for instance?

TEACHER: No. Let's review what you have found already. Pay attention to those facts that you already know. (She points to the board, where a student has been summarizing the responses to their questions.)

STUDENT: Did they have to treat the beaver pelts in some way?

TEACHER: Yes, they did.

STUDENT: Did they use high heat, which made the people go crazy?

TEACHER: They may have used heat, but it was not the primary cause of the problem.

STUDENT: Did they use a chemical?

TEACHER: Yes.

STUDENT: Was it poisonous?

TEACHER: Yes.

STUDENT: Did they inhale the fumes?

TEACHER: That might be a part of it. Do you wish to pose a theory?

STUDENT: The hatters were poisoned by handling a toxic substance used in the making of felt for the hats.

TEACHER: Now, let us ask questions to test this theory or to make it more complete.

STUDENT: Was it arsenic?

TEACHER: No.

STUDENT: Is this poison still in use today?

TEACHER: Yes.

STUDENT: Do they still use it to make hats?

TEACHER: Not to my knowledge.

STUDENT: Do people know that this substance is poisonous?

TEACHER: Yes.

STUDENT: Can we caucus?

TEACHER: Certainly. Remember we are now testing the theory that is written on the board.

STUDENT: (After the caucus) Was the substance mercury?

TEACHER: Yes, it was. So now you can restate your theory to make it more complete. (The students add the word *mercury*.)

The teacher asks the class to state some rules they could draw from the theory they postulated. They say that (1) people may be harmed by a substance when they are unaware of its dangers, and (2) when they do not know all the facts, people may ridicule a group for being different.

The students also discuss how they arrived at their theory and what steps were most helpful in deciding. They note that recording the data during the process was helpful.

A C T I V I T Y   7 . 1

Select one of the problems mentioned in step 1 of the description of the Suchman inquiry model in the first part of this chapter. Research the problem to determine the possible solutions or answers. Develop a lesson plan using this puzzling situation. ■

Summary

The first inquiry model presented in this chapter is primarily based on the work of Richard Suchman. The model uses the steps employed in scientific inquiry to approach problems in general. The second utilizes the Web as a primary source of information as students solve problems through their own investigation.

The inquiry model is appropriate whenever the learning that is to take place requires students to be involved with information actively while challenging and questioning solutions to determine if they are acceptable. Used in conjunction with other models in a design process, the inquiry model provides a stimulating option for solving problems and teaching thinking skills.

WEB RESOURCES

1. **http://curry.edschool.virginia.edu/go/edis771/classwebquests.html**
This is a list of numerous WebQuests organized by subject area and grade level. Each quest was created by a student in Professor Tom Estes's content area reading course at the University of Virginia. Teachers may use any part or the whole of any quest. Students who put their work here did so because they are happy to share.

2. **http://www.multiage-education.com/russportfolio/curriculumtopics/sampleunits.html**
This site presents sample units of instruction done as WebQuests.

3. **http://edweb.sdsu.edu/webquest/webquest.html**
Everything you need to know about WebQuests and more is at this site, maintained by the creator of the idea of WebQuests as problem-based units of study that take advantage of the Web as an instructional tool. By clicking on the "Training Materials" link, you can download a template for a WebQuest to start you on your way to this special form of inquiry teaching. You may directly access the template at http://edweb.sdsu.edu/webquest/LessonTemplate.html. Be sure to see the many different examples of WebQuests that are linked here: http://edweb.sdsu.edu/webquest/matrix.html. This matrix is organized for maximum convenience, with examples categorized by subject area and grade level.

4. **http://www.imsa.edu/team/cpbl/cpbl.html**
This is the home page of the Center for Problem-Based Learning, a resource created and maintained by the Illinois Mathematics and Science Academy. The first link to visit from this page is the excellent tutorial entitled "What Is Problem-Based Learning?" Every teacher should read this description and review the examples offered.

5. **http://edweb.sdsu.edu/clrit/learningtree/PBL/WhatisPBL.html**
This site offers a brief but compelling description of problem-based learning as student-centered, faculty-facilitated learning that is designed to take students beyond content to "the development of flexible, cognitive strategies that help analyze unanticipated, ill-structured situations to produce meaningful solutions."

6. **http://www.bscs.org/index.html**
This is the home page of the Biological Sciences Curriculum Study, a nonprofit, noncommercial organization that has been creating exemplary inquiry-based science

curricula since 1958. The goal of BSCS is to develop tools for teaching that allow students to learn science by doing science, abandoning rote learning in favor of an authentic problem-solving approach to learning. At the BSCS web site, teachers will find the "Integrated Science Guide," which can be used as a map for integrating the science curriculum at the high school level.

7. http://www.exploratorium.edu/ifi/

Visitors to the home page of the Exploratorium Institute for Inquiry should be sure to view the March/April 2000 issue of *Connect* magazine, which highlights six case studies of classroom inquiry, five in elementary grades, one in middle school.

8. http://ilf.crlt.indiana.edu/

The Inquiry Learning Forum is a community of teachers meeting online to share ideas related to inquiry learning. The site is built on the metaphor of a school in which each "room" houses a different resource and assistance in implementing inquiry learning.

9. http://inquiry.uiuc.edu/

The Inquiry Page is a virtual community of teachers and administrators interested in inquiry learning and teaching. At this site you can contact other teachers, share inquiry-based lessons and units, draw on resources and ideas for inquiry activities for your classroom, and more.

10. http://www.biopoint.com/msla/links.html

If you are interested in using the Web in promoting inquiry-based learning, this inquiry links page will save you hours of time in searching for the tools you will need.

NOTES

1. Lewis Thomas, "The Art of Teaching Science," in *Fields of Writing*, ed. N. R. Comley et al. (New York: St. Martin's, 1984), 559–564.

2. J. R. Suchman, *The Elementary School Training Program in Scientific Inquiry*, Report to the U.S. Office of Education, Project Title VII (Urbana: University of Illinois Press, 1962).

3. R. Williams & J. Tollett, *The Non-Designer's Web Book*, 2nd ed. (Berkeley, CA: Peachpit Press, 2000).

4. Robert Sternberg, "Teaching Critical Thinking, Part I: Are We Making Critical Mistakes?" *Phi Delta Kappan* 67 (1985): 194–198.

5. Robert Sternberg, "Teaching Critical Thinking, Part II: Possible Solutions," *Phi Delta Kappan* 67 (1985): 277–280.

6. P. Mayo, M. B. Donnelly, P. P. Nash, & R. W. Schwartz, "Student Perceptions of Tutor Effectiveness in Problem Based Surgery Clerkship," *Teaching and Learning in Medicine* 5 (1993): 228.

7. D. N. Aspy, C. B. Aspy, & P. M. Quimby, "What Doctors Can Teach Teachers about Problem-Based Learning," *Educational Leadership* 50, no. 7 (1993): 22–24.

8. Jerome Bruner, "Act of Discovery," *Harvard Educational Review* 31, no. 1 (1961): 21–32.

8 Synectics

Developing Creative Thinking and Problem Solving

Fog

The fog comes
on little cat feet.
It sits looking
over the harbor and city
on silent haunches
and then moves on.

—Carl Sandburg

Cat feet and fog are very different realities, but when the poet Carl Sandburg put the two together, he created an image that delights and surprises the reader with its accuracy. Likewise, the child who says "Oh, look, Mommy, my ice has porcupines in it!" is creating language to express meaning. Poet and child alike constantly exercise the ultimate creative power of language: the power of metaphor.

By bringing together two literally different ideas, metaphor creates a psychological tension that can be resolved only by seeing an otherwise hidden relationship. The best metaphors are those that lead to the most interesting insights, those that extend the resources of language to allow new meaning to emerge. In the words of the French linguist Paul Ricoeur, the purpose of metaphor is "to shatter and to increase our sense of reality by shattering and increasing our language."[1] In exactly the same way, the synectics model is a structured approach to creating understandings that are not merely novel but are unique to the participants.

William Gordon is credited with the development of the process called synectics, which is derived from the Greek word *synecticos* meaning "understanding together that which is apparently different." Synectics uses group interaction to create new insights through this "understanding together" process. "It is an operational theory," writes Gordon, "for the conscious use of the preconscious psychological mechanisms present in man's creative activity."[2]

The synectics approach was originally developed for groups of individuals responsible for developing new products. Since the 1960s, synectics materials have been developed by Gordon and others as a part of an inventive process. These techniques are particularly effective in teaching creative thinking and writing in all subject areas.

Gordon and associates have developed specific skills to teach youngsters skills to help learners make unique and creative connections between what they know and what they are to learn. Gordon writes: "It is clear that learning by purposeful connection making is efficient because it makes explicit the associative process by which the mind naturally assimilates knowledge. Can the human mind ever understand anything new except by associating it with something with which the mind is already familiar?"[3] Through the use of metaphor, these connections are facilitated in the synectics process.

In synectics, metaphor is broadly defined to include all figures of speech (e.g., simile, personification, oxymoron) that join together different and apparently irrelevant elements through the use of analogy. Three forms are stressed in the synectics model: (1) direct analogy, (2) personal analogy, and (3) symbolic analogy.

A direct analogy is a direct comparison between two objects, ideas, or concepts. For instance, how is a classroom like an anthill, or a teenage crush like a roller coaster? How is math like a crowded bus, or a summer day like watermelon slices? How are the veins in our bodies like a plumbing system? In each of these questions is an implied metaphor or an analogy by metaphor. With practice in analogy by metaphor, students become more able to extend their thought. In the beginning, they will usually see fairly obvious comparisons, such as the sun as a ball of fire. But then the sun may become a chariot, a dragon, lemon custard, or a burning seed. With practice, students are able to increase the tension or strangeness of their analogies.

A personal analogy invites students to become a part of the problem to be solved or the image being explored. How does it feel to be a zipper? How would you feel if you were a tree that had been attacked by acid rain? When does a sewing machine feel anxious? What is it like to be a rose? What if you could defy gravity? The goal here is empathy. Use of the personal analogy in synectics is to provoke the learner into projecting his or her consciousness into the particular object or idea so as to experience an emotional understanding that goes beyond the merely cognitive.

A symbolic analogy, or compressed conflict, involves descriptions that appear to be contradictory but are actually creatively insightful. This type of analogy extends the common understanding of metaphor to the realm of the oxymoron. The word *oxymoron* derives from the Greek *oxys*, meaning sharp or keen, and *moros*, meaning foolish. In ancient Greek, the word is *oxymoros*, pointedly foolish. There are many examples of oxymorons in common language, not mere contradictions but carefully thought-out creations, such as the play title *Alone Together* or the book title *Intimate Strangers*. In discussing this special trope, William Safire cites "cruel kindness," "thunderous silence," "deliberate speed," and "open secret," among others.[4] How can love be both kind and cruel? When is silence deafening? How can love nurture and smother? When is duty both ennobling and unkind? Even young children can participate in this compressed conflict when it is explained in terms of words that fight each other. The fight is the tension of the metaphor in compression. By removing themselves from their realm of immediate personal experience, learners can gain a fresh view of whatever they explore. In addition, as learners participate in the creative experience of this group activity, their shared ideas and creations build a shared pride of authorship.

Three versions of the synectic process are described in this chapter: making the familiar strange, making the strange familiar, and the synectics excursion.

Version One: Making the Familiar Strange

In this version of the model, students are encouraged to see the ordinary and the familiar in a new and different way. Through this process, they can often see unexpected possibilities in what they may have thought to be routine and predictable.

Steps in Synectics: Making the Familiar Strange

1. Describe the topic.
2. Create direct analogies.
3. Describe personal analogies.
4. Identify compressed conflicts.
5. Create a new direct analogy.
6. Reexamine the original topic.
7. Evaluate.

Step 1—Describe the Topic

The teacher begins by asking students to describe a topic with which they are familiar (e.g., a character of fiction, a concept, or an object), either in small-group discussions or by individually writing a paragraph. In the case of young children or students who cannot write, discuss the subject with them and write down their descriptive words and phrases. Or, have them draw a picture or act out their interpretation of the subject. Use this step to frame an initial description of the topic.

When the students have completed their writing or discussion, ask them to share the words they have used to describe the topic. Write them on the chalkboard. (If there is no board space, use sheets of paper that can be torn from a chart and attached to the wall.) List the words or phrases without evaluating them; all student contributions are welcome.

Step 2—Create Direct Analogies

In the second phase of the model, the students form a direct analogy between the descriptive words on the board from step 1 and words from an apparently unrelated category. For instance, the teacher may ask them to examine the list and name a machine that reminds them of as many of those words as possible. Plants, foods, flowers, and animals are other possible categories.

Add each student's contribution to the board, and encourage each person to explain why he or she chose a particular analogy. When the teacher feels that everyone has had an opportunity to participate and the class is ready, the students vote on one particular analogy that they would like to pursue in the next step of the synectics model.

In one class, students produced the following initial list of descriptive words while exploring the word *math:*

difficult	obscure
sometimes hard, sometimes easy	necessary
frightening	a key
rewarding	a mystery

When asked to name a machine that these words reminded them of, they listed the following:

- Computers, because they hold the key but they are hard to learn
- Pianos, because they have keys but they can be obscure and difficult
- A dentist's drill, because it is frightening but necessary

Step 3—Describe Personal Analogies

In the third phase of the synectics model, learners are asked to view reality from the perspective of the metaphorical object that they just selected. After giving students a short time to think, ask them to tell you how it feels to be this object, and list their reactions on the board. Encourage each person to explain why he or she had a particular feeling. It takes older learners more time to accept this step in the model, but once they do, the response can be exhilarating.

A group of teachers participating in a synectics lesson used student behavior in the lunchroom as their subject. The teachers were comparing the children to a swarm of bees, and when asked to consider what it would feel like to be a bee inside a swarm, they expressed the following perceptions:

- Helpless: I have to do what the others are doing.
- Powerful: I am the queen and I can make the others follow me.
- Frightened: I don't know what will happen next.
- Secure: I don't have to make decisions for myself.
- Dangerous: I can harm people with my stinger.
- Carefree: I can fly and I don't have to make decisions.
- Armed: I have my stinger.
- Imprisoned: I have to follow the swarm, and I am inside, and I can't escape.
- Vulnerable: I can be swatted if I get away from the group.
- Independent: I can fly away from trouble.

A group of third-grade students described how it felt to be a rose blooming on a fence:

- It feels like I'm safe because I have thorns all around me.
- I feel fragile because I can't bloom very long and the heat makes me wilted.
- Beautiful and admired: People come by and see how nice I look.

Step 4—Identify Compressed Conflicts

The fourth step is the most exciting and important step in this model. Ask the students to examine the list of descriptive feelings they created in the last step and to put together pairs of words that seem to fight each other. For instance, in our example of the teachers comparing the children to a swarm of bees, some words that fight each other are:

Frightened and secure
Helpless and powerful
Armed and vulnerable
Carefree and frightened
Independent and imprisoned
Armed and carefree

These are all combinations of words that seem to be in conflict, yet each pair is in metaphoric tension.

Take all suggestions and encourage the students to explain why they think the words fight each other. Then have the students vote once again on which combination of words contains the best compressed conflict.

Step 5—Create a New Direct Analogy

Using the compressed conflict chosen by the class, ask the students to create another direct analogy. For instance, if the combination chosen was independent and imprisoned, ask the students to describe an animal that is both independent and imprisoned. Some possible analogies would be:

A tiger in a cage
A human being in society
A powerful dog on a leash
An astronaut in a space shuttle

Then, once again, have the students vote on the best direct analogy.

Another category for the compressed conflict could be that of food: Hot sauce in a bottle or seeds inside an orange are foods that are both independent and imprisoned. The more experience teachers and students have with the model, the more categories they will be able to use with confidence.

Step 6—Reexamine the Original Topic

In this step, return to the last direct analogy chosen by the class and compare it to the original topic. For instance, if the last analogy chosen was "a dog on a leash" and you had begun the process with "a character in a novel," you would ask the class to describe the characteristics of the leashed animal and then to consider the character in terms of those descriptors.

No mention is made of the original subject until this step. The purpose is to get away from the original topic, step by step, and then to return with all the rich imagery that has been developed during the process. An important part of this step is that each student hears the thoughts and relationships expressed by the others.

Asking the students to describe the original topic in writing again gives them the opportunity to use any of the images that were generated during the exercise, not only those of the last analogy. This works particularly well with older learners and with students who are experienced in working with this model. The list of analogies provides the students with a rich resource of words and images.

Step 7—Evaluate

Discuss with the students the process that occurred during the lesson. Ask them to explain why certain images were very powerful to them and why others were not. Ask them to describe their response to the process. If necessary, have an anonymous response sheet that allows them to express their feelings. Because students know that you can recognize their handwriting, this sheet should be designed so that they can check the answer that most closely matches their feelings. For instance,

Doing this activity makes me feel:

_____ excited
_____ interested
_____ bored
_____ frustrated
_____ angry

If a number of students indicate boredom, frustration, or anger at this model, have a class discussion on the problem and ask a fellow teacher to observe the process and give feedback.

Keep samples of the students' writing before and after a synectics activity and monitor their progress toward more powerful writing.

Summary of Steps in Making the Familiar Strange

1. *Describe the topic:* Select a subject to explore with the class. It can be from any discipline: a character from a novel that has been read or a concept such as freedom or justice; a problem, such as behavior on the school bus; or a technique, such as

diving. Ask students to describe the topic. The descriptive words or phrases are written on the board.

2. *Create direct analogies:* Select a category, such as machine, plant, or food, and ask the students to examine the list of words generated in step 1 and describe how those words are like an item in the chosen category. Ask the students to explain the reasons for their choices.

3. *Describe personal analogies:* Have the students select one of the direct analogies and create personal analogies. Ask the students to become the object and describe how it feels and works. Write down the words used by the students to describe their feelings.

4. *Identify compressed conflicts:* Direct the students in creating a series of compressed conflicts using the words from the personal analogy stage. Ask the class to pair words that seem to conflict or fight with each other and that seem charged with tension.

5. *Create a new direct analogy:* For one of the pairs of words from the compressed conflict step, ask the students to create another direct analogy by selecting an object (animal, machine, fruit, etc.) that is described by the paired words.

6. *Reexamine the original topic:* Return to the original idea or task so that the students may produce a product or description that uses the ideas generated. They may concentrate on the final analogy or they may use ideas from the total experience.

7. *Evaluate:* Discuss the experience with the class and develop techniques for determining both individual and group response to the process.

EXERCISE 8.1

The following words were used by a class to describe the character of Tom Sawyer. What vehicle do the words in this list make you think of?

clever	young
naughty	old-fashioned
headstrong	original
brave	funny
smart	

Possible Answers to Exercise 8.1
Some of these responses were given by seventh-grade students:

- Model A Ford, because it is old-fashioned and an original
- Red convertible, because it is naughty and headstrong and makes a person feel young and naughty

- Bicycle built for two, because it is an original and fun
- Roller skates, because they are young and funny and they get you into trouble a lot of times ■

ACTIVITY 8.1

Select a topic and follow the steps of the Making the Familiar Strange model on your own. Then repeat the experience with several friends. Compare the richness of the images created both individually and when in the group. ■

Version Two: Making the Strange Familiar

In this variation of the synectics model, the teacher leads the students through the use of analogies to see relationships between new and unfamiliar material and material with which they already have some information.

Steps in Synectics: Making the Strange Familiar

1. Provide information.
2. Present the analogy.
3. Use personal analogy to create compressed conflicts.
4. Compare the compressed conflict with the subject.
5. Identify differences.
6. Reexamine the original subject.
7. Create new direct analogies.
8. Evaluate.

Step 1—Provide Information

The teacher selects the new material to be learned, perhaps the study of reptiles, adjectives, fractions, or the periodic table. The teacher provides factual information for the topic.

Step 2—Present the Analogy

If the new subject is the Civil War, the teacher might present the analogy by listing the similarities between the Civil War and an earthquake and then discussing these similarities with the class. For example:

a. In an earthquake, the land often splits. The North and the South had been one country and then they split apart violently.

b. In an earthquake, many people are killed by forces they cannot control. In war, the same thing happens.

c. Before an earthquake there are usually warning tremors. Before the Civil War there were warning signs that trouble was coming.

d. After an earthquake, there are usually aftershocks; following the Civil War, aftershocks went on for a long time, especially after the death of President Lincoln.

Step 3—Use Personal Analogy to Create Compressed Conflicts

The teacher asks the students to imagine what it feels like to be an earthquake. The teacher writes these feelings on the board, and the students pair these words to create compressed conflicts. One pair is selected for further exploration. For instance, the students might select *powerful* and *predictable* or *omnipotent* and *ashamed* as their compressed conflict.

Step 4—Compare the Compressed Conflict with the Subject

The class then discusses how the Civil War was both powerful and predictable or how the participants might feel both omnipotent and ashamed. At this point, the teacher might ask the students to write about their feelings on each side of the conflict.

Step 5—Identify Differences

The students might recognize that wars are not unavoidable natural disasters. Wars are caused by people and, unlike earthquakes, they can be prevented. They might also discuss that when earthquakes are over, life usually goes back to normal after a short time, but the effects of war go on and on.

Step 6—Reexamine the Original Subject

At this point, the students are asked to write about or to discuss the original subject in their own words, using images and ideas presented in this activity.

Step 7—Create New Direct Analogies

The students are encouraged to create their own analogies for the Civil War. The teacher instructs them to select analogies that are as far removed as possible from the subject. For instance, one might think of a family feud, but this is quite close to a Civil War. However, a ruptured appendix seems to be very dissimilar but might create some interesting comparisons.

Step 8—Evaluate

Discuss the process with the students and encourage them to describe what parts were the most helpful to their thinking. If a number of people in the class are not responding to the process, use an anonymous survey such as that described previously.

If any individual students are not participating in the process, schedule a personal conference. Encourage them to describe their response to the activity and how they could become more involved.

Keep the students' writing samples and look for effective analogies in their writing.

Summary of Steps in Making the Strange Familiar

1. *Provide information:* Students must understand basic facts and information related to the subject to be explored.
2. *Present the analogy:* Have a prepared analogy involving the subject that will be familiar to the students.
3. *Use personal analogy to create compressed conflicts:* Have students describe how it feels to become the subject; then have them create compressed conflicts.
4. *Compare the compressed conflict with the subject:* Students select one compressed conflict and then compare it to the original subject.
5. *Identify differences:* Students discuss the differences between the original subject and the compressed conflict.
6. *Reexamine the original subject:* Ask the students to write about or to discuss the original subject using the ideas, words, and images in the exercise.
7. *Create new direct analogies:* Encourage students to create new analogies different from the initial one.
8. *Evaluate:* Determine the effectiveness of the procedure on a class and individual basis.

E X E R C I S E   8 . 2

Create an analogy to use with each of the following subjects:

Nutrition	Fractions
Bridges	Declaration of Independence
Nouns	Poetry

Possible Answers to Exercise 8.2
Nutrition: fuel for the auto
Fractions: a map of the United States
Bridges: telephones
Declaration of Independence: alarm clock

Nouns: trumpets
Poetry: ocean ■

Version Three: The Synectics Excursion

The synectics excursion process uses all three forms of analogy—direct, personal, and symbolic—to solve a problem. In addition, fantasy analogies that enable students to control the forces of nature may be useful in this model. Ask students to design a particular product, such as a better mousetrap. Or, ask them to develop procedures to accomplish a task more effectively, such as running a marathon or translating an ancient map to locate a buried treasure.

The steps in the excursion process as presented here are derived from the writings of Gordon[5] as interpreted by G. M. Prince[5] and expanded upon by Wilson, Greer, and Johnson.[6]

Steps in the Synectics Excursion

1. Present the problem.
2. Provide expert information.
3. Question obvious solutions and purge.
4. Generate individual problem statements.
5. Choose one problem statement for focus.
6. Question through the use of analogies.
7. Force analogies to fit the problem.
8. Determine a solution from a new viewpoint.
9. Evaluate.

Step 1—Present the Problem

The problem should be one that will excite the interest and the enthusiasm of the participants and should be stated in general terms by the teacher. For example, one problem is how to design a more efficient process for leaf removal.

Step 2—Provide Expert Information

Information about the situation and as much expert advice as possible are provided to the class. For instance, a catalog containing various rakes and leaf removal machines could be presented. A group of students could report on the current techniques for removing leaves, the problems faced by landfills, and the air pollution from burning leaves. A person from the city garbage collection department could be invited to discuss the problems of removing leaves and dealing with leaves once they arrive at a landfill.

Step 3—Question Obvious Solutions and Purge

The teacher encourages the students to brainstorm obvious solutions to the problem and the relative merits of these. Solutions identified by the group as unworkable are purged from consideration. The problem can be solved in this step if all the class agree to a particular solution; usually, however, the answers that come most readily are the least effective. The teacher should be prepared to assist the students in identifying the flaws. For instance, a student might suggest that the leaves be burned. The teacher might, in turn, question the problem of burning in relation to air pollution.

Step 4—Generate Individual Problem Statements

The students are asked to write and restate the problem individually as each understands it. They are instructed to break the problem down into the component parts and state one of these in their own words. For instance, an individual student might focus on the problem of overcrowded landfills. Another student might focus on the problem and the fire hazard of piles of leaves on the streets awaiting removal.

Step 5—Choose One Problem Statement for Focus

The students read their descriptions of the problem to the class, and the class selects one to pursue further. For instance, one student may have focused on developing a new technique for reducing leaves at the landfill, whereas another student may have focused on treating the leaves as a valuable natural resource. The class must choose to explore one possible approach to the problem.

Step 6—Question through the Use of Analogies

At this point, the teacher presents the students with a number of analogies. For instance:

Direct Analogies
1. A leaf on the ground is like what animal?
2. How is a leaf like an elderly person?
3. What do leaves and garbage have in common? How are they different?
4. How is a leaf like an orphan?

Personal Analogies
1. What would it feel like to be a leaf?
2. What does it feel like to be a machine that collects leaves?
3. What does it feel like to be abandoned?
4. What does it feel like to be a load of leaves in a landfill?

Symbolic Analogies
1. How can a leaf be both free and doomed?

2. How would you describe something that is both essential and a nuisance?
3. How would *useful* and *nuisance* apply to this problem? *Helpful* and *destructive?*

Fantasy Analogies
1. If you could suspend the laws of gravity, how could you prevent the leaves from falling off the tree?
2. If you could control the tree, how could you prevent the leaves from falling?
3. Create an animal that could help solve the problem.

Step 7—Force Analogies to Fit the Problem

The students are asked to return to the problem of designing a better system for leaf removal and to apply the analogies directly to this subject. For instance, the teacher might ask:

1. If leaves are essential to life, why do we consider them a nuisance?
2. If leaves are like orphans, how can we provide more effective homes for them?
3. Allowing the leaves to remain where they fall is like allowing the elderly to remain productive.
4. Placing leaves in mulch piles and learning how to treat the mulch properly is like providing a home where the leaves can continue to be productive.

Step 8—Determine a Solution from a New Viewpoint

Using the force fit of one or more of the analogies, the teacher assists the group in looking at the problem from a new viewpoint. From this viewpoint, the group determines if they have discovered a solution to the problem. For instance, they may have decided that a special type of worm could be genetically engineered that would live in home mulch piles and reduce the leaves to mulch or that a mechanical "worm" could be designed to reduce leaves to mulch.

If students decide that there are still some situations in which leaves must be removed, the class can continue the cycle of exploring analogies leading to additional solutions.

Step 9—Evaluate

Present a new problem to be solved and have the students work in groups following the same procedure. Monitor this practice and help the students when they have difficulty. Each time the model is used, determine if the students are becoming more comfortable with the process.

Discuss the process with a small representative sample of students. Ask them to speak frankly about their reaction to the experience.

Ask other teachers if they have noticed any students using the techniques described in this model in other learning situations.

Summary of Steps in the Synectics Excursion

1. *Present the problem:* Select and then present to the class an interesting and challenging problem.
2. *Provide expert information:* Provide the class with as much expert information as possible.
3. *Question obvious solutions and purge:* Lead the class in an exploration of the most obvious solutions and have the students purge those that are not feasible.
4. *Generate individual problem statements:* Have each student write a statement regarding the problem, giving his or her interpretation or focus.
5. *Choose one problem statement for focus:* The problem statements are read aloud, and one is selected by the class for focus.
6. *Question through the use of analogies:* Present analogies to the class stated in the form of evocative questions.
7. *Force analogies to fit the problem:* Return to the original problem and ask the students to force the analogies to fit the problem.
8. *Determine a solution from a new viewpoint:* Ask students to determine a solution by looking at the problem from a new viewpoint.
9. *Evaluate:* Develop a process for determining if the techniques are becoming effective and habitual.

ACTIVITY 8.2

Select a problem about which you are concerned and go through these steps on your own. Determine if approaching the problem in this manner helps you explore possible solutions effectively. Then repeat the activity while working with a small group of adults, such as a group of fellow teachers, and see if the results are different. ■

Basis for Synectics

Faraday, the chemist; Einstein, the physicist and philosopher; and Keats, the man of letters, all report a feeling of becoming the very thing they were trying to create, a knowing of what it feels like to be a molecule, an atom, the sea itself. Gordon observes, "In both science and art, detached observation and analysis are abandoned in favor of Personal Analogy."[7]

Detached observation and analysis are essential to solving problems, but the ability to use empathy, imagination, and feelings is equally essential. The flashes of insight and creativity that come from our nonrational thinking create unique and extraordinary images and solutions. It is this irrational part of our thinking that synectics is designed to enhance.

The synectics process works most effectively when the objective is for students to look at reality in a different way and experiment with possibilities. Objectives calling for inductive thinking and seeing wholes in relation to parts require that students juxtapose seemingly disparate facts or occurrences. Because students seldom know how to do this, instruction that helps them recognize analogous relationships is very important. Synectics is the ideal means to this end.

Originally, synectics was used in developing new products for industry by having groups play with metaphor in solving problems. In their Cambridge, Massachusetts, laboratory, Gordon and associates developed the idea that led to potato chips in a can. Gordon and Poze comment, "When we searched for a metaphorical parallel we identified the way leaves conform to each other's shape when they are soaked with water and packed tightly. Even when they dried they held their shape and this was the approach we adopted to solve the problem."[8]

Gordon points out that in problem solving "the challenge is to view the problem in a new way. This new viewpoint in turn embodies the potential for a new basic solution."[9] In making the familiar strange, the mind is unlocked from the narrow confines that prevent creative insights and solutions. In making the strange familiar, the mind connects that which is already known to the unknown, thus facilitating the new learning.

In the following passage from a transcription in Gordon's book *Synectics: The Development of Creative Capacity*, the participants are working on the development of a new can opener for a client:

B: We aren't going to get anywhere if we limit our thinking to improvements. My understanding is that the client wants a radically new can opener . . . not a slightly better one.

A: I think you're right. Let's back way off from the problem. . . . What does "open" mean?

E: In nature there are things that are completely closed, then open up . . . a clam for instance.

B: But with a clam the process is reversible. We don't need that for our problem. We don't need to close the can up again.

D: I thought it would be great if we could.

B: I guess not. . . . How about a pea pod? That really opens up along a line . . . it's got a built-in weakness and splits along the weak line.[10]

By playing with the idea of "open" and identifying analogies in nature, the group developed the idea of a container that could be opened along a seam and then reclosed, a revolutionary new design concept.

Contrary to the common belief that creativity is an isolated activity that cannot really be understood or taught, Gordon maintains that it can be taught and that learners can understand how to use the process in solving problems or in developing more insight into descriptions and analyses. Using synectics in a group can actually enhance the creative process for many individuals. It provides an important kind of interaction: the sparking of ideas from one person to another. "A synectics group can compress into a few hours the kind of semiconscious mental activity that might take months of incubation for a single person."[11]

Synectics also encourages interdisciplinary relationships. The act of combining seemingly unlike entities causes both students and teachers to search for relationships across the artificial boundaries of knowledge that can be so restrictive. How are volcanic eruptions and civil wars alike? Frost's poetry and Euclid's geometry? Paragraphs and biological classification? Grammar and diplomatic protocol? Maps and story plots?

This ability to hold two very different concepts together in the mind has been described as Janusian thinking, after the Roman god with two faces, Janus. Janusian thinking consists of actively conceiving two or more opposite or antithetical concepts, ideas, or images simultaneously, as existing side by side, as equally operative or equally true, or as both. In apparent defiance of logic or matters of physical impossibility, the creative person formulates two or more opposites or antitheses coexisting and simultaneously operating, a formulation that leads to interrelated concepts, images, and creations.[12]

The ultimate goal of synectics is to find practical and realistic solutions to problems and more effective and powerful ways of communicating ideas. Yet the means used to achieve these goals is unique to the process. By insisting on the involvement of the irrational and emotional part of the brain before engaging the rational and the analytical, synectics seeks to open new dimensions of thought and new possibilities for problem solving.

George Prince, one of the founders of Synectics Corporation, who has studied the creative process for many years, writes: "Connection-making is at the very heart of learning and creativity. As children grow older, they become less and less willing to make bold connections. . . . From our study of creativity and learning we know that the essential building block for learning is connection-making."[13]

Scenario for Making the Familiar Strange

Mrs. DiMare's seventh-grade class has been studying the early colonists in New England, and they are about to begin a unit on the Salem witch trials. Mrs. DiMare asks the class to write a paragraph describing witches, a subject that would seem to be very familiar to them because most youngsters have a wide variety of exposure to the topic through comic strips, fairy tales, Halloween, television characters, and so on.

Step 1—Describe the Topic

Under the topic *witches* on the chalkboard, the teacher writes the ideas the students share about the topic based on their writing.

> **TEACHER:**   What words or phrases did you use to describe witches?
>
> **STUDENT A:**   They are spooky.
>
> **TEACHER:**   Why do you think they are spooky?

STUDENT A: Well, you never know what they are going to do, and people are afraid of them.

TEACHER: Would you say that they are unpredictable?

STUDENT A: Yes, that is a good word.

STUDENT B: I think they are powerful because they can make magic happen and they can cast a spell on people if they want to.

STUDENT C: I think that witches are evil; some people think that they do the work of the devil.

STUDENT D: There are good witches too. Remember in *The Wizard of Oz*, it was a good witch who saved Dorothy. I said that witches are like people, some good, some bad.

STUDENT E: I said that they don't really exist. They are just based on superstition and ignorance.

STUDENT F: When I was little I used to love to dress up like a witch at Halloween in a long black cloak and a pointed hat.

STUDENT G: Me, too. I put a big wart on my nose with clay and used an old mop to make stringy hair.

TEACHER: I will add *looks strange* and *wears weird clothes* to the list.

STUDENT H: Don't forget that they fly around on brooms.

Step 2—Create Direct Analogies

TEACHER: This is quite a list of descriptors. Look at it closely for a few minutes and then tell me what plant comes into your mind when you look at some of these words.

STUDENT B: I think of a Venus's-flytrap because they can be beautiful but they trap insects.

STUDENT A: How about an old oak tree in a swamp with moss hanging from the branches? I saw one like that on a trip and it made me feel really spooky.

STUDENT D: How about a dead tree standing all alone in a field?

STUDENT C: I think of those trees in the swamps with the big roots that grow down into the water.

TEACHER: Are you thinking of a cypress tree?

STUDENT C: Yes, that's the one. They seem to be powerful but they are frightening, too. They aren't really evil, but they can make you feel uncomfortable not knowing what is down below those roots.

STUDENT G: It seems strange but it makes me think of a weeping willow blowing in the wind. They always seem to be flying and they make me feel sorry for them.

STUDENT H: Well, I think about a potato. They usually have warts on them and they have rough, ugly skins.

TEACHER: This is a good list. Let's vote on these and see which of the images you would like to pursue. (A vote is taken.)

Step 3—Describe Personal Analogies

TEACHER: It looks like the oak tree hanging with moss has been selected. Close your eyes and imagine what it would be like to be a tree like this.

STUDENT B: It feels lonely. There aren't any other trees around that are like me. I am old and different.

STUDENT A: It feels like I am being used, with all this moss hanging on me. I can't get away and this moss is taking advantage of me.

STUDENT D: I feel strong and powerful. I am bigger than everyone else and this moss needs me.

STUDENT G: I feel peaceful. It is very quiet here and the wind is stirring in my branches.

STUDENT H: I feel trapped because I can't get away. I just have to stay here in this one spot forever.

STUDENT I: I feel independent. There is no one around, and I am free.

Step 4—Identify Compressed Conflicts

TEACHER: Look at this list and pick out pairs of words that seem to fight with each other and have very different meanings.

STUDENT A: How about *powerful* and *trapped?*

TEACHER: Why do those two words seem to fight with each other?

STUDENT A: Because if you are powerful you should be able to get away and not be trapped.

STUDENT C: I think that *lonely* and *peaceful* fight with each other. If you are peaceful you don't usually feel lonely.

STUDENT G: *Powerful* and *taken advantage of,* because if you are powerful you should be able to keep people from taking advantage of you.

STUDENT B: *Lonely* and *powerful,* because if you are powerful you shouldn't be lonely.

STUDENT A: How about *needed* and *taken advantage of?* Usually when people feel needed they don't feel that they are being taken advantage of.

STUDENT E: How about *trapped* and *independent?* Those two words really don't seem to belong together.

TEACHER: Let's vote again and see which of these compressed conflicts we want to work with in the next step. (A vote is taken.) It looks like *trapped* and *independent* will be our compressed conflict.

Step 5—Create a New Direct Analogy

> **TEACHER:** Let's try an animal for our direct analogy in this step. What animal seems to be both trapped and independent?

> **STUDENT A:** A horse in a corral. It is trapped but it is still very independent in the way it moves about.

> **STUDENT E:** It reminds me of an animal—a leopard—in one of those zoos where the animals seem to be free but they really can't get away.

> **STUDENT G:** I know what you mean. You just walk around and there aren't any cages or bars. The animals seem to be free but you hope they really can't get away. There is always something that is stopping them. There was this beautiful big parrot that couldn't get away because its wings had been clipped.

> **STUDENT H:** I saw a film about trapping otters. The animals caught in the trap always seemed to be independent and fierce even when they were bleeding and in pain.

> **STUDENT G:** My grandmother has a parrot and that bird is so independent. She won't talk or do anything unless she wants to, but she *is* still in that cage.

> **STUDENT D:** My cat is like that. Even though she has to stay in the apartment and she can only sit in the window and look out, she is still independent.

> **TEACHER:** Let us select one of these that seems to be the best example of something that is both independent and trapped. (A vote is taken.) It will be the otter caught in the trap that we will examine further.

Step 6—Reexamine the Original Topic

> **TEACHER:** Now, here is the question. Suppose you lived back in the days when witches were condemned and put to death. How is a person who has been condemned as a witch like an otter caught in a trap?

> **STUDENT C:** They would probably be fighting for their lives and would try anything to escape.

> **STUDENT D:** Trapping animals is illegal in most states now because it is so cruel to the animals. We don't believe that people should be called witches anymore either.

> **STUDENT A:** The animals are often hunted and trapped because they are beautiful. Sometimes people were jealous of the witches because they were different and people wanted to destroy them.

> **STUDENT E:** People used to trap animals because they didn't know any better and that was the way it was with witches. They just didn't know how wrong it was. There are still people today that think that it is OK to trap animals just like there are still people who believe in witchcraft.

> **TEACHER:** Using any of the images that we have on the board today, write another description of witches.

When the steps were completed the information on the board looked like this:

1. *List of descriptors.* Question: What words would you use to describe witches?

   spooky   unpredictable

   powerful   cast spells

   some good/some bad   imaginary

   based on superstition and ignorance   look strange

   wear funny clothes   fly on brooms

2. *Direct analogy.* Question: What plant does the list of words in step 1 bring to mind? *Venus's-flytrap, old oak tree in a swamp with moss* (chosen by the class), *weeping willow, cypress tree, potato*

3. *Personal analogy.* Question: How does it feel to be an old oak tree in a swamp?

   lonely   needed

   old   trapped

   powerful   independent

   different   used

   taken advantage of strong

   peaceful   free

4. *Compressed conflict.* Question: What words from the list in step 3 seem to be in conflict or to fight with each other?

   powerful and *trapped*   *lonely* and *peaceful*

   trapped and *free*   *powerful* and *taken advantage of*

   needed and *taken advantage of*   *trapped* and *independent* (chosen by the class)

5. *New direct analogy.* Question: What animal could be described as being both trapped and independent?

   horse in a corral   leopard in a zoo

   parrot with clipped wings otter in a trap (chosen by the class)

   cat in a window

6. *Reexamine the original topic.* Question: How is a person who has been condemned as a witch like an otter in a trap?

Step 7—Evaluate

The writing assignment should provide an effective evaluation. You might also ask students to create their own analogies for a topic.

The following example of a before-and-after writing exercise on witches gives a flavor of the effect of the synectics exercise on the students' thinking. Here are two examples written before the synectics exercise:

I. Witches are really spooky. They fly around on brooms and they snatch little children who are not inside their houses.

II. Witches used to be taken seriously and people hung them and put them to death. I don't really believe in witches, but I think that it is fun to pretend that they really exist.

And two examples from after the exercise:

I. People who were called witches must have felt like animals caught in a trap. The trap is really superstition and ignorance, because people want to blame someone for things that are wrong with the world.

II. People who were called witches must have felt very lonely, like a tree standing all alone in the field when a lightning storm comes.

In the second writing, the students have gained insight into the problem, and their language has deepened in power and imagery. Now the teacher can continue the lesson on the Salem witch trials, knowing the students have a heightened awareness of the subject. What seemed like a common and familiar concept has taken on new meanings.

This activity's value is that the students were doing most of the talking and drawing most of the conclusions. The teacher is in control of the process and can intervene at any time, but the ideas come from the students. When students think about values during this process, they are coming up with ideas on their own rather than being lectured to by the teacher.

ACTIVITY 8.3

Design a lesson in which synectics is used as an advance organizer for a unit. For instance, a unit on the study of amphibians could begin with a synectics lesson on toads, or a unit on the seasons could begin with a synectics lesson on summer. ▪

Summary

Synectics is a process that uses the power of metaphor to expand imagination and creative thinking. Students are encouraged to look at problems in new and more dynamic ways and to express their ideas forcefully. The key to its success lies in getting learners to see relationships among ideas they might otherwise have never associated. The result alters the way the learner sees information and ideas to be learned.

Synectics can be used with learners of all ages. Students and teachers enjoy the process and are often astounded at the interesting and imaginative results. Although synectics is particularly effective in teaching writing, it is also effective in any type of learning where the objective is to develop new and creative insights into a problem. Participants—both teachers and students—are amazed at the power of metaphor to capture the imagination of learners.

WEB RESOURCES

1. **http://www.writedesignonline.com/organizers/index.html**
   This site describes a number of graphic organizers, including a version of synectics.

2. **http://www.synecticsworld.com/library/synectics-reading.htm**
   This site describes a Synectics training program designed primarily for industry. Also at this site are materials and books that may be ordered, and at the helpdesk is a chart describing actions that encourage creativity and actions that discourage it.

3. **http://www.nade.net/h3a__scp99.htm**
   This interesting paper, entitled "Strategies for Using the Arts in Developmental Education," offers a good explanation of metaphoric thinking.

4. **http://edweb.sdsu.edu/courses/edtec670/Cardboard/card/c/CerebralFlat.html**
   This site provides a description of a classroom game for high school students that is based on synectics. Directions are given both for playing the game and for creating the materials needed for the game.

NOTES

1. Paul Ricoeur, "Creativity in Language: Word, Polysemy, Metaphor," *Philosophy Today* 17, no. 2 (1973): 111.

2. William J. J. Gordon, *Synectics: The Development of Creative Capacity* (New York: Harper and Row, 1961), 3.

3. William J. J. Gordon and Tony Poze, "Learning Dysfunction and Connection Making," *Psychiatric Annals* 8, no. 3 (1978): 79.

4. William Safire, "Whose Oxymoron Is Gored?" *New York Times*, June 2, 1985, Sec. 6, 16–18.

5. G. M. Prince, "The Operational Mechanism of Synectics," *Journal of Creative Behavior* 2 (March 1967): 1–9.

6. Sandra H. Wilson, Jack F. Greer, and Russell M. Johnson, "Synectics: A Creative Problem-Solving Technique for the Gifted," *Gifted Child Quarterly* 17 (1963): 260–266.

7. Gordon, 38.

8. William J. J. Gordon and Tony Poze, *The Metaphysical Way of Learning and Knowing* (Cambridge, MA: Porpoise Books, 1979), 3.

9. Gordon, 34.

10. Gordon, 125–126.

11. Gordon, 10.

12. Albert Rothenberg, "Einstein's Creative Thinking and the General Theory of Relativity: A Documented Report," *American Journal of Psychiatry* 136 (January 1979): 39–40.

13. G. Prince, W. Weaver, and K. Logan-Prince, "Liberating Creativity and Learning" in *Creative Education: Educating a Nation of Innovators*, ed. Vincent Nolan (London: Synectics Education Initiative, 2000), 3–28.

9 The Cause and Effect Model

Influencing Events by Analyzing Causality

> Plot makes us aware of events not merely as elements in a temporal series but also as an intricate pattern of cause and effect. . . . Surely our sense of the meaning of experience is closely tied to our understanding of what causes what, and it is the business of plot to clarify causal relationships.[1]
>
> —William Kenney

William Kenney makes the point that human behavior, reduced to its simplest terms, is a study of cause and effect. In addition to literature, history, because it is a recording of past human behavior, is also a study of cause and effect. Science, although its subjects are not necessarily human, is an analysis of data in terms of cause and effect. Yet most of us have never formally explored the logical connections between causes and effects.

Cause and effect are frequently confused with mere association or sequence. The field of advertising capitalizes on this. We are shown a pretty young woman using an expensive perfume. Next we see the same young woman with an attractive boyfriend. Ergo: Women who use this perfume will acquire attractive boyfriends.

If students do have a grasp of cause and effect, it is often a very simplistic one. For example, if Tom hit Russ first, then Tom started the fight. The students may not bother to find out that Russ had been taunting Tom about his girlfriend for some time. Youngsters seldom think to ask about underlying causes.

Most of us have direct contact with many people in our personal and professional lives. The caliber of that contact to a great extent dictates the degree of fulfillment we feel. If we are to attain our goals at work or at home, we must exert some control over the normal flow of events. To do this successfully, we must understand some of the complexities of causality.

The model presented in this chapter, based on one strategy from the work of educator Hilda Taba,[2] leads students through an investigation of a significant action, situation, condition, or conflict. Through a process of inference, students hypothesize about causes and effects, prior causes, and subsequent effects. Finally, they draw conclusions and arrive at generalizations about how people usually behave in similar situations. The teacher remains facilitator, asking set questions, not contributing to or commenting on the contributions except to ask follow-up questions.

In history, anything from a single action to a war to the passing of a bill to the election of a candidate can lead to fruitful discussion. Almost any experiment or condition in science will lend itself to this model. When a class has finished a piece of literature in English, a significant action or a climax or a pivotal moment makes a stimulating topic. Newspaper articles, particularly advice columns, can lead to exciting discussions, especially if the subject is important to the students. Using situations such as students coming late to class or disrupting class as the topic will enable students to understand the reasons behind certain rules.

Once an individual has performed this model in a group several times, he or she can perform it alone. It can become an extremely valuable tool in that individual's repertoire of techniques for problem solving, generating ideas, making decisions, and analyzing data. The value of group explorations, however, cannot be overestimated. Hearing the ideas of others opens up many possibilities that students say would never have occurred to them on their own. They become more flexible thinkers.

Steps in the Cause and Effect Model

1. Choose the data, topic, action, or problem to be analyzed.
2. Ask for causes and support for those causes.
3. Ask for effects and support.
4. Ask for prior causes and support.
5. Ask for subsequent effects and support.
6. Ask for conclusions. Conclusions are statements we infer about the behavior of the persons in the situation under study. Ask the students to support their conclusions.
7. Ask for generalizations. Generalizations are statements of inference about how people in general behave in situations similar to the one under study.
8. Evaluating students' performances is optional, but feedback, either individual or group, is important.

Practice Sheet

The teacher should have the following chart on the chalkboard, visible to all students, when a discussion starts. Occasionally, the students will not have enough information to perform all seven steps of the model. Performing part of the model can be very fruitful. The numbers indicate sequence. The data should be filled in.

4	2	1	3	5
Prior Causes	**Causes**	**Topic to Be Analyzed** (Situation under scrutiny)	**Effects**	**Subsequent Effects**

6. Conclusions:

7. Generalizations:

The Steps in More Detail

The discussion of the steps of the cause and eff~£t model for high school students will focus on the novel *A Separate Peace*. This novel is about two best friends in a boarding school who are also deadly rivals in the eyes of one. Finny is a superb athlete. His roommate and best friend, Gene, is working hard to be class valedictorian. Finny keeps distracting Gene from studying by urging him to try various physical games and feats, and Gene begins to suspect that Finny is trying to sabotage his chance to be valedictorian. This is not true: Finny believes that Gene's academic ability comes with no effort, as Finny's athletic ability does.

The discussion of the steps for lower-grade elementary school students will focus on Watty Piper's well-known story *The Little Engine That Could*. In this story, a small engine breaks down that has been carrying Christmas presents and food to the little boys and girls on the other side of a mountain. The dolls and clowns and toys beg several large engines to pull them over the mountain; they refuse. Finally, a little blue engine comes along and, in spite of her size, says she will do this. She pulls and strains and repeats "I think I can" over and over, and finally she is successful.[3] The data or question discussed by these young students is why the little blue engine was willing to try something that larger engines had refused to try.

Elementary students can handle the concepts and ideas in this model if the teacher simplifies the questions and the vocabulary. One of the advantages of the cause and effect model is that each class will take the discussion to its appropriate level of complexity, because all the responses come from the students. In addition, seeing their contributions written on the board is a good lesson in reading for the young students. They are amazingly adept at remembering the ideas mentioned, and the teacher can repeat them when necessary.

Following is an overview of some of the items on the chalkboard after a ninth-grade class performed this model on the novel *A Separate Peace*.[4]

Analysis of **A Separate Peace**

4 Prior Causes	2 Causes	1 Topic to Be Analyzed	3 Effects	5 Subsequent Effects
Gene's insecurity	Gene's fear of double jump	Gene jounced the limb Finny was on causing Finny to fall. Why?	Finny's broken leg	Finny's death
Finny's silver tongue	Gene's fear of being unworthy		Gene's guilt	Gene returns to Devon
Finny's athletic ability	Gene's low self-esteem		Finny's dependence upon Gene	
Gene's suspicions about Finny	Gene's guilt about his suspicions		Gene's knowledge that he is Finny's least trustworthy friend	Gene forgives himself
Gene's desire to be valedictorian	Gene's con-viction that Finny is disrupting his studies			
	Gene's anger at self		Finny's continued trust in Gene	Gene's separate peace
			Gene's increased guilt	

Conclusions: Judgments or ideas about human behavior inherent in the story often can be found by reading related items on the board from left to right or top to bottom as shown in the following list. As the teacher, you will have to give students examples of conclusions the first few times they perform the model.

1. Once suspicious of a plot, Gene saw all of Finny's actions in terms of the imag-ined plot. (prior cause → cause)
2. Feeling totally inferior made Gene lash out. (cause → topic)
3. Finny denied the possibility of Gene's guilt, thereby making Gene feel even guiltier. (effect → increased effect)

Generalizations: Generalizations are conclusions expressed in general terms. They are also themes. Many students find it very difficult to extract themes from a work of art. Those who use this model find they are able to generate themes more easily.

1. (conclusion 1 expressed in general terms) We see events through a filter made up of our own ideas and prejudices.
2. (conclusion 2) Feeling inferior can make one aggressive.
3. (conclusion 3) Being defended by someone we have wronged increases our guilt.

The more frequently a class performs the model, the more items the students are able to generate at each step. Not all the items produced by the class in this example have been listed here. To illustrate the richness and variety of ideas that classes become able to generate, the following are the additional causes the students listed:

> Gene's frustration because he does not have time to study
> The rivalry in Gene's eyes
> Gene's unconscious need to rid himself of this competition
> Gene's very rational fear of falling
> Gene's discovery of his own self-deception
> Gene's realization that Finny is a much bigger person

One student's idea will trigger another student's thoughts. For this reason, it is important not to move too quickly to the next step and to be sure all the students' ideas have been expressed.

Step 1—Choose the Data or Topic, Action, or Problem to Be Analyzed

This may be a significant action, event, condition, or conflict. It may be fictional, hypothetical, or real. It may come from any discipline being taught. Write the data or topic in the center of the chalkboard or on a large tablet.

High school topic: Gene jounced the limb that Finny was on.

Elementary topic: The little blue engine was able to pull all the cars filled with dolls and toys and goodies over the mountain when bigger, stronger engines could not or would not.

Step 2—Ask for Causes and Support for Those Causes

In step 2, the students look for reasons for the situation. Some questions for the high school students are "What do you think are some of the causes of Gene's jouncing the limb?" and "What else could have caused this action?" Ask the students to support their responses. For example, "Why did Gene's fear of falling make him lash out?" Write all responses on the chalkboard under Causes.

Elementary teacher's question: "Why do you think the little blue engine was able to pull all those dolls and toys and presents over the mountain?" or "Why was such a little engine able to do something that bigger engines had said they could not do?" Ask for support: "What makes you think that?"

Step 3—Ask for Effects and Support

Moving to the right side of the topic column, ask for effects. A question for the high school students is "What are some of the effects of Gene's jouncing the limb?" or "What are some of the things that happened because Gene jounced the limb?" Ask for support: "Why do you think that?"

Elementary teacher's question: "What are some of the things that happened because the little blue engine was able to pull all those presents over the mountain?" Ask for support: "What makes you think that?"

Step 4—Ask for Prior Causes and Support

Moving to the left side of the chalkboard, ask for prior causes. Take each cause and ask for the causes of those causes, the prior causes. For example, "What caused Gene's low self-esteem?" Then ask for support: "How did Finny's athletic ability increase Gene's low self-esteem?"

Elementary teacher's question: "Why did having done hard things before make it easier for the little blue engine to pull all those presents over the mountain?" Ask for support: Why did believing in herself help the little blue engine? Repeat the procedure, asking for the causes of each cause.

Step 5—Ask for Subsequent Effects and Support

After repeating the request for prior causes several times, when students seem to be completely out of ideas, move to the far right of the board and ask for subsequent effects. Taking each effect separately, ask the high school students, "What were the effects of Gene's guilt?" Then ask for support for the subsequent effect: "Why was Gene's return to Devon a result of his guilt?" or simply "What makes you think that?"

Elementary teacher's questions: "What were some of the things that you think happened because all the children in the city had happy Christmases?" and "What do you think happened because the little engine felt wonderful?" Ask for support.

ACTIVITY 9.1

If you were appointed principal of a school where you had either studied or taught, think of a change in policy that you would initiate. Now list three effects and three subsequent effects that you think would occur. ∎

Step 6—Ask for Conclusions

Conclusions are statements we infer about the behavior of the persons in the situation under study. Conclusions can come from reading related items on the board from left to right or top to bottom. Ask the high school students, "Looking over the whole chalkboard, what can we say about the way the people in this situation behaved?" Initially, you will have to give them several examples of conclusions. Ask the students to support their conclusions.

Examples of Conclusions

1. When Gene became convinced Finny was sabotaging his studies, he became suspicious of everything Finny did.
2. Discovering that Finny had not been competing with him made Gene lash out. This sounds contradictory, but discovering that Finny's plotting had existed only in Gene's mind made Gene feel even more inferior and increased his need to lash out.
3. Gene's fear of falling made him jounce the limb in self-defense.
4. Gene's own insecurity made him want to believe the worst of Finny.

Elementary teacher's question: "Thinking back about the story, what can we say about how the engines behaved when faced with a hard job?"

Elementary Conclusions

1. Proud engines can become mean.
2. Big engines think they're more important than little engines.
3. Engines with hearts are stronger.
4. Old, tired engines lose their belief in themselves.
5. Engines that believe in themselves can do lots of things.

Step 6 is the most difficult because it involves the most abstract thinking. As noted earlier, you will initially have to give the students several examples of conclusions drawn from the situation being discussed. Performing the model as a class and then in small groups will allow students to see numerous examples of conclusions, yours and those of other students, and, frequently, many catch on to how one thinks abstractly. Thinking abstractly seems to be one of those "lightbulb" experiences where examples suddenly clarify the necessary thought processes.

Step 7—Ask for Generalizations

Generalizations are conclusions expressed in general terms—that is, terms not specific to the topic or the people involved. Students should simply replace the specific names in the conclusions with general names such as *people* or *one*. The teacher may ask, "What can we say about how people we know might behave when faced with a situation like that of Gene and Finny?"

Here are some of the conclusions for the high school students expressed as generalizations:

1. Discovering that our suspicions about a friend are incorrect can make us angry at ourselves.
2. Being in physical danger can make us aggressive.
3. Feeling inferior makes us want to believe others share our shortcomings.
4. People who are very capable in one area sometimes assume others are also.

Elementary teacher's question: "If this were a story about people, would the people have behaved the way the engines did or would they have behaved differently?"

Elementary Generalizations
1. When asked to do hard things, sometimes big, important people will not make the effort.
2. People who do not care about others will not make an effort to do hard things for others.
3. People who have self-confidence will try hard things.

Step 8—Evaluate Students' Performances

Although evaluation is optional, feedback, either individual or group, is important. Students need to learn certain rules of behavior before they can conduct constructive discussions. Even well-behaved students need to learn the value of listening, really listening, to the ideas of others. In addition, they need to learn that they may actually change their minds about an issue and that being flexible is something you value. Talk about our habit of only partially listening to someone else as we marshal our own thoughts and decide how to articulate them. Tell the students to jot their ideas on paper if they are afraid they will forget them, so that they can concentrate on what others are saying. Next let them know that disagreement can be very productive if it is voiced politely. Finally, tell them that initially you will be grading more on manners than on the content of their contributions. Later the thoughtfulness and originality of their ideas will be given more weight.

Summary of Steps in the Cause and Effect Model

1. *Choose the data or topic, action, or problem to be analyzed.* When your students are familiar with the model, you may want to ask older students to choose the critical action or situation to be analyzed in a chapter in history, a novel, short story, or poem in literature, or a situation in science.
2. *Ask for causes and support for those causes.* Try to elicit as many as possible. We tend to think simplistically in terms of a single cause as opposed to multiple causes.
3. *Ask for effects and support.* Again, elicit as many as possible.
4. *Ask for prior causes and support.*

5. *Ask for subsequent effects and support.* Comment occasionally on the connections between prior causes and subsequent effects. Seemingly unimportant actions can build into major effects.

6. *Ask for conclusions.* Conclusions are statements we infer about the behavior of the persons in the situation under study. Ask the students to support their conclusions.

7. *Ask for generalizations.* Generalizations are statements of inference about how people in general behave in situations similar to those under study.

8. *Evaluate students' performances.* This step is optional, but feedback, either individual or group, is important.

Comments on Conducting the Model

Time: Take plenty of time. The more often groups perform the model, the more items they will generate. Your hesitation to go on to the next step will signal to the students that there may be other ideas they might consider.

Support: Once the students are comfortable with the model, in each step, after each contribution, ask the student to support his or her thinking:

"Joan, why do you think _____ caused _____?"

"Why do you think Finny became dependent upon Gene after his fall?"

"Kip, can you support that?"

If you think that the reason is very obvious or that a student may have trouble articulating his or her reasoning, you might omit this step initially or open the question to all students by asking, "Can any of you support this point?" It is not necessary to write this support on the chalkboard, but it is important for students to substantiate their thinking.

Placement: The reason for the placement of items from left to right on the chart is so that the items will appear chronologically. Use of this model helps students visualize chronology.

Sequence: Going from causes to effects then from prior causes to subsequent effects may reveal the connections between these events more effectively. However, you may feel that establishing the cause-to-prior-cause or effect-to-subsequent-effect relationship is easier for students to grasp initially. Trust your instincts.

Function: In addition to the use described here, you may employ this model for review of content area material. Using their books, ask students to use crucial events as their data. They may do this as a class or in small groups or individually.

An Abbreviated Example of the Cause and Effect Model from Science

Data: High blood sugar levels

Causes: Beta cells of pancreas hyposecrete (undersecrete) the hormone insulin; diabetes mellitus

Prior causes: Heredity; age; obesity; destructive or infectious condition of pancreas

Effects: Glucose not absorbed into cells; glucose accumulates in plasma; excess sugar excreted in urine; less H_2O absorbed into blood by kidney tubules; because glucose not available, a shift in cellular metabolism to fats and proteins for energy production

Subsequent effects: Extreme thirst; some fats may be deposited in blood vessels causing a variety of vascular problems (e.g., if retinal vessels are affected, blindness can result; or when limbs and feet are affected, gangrene can result); many fats completely oxidized producing acidosis, which can result in diabetic coma

Conclusion: When glucose accumulates in plasma, excess sugar is excreted into urine.

Generalization: What happens in one part of the body affects other parts of the body.[5]

An Abbreviated Example from History

Data: In 1860 America was a nation of farmers. Just 60 years later, the majority of working Americans were in cities. What were some of the causes and effects of this rapid change?

Causes: Advanced machinery, new breed of entrepreneurs, European immigration to cities, railroads, assembly lines increased production, depletion of farm land

Prior causes: In 1860: country had abundance of timber, water, and clean air; belief that hard work brings large rewards, limited travel

Effects: Blast furnaces, belching chimneys, women and children used for labor, increased production

Subsequent effects: Few labor laws, mass production, natural resources ravaged, monopolies created, economic growth

Conclusions: A rapid population expansion was caused by immigration to the cities and a shift from farming to manufacturing.

Generalizations:

1. Population is drawn to job opportunities.
2. When competitors join forces, they create monopolies, frequently raising prices, increasing profits, and reducing wages.

Overview or "Cheat Sheet."   At first, the model seems long and complex, but once you have performed it a few times and learn the sequence of the steps, it takes little or *no* preparation. The students provide all the input. If you had to perform the model in class tomorrow, however, what would you need to do?

Before class:

1. On a practice sheet (shown earlier), write the data or topic to be analyzed.
2. Just before the discussion, write the *topic to be analyzed*, the *causes, prior causes*, and so forth, on a chalkboard. Write the topic under *data*.

3. Normally that would be sufficient, but the first few times, you will need to provide the students with a few examples of conclusions and generalizations.
4. Use the summary of steps until you feel sure of the sequence.

EXERCISE 9.1

Because producing conclusions involves complex abstract thinking, you may want to try the following exercise. It is not a part of the model, but it can help your students (or participants in your group) understand and produce conclusions more easily.

Remind older students that a *fact* is true (able to be proved beyond a reasonable doubt), whereas a *conclusion* is an inference built on supporting evidence. If the students are in elementary school, simply call the terms *facts* and *opinions*.

Ask each student to write down one fact and one conclusion (or opinion) about some material you have just completed. Put a few of their contributions on the board without revealing the students' names or labels. Ask the class to decide whether the contributions are facts or conclusions. Remain outside of the discussion as much as possible.

Often the students cannot agree and are afraid that their inability to reach an agreement is a weakness. Tell them it is not their decision but the caliber of the support for their reasoning that matters. Once they realize this, they become quite adept at defending their positions. In this exercise, there is not always a right and a wrong answer; it is often a matter of interpretation. The process of deciding which statements are facts and which are opinions does not become easier. It actually becomes more complex; however, the students' grasp of the process and their ability to think in complex ways increases by participating in these discussions.

The following is an example:

Statement	Discussion	Fact or Opinion?
Elementary School:		
The freight train in *The Little Engine That Could* was right when he said the machines that print books and newspapers that he carried over the mountain were more important than the dolls and toys and food and treats for the boys and girls. ■	At first the students said this was a fact. Then one student mentioned the oranges and apples and milk. She said food for poor children was more important than books and newspapers. After a lengthy discussion about the importance of books and news, the class agreed.	Originally fact. Found to be faulty and changed to opinion.

A C T I V I T Y   9 . 2

Identify and write three facts and three conclusions about this model. ■

Variations on the Cause and Effect Model

One of the exciting aspects of several of the models in this book is that the students can perform many important intellectual tasks while they are trying to achieve the models' stated goals. The cause and effect model is no exception. Here are a few of the most important tasks they can perform:

1. *Writing creatively:* William Faulkner said that his novel *The Sound and the Fury*[6] was inspired when he saw a little girl climbing a tree and looking into a second-floor window. Her brothers were on lower branches following her up. From this single image an entire novel grew. Have students pick a single image or a single action as their topic or data. Ask them to think up some causes and prior causes for this image or action, then some effects and subsequent effects. The result will be a plot for a short story. Initially, you might have the entire class or small groups do this together. This strategy allows students to become conscious of the point of the quote from William Kenney at the beginning of the chapter: "Plot makes us aware of events not merely as elements in a temporal series but also as an intricate pattern of cause and effect."

2. *Writing critical essays:* The most difficult step in writing a critical essay is arriving at an interesting thesis, one that is neither so obvious that it is boring nor so obscure that it is not provable. The chart on the chalkboard after a discussion can become a blueprint for a critical essay. The conclusions are potential theses, and the actions listed are potential supporting evidence.

3. *Producing themes:* A litmus test of whether students can think in abstract terms is to ask them to produce themes. Even students who can generate them may be unable to retrace their mental steps. One day, after performing this model, a student was studying the board and said he thought the initial steps in the model mirror the way we reach a theme. He said we perform them so rapidly that we are unaware of what we are doing. He thought we isolate a problem in a book (data), mentally connect related causes and effects, and come up with one of the author's "umbrella" ideas or views on life. An example would be John Knowles's idea in *A Separate Peace* that fear can make people lash out. The resulting generalizations are themes.

4. *Making predictions:* Once students are familiar with the cause and effect model, have them stop reading a piece of literature either just before or just after the climax or a chapter in history at a pivotal point or a scientific experiment before the results are clear. Ask the students to predict what will happen. What will be the effects and subsequent effects of what has happened so far? Later, compare their predictions with what the author wrote or with what actually happened. Why were their predictions accurate? Inaccurate? Which sequence do they prefer? Why? Why do they think the author had the characters act in certain ways? Did the people in history act the way the students themselves might have? Why did the experiment turn out as they predicted? Why did it not? Making predictions is not a new idea, but there is more precision involved when the students are familiar with breaking their thinking down into the different steps in this model.

Basis for the Cause and Effect Model

The cause and effect model begins by examining a specific situation and ends by generalizing about courses of action in similar situations. Students have an opportunity to study a situation in detail, to put names to mental activities they have used in their own thinking, and to hear the thinking of others. They also have an opportunity to speculate about different courses of action and their consequences.

Taba makes several important points about generalizations. Concepts, she says, are often confused with generalizations. They are, however, quite different. "Generalizations are . . . verbalized formulations of relations among concepts. [We must confine] the concept label to single words and the generalization label to sentences. Generalizations are about the relations among concepts."[7] Taba also states, "Generalizations should play an important role in directing students' thinking as they search for meanings in the data of social studies, English, science, and mathematics."[8] Next she argues that it is far more important for students to arrive at their own generalizations than for them to simply study the generalizations others have reached. Finally, she states that generalizations are by their nature tentative, not statements of absolute truth, because "there is always more information on a particular topic than can ever be known by the human beings who generalize about it." Thus "those most proficient with language are the ones who most frequently use language to express tentativeness."[9]

L. L. Thurstone discusses the importance of considering hypothetical courses of action before acting:

> A key aspect of intelligence . . . is the inhibition of impulsiveness. By inhibiting impulses before they develop into overt behavior, and focusing on them consciously while they are still relatively general, one gains latitude of choice with respect to the different ways in which one's needs or desires might be satisfied.
>
> Intelligence is therefore the capacity of abstraction, which is an inhibitory process. In the intelligent moment the impulse is inhibited while it is still only loosely organized. It is the ability to consider and evaluate possible courses of action without actually engaging them that distinguishes between intelligent and unintelligent life forms, and the more intelligent the individual the higher the level of abstraction and the greater the degree of flexibility of choice attained.[10]

Because thoughtful action is action for which the consequences have been anticipated, attempting to predict behavior is a crucial, although inexact, exercise. Examining behavior in specific situations and arriving at generalizations about how the people in those situations behaved is the most efficient way to predict and, therefore, guide behavior.

Hypothesizing about our own potential courses of action before choosing one will allow us to avoid many of the pitfalls that result from acting impulsively or allowing mood swings to dictate our behavior. Most of us do anticipate the results of potential actions informally, but familiarity with this model gives us a tool that is more precise when anticipating the consequences of daily decisions or important changes. Its use breaks what may be vague ruminations into specific parts and sharpens and increases the number of specifics we consider.

That educators have come to recognize the importance of active learning in general and students' grasp of cause and effect in particular is apparent in the standards and goals they have established for students. For example, in the *National Standards for History*, 1996, the general section on historical understanding begins,

> History, properly developed for children in the early years of schooling, can open important opportunities to analyze and develop appreciation for all these spheres of human activity and of the interactions among them. To do so requires that children be engaged in ACTIVE questioning and learning, and not merely in the passive absorption of facts, names, and dates. Real historical understanding requires that students engage in historical reasoning; listen to and read historical stories, narratives, and literature with meaning; think through cause-effect relationships.[11]

Standard 1 of the historical thinking standards of the *National Standards for History* concerns chronological thinking. The first paragraph in the overview about this standard reads,

> Chronological thinking is at the heart of historical reasoning. Without a clear sense of historical time—time past, present, and future—students are bound to see events as one great tangled mess. Without a strong sense of chronology—of when events occurred and in what temporal order—it is impossible for students to examine relationships among them or to explain historical causality. Chronology provides the mental scaffolding for organizing historical thought.[12]

Many of the specific capabilities in subsequent standards directly involve cause and effect. For example, under standard 3, "historical analysis and interpretation," is the charge "Explain causes in analyzing historical actions."[13] Under standard 5, "historical issues—analysis and decision making," are the charges "Identify the causes of the problem or dilemma" and "Evaluate the consequences of a decision."[14] This model allows students to visualize chronology.

One final aspect to consider in a discussion of cause and effect, as well as in all other types of thinking, is bias. The book *Psychology of Intelligence Analysis* by Richards Heuer, Jr., of the Central Intelligence Agency contains an excellent chapter entitled "Biases in Perception of Cause and Effect." The chapter begins, "Judgments about cause and effect are necessary to explain the past, understand the present, and estimate the future. These judgments are often biased by factors over which people exercise little conscious control."[15]

Heuer makes the point that when we study the behavior of other countries we attempt to explain the past in terms of cause and effect. We assign causes where clear-cut causes may not have existed, where random acts may have occurred. In attempting to understand the past and possibly affect the future, we then have an orderly, albeit inaccurate, picture of that past. This point seems equally true of our perception of the behavior of other individuals in our lives. We want our thinking to be objective and open to many possibilities, yet, in reality, we find ourselves assigning reasons where the reasons may have been completely different or where impulse played the major role. So we caution that in analyzing human behavior using the model in this chapter, we must be conscious that we are unable to put ourselves in the position of another person and that our conclusions must remain tentative and open to further scrutiny.

Scenario

Mrs. Coffey's advanced senior class had just finished studying *Hamlet*. She felt there were certain issues they had not grappled with sufficiently. She decided to use the cause and effect model with one of the play's central issues: why Hamlet continued to hesitate to act against Claudius. This hesitation led to the death of all of the royalty at Elsinore Castle.

The emphasis would be on causes and prior causes, because the effects and subsequent effects were obvious. Mrs. Coffey wrote, "Hamlet continues to hesitate to take action against Claudius" under the heading *topic* in the center of the chalkboard. She began by asking for causes:

JEROME: Hamlet was squeamish; he couldn't kill in cold blood. He couldn't even kill Claudius after the play, when he had proof.

JUDY: But remember Hamlet's previous reputation for bravery and his military success against the older Fortinbras.

JOSÉ: Hamlet wasn't sure about the ghost. It could have been a trick. People in those days believed ghosts could be real or could be messengers of the devil.

MARIA: Hamlet was sort of in shock. Everyone at the castle was acting strangely—not like they had always acted. So he hesitated until he could figure out what was going on.

PHIL: Like the suddenness of the queen's second marriage.

JANE: Hamlet didn't know whom to trust, except for Horatio.

ANDY: He was afraid of death. That's what it says in his soliloquy.

ANNE: But he seems more afraid of not setting his father's ghost free.

PHIL: But if he takes action, everyone else might think he just wanted to be king.

MARIA: No one else suspects the king. It's really odd.

ANDY: Hamlet overanalyzes everything.

MARIA: Well, what do you think he should have done?

ANDY: He should have killed Claudius after the play.

PHIL: And be thought of as a power-hungry murderer?

ANDY: Couldn't Horatio have defended him?

PHIL: But it's only Horatio, and he didn't even hear what the ghost said.

CANEKA: He wants others to see what he sees: Claudius's guilt.

MARIA: He hesitates because he hates Claudius so much.

EVERYBODY: But that's a reason to kill him.

MARIA: No, you don't understand. Hamlet has this sense of justice. If he's wrong, and he kills him, then he's worse than Claudius. That's why he has to expose him first.

> (The others began to see Maria's point. Some agreed.)

MRS. COFFEY: Where should I put his sense of justice?

MARIA: I guess that's a prior cause.

> (They moved to prior causes.)

PHIL: I guess the main prior cause is his father's death or murder.

RASHAD: The ghost's request for revenge.

CANEKA: He's got to be careful. These are all people who cared about him and he cared about: his mother, Ophelia, Horatio, Laertes, even Polonius.

JEROME: And Yorick, and Fortinbras admired him.

JANE: You know, I don't think all these people would have been fooled. I think Maria's right. If Hamlet had been evil or overly ambitious, they would not have cared for him quite so much. I think he does feel some princely responsibilities, and he does have a sense of justice. He isn't afraid for himself. He wants to be sure; he wants to do the right thing. It's ironic that people keep getting hurt because Hamlet is trying to do what is right. (They all began to agree with this perspective.)

Mrs. Coffey felt they had reached a depth of understanding of the play and of its main character that they might not have reached without this model.

Conclusions
1. Hamlet's hatred of Claudius caused him to be especially careful in trying to find proof of his guilt.
2. Hamlet understands that he must prove conclusively that Claudius is guilty or people will think Hamlet simply wanted to be king.
3. Hamlet realizes that if he takes action against Claudius, and Claudius is innocent, that he, Hamlet, is far more guilty than Claudius.

Generalizations
1. In trying to find proof of guilt, we must attempt to be objective, or the proof may be suspect.
2. Guilt must be proved convincingly or justice will not have been served.
3. If we wrongly convict an innocent man, we are guilty of the injustice we have accused him of.

Summary

One of the primary goals of the models discussed in this book is to have students become active participants in the learning process rather than passive recipients of information. Once a class has performed the cause and effect model several times, the students tend to take over in the sense that they react to one another's contributions, are stimulated by one another's ideas, and challenge one another's points of view. The most provocative ideas are products of this tension between opposing views. Surprisingly young students, even lower-grade elementary students, can hold very thoughtful discussions.

The quote at the beginning of this chapter that reads "Surely our sense of the meaning of experience is closely tied to our understanding of what causes what" relays a concept that some of our students seem to have grasped. It is difficult to gauge whether anything that occurs in class goes beyond class and has an impact on students' lives. Students have left our classes saying such things as "And if I do this what will he do? Would it be better to. . . ?" Several students have become interested in becoming mediators at school. This might have occurred in any case, but their ability to search for underlying and multiple causes in addition to future consequences in their own lives and the lives of others has been enhanced.

WEB RESOURCES

1. **http://www.cia.gov/csi/books/19104/index.html**
   This site describes the book *Psychology of Intelligence Analysis*, written by Richards J. Heuer, Jr. Chapter 11 is on biases in the perception of cause and effect. The book was published in 1999 by the Center for the Study of Intelligence, Central Intelligence Agency. It is available in the government documents division of most libraries or may be ordered from the Library of Congress, Fax no. (202) 707-0380.

2. **http://www.terraquest.com/galapagos/wildlife/island/finch.html**
   Through the Education Workbook at this site, students can discover how one species has adapted to an environment in order to survive. This cause and effect investigation can be expanded through consideration of the question "In what physiological ways will the human species have to adapt to survive in space?"

3. **http://trochim.human.cornell.edu/kb/causeeff.htm**
   This site, entitled "Establishing a Cause-Effect Relationship," describes three criteria that are necessary to the claim of a cause-effect relationship.

4. http://www.education-world.com/a_curr/curr376/.shtml

This site begins with an article describing the use of cause and effect writing as a teaching approach. Following the article are links to additional cause and effect writing resources.

5. http://www.usask.ca/education/ideas/tplan/sslp/cubanm~1.htm

This site presents the sequence of events leading to the Cuban Missile Crisis of 1962 as a context for a lesson in cause and effect with regard to historical events.

6. http://www.accd.edu/sac/english/mgarcia/writfils/modcause.htm

Eight methods of writing development are discussed, one of which is the composition of cause and effect essays. The discussion includes an outline for cause and effect writing.

NOTES

1. William Kenney, *How to Analyze Fiction* (New York: Simon and Schuster, 1966), 14, 23.

2. Hilda Taba, *Hilda Taba Teaching Strategies Program*, Unit II, Secondary Edition (Miami: Institute for Staff Development, 1971), 13–16. Two of Dr. Taba's steps have been separated in the model presented in this chapter.

3. Watty Piper, *The Little Engine That Could* (New York: Platt & Munk, 1930; New York: Putnam Publishing Group, 1984).

4. John Knowles, *A Separate Peace* (New York: Macmillan, 1960).

5. The first five steps of this science example were prepared by Willa Powell, former science teacher at Charlottesville High School, Charlottesville, VA.

6. William Faulkner's remarks to a graduate class in American literature at the University of Virginia that Jan Schwab attended (Charlottesville, VA, 1957).

7. Taba, 140.

8. Taba, 137.

9. Taba, 142.

10. L. L. Thurstone, *The Nature of Intelligence* (London: Routledge and Kegan Paul, 1924; Patterson, NJ: Littlefield Adams, 1960), 159.

11. National Center for History in the Schools, *National Standards for History* (Los Angeles: University of California, 1996), 6.

12. National Center for History in the Schools, 17.

13. National Center for History in the Schools, 16.

14. National Center for History in the Schools, 16.

15. Richards J. Heuer, Jr., *Psychology of Intelligence Analysis* (Washington, DC: Center for the Study of Intelligence, Central Intelligence Agency, Superintendent of Documents, 1999), 127.

10 The Classroom Discussion Model

Conducting Classroom Discussions Based on the Preparation of Factual, Interpretive, and Evaluative Questions

An 11-year-old named Abby, making a guest appearance on a television show, was asked what school was like. "School is taking in what the teachers dish out and then just . . . spitting it back!" she replied. Teachers often hear comments akin to this one. Questions such as "Will this be on the next test?" or "Do we have to remember this for the final exam?" have the common implication that learning in school can be very temporary. School learning is borrowing information to be given back later as proof that the learner was able to retain it in approximately the same form it was given for at least a short time.

Test yourself on the difference between learning by borrowing and learning by owning with this experiment. Think of some of the things you remember learning in school. For example, you can probably remember learning the Pythagorean theorem, the quadratic equation, Wilson's 14 points, the date of the Battle of Hastings, the atomic weights of the inert elements, the causes for the seasonal changes on Earth, an interpretation of Robert Frost's "Stopping by Woods on a Snowy Evening," and many other details both important and trivial. Try to list 12 remembrances of school learnings. For each, rate your present understanding on a scale of 1 to 5, with 1 for low and 5 for high. Do you agree that the things you remember only vaguely or understand imperfectly now are the things you merely borrowed to give back on a test? By contrast, aren't the things you remember very well or understand perfectly now (after what may be years) the learnings of which you took *ownership*? What was the difference, if you recall any, between the way you were taught or learned these different things? What, for you, distinguishes learning by borrowing and learning by owning?

Many of the models described in this book are designed for learning by taking ownership, to give students a way to generate their own ideas and thus to possess them, to make them their own once and forever. Also, many of the suggested instructional approaches involve elaboration and discussion between teachers and students. Often, the quality of those discussions determines the extent and quality of students' learning. The better the discussion with respect to its intellectual demand and objective, the better the students' thinking and the more permanent their learning.

Because discussion has such a central place in good classroom teaching, in this chapter we offer a model focused directly on the issue of discussion, the kind of discussion where teachers, through a process of thoughtful questioning, stimulate students to arrive at their own exciting insights. We suggest this model as a most broadly applicable guide to the conduct of classroom discussion in all grades—kindergarten through grade 12—and in all disciplines where the teacher wants to expose the students to the areas of ambiguity and complexity, indeed to the areas of deepest meaning.

We owe much to the Great Books Foundation, an independent, nonprofit educational corporation in Chicago, for many of the ideas presented in this chapter.[1] We believe, however, that the method of discussion proposed here is applicable to any work of fiction or nonfiction, indeed to any topic, that is rich in ideas. The more substantive the work is, the more fruitful the discussion is likely to be. Many fine works of literature are too unambiguous to support interpretive discussion. A useful test is whether you can read the material more than one way or whether you can ask questions for which there is more than one valid answer.

In science and social studies, discussion material should be sources that are individually complex in meaning or that when grouped together yield divergent meanings. Textbooks are seldom useful except as sources of original documents because they try to summarize subjects in simple terms. Discussion should focus on the selected materials so that all participants have a shared body of knowledge to support their reasoning.

Materials to be discussed can be more difficult than those used for other classroom purposes because discussion gives students support and motivation for comprehension. The materials should, however, be short enough for students to review during the discussion to find specific passages to back up their opinions. Novels or longer works lead to fruitful discussion if students can quickly locate sections or if the focus is on one or two particular chapters.

Steps in the Classroom Discussion Model

1. Read the material and prepare the questions.
2. Plan and cluster the questions.
3. Introduce the model to the students.
4. Conduct the discussion.
5. Review the process and summarize the students' observations.
6. (Optional) Evaluate the discussion.

Step 1—Read the Material and Prepare the Questions

Because the caliber of a discussion is directly dependent on the caliber of the questions asked, the first half of this chapter presents a specific system for asking meaningful questions. The second half of the chapter offers a step-by-step process for conducting productive discussions. The Great Books Foundation distinguishes between three types of questions: *factual, interpretive,* and *evaluative.*[2] Understanding the distinctions between these three types of questions makes it much easier to generate provocative questions.

Types of Questions

Factual Questions. Questions that can be answered directly by the actual words of the text under scrutiny are factual questions. Facts, in this context, are defined as everything stated in the text. Even if the text asserts things that have been refuted or that run counter to one's personal conception of reality, these assertions are considered facts in the discussion. For example, the existence of rabbit holes through which humans can fall for miles is a fact in *Alice in Wonderland.* However, the personal experiences of the readers are not a source of facts. The readers must learn to step into another world and to perceive reality from the author's perspective. Inferences, in this model, can take the force of facts, as described in the following quote from the Great Books Foundation.

> Sometimes, however, a question of fact cannot be answered by pointing to any single place in the text; rather, its answer must be inferred from other facts available in the selection. For instance, the answer to the question "Did Jack plan to steal from the ogre when he climbed the beanstalk for the first time?" does not appear explicitly in the story. But we can conclude that since this was Jack's first climb (a fact), he could not have had knowledge of the ogre and so could not have planned to steal from him (reasonable inference). Since this inference represents the only logical conclusion, it takes the force of a "fact."[3]

Examples of Factual Questions

I. From literature:

   A. From "The Ugly Duckling"
      1. What was the significance of the red rag around the old duck's leg?
      2. What did the girl who fed the ducks do to the ugly duckling?
   B. From *Antigone*
      1. Who is Creon?
      2. What reasons does Creon state for refusing to bury Polynices?

II. From science:

   A. What is the geocentric theory?
   B. Who first proposed the heliocentric theory?

III. From social studies:

    A. What is an indentured servant?

    B. When did the women's suffrage movement begin?

Comments: The questions on "The Ugly Duckling" may sound interpretive. In the first, "What was the significance of the red rag around the old duck's leg?" the word *significance* is a broad, subjective term; the mother duck, however, tells us precisely what the red rag means. The answer to the second question, "What did the girl who fed the ducks do to the ugly duckling?" is that she kicked him. She also hurt him both physically and emotionally. This, too, sounds like a conclusion; we can hardly conclude otherwise, however, because being kicked hurts and because the ugly duckling specifically mentions his feelings about having been kicked.

Interpretive Questions.   Interpretive questions explore not only what the author says but also what the text means. All speakers and writers would like to think that they say precisely what they mean, but all are limited by their particular perspectives, by the meanings they attach to certain words, by the personal experiences that have formed the concepts and generalizations by which they live, by the limits of their ability to translate thoughts and feelings into words, and by the gap between their personal experiences and those of the reader. Interpretive questions are framed to explore these areas of ambiguity in the quest for successful communication.

Interpretive questions may "have more than one reasonable answer that can be supported with evidence from the text."[4] The ultimate justification for interpretation is found in the text itself; in answering an interpretive question, readers must be able to cite the parts of the text that gave them their ideas about the question's meaning. Finally, the ultimate burden of interpretation is on readers. Each person must consider possibilities and then decide which interpretation makes the most sense to him or her; there is no single right answer. Interpretive questions are meant to tease out all possible interpretations.

Examples of Interpretive Questions

  I. From literature:

    A. From "The Ugly Duckling"

      1. Why do the hen and the cat feel that their lifestyle should be imposed on others?

      2. What does the old woman mean when she says, "I tell you unpleasant things, but that's the way to know one's real friends"?

    B. From *Antigone*

      1. Why does Antigone attempt to bury Polynices twice?

      2. What reasons does Creon have for refusing to bury Polynices?

  II. From science:

    A. Why was it difficult for Newton's fellow scientists to accept his thesis that "white" light is a mixture of colors?

    B. Why did it take so long for the theory of spontaneous generation to be disproved?

III. From social studies:

    A. Is it proper to blame a person's actions even partially on society?

    B. What did Stephen Douglas mean when he said that in theory he favored the Dred Scott decision but in practice he remained true to the principle of popular sovereignty?

Evaluative Questions. Evaluative questions ask to what extent the ideas in the text square with the reader's own perception of life. Evaluative questions probe the relevance of the text for its readers. Before being able to judge relevance, however, readers must clearly understand the ideas presented. Evaluative questions, therefore, should not be asked until readers can demonstrate their understanding of the text. These questions ask the reader to make value judgments.

Evaluative questions require the reader to:

> relate ideas in the book to his personal experiences and to his own (often latent) standards of value (of truth, beauty, happiness, goodness, etc.). . . . Questions of fact are verified by turning to the book; questions of evaluation by turning to those facts of experience all participants can reasonably be expected to have in common.[5]

Examples of Evaluative Questions

  I. From literature:

    A. From "The Ugly Duckling"
      1. If someone feels his or her lifestyle is superior to other people's, should one attempt to impose it upon others?
      2. Do you agree with the old woman that telling someone unpleasant things is an act of friendship? Has this happened to you?

    B. From *Antigone*
      1. Is Antigone's attempt to bury Polynices a second time a reasonable or a fanatical act?
      2. Do you agree with Creon's argument that a ruler should overlook personal morality to protect the state? Can you think of a similar situation in modern times?

  II. From science:

    A. Knowing that Earth revolves around the Sun, do you see humanity as an unimportant part of the universe?

    B. Do you see the possibility of life in outer space as an advantage or a disadvantage to "earthlings"? Why?

  III. From social studies:

    A. How do you think President Lincoln should have responded to the problem at Fort Sumter?

    B. Would you buy a product from a company that uses child labor?

Guidelines to Framing Good Discussion Questions

1. Precision in wording questions is very important. For example, the question "What reasons does Creon state for refusing to bury Polynices?" is factual because it can be answered by turning to a passage in the book, whereas "What reasons does Creon have for refusing to bury Polynices?" is interpretive because Creon may have had many unstated reasons. A question such as "Why is there a moral at the end of Aesop's fables?" sounds straightforward but could be ambiguous. A student might interpret the question as asking why he or she thinks there is a moral at the end or what values morals have. The question might also be interpreted as asking why Aesop put a moral there. One must be careful to make the intent of the question clear.

2. Just as precision in wording questions is important, so is precision in reading the author's words. Thus questions about the author's wording make excellent interpretive questions. The meaning of one word can become the subject for an entire cluster of questions. What does the word *jealous* mean in a short story, or to whom did the word *ourselves* refer in the first draft of the Constitution? A good strategy is to read the sentence where the word first appears and ask different students to venture a definition. Then read other passages where the word appears and ask which definition seems most applicable and why. Does the definition need revision? The meanings of sentences, paragraphs, or whole pages make excellent questions. Reading particularly puzzling sections and allowing students to sense that you are puzzled and looking to them for ideas gives participants confidence.

3. Discussion questions should not be too broad. A discussion needs to be focused, and the questions act as lenses, singling out particular areas. For example, in discussing the short story "Charles" by Shirley Jackson, asking why the boy in the story, Laurie, invented Charles is too broad a question. But some questions—What does the first sentence tell us about Laurie? What is Laurie's attitude toward school? What is Laurie's mother's attitude toward him? Why do Laurie's parents encourage him to talk about Charles?—serve to narrow the discussion and give it direction.

4. Finally, the most important rule regarding good questions is that they must reflect real doubt. The best test of real doubt is whether the person asking the question can think of at least two distinct answers to the question. This should not be an emotional "doubt" but a rational "doubt" that could be demonstrated to anyone. In addition:

> Doubt means that after identifying and considering a problem of meaning, you are still unsure about how best to resolve it. . . . Doubt does not mean, "I know the best answer, but my participants may not." Questions meant to lead your participants to a single answer or to an insight you think is important . . . do not help participants work with and develop their own ideas.[6]

Questions that you know may be answered in several different ways, supported by evidence from the text, force the discussion of real problems of meaning and call forth the students' best attempts to comprehend. It is these questions that lead the discussion into that realm of author's intent. Also, those parts of the text that bother you or puzzle you, the discussion leader, make excellent questions. Remember, you never supply answers, but it is helpful if the students sense that you are truly searching, that their ideas are valuable to you and to one another.

It is not necessary to "talk down" to younger students. Although you may want to simplify vocabulary, even elementary students can grasp complex ideas. Their honesty is refreshing. "Experience is a two-edged sword; it can broaden our understanding and strengthen our rational convictions; but it can also narrow our interests and shore up our prejudices."[7]

There are many systems for classifying questions. The approach described here seems particularly effective because most people, particularly students, tend to ask and to think in terms of factual questions or evaluative questions. Because factual questions have one right answer, and because evaluative questions are matters of opinion, they rarely lead to discussion as provocative as that produced by interpretive questions. Learning to classify questions can help teachers and students ask more thought-provoking questions in the classroom.

EXERCISE 10.1

Identify the following questions by type:

1. In the prologue to *Romeo and Juliet*, what does the chorus tell us about the play?
2. How does the chorus help to prepare us for the story that follows?
3. How does Juliet feel about marriage before she meets Romeo?
4. Did Romeo believe that his fate was in his own hands?
5. What would you have done in Juliet's place when her father ordered her to marry Paris?

Answers to Exercise 10.1

1. Factual (depending upon your interpretation of the word *tell*). The words of the chorus are clearly delineated in the prologue.
2. Interpretive. Unlike the first question, this calls for an interpretation of the facts given in the prologue and their effect on us.
3. Factual. Although it requires drawing an inference, Juliet's statement that marriage is an honor she dreams not of can only be read as indicating dislike of her father's plan.
4. Interpretive. Many of Romeo's words indicate a belief in fate; yet his actions indicate a sense of being able to control events to some degree. One could argue that Romeo is or is not a fatalist; thus the question is interpretive.
5. Evaluative. This question asks the participants to evaluate their own responses to the situation. ■

Step 2—Plan and Cluster the Questions

The Great Books Foundation highly recommends co-leaders rather than single leaders for its discussion groups. This arrangement, if possible, is very desirable for classroom discussions. A discussion co-leader can be a willing parent, a guidance counselor, a friend, another teacher, or a student from the class. After students become familiar with the process of discussion, we suggest that you teach students (middle school and older) the types of questions used. With experience, students can not only help you; they can pair up and take the role of discussion leaders themselves. The only preparation necessary is that they have read the material carefully and thoughtfully, planned clusters of questions with you (later with another student), and care about the issues raised in the questions.

Talk about the material with your co-leader. Compare ideas, reactions, and questions. Jot down questions that puzzle you, mark passages that seem significant, and share reactions that interest you. Combine your ideas. Just as a group discussion generates deeper insights than one can generate alone, so planning with someone generates better questions than planning alone. Once again, the students can be very helpful. If you and your co-leader have trouble generating enough questions (it becomes easier as you use the model more frequently), ask each student to generate two or three "thinking type" questions about the material you will be discussing. The students are usually an excellent source of questions.

Basic and Cluster Questions.   Next, "group" the questions by topic. Then identify *basic* questions and *cluster* questions. A basic question is an "umbrella" question: an interpretive question, fairly broad in scope, that raises an issue. Cluster questions are interpretive questions that develop that issue. Together they make up a cluster. A cluster, as illustrated in Figure 10.1, consists of one basic (broad) question and six or eight more focused interpretive questions. Having several different vantage points (i.e., cluster questions) affords different entrances to the issue being discussed. This allows participants to go beyond their initial reactions to the basic question and look at a broad spectrum of information before settling upon an answer.

Clustering, therefore, allows the answers to the basic interpretive questions to become predicated upon data supplied by the answers to the cluster questions. It must be remembered that basic questions may be answered in several different ways; the strength of supporting data from the text determines the validity of individual answers. If a question points to only one answer, it is not a basic question. The essence of an issue is that one may marshal valid reasons on more than one side. Basic questions are "issue" questions; they trigger extended discussion. Basic questions are exciting; "you care about finding an answer."[8]

Two or three clusters should provide ample questions for a discussion, unless the participants are very young (first or second grade) or are unfamiliar with discussion techniques. The more frequently a class engages in discussion stemming from clusters of questions, however, the fewer questions they will cover; the tendency will be to go into each question in more depth. Some high school classes will often productively discuss one cluster for an entire class period. If the group, through

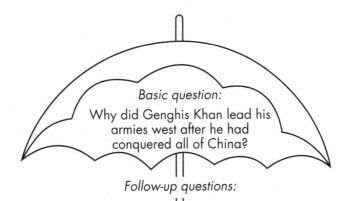

Basic question:
Why did Genghis Khan lead his armies west after he had conquered all of China?

Follow-up questions:

1. What was Genghis Khan's birthright?

2. What puzzled Genghis Khan about trading in the Mongolian camp he visited?

3. What effect did Genghis Khan's father's death have on the family?

4. What made the people want to follow Genghis Khan after he escaped his captors?

5. What made Genghis Khan such an effective leader?

6. What advantages did Genghis Khan's men have over the soldiers they fought?

7. Why was Genghis Khan not satisfied with his conquest of China?

8. What might have happened if Genghis Khan had stopped his conquests in 1215?

(Repeat basic question)

FIGURE 10.1   Sample Cluster—Subject: Genghis Khan

individual contributions, touches on pertinent areas of the text on their own, there is no need to interrupt this flow. If, however, the group strays from the original topic, another cluster question will refocus the discussion.

The following is another example of clustering:

From Edgar Allan Poe's short story "The Cask of Amontillado":
Basic Question: *Why isn't Fortunato more suspicious of Montresor?*

Cluster Questions
1. Why does Montresor call Fortunato his friend when he meets him?
2. Why doesn't Fortunato find it suspicious that Montresor carries a trowel?

3. Why doesn't Fortunato find it odd that the wine is so very far away?
4. Why doesn't the family motto warn Fortunato?
5. Why doesn't Fortunato turn back when the narrator repeatedly suggests it?
6. If Fortunato has grievously injured Montresor, why is Fortunato so trusting?

Repeat the basic question: *Why isn't Fortunato more suspicious of Montresor?*

Sequence.   One issue in planning a discussion is sequence. Some discussion leaders begin with a few factual questions to ground the students in the material. We believe, however, that this should be done during the readings if possible so that the entire discussion can focus on interpretation and evaluation. Ensuring that the students know the material may be done in many ways. If the students are very young, read the story aloud and discuss the plot and take questions. To keep the students focused on a second reading, you can ask them to look for the answers to three or four factual questions as you play a tape of you reading the story. Young students are fascinated by hearing their teacher's voice on a tape recorder. Having them follow along helps them learn to read. Ask them to raise their hands when they have the answer to the first question. You may want to stop the recorder and discuss the answer or, if they seem confused or distracted, stop and find out what the problem is. Giving older students questions to answer during a second reading keeps them focused. Asking students to generate their own questions for you either individually or in pairs also keeps them on task. Using some of their questions makes your planning much easier. Learning the value of second readings is an important lesson for students.

Begin the discussion by asking the basic question in your first cluster. Next ask your first cluster question. Because most good interpretive questions have several possible answers, ask each cluster question two or three times. The students will learn that you are not repeating the questions because you are dissatisfied with their answers but because there may be several good answers. When these have been discussed thoroughly, with responses from several students to each question, reintroduce the basic question. The students' subsequent responses are usually far more thoughtful than their initial responses, because they are based on a pattern of data.

During the discussion, ask many follow-up questions. *Follow-up* is an umbrella term meaning many things:

1. If a student's comment is not clear, ask the student to explain what he or she means. If the student is reticent, ask "Do you mean . . . ?" or "Are you saying that . . . ?"
2. If the comment is clear and provocative, ask other students to respond: "Jamie, what do you think about what Diane just said?" or "Terry, do you agree with Aaron?" Take plenty of time with each new contribution to get other participants' reactions. Encourage other opinions.
3. Ask the students to expand on their ideas, and, most important, ask them to support their ideas with passages from the text. If students are new to discussion or are reluctant to talk, ask all the students to help find support in the text for the idea under discussion.

Even though your planning follows a particular sequence, be prepared to deviate from that sequence in the discussion. A good leader is flexible, because the students' responses should dictate the discussion's direction. This is not easy and can make a teacher feel insecure. There are so many implicit messages in education that teachers must maintain control in a behavioral sense that the message spills over into every facet of teaching. It takes courage and experience to let go of the control of ideas. Even here, because you are asking the questions, you are not relinquishing complete control.

The teacher's goal, however, should be to listen, really listen, to the students and not to steer the discussion to a preconceived view of the material. If, in following the students' leads, you find that you are discussing something you had planned to discuss later, that is perfectly all right. When you get to the subject later you can skip that question, or, if you forget and ask the question, you may get more thoughtful answers. Do not be afraid of repetition. A thoughtful discussion proceeds slowly and carefully, with pauses for reassessment.

Good discussions frequently dictate their own directions and build their own momentum. Allow this to happen. When the particular topic has been covered and you need a short time to reassess, ask the students to stop and think of one or two questions they would like to ask at this point. This will give you a moment to reconsider direction. You might want to use some of their questions. Using their questions can give you insight into their perceptions, which can be different from your own. Or you might prefer to take a new direction or begin a new cluster. Leading a discussion sounds complex, but it becomes easier with practice. It is always exciting!

ACTIVITY 10.1

Form one basic question and several cluster questions that might be useful in a discussion with students in a class you teach or would like to teach. The main criterion for judging your questions is whether they focus on an interpretable issue. Your basic question should be at a higher level of generality than the cluster questions. ■

Step 3—Introduce the Model to the Students

Students learn more when they are told not only what they are going to do but why they are going to do it. As an introduction to these discussions, we suggest that you ask the students what they would like school to do for them. What, specifically, do they want to learn? What should they know? Do they think that it is important to learn any skills? If so, which ones? Is thinking a skill? If so, can this skill be improved by practice? What is thinking? When do they do it? How do they do it? What happens when they do it? You might show them a picture of Rodin's sculpture *The Thinker*, which portrays the solitary nature of the thinking process. This is a kind of thinking but only one kind. Good thinking also occurs when people have a chance to express their ideas, to hear the ideas of others, and to react to them. Let students know that a major purpose of the classroom discussions is to help them learn to think for themselves in intellectual interaction with others.

Tell the students that figuring out what other people mean is an important part of getting along in the real world. This is not easy, because sometimes people do not want to say what they really mean, and even when they do, they often have trouble expressing their thoughts and feelings precisely. Reading people takes practice, just as reading text takes practice.

We tend to think of the written word as fairly explicit, more explicit than conversation. Actually, in conversation, we have body language, facial expression, and tone to help us translate meaning. People frequently have to think long and carefully to figure out what a piece of writing means. Writers strive to say what they mean in clear terms, but there are always gaps between a writer's and a reader's personal experiences and the meanings they give to words and phrases. Different people can read the same piece of writing and come up with different ideas about what it means. If they discuss their ideas together, they will all come to a clearer understanding of the text. Explain that during the next session the class will discuss a reading passage by answering a set of questions.

Ask older students to read the material to be discussed for homework. You may want to quiz them on it. Next, read it aloud in class. It is crucial that students read the material at least twice. Becoming familiar with the art of discussion and the need to refer to the text frequently helps teach students the value of second readings. Also, they should have worked on the material in some way: kept a reading log, generated questions, and so forth.

Step 4—Conduct the Discussion

Prediscussion Instructions for Students
1. Ask the students to put their chairs or desks in a circle. This enables you and your co-leader to assume the role of participants rather than the role of authority figures.
2. Each student should have a copy of the material, a pencil, and paper. Encourage the students to jot down ideas that excite them or to jot down their own contributions. This allows them to follow the discussion without the risk of forgetting their ideas, until you have an opportunity to call on them.
3. Tell the students that the questions you will ask are ones about which you have real doubt, that you are not sure how you would answer them. You want them to feel free to share their own concerns about the reading as well. Many questions that arise will have no one right answer. For most, there are several good answers.
4. Tell the students that there is only one rule that must be followed: They must not talk or contribute until they have been recognized.
5. Next, let the students know that they are to respond to one another's ideas as well as to your questions when you call on them. Later, when they have become used to the process, encourage them to speak directly to one another about areas of agreement or disagreement, and to ask questions.
6. Finally, tell them that you may ask them to support their ideas with specific references to the material. It often will not be easy for them to pinpoint exactly

what has given them a particular impression or idea. Give them plenty of time. Other students should try to help them.

Conducting the Discussion. When leading the discussion, frequently ask follow-up questions that force students to reason aloud, to air their work so to speak. The tone of your probing should encourage: Tell me what you think. Why do you think so? Can you support that from the text? Could you expand on that? Could you explain that idea? Could you rephrase that? I am not sure I understand fully. Can you develop that further? Julio, do you agree with Peter? Amber, what do you think?

After asking a question, allow sufficient time before eliciting an answer. Wait until many hands are up and do not always call on the same people or on those whose hands went up first. The students will begin to understand that you prefer them to take time to consider a response. Again, ask for several students' opinions before asking another question. For each idea, ask follow-up questions about why the student thinks that and what evidence he or she can cite in the text. Others' insights help students develop their own ideas. It is the richness of varying perspectives that makes the insights so penetrating.

If you feel that a student's comment is not valid, ask the student to support it from the text. If, however, neither he or she nor the other students see that this inference may be unsupported, you should not point that out; you should only ask further questions. Most students have very little confidence in their own abilities to solve problems or make decisions. If you step in and provide answers when they are floundering, they may learn more about the specific point you are discussing, but does that knowledge outweigh the imperceptible loss of confidence in themselves? When faced with the next tough question, will they defer to you? The need for a pattern of supporting evidence for an idea will become clear through repeated discussions, and self-confidence will be built in the process.

Remember that the questions you ask should be open-ended questions, not questions to which you have specific answers. One of the most important purposes of the model—if not *the* most important—is to increase the students' confidence in their own ideas. You are asserting *their* individual abilities to generate important ideas and the ability of the group to discern valid and invalid assertions. There are many times when answers are appropriate, when direct instruction is the best way to approach material, but when using this particular model, we think that holding back may pay long-term dividends.

One further word of caution: It is only natural to question less stringently those answers with which you agree. Try to guard against this and to ask for supporting evidence for comments that seem true to you but that have not been adequately supported.

Because the stress in this model is on the *process* of discussion rather than the achievement of one specific conclusion, there is no closure in the sense of reaching a stated conclusion. Instead, participants come to feel that they have developed their own ideas fully, that they have little more to ask or to say for now about the basic question. They may want to explore other questions. This seems appropriate because one characteristic that distinguishes superior writing from mediocre writing is that superior writing leads to more and more questions, ambiguities, and complexities. The idea that there is no one right conclusion is difficult for students to grasp, but it is good if they come to grips with this concept. It is also good if they see that disagreement can be healthy and can lead to greater insights.

Step 5—Review the Process and Summarize the Students' Observations

At the conclusion, ask the students to review the discussion's main points. What was said that particularly impressed them? What ideas do they remember? Discuss the value of different points of view and encourage students to share the way their perceptions of the material changed. You may want them to write their responses to one of the basic questions now that they have explored the topic through discussion.

Step 6—(Optional) Evaluate the Discussion

The etymology of the verb *educate* includes the concept leading out, drawing out, or bringing up. Jerome Bruner emphasizes this aspect when he observes that "thinking, for all its benefits from acquired knowledge, is not the acquisition of knowledge, but is its deployment in the interest of solving problems."[9]

The classroom discussion model is an excellent tool for students to use when thinking independently, when solving problems of interpretation, and when thinking in concert with or in opposition to their peers. But how does one evaluate this activity? We do not suggest evaluating student performances until the students have become comfortable with the discussion process. Evaluating students may not be necessary at all. However, you may wish to evaluate student progress or to validate progress in your own performance. There are several ways to do both:

1. To evaluate your own performance, talk with your co-leader as soon as possible after the discussion; if you did not have a co-leader, review your questions yourself. Did you deviate from your plan? When? Why? How did you return to the questions again? Did you feel that you followed students' leads? Did you feel that you missed some opportunities? Were you pleased with the discussion? Did the students become involved? Seem excited? Remember to be easy on yourself, however! Veteran co-leaders make mistakes in sequence, fail to pick up important points, and so forth. There is no perfect discussion.

2. To evaluate students' performances, first go over your and your co-leader's initial impressions. As soon as possible after the discussion, jot down approximate grades, being very generous. When judging student performances, consider:

- The ability to contribute insights that take the class to a deeper level of understanding
- The ability to respond to the ideas of the other students
- The ability to support insights with references to the text

- The ability to listen carefully and to be open-minded
- The ability to be quietly patient but involved and enthusiastic while others are discussing

Although this list sounds subjective and difficult, it is surprising how accurate these initial impressions are. Compare your results with those of your co-leader; the grades will probably be very similar. You may want to tape record the discussion.

Let your students know what you seek in a discussion. Give older students a copy of the list of abilities you value to keep in their notebooks. This model demands a great deal from students; be very charitable, especially until the students are comfortable with the procedure. Some students will be more inhibited and will not think on their feet as easily as others. Try to bring these students out, and try to get contributions from everyone. Reward and encourage growth.

Make a comment about open-mindedness. You are looking for the ability to listen actively. If, after listening to other points of view, a student remains adamant about a response, that is good. You want students to have the courage of their convictions. However, a response that does not take other perspectives into account is usually not a strong response. A response that builds on or refutes other responses with specific reasons is a strong response.

Baron and Sternberg, in their book on thinking skills, comment:

> If open-mindedness is a criterion for evaluating thinking, the teachers and students can look for the extent to which open-mindedness is reflected by the participants in the discussion. The same can be true for focusing on the extent to which the students are providing reasons and evidence for their opinions, building upon their ideas, and making connections.[10]

3. In addition to evaluating overall performance, there are many specific ways of evaluating aspects of this model. For example, you can require all students to prepare some factual, interpretive, and evaluative questions before the discussion. This helps them read more carefully, helps you plan more easily, and gives you an idea about how carefully they have prepared. The caliber of the prediscussion questions can be evaluated. This activity may be performed individually or in pairs, with each pair generating two clusters and some evaluative questions.

4. The Great Books Foundation asks students to jot down their initial responses to the basic questions when they are asked. The students could also write down their final answers after the discussion or for homework. Ask them to support these with evidence from the text. These can be evaluated.

5. Ask older students to generate three interpretive questions. They can then answer them, giving support for their answers from the text. Their answers become possible theses for critical essays. This process gives students techniques for generating original ideas. It is difficult to generate good theses. If a thesis is too obscure, it is difficult to prove and may not be valid. If it is too obvious, it is not interesting. Having students generate interpretive questions is a good way to help them select ideas that are neither too broad nor too narrow.

As noted earlier, it is usually preferable to defer grading as evaluation until students are comfortable with the model. Your major goal is to generate excitement for discussing, discovering, and responding to ideas. Do not allow the evaluation process to interfere with this excitement.

Summary of Steps in the Classroom Discussion Model

1. *Read the material and prepare the questions:* Select and prepare the material for discussion by reading and rereading the text and developing factual, interpretive, and evaluative questions.

2. *Plan and cluster the questions:* Preferably with a co-leader, compare ideas, reactions, and questions. The questions are clustered and sequenced in preparation for the discussion.

3. *Introduce the model to the students:* Through a series of questions about what students think they should learn, explain the benefits of the discussion model. Next, introduce the students to the process and assign the reading. Finally, ask the students to prepare questions for the discussion. (Gradually, older students learn how to prepare factual, interpretive, and evaluative questions. Use these to help you plan.) Then give the students time to reread the material carefully before the discussion.

4. *Conduct the discussion:* Conduct the discussion and maintain a nondirective role as much as possible. Encourage the students to listen carefully and respond to the opinions of others and to validate their own opinions by referring to the text whenever possible.

5. *Review the discussion and summarize the students' observations:* Review the major points made during the discussion or encourage the students to jot down ideas that impressed them. Ask for their contributions. You might also ask if any students changed their minds during the discussion about the answers to the basic questions. How did their ideas change and why?

6. *(Optional) Evaluate the discussion:* Talk with your co-leader about the direction of the discussion, the enthusiasm of the students, and the caliber of their contributions. If necessary, make suggestions for the next discussion.

Basis for the Classroom Discussion Model

The practice of teaching by holding discussions and generating thoughtful questions dates at least to Socrates; however, the Great Books' method of discussion as we know it today began to evolve at Columbia University. In 1919, John Erskine, an English professor, conducted discussions of this type in his general honors course. One participant in the discussions at Columbia was Mortimer Adler. With the backing of Robert Maynard Hutchins, president of the University of Chicago, Adler initiated discussions at that institution. Adult discussion groups were also started in Chicago.

In the 1972 revision of *How to Read a Book*, Adler and Van Doren write that one should never say "I disagree" until one can say, "I understand."[11] This level of understanding requires looking at a text from the author's vantage point. It involves trying to infer the meaning and use of particular words in an effort to comprehend not only what is said but also how and why the author reached a certain conclusion or held a certain point of view.

To help readers reach this level of understanding, discussion leaders raise questions about a text, questions in which they themselves express genuine curiosity, such as: What does the word *right* mean in the Declaration of Independence? To whom does the word *men* refer in the opening paragraph? What is the common appeal of the Golden Mean in art, architecture, and mathematics? What might be a good analogy to express the relationships among community, conservation, harmony, and friendship? Questions such as these are clustered around a specific area of inquiry to give the discussion direction. Furthermore, these kinds of questions require readers to think and never to read passively.

How does this model alleviate the problem of overreliance on memorization and student passivity in the classroom? By presenting complex problems for the students to solve, the teacher affirms a belief in their ability to infer, to make connections, to find answers—in short, to think well and to *create*—rather than to memorize ideas.

By offering a method of distinguishing thoughtful questions from dead-end questions, this model increases the teacher's ability to require students to use higher-level thinking skills. Dolores Durkin's research has suggested that teachers in elementary grades only rarely ask questions of students that have any bearing on *how* to think about text[12]; John Goodlad's observations of secondary classrooms suggest that only 1 percent of teachers' questions require of students anything but the most superficial thought.[13]

The point was made in Chapter 6 that for new words to become a permanent part of a youngster's working vocabulary, a concept must be in place. Then, when the correct tag is supplied, the new word is truly acquired. Research by Steven Stahl and Charles Clark found that fifth-grade students who were regularly engaged in discussions of scientific material containing new vocabulary were more successful at retaining the concepts and the words than students who did not engage in such discussions.[14]

Based on the later Gestalt theories and the psychology of John Dewey, Maurice Hunt and Lawrence Metcalf made an impressive case for emphasizing "conceptualization and reflection, and insightful learning of skills and habits" over "the learning of skills, habits, and memorized relationships, according to the principle of repetitive drill."[15] They saw discussion as the most effective way to generate this reflection. Moreover, they viewed discussion as *the* tool in social studies with which to ensure our democratic heritage. "Perhaps the chief difference between totalitarian cultures and our own is that in the former *all* controversial fields are closed—and closed uniformly and consistently. In a culture with democratic inclinations fewer areas are closed to open discussion, and, in certain places—as in the universities—there may be none closed at all."[16]

Most important, Hunt and Metcalf saw discussion as the chief tool in encouraging people to be flexible and change their ideas. "If they can independently explore a problem, feeling no authoritarian pressure from above to . . . emerge with particular conclusions, they are much more likely than otherwise to undergo real permanent changes in conceptual and behavioral patterns."[17]

In writing about how an individual's thinking changes, Roger Holmes, in *The Rhyme of Reason*, asserts that an individual's thinking matures as a series of steps in which one alternates between analyzing presently held beliefs and synthesizing these beliefs with new ideas:

> On the plateaus we employ the traditional deductive logic, elaborating by way of analysis an already acquired set of judgments and avoiding contradictions. These stages are static, and for most of us, complacent. But they are essential to profound thinking. The more we analyze our position the more we understand it. And the more we understand it the sooner we see the inadequacies and begin to doubt. And when we begin to doubt we are ready for another step upward. . . . The dynamic, and more humble, stage is that in which we courageously leave one plateau and work toward another. This is the process that all education in general, and all logic in particular, should emphasize. In this stage contradictions are welcome and new syntheses sought.[18]

The thinking that occurs during a class discussion encourages new syntheses; opposing views are expressed, explored, and argued. Thus richer, more advanced views emerge. The presence of opposing views pushes the students to take steps up in their thinking. This is not always a comfortable process, but its value in fostering intellectual growth is borne out by the astuteness of the conclusions students reach.

Lee Shulman asserts that teaching reform must be built "on the idea of teaching that emphasizes comprehension and reasoning, transformation and reflection."[19] Most teachers are considered effective today, Shulman says, if they manage behavior well. Too few let their teaching methods be dictated by the ideas inherent in the material. "We find few descriptions or analyses of teachers that give careful attention not only to the management of students in classrooms, but also to the management of *ideas* within classroom discourse."[20]

Shulman cites a veteran teacher who divides her approach to guiding the students' understanding of literature into four levels: literal, connotative, interpretive, and evaluative. This is, of course, very similar to the model presented in this chapter. The strength of the approach in both cases comes from allowing "what" you teach to dictate in part "how" you teach. Serious literature contains complex, subtle, and often ambiguous ideas. Unless students are allowed to approach, manipulate, and weigh these ideas in light of their own experiences, beliefs, and values, the ideas will not affect their thinking in any permanent way.

Scenario

Mrs. Jones's class was discussing "The Ledge," by Lawrence Hall,[21] a chilling story of death on a duck hunting trip. The story's central character has earned a reputation for being a first-rate fisherman and hunter, always in control of himself and the situation. The following is a discussion of this story by Mrs. Jones's advanced 10th-grade class. This class was experienced in classroom discussions.

The first basic question Mrs. Jones asked was:

1. Why did the fisherman go hunting on Christmas morning? (Pause.)

> **JANIE:** It says on page 1, 2nd paragraph (students turn to that page), "But he had promised his son, thirteen, and his nephew, fifteen, who came from inland." I don't think he wanted to go back on his promise.

> **JULIA:** But that sentence starts with *But*. And right before that it says, "It was a home day, which made it natural to think of the outer ledge merely as some place he had shot ducks in the past." I don't think he wanted to go.

> **JANIE:** But he had promised, and he seemed to want to be a man of his word.

> **TED:** It also says in the next paragraph "Above the snug murmur of his wife's protest he heard the wind in the pines and knew it was easterly as the boys had hoped and he had surmised the night before. Conditions would be ideal, and when they were, anybody ought to take advantage of them. The birds would be flying." I think this is how he always made his decisions to go—or not to go—fishing or hunting. It was always a gamble, but he had to take advantage of good conditions, and pay attention to bad ones.

> **CARL:** Also, it says somewhere that he always had the best equipment—wait a minute, I'll find it.

> **KATHY:** It's on the top of page 4. "He had the best of equipment, and he kept it in the best of condition."

> **CARL:** Thanks. Yeah, my point is that to get and keep the best equipment costs money. You have to catch more fish and shoot more birds than anyone else. You have to go when you can. You have to play it close to the edge.

> **BETTY:** But he was only taking his son and nephew. That didn't have anything to do with making money.

> **CARL:** I don't think he thought that way. He had always let conditions dictate his decisions.

> **KATHY:** In the first paragraph of the story, it describes him as a "big, raw man, with too much strength, whose delight in winter was to hunt the sea ducks that flew in to feed by the outer ledges, bare at low tide." So he got his kicks playing it close.

NICOLE: Also, the fact that he had kind of wanted to stay home might have frightened him. He might be afraid he's getting soft. He's got to keep proving he's tough to himself.

MRS. JONES: Do you all agree? (Pause.)

PETER: He needed that toughness. I'm not sure why. Something else . . . he had a reputation. Not going out that day might hurt his reputation.

MRS. JONES: Why do you think he needed that reputation?

CARL: Well, if you get soft, you might let down your standards, not do all the things you should, forget something, and that could be dangerous.

JANIE: But if he hadn't been so tough, he might not have gone out and they wouldn't have drowned. (Pause.)

MRS. JONES: So, Ann, why do you think he went hunting that day?

ANN: On the bottom of page 2 it says, "People thought him a hard man, and gave him the reputation of being all out for himself because he was inclined to brag and be disdainful. If it was true, and his own brother was one who felt strongly it was, they lived better than others."

MRS. JONES: What do you conclude from that?

ANN: Well, I agree with Carl. The fisherman had been doing things successfully for a long time and he was afraid of change. Also, he probably liked his rep of being strong. He probably felt it was good, because if you were strong and kept to your rules you were safer.

MRS. JONES: Can anyone think of any other reasons the fisherman might have had for going out that morning? (Long pause.) Then, Julia, would you summarize what we've said?

JULIA: Well, a part of the fisherman wanted to stay home and relax, but he had promised the boys. Also, he was a little afraid of getting soft, of that part of him that wanted to stay. So he allowed himself to share the old excitement with the boys. He felt the conditions were perfect and he should take advantage of them.

MRS. JONES: Does anyone want to add anything?

JOHN: Yes, he had a reputation to uphold so he didn't allow himself to think, like his wife, about how far out they would be, about how few people would be out there, about the danger. I guess he couldn't dwell on those things or he would never have led the life he did.

They felt they had covered the subject, so Mrs. Jones went to her next cluster.

2. Why is the hunter so upset when he realizes he has forgotten his tobacco?

ANN: Well, there's the obvious reason—his own enjoyment. He couldn't imagine a whole day out without his pipe.

JOHN: But it says, bottom of page 5, "Groping in his pocket for his pipe, the fisherman suddenly had his high spirits rocked by the discovery that he had left his tobacco at home. . . . He was incredulous." That sounds like more than the loss of some enjoyment.

BETTY: It goes on to say, "He was a man who did things the way he set out to do." He had a kind of ritual. To forget something could be dangerous.

TED: Yeah. I've been fishing with a friend of my father's. He had checklists. I mean you need coolers and drinks and food and water and suntan lotion and rain gear and sweaters and first aid stuff, and that's only the personal stuff. He needed gas and extra oil and tools and life preservers and radios and forecasts and ropes in special places tied certain ways. We had to get up at 4:30 to get ready. But my point is that without some of this stuff it's really dangerous out there.

JOHN: It's sort of the beginning of his losing control.

MRS. JONES: What do you mean, John?

JOHN: Well, he forgot the tobacco. What else could he have forgotten? He got the boys to check the whiskey. It's like he had a premonition. I mean it was his forgetting to pull the skiff up that caused them to drown.

KATHY: Yes, he had even said—wait, I'll find it . . . on page 9, bottom: "Exultantly the boys dropped their guns, jumped up and scrambled for the skiff. 'I'll handle the skiff!' the fisherman shouted at them." He had somehow known how dangerous it was for him to have forgotten the tobacco. It was the beginning of his losing control.

TED: Being in control is life and death on the water. There are so many things you can't control—wind, tides, and so on, that you have to control what you can so you can cope with emergencies.

JULIA: I guess that necessity to control creeps into other aspects of life. You just make a habit of controlling.

KATHY: That's probably why everyone thought he was so hard. What was it his wife said? Wait a minute.

JANIE: On page 3 she says he's dangerous and refers to his unsympathetic competence. Is that what you mean?

JULIA: Yes. I guess you can be sympathetically competent, but he had to be almost ruthlessly competent to be really good and to survive. He probably felt no one understood that.

CARL: That's why he enjoyed the reputation, the distance from others. It meant he was in control.

NICOLE: That's interesting. He got a reputation by being in control and now that reputation was sort of controlling him.

MRS. JONES: Could you expand on that a little?

NICOLE: Well, he couldn't control the elements, but to survive, he had to control everything he could. This habit crept into every facet of his life—his dealings with people. He enjoyed his reputation for being hard and in control. In a way, though, it began to control him. I think a part of him wanted to stay home and relax, but he had to live up to his reputation by being strong—"macho"—and going.

There was not time to explore this idea further. Mrs. Jones asked the students to write down the idea or ideas that they had found exciting or significant. Her planning for this class had been similar to the planning she would have done for a beginning class, except that she would have prepared one more cluster. She had not needed to ask several of her cluster questions, because the class brought up the topics themselves. In addition, they responded directly to one another. Her first cluster had been:

1. Why did the fisherman go hunting on Christmas morning?

Her cluster questions had been: Do you think he wanted to go? How did his wife feel about his going? Why did his son and nephew want to go? What factors did the fisherman take into consideration? Were there other reasons the fisherman might have wanted to go or not to go? Repeat: Why did the fisherman go hunting on Christmas morning?

She had considered her own responses to the questions, not because she would mention them or ask leading questions, but because it helped her to know when to move on. For example, the points she hoped the students would touch on were that he was tempted to stay, the promise, the conditions, the necessity of taking advantage of favorable conditions, the desire not to grow soft, and so on. If she thought that they had overlooked something important, she might have asked for any other ideas or she might have probed a little more. If there were no additional comments, she would go on. Actually, to her delight, the students had gone farther than she had, which was often the case.

Obviously this class had learned to respond to one another, to listen carefully to one another without interrupting, and to refer to the text when indicated. Mrs. Jones was pleased because they had referred to the text more in this discussion than in any other. This was important. If, for example, Janie had not begun by reading the exact words, Julia would not have heard the word *But* at the beginning and may not have felt that the fisherman had some doubts. Mrs. Jones enjoyed seeing them press each other, and they had made some very perceptive comments. She wished she had had more time on this discussion.

Her own role would have been a little different had this been a beginning class. She probably would have had to remind the students not to interrupt and to go to the text more frequently. Undoubtedly she would have had to ask more follow-up questions: "What do you mean?" "Could you expand on that?" "Could you explain further?" "Why do you say that?" These words, delivered in a proper and appropriate tone, imply, "Yes, I like that. Could you expand on that idea?" This gentle questioning encourages students to articulate what were initially only vaguely felt subtleties. The students in this class had learned to do that for each other.

A Word to the Reader.   No one could possibly remember to do all the things suggested in this chapter. We have used this discussion technique for over 15 years in real classes with real students and still finish discussions knowing that many points have been overlooked. It has been, however, a very productive tool in a long search for techniques that excite students and that invite them to participate actively in the learning process. It would be ideal to present the model as a series of overlays, introducing only one or two aspects at a time. Try the strategy in easy chunks. Here are some suggestions:

1. Start by generating as many single interpretive questions as you can, and ask them in class or on quizzes or tests.
2. Create one cluster on material the class is currently using and have students discuss it.
3. Plan (with a co-leader if possible) your clusters over the summer when you have more time.
4. Start by concentrating on asking basic and cluster questions and repeating the cluster questions. When you feel comfortable, concentrate more on follow-up questions. Next, concentrate on asking students to support their ideas with references to the text. Later, skim this chapter again for some of the more subtle points, such as stringent questioning of ideas with which you agree.

Do not worry if, in concentrating on one aspect, you forget other aspects. Just begin where it seems easiest. Be patient with yourself. Eventually students will be able to tackle new and puzzling material on their own. Once they begin to learn the questioning techniques—and this is an on-going process—they can plan discussions. When you lead discussions, you actually model the process for them. It is surprising how quickly they catch on to the main points a discussion leader needs to remember. When the students lead a discussion, remind them that they do not have to have answers, only good questions. Usually they are surprised and pleased with how many new ideas the class generates from their questions, ideas they had not considered.

ACTIVITY 10.2

Almost all textbooks place questions for discussion at the end of each chapter. Survey these questions in several textbooks appropriate to your teaching specialty. What proportion of the questions are at a factual level? An interpretive level? An evaluative level? Do the questions seem to pursue a line of thought, or are they disconnected? How could you make the best use of these questions in conducting discussions with the students in a class? ■

Summary

The classroom discussion model encourages more than one right answer to complex questions and welcomes opposing points of view in the hope that these will lead to newer, richer, and more advanced ideas. The underlying premise of the model is that discussion—the true and honest interchange of ideas—produces ideas over and above those that solitary reading and study can generate. Implicit in this premise lies a curious paradox: When students read merely to remember, they will forget; when they read to understand, they will remember.

In synectics (Chapter 8), the juxtaposition of seemingly opposite traits (e.g., passionately cold, calmly furious) leads to a deeper, more sophisticated appreciation of the subject being explored. In this chapter, something similar happens. By presenting different and even conflicting views, the students push one another forward in their thinking, thereby coming much closer to grasping the richness of the presented material than would have been possible without the conflict of varying perspectives.

WEB RESOURCES

1. **http://www.goodcharacter.com/Articles.html**
   Focused on classroom discussion techniques, this site contains articles on the Socratic method and its effectiveness in character education, the use of this method with at-risk students, and more.

2. **http://www.accessexcellence.org/21st/TE/BE**
   After explaining why discussion of bioethical issues fosters critical thinking skills, this site gives suggestions for facilitating classroom discussion in this important area. Also presented is a list of valuable resources on this issue.

3. **http://www.nexus.edu.au/teachstud/gat/painter.htm**
   Author Jo Painter explains techniques for framing questions: including open, closed, rhetorical, and Socratic questions. She also provides an excellent list of resources that can be used for creating different types of questions.

4. **http://www.petech.ac.za/robert/questioning/Default.htm**
   This site offers clear, concise information on framing different types of questions using the Bloom-Turney and Barnes models. This information is presented using graphic organizers in the form of slide presentations.

5. **http://www.covington.k12.tn.us/resources/question.htm**
   After offering guidelines for using Socratic questioning techniques, this site presents sections on questions that probe assumptions, questions that probe reason and evidence, questions about viewpoints or perspectives, questions that probe implications and consequences, and questions about the questions asked. Also included are links to critical thinking skills activities.

6. **http://www.hcc.hawaii.edu/intranet/committees/FacDevCom/guidebk/teachtip/effquest.htm**
   This site gives suggestions for phrasing questions clearly and specifically. Also useful is the page on framing questions based on Bloom's taxonomy located at http://www.hcc.hawaii.edu/intranet/committees/FacDevCom/guidebk/teachtip/teachtip.htm#Questions.

7. **http://www.greatbooks.org**
   On this site, which is the Great Books Foundation homepage, valuable information regarding shared inquiry is available.

NOTES

1. The authors particularly want to acknowledge Margo Criscuola, senior editor of the Great Books Foundation, for her work in helping to update this chapter. Established in 1947, the Great Books Foundation selects and publishes paperback sets of readings for discussion and administers courses that prepare volunteers, teachers, and librarians to conduct Junior and Adult Great Books groups using the foundation's reading materials. The Junior Great Books program is available for every grade from second through twelfth. Most Junior Great Books groups are part of school programs. Adult Great Books groups meet in libraries, offices, homes, churches, and community centers across the United States. Information is available from the Great Books Foundation, 35 East Wacker Drive, Chicago, IL 60601. The foundation has not sponsored and is not otherwise associated with this book.

2. The authors acknowledge that the phrases and terms *interpretive question, evaluative question,* and *clustering* were coined by the Great Books Foundation in the context of its explanation of shared inquiry and have been used consistently as central terms in Great Books courses and materials since 1947. See the foundation's manual *An Introduction to Shared Inquiry,* 1987, for Great Books' use and explanation of these terms.

Under the direction of Margo Criscuola, the Great Books Foundation is currently developing a writing program. The program will teach students from 7th through 12th grades to identify the issues in a piece of writing by generating and responding to interpretive questions, thereby helping students participate in shared inquiry. The foundation is also extending shared inquiry into new areas with high school readings on social studies and biology. In addition, the foundation is compiling a high school poetry anthology.

3. Great Books Foundation, *An Introduction to Shared Inquiry,* 3rd ed. (Chicago: Author, 1992), 7.

4. Great Books Foundation, *An Introduction to Shared Inquiry,* 7.

5. Great Books Foundation, *Manual for Co-leaders* (Chicago: Author, 1965), 21–22.

6. Great Books Foundation, *An Introduction to Shared Inquiry,* 25–26.

7. Great Books Foundation, *Manual for Co-leaders,* 93.

8. Great Books Foundation, *Manual for Co-leaders,* 36.

9. Jerome S. Bruner, *A Study of Thinking* (New Brunswick, NJ: Transaction Books, 1986), xi.

10. Joan Boykoff Baron and Robert J. Sternberg, *Teaching Thinking Skills* (New York: W. H. Freeman, 1987), 227.

11. Mortimer J. Adler and Charles Van Doren, *How to Read a Book* (New York: Simon and Schuster, 1972), 142–143.

12. Dolores Durkin, "What Classroom Observations Reveal about Reading Comprehension Instruction," *Reading Research Quarterly,* 14 (1978–1979): 481–533.

13. John Goodlad, *A Place Called School: Prospects for the Future* (New York: McGraw-Hill, 1984).

14. Steven Stahl and Charles Clark, "The Effects of Participatory Expectations in Classroom Discussion on the Learning of Science Vocabulary," *American Educational Research Journal* 24 (1987): 541–555.

15. Maurice P. Hunt and Lawrence P. Metcalf, *Teaching High School Social Studies* (New York: Harper and Row, 1955), 21.

16. Hunt and Metcalf, 6.

17. Hunt and Metcalf, 150.

18. Roger W. Holmes, *The Rhyme of Reason* (New York: Appleton-Century-Crofts, 1939), 419.

19. Lee S. Shulman, "Knowledge and Teaching: Foundations of the New Reform," *Harvard Educational Review* 57, no. 1 (1987): 1.

20. Shulman, 1.

21. "The Ledge," by Lawrence Sargent Hall, is anthologized in *Best American Short Stories of the Century,* edited by John Updike (Boston: Houghton Mifflin, 1999).

11 The Vocabulary Acquisition Model

Learning the Spellings and Meanings of Words

In teaching the difference between physical and chemical changes, the teacher opened with concept attainment lessons based on the two words *physical* and *chemical* to create a conceptual distinction between these different kinds of changes. At one point in the discussion, the word *physics* was written on the chalkboard and the students were asked if they knew of other words in which *physics* is embedded. To get at the concept of what we call physical, this question was posed: "Does anyone know how to spell *physician?*" The response of the students was quite innocent; one answered, "Oh, gosh, we had that word last week," meaning that it was a spelling word memorized for the previous Friday. Despite some modest pressure to remember, not one child was confident of the word's spelling. They had memorized its spelling, but they did not know how to spell it. They might have spelled it correctly on Friday's test, but even then they did not know *how* the word is spelled. They did not have the slightest notion of how the spelling and the meaning of the word are connected, and so they completely missed an insight that makes a seemingly difficult word like *physician* easy to spell and reveals its meaning at the same time.

Physics is the plural of *physic*, an archaic word once used to refer to the profession of medicine, deriving in meaning from *nature* and natural science. The suffix *ian* adds the meaning "of, or related to." This is not the way the word *physician* is taught, however. It is taught as a difficult word to spell because of the way it is pronounced, a phonetic oddity of English. These "oddities" include *physical, physiology, physique,* and *physiognomy.* But only at a phonetic level are they odd; at the level of meaning they are fairly regular words, spelled according to their meaning. All these words have a relationship to the word *physical*, an adjective referring to matter, distinct from things immaterial or spiritual.

The authors are indebted to Dr. Deborah Pettit, assistant superintendent for instruction, Louisa County Schools, and to the teachers of Louisa Middle School, Mineral, Virginia, for their contributions to this chapter.

Unfortunately, the connection between spelling and meaning is ignored in most spelling instruction, just one of a number of peculiarities about the ways in which vocabulary is taught in school. The expressions "vocabulary words" and "spelling words" would be redundant anywhere but in school. But virtually anyone, in school or out, would recognize that these expressions refer to words studied in school, usually in lists, *as* vocabulary words or spelling words, with focus on their definitions, spellings, or both. Furthermore, there is probably nothing more universal in education than the way those words are studied. This usually begins with a list of words more or less arbitrarily grouped together and assigned to students weekly. The accompanying instructions generally require activities such as "Look the words up in a dictionary, use each one in a sentence, and learn their correct spellings and definitions for a test on Friday."

Sometimes, of course, students are required merely to memorize the spellings of the words by looking at each word to get an image of its spelling, copying the word in their own handwriting, and writing the word, correctly spelled, ten times without looking at the correct spelling. Endless hours are spent in activities like this every week of the school year! One has to wonder how many Thursday nights find parents "calling words" to their children, not just for language arts or English class but for every subject in school at one time or another.

Despite all this effort, the cost-effectiveness of this experience is extremely meager because of two major problems with trying to learn lists of words: (1) Whatever the students learn from the experience of memorizing words is mostly lost within a few hours or days of the test, and (2) the students learn practically nothing about the *system* of English spelling and word meaning. The experience of many people who have studied words in the traditional ways just described illustrates each of these two shortcomings.

The first shortcoming can be tested any time a teacher wants to quiz the students. Imagine a teacher saying, first thing one Monday morning, that Friday's test was lost in a flood and that the students will have to retake the test now. To require that students spell or define words on Monday that they learned for Friday would loudly be met with cries of "Unfair! We need time to study! Let us have at least 10 minutes."

The second shortcoming is easiest to illustrate by listing a few words that many people have difficulty spelling because they have little knowledge of how meaning and spelling are connected. Here's a simple example. What do all the following words have in common?

adequate
advent
accustom
accommodate
arrange
affirm
aggravate

       acknowledge
       allocate
       appall
       acquire
       assist
       attain

These words are difficult to spell, even for some adults. It's the rare speller who realizes that each of these words begins with a form of the prefix *ad* meaning "at, or toward." Thus *adequate* means "to move toward equal" (the root of the word can be seen in *equate*), and *advent* means "toward the coming." *Vent* is from the Latin word for "come," as in the familiar quote from Julius Caesar, "Veni, vidi, vici," or "I came, I saw, I conquered." Likewise, and despite the spelling changes, *accustom* means "to move toward custom"; *accommodate* means "to move toward common"; *arrange* means "to move into line" (*range* being a word for *line*, as in "range of colors"); and so on down this list of words and many others that begin either with *ad* or with *a* followed by a double consonant. The double consonant following the initial letter *a* is likely to be the prefix *ad* assimilated to the root word. Incidentally, the word *assimilate* is an example of assimilation. The root of the word is *similar*, and *assimilate* means "to move toward similar." At some point it must have been spelled and pronounced something like *adsimilate.* But precisely because such a spelling was difficult to articulate, English speakers gradually began to pronounce the *d* as if it were similar to the letter following, and so the *d* in *ad* is frequently assimilated to the initial consonant of the root word to which it is attached. (Two words on the above list have double assimilated letters. In *acknowledge* and *acquire*, the *k* sound of the *c* is assimilated to the sound of *k* or *q*.) This example is not a mini-lesson in linguistics, but it illustrates a crucial feature of the system of the English language: The spelling of words in English is based on meaning, not just on sound, and the connection between meaning and sound is an important part of the basis for spelling. But that is generally *not* the way spelling and meaning are taught in school.

Each of these two shortcomings of vocabulary and spelling instruction—the great loss of memory for what is memorized and the failure of instruction to acknowledge the system governing the connection of spoken and written language—is predictable in light of what has been learned recently about characteristics of the brain, the organ of learning. It would be no exaggeration to say that requirements to "look the words up in a dictionary, use each one in a sentence, and memorize their correct spellings and definitions for a test on Friday" are contrary to the way the human brain works.

The brain is a pattern-seeking machine, an organ designed specifically to look for pattern and meaning and to ignore what it judges to be random or meaningless information. Fortunately, the vocabulary of English is neither random nor meaningless. In fact, it is systematic and meaningful. This can guide the study of the spellings and definitions of words *precisely because the human brain thrives on pattern and meaning.* The vocabulary acquisition model described here honors this insight.

Steps in the Vocabulary Acquisition Model

1. Pretest knowledge of words critical to content.
2. Elaborate upon and discuss invented spellings and hypothesized meanings.
3. Explore patterns of meaning.
4. Read and study.
5. Evaluate and posttest.

Step 1—Pretest Knowledge of Words Critical to Content

At the beginning of any unit of study or new topic, students can profit from a pretest of knowledge of words critical to the content under study. The *unannounced* pretest is an opportunity for students to show what they know and can be a place to begin learning more. As you call each word out to them, ask students to spell and define the words the best they can. Emphasize that this is a test not to find out what they *do not* know but a test to find out what they *do* know. Teaching and learning has to proceed from the known to the new, so the first step in learning is often to identify the known.

To generate the list of words to be pretested, carefully examine the information to be taught—the textbook or other source(s) of information—and identify the basic vocabulary in which that information is expressed. These need not be technical words, but they must be words that express the basic concepts underlying the information. Keep the list short, as the goal is to teach a few words so well that the understandings will generalize to many other words. As an example, consider parts of a science lesson at the fifth-grade level on the topic *Changing Forms of Energy*. Perusing the textbook chapter carefully, we identified and pretested the following five words: *energy, potential, kinetic, conservation,* and *transformation*. As we expected, our fifth-grade students gave us quite a number of spellings and a great variety of definitions for each word. This particular pretest and the conversation that followed are used in the following sections to illustrate the steps in this model.

Step 2—Elaborate upon and Discuss Invented Spellings and Hypothesized Meanings

Students usually come to believe that school is a place that honors being right, without error. The basic idea of the pretest is to acknowledge that "error" is a judgment of what is more or less conventional, such as whether a spelling attempt matches its correct form. This right or wrong evaluation, however, is only one possible judgment. "State of knowledge" is another, potentially more useful, judgment. It opens up a greater range of possibilities for the teacher and admits a greater range of thought on the part of the learner. Certainly it is more respectful in conveying to the learner that every person's knowledge is incomplete. Some things we do not know; a few things we cannot know. Knowledge of language in any aspect (spelling and word meaning in speaking, listening, reading, and writing) is never an all-or-nothing affair.

If possible, display the various spellings and meanings given for each word for all to see, with the names of the students deleted. Emphasize that each attempted spelling and each meaning given reflects some knowledge of the ideas and words that represent them. Many misspellings are phonetically derived; they are attempts to represent sound with print. But English spelling is based on meaning as well as sound. (Thus "spelling demons" such as the word *separate* are really very easy to spell once one recognizes that the root meaning of the word is "to pare, or cut apart." Once the source of the letter *a* in the second syllable is recognized in the idea of "part," the spelling becomes more certain.) Students recognize this on an intuitive level when they misspell a word by spelling another word whose sound pattern is similar and with whose meaning they are familiar, or when they assign a definition to a word that is actually the definition of a word that merely sounds like the word given them to define.

Examine each of the words on the pretest and discuss the relationships of their sound, their meaning, and their spelling. In our "Changing Forms of Energy" pretest, 28 of 37 students spelled *energy* correctly. The other 9 students offered a total of 8 different spellings such as *energey* and *inergi* and *entergy*. But half of the students who produced the alternative spellings did, however unknowingly, preserve the root of the word, *erg*, from the Greek *ergon*, meaning "work." Although this root is not something these fifth-grade students know, it is something they are ready to learn. Definitions of *energy* offered by the students fell into two categories, and each definition related to one or the other meaning. Thus the students defined the word in relation to the idea of work or in relation solely to a human quality, as in "full of energy." But here, as in the spellings, the connections are in place for an excellent lesson in why the word *energy* means what it does and is spelled as it is.

The word *potential* presented more challenge to these students, as might be expected. Only 7 of the 37 students spelled the word correctly. Most of the misspellings occurred in the *tial* ending of the word, a phonetically strange construction in which the ending of the base word, *potent*, is attached to the suffix, *ial*, and the sound of *t* changes to *sh*. This is another example of assimilation, where the pronunciation of a letter is changed when it occurs immediately before or after another sound that makes it difficult to enunciate. (Try saying *potent* and then adding *ial*.) Thus *potent* shifts in its pronunciation when the suffix *ial* is added, creating *po/ten/tial*. Yet *ial* is a key to the meaning and the spelling of this word: These letters form a suffix with the meaning "of, or related to," as seen in words such as *residential, presidential, tutorial,* and *special*. (Even the word *special* follows this rule. The literal meaning of *special* is "of, or related to, a particular species, kind, or form.") With an understanding of the suffix *ial*, students can see that the base of *potential* is a word that they may have seen or heard before: *potent*, meaning "powerful," from a Latin word meaning "to be able." Potential energy, then, is energy that can be used when called upon but that is not at the moment being used.

The word *kinetic* was spelled correctly by only 3 of the 37 students, although 18 students did show that the word was somehow related to the concept of energy (12 students) or electricity (5 students.) Mainly the students tried to spell the word as a word they did know whose sound was similar and whose meaning was familiar: *connect* or *Connecticut* or *conversation*. As it happens, there is one other familiar word that they did not associate with *kinetic: cinema*. The key to teaching the word *kinetic* lies in the concepts associated with the movies. Movie is a synonym for *cinema*, short for cinematograph, a picture of motion, or motion picture. *Cinema* derives from the Greek word *kinema* meaning "motion," from the idea of movement, a concept expressed in science as *kinesis* and *kinetic*. Kinetic energy, then, is energy achieved by motion. This is key to understanding the idea of inertia when this concept arises later in the curriculum.

Conservation fared little better with these students than did kinetic. Although 19 of the 37 spelled it correctly, no student defined the word in relation to energy. Eleven students connected the word to science in one way, in the concept of ecology. But most of the students spelled and defined the word in relation to some other word they knew, such as *conversation, convention, observation, concentration,* or *concern*. The bright spot, and the initial instructional handle, was that 26 students spelled the *ser* part of the word correctly. Although unknown to these students, like the root *erg* of *energy, ser* is a root that means "to protect." It occurs in words like *preserve, reserve, reservoir,* and, oddly, in the word *hero*, which in its Greek form is the source of this root. Perhaps a hero is one who protects, as to conserve is to protect.

The last of the five words, *transformation*, was spelled correctly by 20 of the 37 students and defined in relation to the idea of "change" by 24 students. Although a few students confused the word with *transportation*, for the most part they all had some idea of the word's meaning. One student at least vaguely connected the word to the concept of energy. What all the students revealed in their spellings and their definitions of this last word was a readiness to learn the concept of changing forms. The first step in their instruction might be to connect *transformation* to *transformer*, a kind of toy many of them have played with.

Words like these five that students are asked to spell on a pretest are not likely to be easy for them. After all, these are words labeling the concepts they are going to be taught, not things they necessarily already know. But by examining the knowledge they do have, as revealed in their best attempts at spelling and definition, a conversation arises that forms the basis of teaching what we want students to know on the basis of what they do know.

Step 3—Explore Patterns of Meaning

The *Teacher's Guide* for the *Iowa Tests of Basic Skills* (ITBS), which is one of the most widely used benchmarks of educational attainment, offers an interesting list of suggestions for improving vocabulary. We do not want to imply that improved Iowa scores are the point of vocabulary instruction, but if a test like the vocabulary subtest of ITBS has any validity (as we think it does), then improvements in vocabulary will show up in the test scores of students. This is what the authors of the ITBS manual have to say about vocabulary improvement:

> Understanding the meanings of words is essential to all communication and learning. In general, the school can contribute to vocabulary power through a) planned,

systematic instruction; b) informal instruction whenever the opportunity arises; c) wide reading of a variety of materials; and d) activities and experience, field trips, etc. One of the most important responsibilities of teachers in each subject area is to provide pupils with an understanding of the specialized vocabulary and concepts of the subject.

There are no known shortcuts to vocabulary instruction; vocabulary development is a continuous program. The following suggestions may prove helpful:

1. Keep the emphasis upon meaning rather than upon mere recognition or mechanical pronunciation of words.
2. Teach words in context, not in isolation.
3. Teach children to ask about any new, confusing, or unusual words as they encounter them.
4. Put such words on the board, and encourage their frequent use.
5. Make definite provision for word study and word building: explain origins of words, roots, affixes, compound words, etc.
6. Have frequent oral tests covering new words, using them in sentences, and discussing their meanings.
7. Give practice in synonyms and antonyms, both for words and for phrases.
8. Conduct discussions of differences in meaning of words that are similar but not identical. (Most dictionaries have "usage notes" and cross-references that provide excellent materials for this purpose.)
9. Give pupils, particularly in the upper grades, experience using a thesaurus.
10. Encourage children of different language backgrounds to share interesting words, concepts, and idioms.[1]

A test manual may be an unlikely place to find a prescription for success in vocabulary instruction, but one group of teachers we know took this page of the ITBS manual as exactly that. The following suggestions are distilled from those teachers' experience with this model of vocabulary development interpreted through the lens of the ITBS suggestions. The teachers we are referring to work at Louisa Middle School in Mineral, Virginia.

These are the steps the Louisa teachers take in their application of the vocabulary acquisition model:

1. *I* Involve the students: Invite them to share *their* ideas about how a target word is spelled and defined.
2. *T* Tell them about the word: Show correct spelling, meaning, and derivation; reinforce elements of their ideas that relate to the correct information; tell the story of the word's origin if it is known.
3. *B* Brainstorm with the students, accepting the words they believe to be synonymous with the target word as well as words that they think are related in meaning to the target word. Using your knowledge and various reference sources, model for and lead the students in an analysis of the words on the brainstormed list by having them compare meanings of those words to the definition of the target word.
4. *S* Sentences: Have each student select one of the words from the list they generated or select the target word and use the selected word in a sentence; discuss parts of speech and word usage within the sentences they share.

Each teacher in the school chooses the words he or she will teach in a particular week. It may be a single word per week or several words. In general, the words chosen for teaching are core concept words in the content area—words like *energy* in science, *fraction* in math, *federal* in social studies, *participle* in grammar, and *descriptive* in literature.

To begin, the teacher asks the students to spell and define the target word as best they can. Next, they share their spellings and definitions with a partner or in a small group. To conclude this first step, the pair or group composes one spelling and definition and writes it on the chalkboard.

Each student receives or draws, in a personal vocabulary journal, a copy of the graphic organizer for vocabulary acquisition shown in Figure 11.1. The target word, correctly spelled, is written in the center of the graphic by the teacher and copied by the students. They compare their spellings and begin to discuss differences. Then, the teacher writes the prime dictionary definition in the appropriate space on the graphic. Again, the students compare their definitions. They discuss similarities between spellings and definitions, with emphasis on why the word is spelled as it is and why it

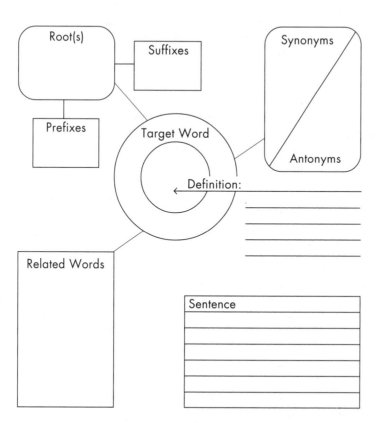

FIGURE 11.1 Graphic Organizer for Vocabulary Acquisition

means what it means. Often, the students are very close in their spellings and definitions, and because learning what a thing is *not* can be very helpful in understanding what it *is*, the discussion of differences between the conventional and unconventional spellings and definitions helps everyone get closer to actually knowing the word.

Next, the students' proposed sentences are examined in the same spirit as the spellings and definitions. The teacher and students create an exemplary sentence using the target word, based on what they have found together to that point. The teacher refers the students to the actual spelling and definition as the context of the discussion requires. This keeps the focus on the actual target of the lesson.

Next, the brainstormed words are examined to see which are related words, which are synonyms, and which are antonyms. At this point students can offer additional words to be included on the chart. Related words are words with the same root, words that form a "meaning" family. Synonyms are words of similar meaning, and antonyms are words of opposite meaning. Knowing a word often means knowing words it is like and words it is not like; acquiring this knowledge is, of course, the point of the exercise.

At the same time that the class is discussing related words, synonyms, and antonyms, possible prefixes, roots, and suffixes can be brought to light. English is a system of combinations. Young readers need to learn to combine, or blend, sounds into words as they decode print to speech. But beyond the basic phonics patterns, readers need to see the patterns of meaning that are also encoded in print. Why is there a silent *g* in *sign*, for example? The answer is that the *g* is needed to maintain the meaning connection between *sign* and *signal* and any number of other words of the same meaning family. Why do we say *rented*, *walked*, and *roused*, in each case spelling the "-ed" part the same but pronouncing it differently? We spell this part of each word the same to maintain the similar function of the word part in each word. We pronounce the endings differently because we gravitate, over time, to the easiest way to say words, a fact that often has led to a mismatch between sound and spelling. There are thousands of similar examples. Bearing in mind that English is a combinatorial system that works to encode both meaning and sound can help readers enormously in their quest for understanding, which is, after all, the point of reading.

Step 4—Read and Study

Once the target ideas and vocabulary are introduced and discussed in the vocabulary acquisition model, reading and study may be guided by any companion model such as concept development, classroom discussion, or cooperative learning. Encourage the students to observe carefully how the words they have studied are used in the text(s) they will read. Seeing a new word used in an appropriate context is another step in vocabulary acquisition. In addition, the students can listen for uses of any of the words in conversation, on radio, or on television or watch for uses of the word in readings other than their textbook. Fiction and nonfiction alike will use all these words in many ways. It is likely, in fact, that wide reading is the single best way to improve one's vocabulary, but only if one is sensitive to the subtle distinctions that writers achieve by the careful use of language. Conversation and discussion before reading and study in the vocabulary acquisition model will heighten this sensitivity for many learners.

Step 5—Evaluate and Posttest

The effects of the vocabulary acquisition model are relatively easy to assess. The model begins with a pretest and ends with a posttest of the spellings and meanings of the same words. One can expect very large differences in the scores on these two tests, considering the intensity of vocabulary study. In this model, mastery is the goal and near perfect scores the intent.

The posttest can include more than spellings and definitions of words, although those might be the basis of grading the posttest. It is critical that learners see beyond words and their definitions, that they understand the ideas of synonymity, usage, and etymology. Use the posttest, then, as an opportunity to probe beyond mere spelling and definition. Ask for synonyms, examples of use, and explanations of etymology. Vocabulary instruction is not merely about the words that are taught. The point is the insight into language and ideas that students gain from their discussion and study, insights that will generalize across many different words because of the ways in which all language is connected at the level of roots, base words, and affixes. When these connections are emphasized, students can be fairly tested with the expectation that they will excel.

Part of the evaluation of language is always informal. We all commonly make judgments about a person when we hear the person speak or see the person's writing. The conversation about the vocabulary that has been taught with the vocabulary acquisition model will continue across time, and in that conversation, evaluation and encouragement to use more precise language will be inevitable. Keep an informal tally of how often the words taught in past lessons are used. Draw the students' attention to places where a recently discussed word may say more precisely what they mean. Such informal diagnostic attention to the words students own and use might be the best part of evaluation for the vocabulary acquisition model.

When testing learners about what they have been expected to learn from their study, include a spelling and meaning test covering the words and concepts targeted in the vocabulary acquisition lesson. The results will show marked improvement of understandings of spellings and meanings of words. The effect will be significantly higher grades, with the added benefit of reinforcing vocabulary study. Furthermore, teaching using this model will greatly enhance the chances that if last Friday's test is washed away in a weekend flood, the students will do just fine on Monday's retest.

Summary of Steps in the Vocabulary Acquisition Model

1. *Pretest knowledge of words critical to content:* This test will establish baseline information for the teacher and students alike, information on what students already know about the fundamental concepts of a topic to be taught. By how they spell and define words, students provide a window on their understandings and a starting point for the instruction.

2. *Elaborate upon and discuss invented spellings and hypothesized meanings:* Invention and hypothesis form the basis of instruction and growth in understanding. New understandings are built on prior knowledge, and whatever students attempt in spelling and defining words can become the basis for growth in understanding.

3. *Explore patterns of meaning:* Discuss how words fit together with their synonyms, how words are used in the language, and how words came into existence in modern English. Spelling is more than speech represented in print. English is a morphophonemic system, which means that a word in print gives clues to its pronunciation and to its meaning. Thus how a word is spelled often has as much to do with what the word means as with how it sounds in speech.

4. *Read and study:* Exploring basic concepts before reading and study creates a context in which students can confirm what they already know while they elaborate and refine their understandings.

5. *Evaluate and posttest:* The evaluation of learning makes best sense when the teacher and students can examine an outcome measure, a test following instruction, against a preinstructional measure of the same information. The steps of the vocabulary acquisition model are set up to ensure marked growth in understandings and knowledge of words and their associated concepts.

Basis for the Vocabulary Acquisition Model

The model for vocabulary acquisition described here rests on the following three principles:

- *Principle 1: The principle of system.* Language is nonarbitrary and metaphoric; it is fundamentally a tool for communicating about unfamiliar things in terms related to familiar things.

    The study of any subject, in school or otherwise, is an exploration of a way of knowing and thinking about the topics that constitute the subject as well as the language in which that knowing and thinking are expressed. Much successful teaching hinges on the relationship between concepts and vocabulary, between ideas and the language in which those ideas are expressed. Words do not arbitrarily label ideas, concepts, or things. To the contrary, words in English make up a system that mirrors the connections among ideas, concepts, and things.

- *Principle 2: The principle of incidence.* Vocabulary is naturally and incidentally acquired as a means for expression of understandings.

    People generally acquire only those words that are important and necessary to the expression of ideas they understand and care about. They usually do this incidentally, as in conversation with someone else who cares about the same thing or in reading about something in which they are interested.

■ *Principle 3: The principle of conceptualization.* Teaching vocabulary is a matter of helping learners move simultaneously to greater sophistication in their understanding of concepts and their understanding of language.

Every subject taught and studied in school is more than a body of arbitrary facts. The academic disciplines are ways of thinking about the world in words particular to those disciplines. We can think of all that is taught in school—each discipline and subject area of school—as the product of a conversation that has been going on for a long time (perhaps many thousands of years, probably since the dawn of consciousness in humankind). This is a conversation in which fine distinctions are created. It is helpful also to remember that the conversation is conducted in words that do not merely label things but label distinctions among things. Thus each subject area of the curriculum is grounded in a particular way of viewing, interpreting, and describing the world. Each generates a way of talking about the world, a particular conversation embedded in a general conversation, a special language embedded in ordinary language.

What would these principles look like in teaching? How might these principles change the way teachers interact with students regarding the various topics of the curriculum? Certainly the instructional conversation should include discussion *about* the language in which ideas and information are expressed as well as discussion of ideas and information *in* the language of the topic. The plan for teaching that honors the principles of system, incidence, and conceptualization would include plans for teaching the vocabulary in which ideas and information are expressed.

Part of the answer to the oft-repeated question "What should schools teach?" is to say "Teach students to participate in the great conversations that have defined what it means to be educated." Teach them the joy of language in which distinctions of thought are reflected. Conduct their way into the particular conversations that have contributed to humankind's knowledge. Use the language of the discipline, and, more important, invite the students to adopt the language as their own as they come to see how the language they are acquiring ties together the concepts they are studying.

Think of teaching as a conversation, a special conversation in which comments of the teacher and texts lead students toward inquiry and curiosity about the concepts under study and about the language in which those concepts are expressed. (The root of the word *educate* means "to lead." Teachers and textbooks alike must, if they are to achieve their purpose, lead learners toward new ideas and concepts by drawing from them the connections between what they know and what they are trying to learn.) This conversation, teaching, is extraordinary in several ways. One conversational participant usually knows a great deal more than the others about the point of the conversation, and that same one, the teacher or author, usually talks more than the others. The purpose of that talk, though, is to engage the other participants in thinking that leads to insights and understandings. Such conversation might accurately be seen as a shared inquiry. The major goal of education is to introduce learners to the conversation that has created the concepts they are trying to learn, extending to them an invitation to contribute to the creation itself.

The special conversation that is teaching is conducted in language particular to the topic under discussion. Concepts and ideas new to the learners are initially framed in language familiar to them. As understandings emerge in the learner, the teacher and text may introduce language that expands the thinking and the range of such understandings. Students participate in that conversation to become conversant with the curriculum topics.

The success of students' learning requires that they learn two things simultaneously. First, learners must understand what they are taught well enough to put their understandings in their "own" words. Second, they must "own" the language in which the understandings they have acquired are typically expressed by experts. Learners need to see experts' vocabulary as both a way of labeling concepts and a way of tying those concepts into the structure of human knowledge.

It seems impossible that someone could understand a subject such as geometry or a topic such as right triangles within that subject and lack the language with which to express that understanding. Likewise, it is difficult to imagine how one might understand social studies or a topic such as forms of government within social studies and yet have no technical language to discuss those forms. Every subject and every topic in the curriculum is couched in a language peculiar to its expression. Think, for example, of the words and phrases associated with the topic of right triangles: *right angle*, *hypotenuse*, *square*, and *square root*, just to name the basics. Likewise, the terms associated with forms of government are essential to expression of what one understands about governments. Among these terms are the words *represent*, *govern*, and the root *archy* in its many forms. Also in that group is *polis* with the meaning "city," the common root of words such as *politic*, *police*, *polish*, *cosmopolitan*, and *polite*.

A C T I V I T Y   1 1 . 1

In most textbooks, a list of words appears at the beginning of each chapter. These are the key words for the chapter. Students also encounter bold-faced or otherwise highlighted words in their reading, words that are important to the topic under scrutiny and that are probably included in the glossary at the end of the text. Examine a textbook, perhaps the one you are using in teaching, to see how words' meanings are conveyed to the reader. Can you find any discussion of why the words mean what they do or why they are spelled as they are? ■

There is no shortcut to knowledge, yet obviously there are more ways to be expert in a topic than firsthand experience. Much that we know, that we claim to be expert in, we gain from conversation. In instructional conversation, ideas and experiences are gained vicariously and the learner is free to take risks, to be wrong, or to be right in unique ways. Learners test ideas and understandings by participation in this conversation. "To risk, to try, or to test out" is the core meaning of the Latin root of *expert* (the root also appears in *peril* and, less obviously, in *pirate*), and the most efficient way to try or test ideas is in conversation. Imagine classroom conversations marked by the qualities associated with expertise, and you begin to get an idea of an aim that is possible in teaching: learners who are virtual experts in their studies.

This aim will be realized when teachers see themselves as more than conveyors of information, when they define themselves as conductors of and participants in a conversation to which students are invited to participate. This conversation is about more than the topic under study, however. It is a conversation simultaneously about a topic and about the language in which the topic has come to be expressed. The guide to that conversation is as follows:

1. Teach the topics of the curriculum as bodies of knowledge, information, and concepts that are born in language, live in language, and expand in language.
2. Teach as if everything to be taught and everything to be learned existed and was understandable in language created precisely for its expression.
3. Teach the topics of the curriculum *as* language.

Learners young and old all acquire vocabulary in fundamentally the same way: from the conversations they engage in, first with intimate caretakers, later with teachers and with authors of texts removed in space and time. *Vocabulary* shares a common root with *vocation*: *voc*, meaning "to call." So vocabulary is the lexicon, or glossary, of a calling and the means by which experts express their callings. In formal study, vocabulary is the language particular to a subject, created as a means of expression for understandings and ideas gained from experience. When learners acquire understandings and words to express those understandings, they replicate, in microcosm, the evolution of the information they are gaining. Put another way, as learners become experts, their understandings evolve through the stages in which those understandings originally evolved. The differences lie in efficiency and timeliness. The teacher saves the learner the trouble of re-creating knowledge, all the while realizing that creating their "own" knowledge is precisely what learners must do in the context of the conversation they are invited into. Seen as conversation, teaching requires of the teacher two

kinds of expertise: expertise in the subject to be taught and expertise in the language of the subject.

ACTIVITY 11.2

Take a close look at the next lesson you are going to teach or a lesson you have taught. Pick out the key concepts—the three or four really big ideas—in that lesson. Now look at the words in which those ideas are expressed. Using one or more of the resources and tools listed in the Essential Resources section at the end of this chapter, examine the words carefully to figure out why they mean what they mean. How could you use this knowledge to better teach these concepts? ■

Mastering Vocabulary

The relationship between reading comprehension and vocabulary knowledge is strong and unequivocal. The problem with teaching vocabulary is that, although the finding may be intuitively contradictory, research has repeatedly demonstrated that the least effective way to teach vocabulary is through the direct teaching of word meanings—for example, by having students look up the meanings of words in a list and use the words in a sentence. Instead, the vocabulary of a reader will improve as he or she learns strategies for learning word meanings independently and as he or she reads widely. Here, in one sentence, is a summary of what years of research into vocabulary development has taught us: *All vocabulary instruction should aim at skills and strategies that help students become independent word learners, able to figure out the meanings of unfamiliar words they encounter in frequent, wide reading.*

Where should educators begin when focusing on vocabulary instruction? Here is a possibility: It is estimated that 65 percent of the English words in common use are made up partly or entirely of prefixes and roots derived from Latin and Greek (55% from Latin, 10% from Greek).[2] Table 11.1 presents 14 of these words. Most of the words in the table are common in the vocabularies of school-age children today, and thousands of words that students will encounter in their reading will contain the prefixes, roots, and suffixes found in the table. Teachers can begin by teaching this list. Then, they can have students brainstorm additions to the list. As the students come to understand these combinations, they will gain the ability to access the meanings of many more new words. There is nothing magical about the number 14, but these particular words will put any learner on the road to understanding some very important things about how language works.

Latin, Greek, and English are related in at least two important ways. The most obvious connection lies in the number of words that came into English almost directly from Latin and are spelled as roots in English words much as they were spelled in Latin. (An example is *duc* in *conductor* and *viaduct*.) A less obvious relationship lies in the fact that Greek, Latin, and English derive from the same ancient mother tongue, Indo-European, a language spoken some 7,000 years ago over vast territories of what

TABLE 11.1 Fourteen Master Words

Word	Prefix	Meaning	Latin Root (Indo-European Root)	Meaning
acceptance	ac- (ad-)	toward	*capere* (*kap-*) as seen in *captive*, *caption*, and *captain* (and in *catch*, *except*, and *inception*)	to grasp, take, or seize
pretends	pre-	before, in front	*tenere* (*ten-*) as seen in *tent*, *tendon*, and *extend* (and in *obtain*, *continue*, and *tone*)	to stretch, hold, or have
permitted	per-	forward, through	*mittere* (*mittere*) as seen in *commit*, *remit*, and *committee* (and in *dismiss*, *premise*, and *message*)	to send or let go
transferable	trans-	across	*ferre* (*bher*) as seen in *ferry*, *offer*, and *circumference* (and in *bear*, *birth*, and *metaphor*)	to carry, to bear, or to present
interstates	inter-	between	*status* (*st-*) as seen in *stage*, *rest*, and *stem* (and in *constitution*, *substitute*, and *persist*)	stand, manner, or condition
defective	de-	away, from	*facere* (*dh-*) as seen in *fact*, *manufacture*, and *facilitate* (and in *perfect*, *defeat*, or *face*)	to set, to put, to make or do
biography	bio-	life	*graphein* (*gerbh-*) as seen in spelling of *graph*, *paragraph*, and *biography* (and in *program*, *grammar*, and *crab*)	to write
epilogue	epi-	after	*logos* (*leg-*) as seen in *logic*, *catalog*, and *apology* (and in *legend*, *lecture*, or *elect*)	word, speech
respectful	re-	again, anew	*specere* (*spek-*) as seen in *spectator*, *suspect*, and *inspect* (and in *telescope*, *special*, and *despise*)	to observe, to see
application	ap-	toward, against	*plicare* (*plek-*) as seen in *implicate*, *complicate*, and *replicate* (and in *complex*, *display*, and *plait*)	to fold together
productivity	pro-	from, for	*ducere* (*deuk-*) as seen in *educate*, *conduct*, and *introduce* (and in *dock*)	to lead
supporter	sub-	under	*portare* (*per-*) as seen in *port*, *export*, and *report* (and in *opportunity*, *porch*, and *ford*)	to carry
contractor	con-	together, with	*tract* (*tragh-*) as seen in *tractor*, *subtract*, and *attract* (and in *train*, *retreat*, and *trace*)	to pull or drag
describer	de-	off, away from	*scribe* (*skr-*) as seen in *describe*, *subscribe*, and *circumscribe* (and in *scripture*, *scribble*, and *script*)	to write down

later became modern Europe, India, and Central Asia. The Indo-European roots of English are often not easy to see in modern spellings of words, but it is important to keep this source of English in mind. Words that are inherited directly from Indo-European, though a small proportion of the total of all English vocabulary, are the true core language. Virtually all of the 200 most common words in our language come straight from Indo-European.[3] The Indo-European roots are given in parentheses in Table 11.1 following the Latin roots.

At times, the modern spelling of a word may obscure the root, and sometimes the same word part may have different meanings in different words. Because older readers can begin to deal with these ambiguities, a few examples of these variations are given in parentheses following the more obvious roots.

The table is not meant as a handout for students, but as a brief introduction and guide for deciding how to point out to students the meaning patterns of language. Just as children in the primary grades refer to patterns of rhyme, students in the intermediate grades can begin to look at patterns of meaning—words with common roots, prefixes, and suffixes that have some commonalities of meaning.

Arguably the most important approach to vocabulary instruction is the "incidental" conversation. During class, model for students your own curiosity about the meaning elements of language by frequently calling attention to word elements that you come across in print. Frequently model using a dictionary to learn the meaning of word parts. There is nothing wrong with a little old-fashioned drill on these elements, done sparingly and with students' help. You might also hold a spelling bee in which students get one point for the correct spelling of a word and an additional point for identifying each meaning part of the word. Additional strategies include the following:

- Display meaning elements of words on wall charts.
- Using index cards, write a word part on one side of a card and a key word illustrating the element on the other side.
- Use strategies such as the graphic organizer shown in Figure 11.1 and the semantic feature analysis and semantic mapping technique described in the Web Resources section to explore the relationships of words, word parts, and the concepts they represent. (This is step 3 of the vocabulary acquisition model: explore patterns of memory.)

Scenario

In planning a 2-day lesson on the early Middle Ages, Mr. Torres chose to focus the initial discussion on two words, *middle* and *crusade*. He began by asking his sixth-grade students to write down anything they associated with each of these words. (This was his pretest of knowledge of the two words.) Most of the students spelled *middle* correctly, but the associations varied widely. The most common idea was the concept of "between." Associations included *middle aged*, *middle ages*, *middle school*, *Middle East*, *middle ear*, and *middleman*. The word *crusade*, by contrast, was spelled in several different ways and defined in reference to war, religion, and Robin Hood. (Several students recalled that the movie version of the story begins with Robin's escape from prison while on a crusade to somewhere.)

With this variety of spellings and associations written on the chalkboard (the students shared their guesses orally to begin the discussion), the following conversation ensued:

MR. TORRES: Look first at the word *middle* in the phrase Middle Ages. Middle of what? What does it mean to say of anything that it's in the middle?

KAREN: It's between two other things. Ages.

MR. TORRES: Like middle school is between elementary and high school. And a middle child is between an older and younger sibling.

MARCUS: But Middle Ages is between old age and young age?

KAREN: Sure—between ancient times and modern times. Right?

MR. TORRES: Right. But of course, when it was happening, the people living then didn't call it the Middle Ages. They probably called when they lived "modern." Like we do today. Let's look a little more closely at the idea of middle. Sometimes in English, it gets spelled *med.* Like in *medium.* That's the same idea. Can you think of other words in which *med* occurs? Let's see if they have anything to do with middle.

JASON: *Medium.*

DOMINIQUE: *Median,* like in a road.

SUSAN: I've heard of *medieval.* Is that the same thing?

MR. TORRES: That's an adjective describing something from the Middle Ages. "Chivalry was a medieval custom," for example. You could say that instead of saying "Middle Age custom." But you see how the idea of "middle" is in all these words?

MARCUS: How about *mediterranean?*

RACHEL: Or *medical?*

MR. TORRES: Well, think about it. Look at the map and see where the Mediterranean Sea is.

JASON: Like between Africa and Europe?

MARCUS: But in the middle of what?

SUSAN: All that land. Like it's surrounded by land, almost.

MR. TORRES: Good thinking. You've got it, I think. I also think I don't know what to say about *medical,* Rachel. Where's our dictionary? Somebody look that word up and see what you can find.

This word proved too much of a stretch for the students, so Mr. Torres had to take it home to work on, with the promise to return with information the next day. What he found is that all of the *med* words are related to the basic idea of measure. *Medical* is related to this group in two ways. One way is through the idea of "diagnostic, to take appropriate measures," which is what medical doctors do. When you go to the doctor, the first thing he or she does is take your temperature, which is an appropriate measure. The other sense in which *med* draws medicine in relates to the word *meditate*, to take apart, literally to cut in half, by thought, which is related to diagnostics in the case of medicine. Incidents like this, where the student stumps the teacher, are part of the joy of teaching, reminding us all that we are no less students of the English language than the students we teach. It should please us to demonstrate that as often as possible.

But what about Middle Ages? Did Mr. Torres forget the point of the lesson? On the contrary, he now had all he needed to explain why this period of about a thousand years is referred to as the Middle Ages: It was *between* two other times, one called ancient (ending with the fall of the Holy Roman Empire) and the other called modern (beginning with the Renaissance).

The idea of crusade proved even easier to get across than the concept of middle. The conversation began with *ade*, which the teacher pointed out means "furnished with." The students thought of *lemonade*, *Kool-Aid*, and *orangeade*. All are flavored drinks "furnished" with sweeteners. Mr. Torres provided the information that the word element *crus* means "cross." Those who marched on the crusades (like the young Robin Hood of the movie version of the story) were furnished with a cross and were sent to the Middle East to furnish the cross to the "barbarians" who were occupying the territory after the fall of the Holy Roman Empire.

Lessons with conversations like these focus attention on information and the language in which information is expressed. Synonyms, word usage, and etymology can be wrapped in conversation that builds readiness for reading and study. Such conversations are about more than words. They are conversations that explore the ideas on which a lesson is built.

Summary

Vocabulary is notoriously badly taught in schools, with endless memorization and consequent forgetting. Our hope is to provide an alternative that has been missing. We also hope that when this model is adopted, the results will be lasting understandings of the language learned in school.

The model is intended to create a conversation that begins with what students know about words essential to their study, the words that carry the brunt of the conceptual load of their school topics. Beginning with an unannounced pretest, this conversation would turn next to the place of these words in the English language: the synonyms of the words, various uses of the words, and the origin and historical development of the words. The metaphor of family has been used in discussing these word features. Following this part of the discussion, students turn to their reading and study, which should now be much more successful than they might have been otherwise. After all, students should be fairly familiar with the basic concepts of their study before their reading begins. The model ends with a posttest. Scores on this test of spellings and definitions should be much higher than the pretest scores. The intent of the model is to have students achieve mastery of the topics of their study; thus their grades in school might soar. If that happens, we think the vocabulary development model is well worth the time and effort. If students catch a glimpse of the joy of language that can live with them from that point forward, they will leave school with a gift for language that will be distinguishing.

Essential Resources for Language Study

The study of English vocabulary requires multiple sources. Most teachers are not linguists, but all teachers teach language and, particularly, the vocabulary of their disciplines. Every teacher's teaching will be greatly enhanced by knowing a bit about the way English works. The following are essential tools with which to approach this subject. Each contains a great deal of information that can enhance almost any instruction.

The American Heritage Dictionary of the English Language. 4th ed. Boston: Houghton Mifflin, 2000. (Also available in CD-ROM version that makes searching very easy. With this version, for example, you can search for all words with the same root, suffix, or prefix.)

Bryson, Bill. *The Mother Tongue: English and How It Got That Way.* New York: William Morrow, 1990.

Crystal, David, ed. *Cambridge Encyclopedia of the English Language.* 2nd ed. Cambridge: Cambridge University Press, 1995.

Morris, William, and Mary Morris. *Dictionary of Word and Phrase Origins.* 2nd ed. New York: Harper and Row, 1988.

Partridge, Eric. *Origins: A Short Etymological Dictionary of Modern English.* New York: Greenwich House, 1983.

Watkins, Calvert, and Benjamin W. Fortson, IV. *The American Heritage Dictionary of Indo-European Roots.* 2nd ed. Boston: Houghton Mifflin, 2000.

W E B   R E S O U R C E S

1. http://www.k12.ky.us/oapd/curric/Publications/Transformations/grahicorgan. html

Visit this site to view a good library of printable graphic organizers, each of which can be used before, during, and after instruction as an aid to predicting, understanding, and remembering information presented in a lesson.

2. http://www.pen.k12.va.us/VDOE/Instruction/Reading/wordsalive_voc_acq. html

This site describes Wordsalive, the Virginia Department of Education's vocabulary acquisition approach that is similar to the graphic organizer in Figure 11.1. The site includes a PowerPoint presentation explaining the approach and a set of blackline masters for classroom use.

3. http://www.vocabulary.com/index.html

Home of Vocabulary University, this site provides interesting ideas for educators. Meet Sam Mantics and Cinny Nym as you explore the vocabulary puzzles. If you choose, register your school to become part of Vocabulary U.

4. http://www.puzzledepot.com/java/czplayer.shtml

If you love crossword puzzles and want to make one for your class with the words of the topic you are studying (or the topic of your WebQuest), give this site a try. It is a crossword puzzle generator!

5. http://idea.uoregon.edu/~ncite/documents/techrep/tech13.html

Visit this site to read "Vocabulary Acquisition: Synthesis of the Research," a report prepared by the National Center to Improve the Tools of Educators. Though the document is long, it will bring you up to date on what is known about vocabulary development. Of particular note, the report highlights the differences between students with poor and rich vocabularies in their vocabulary development and their use of strategies to figure out unfamiliar words.

6. http://www.m-w.com/

This is the Merriam-Webster OnLine Language Center. The site contains a wealth of ideas and resources, including the dictionary and thesaurus in hypertext format. You will want to bookmark this site on every computer you own! As you explore the site, think of all the exercises you could design to teach with it.

There is even a dictionary lookup button that you can add to your computer's personal toolbar for Internet Explorer or Netscape. Once the button is added, you can highlight any word in any browser-viewed page and get a definition immediately (assuming your browser is Internet connected).

7. http://www.abasiccurriculum.com/homeschool/roots/

This site links you to an online book entitled *A Selection of Latin and Greek Roots, Combining Forms, Words, and Prefixes*, which can be read on-line for free and printed for a small fee. Once you get to the main page, click on http://www.abasiccurriculum.com/homeschool/roots/latin/ to get started. Then go to http://www.abasiccurriculum.com/homeschool/roots/greek/.

N O T E S

1. *Teacher's Guide, Iowa Tests of Basic Skills, Multilevel Battery, Levels 9–14* (Chicago: Riverside Publishing, 1986), 47.

2. King, Diana Henbury. *English Isn't Crazy: The Elements of Our Language and How to Teach Them* (Baltimore: York Press, 2000), 83.

3. Watkins, Calvert. *The American Heritage Dictionary of Indo-European Roots*, 2nd ed. (Boston: Houghton Mifflin, 2000).

12 The Resolution of Conflict Model

Reaching Solutions through Shared Perspectives

The Mock Turtle, the Gryphon, and Alice were discussing education. The Mock Turtle said with a sigh,

> "I only took the regular course."
>
> "What was that?" enquired Alice.
>
> "Reeling and Writing, of course, to begin with," the Mock Turtle replied, "and then the different branches of Arithmetic—Ambition, Distraction, Uglification and Derision."
>
> The Gryphon, who had gone to the Classical master, declared, "He was an old crab, HE was."
>
> "I never went to him," the Mock Turtle said with a sigh. "He taught Laughing and Grief."[1]

Educators today might applaud the topics included in the education of the Mock Turtle and the Gryphon, because the current belief is that engaging the emotions of the learner is essential to effective learning. The model presented in this chapter[2] offers precise questioning techniques for the exploration and study of feelings. It allows students from elementary school through high school to examine and express their own thoughts and feelings about a situation or conflict. In addition, students explore the thoughts and feelings of the other people involved. Gradually they learn that others may have very different perspectives and that the same event may be interpreted in a variety of ways. This is an invaluable lesson in relative point of view. It also constitutes the first step in successful conflict resolution. Only when we understand how and why different persons may view the same situation in a variety of ways can we achieve a satisfactory resolution.

Choosing a Conflict

Conflicts for class discussion may derive from a curriculum or course of study. History, science, mathematics, literature, current events, and events in the immediate world of the learners are full of appropriate issues or conflicts. For instance, advances in genetic engineering, such as cloning and stem cell research, are creating ethical conflicts that must be resolved in the political arena. The "new physics," described eloquently by Margaret Wheatley in *Leadership and the New Science*,[3] has dramatically altered our understanding of human relationships. Issues from current events such as these contain conflicts appropriate for class discussion.

History is rife with conflict. To better understand the actions of the persons involved in historical events, students should view these conflicts from different vantage points. What were the circumstances Lincoln faced just before the Civil War? What was he feeling? Why? What might he have done? These questions are the subject of the high school scenario at the end of this chapter.

The resolution of conflict model also provides an excellent analytical tool for discovering an author's fundamental ideas in a work of literature. In addition to applying the model to the work as a whole, the teacher could have students stop reading a short story, novel, play, or poem immediately after the central conflict arises and before it is resolved. The students could discuss the feelings of the different characters involved in the conflict and the reasons for those feelings. Next, the students could decide what the characters might do, given their personalities and previous actions, not what the students themselves might do. Later they could discuss how they would have resolved the conflict. They should express the values that dictated their resolutions.

Newspaper columns relate interesting personal and global conflicts. The model may be used for discussion of an actual happening from current events, from school activities, or from the students' lives. It is easier for students to begin to talk about conflicts hypothetically. Discussing conflicts in a discipline or from an outside source lays the foundation for discussing more personal conflicts. Because the model is personally relevant, its use can contribute to a healthier classroom atmosphere. Looking at conflicts and talking about feelings together does much to foster camaraderie and team spirit within a class.

Steps in the Conflict Resolution Model

1. Students list all the *facts* pertinent to the conflict, including the major actions of the participants.
2. Students identify the *reasons* for the actions, the *feelings* of the participants, and the *reasons* for those feelings.
3. Students list alternative solutions—what the participants *could do*—and what the reactions and effects would be.
4. Students list the appropriate solutions—what the participants *should do*—and what the consequences would be.
5. Students describe any *similar situations* that they, or someone they know, have experienced, including the actions taken. They make inferences about the *feelings* experienced and the *reasons* for those feelings.
6. Students evaluate the course of action chosen. In addition, they look for *alternative solutions* to the similar situations and their consequences.

7. Students arrive at *generalizations* about how people in the situation under scrutiny and in similar situations behave.
8. (Optional) The teacher evaluates the students' participation.[4]

Comments about Conducting a Discussion

Support: If the reason for a student response is not clear, the teacher should ask the student to support his or her response. This should not indicate disagreement; merely ask "Why do you think that?" or "Why do you feel that way?" If you think a student may be uncomfortable, open the question to the class: "Can any of you support this point?" It is excellent practice for students to articulate their reasoning.

Time: Move slowly. Give students time to think. Let them know you value thoughtful answers by not always calling on those students whose hands go up first.

Listen: Evaluators claim that teachers are poor listeners. It is not surprising, particularly in a discussion, because a teacher is supposed to listen carefully to students and, at the same time, consider the direction that the discussion should take. Try very hard to do both, but if that is not possible, follow the students. They will frequently raise ideas you had not thought of. If you do lose the train of thought, ask the students to jot down some questions they would like to ask later while you regroup. Another suggestion is to periodically ask a student to recap a point that has just been made. That helps you, and it keeps the students focused.

The Steps in More Detail

A national news story about a young boy who had been abducted upset Mrs. Juliano. It reminded her that she had wanted to find out how much her third-grade students knew about not becoming involved with strangers. She did not want to unduly frighten the students, so she decided to use the resolution of conflict model on "Red Riding Hood,"[5] which they had just read, to remind them of the mother's instructions. Then she would switch the focus to how children should behave today if they are traveling without an adult as Red Riding Hood was. Normally, one would use just one conflict.

Step 1—List All the Facts Pertinent to the Conflict

These facts (not assumptions) form the database for further deliberation. They should be written on a chalkboard or a large pad of paper and posted where they are visible. Mrs. Juliano wrote the students' contributions on the chalkboard:

> *Sample Database*
>
> Red Riding Hood's mother told her that her grandmother was not well and that she should take a basket of goodies to her. She was to go straight there and "not to loiter."
>
> Along the way the little girl was spotted by a wolf, who thought her a "delicious looking morsel."
>
> The wolf began talking to her and found out where she was going and why. She trusted him because she did not know that he was dangerous.
>
> To gain time, he admired the pretty spring flowers, hoping Red Riding Hood would decide to stop and pick some, giving the wolf time to eat the grandmother and disguise himself as the grandmother.

Step 2—Identify the Reasons for the Actions, the Feelings of the Participants, and the Reasons for Those Feelings

Mrs. Juliano asked why the wolf had distracted Red Riding Hood and why she had stopped to pick flowers when her mother had told her not to.

The students said the wolf had distracted Red Riding Hood so that he could beat her to her grandmother's. They said Red Riding Hood stopped to pick flowers because the wolf had admired them and because she thought her grandmother would like them.

Mrs. Juliano asked how the wolf and Red Riding Hood and the grandmother were feeling and why.

The students said the wolf was feeling hungry because he was licking his lips, Red Riding Hood was feeling happy because the flowers were so pretty, and the grandmother was terrified because she knew the wolf was dangerous.

Step 3—Propose Solutions and Review Their Possible Effects

Mrs. Juliano asked what choices Red Riding Hood had, and what the results of each choice would have been.

The students said she could have ignored the wolf and not stopped to do anything. She could have done what her mother had told her to do. Some said she could have screamed. Others said no, she would not have done that because she did not know the wolf was dangerous.

Step 4—Decide on the Best Resolution and Hypothesize What the Consequences Would Be

Mrs. Juliano asked what Red Riding Hood should have done and what the result would have been.

The students said that if she had ignored the wolf and had not stopped to pick flowers, the wolf could not have disguised himself, and Red Riding Hood and her grandmother would not have been eaten. They also said that her mother should have warned her about wolves.

Step 5—Discuss Similar Situations

Mrs. Juliano switched focus now from Red Riding Hood to a current problem. She said that we do not have wolves on our streets, but we do have people who can cause trouble. She asked if anyone had been in a similar situation and what they should do if a strange adult came up and spoke to them the way the wolf spoke to Red Riding Hood.

Only one student had had a strange adult speak to her, to ask if she were lost. At that moment her mother had walked up. Her mother did ask her what the woman had said. Her mother also said she should never speak to a strange adult, even if that adult seemed to be trying to help.

Mrs. Juliano asked how she had felt. The student said she had not been frightened because she had not known adults who looked friendly could be dangerous.

Step 6—Evaluate the Decision and Look for Alternative Solutions

Mrs. Juliano realized that most of the students had not known that there was danger. She asked what the students would do in the future and what would happen if they took those actions.

One student said if she had been approached she would not have run away because it seemed rude to run when someone was trying to help you. One of the boys said that it might be rude, but that's what you should do. His parents had watched a TV program with him that told children not to speak to anyone they did not know, to run away, and to scream if the adult followed.

Mrs. Juliano said it was sad because most adults want to be helpful, but unfortunately the adults who approach children are often the ones who are not well and they could hurt the children. They are the ones who try very hard to look friendly and nice, just as the wolf had. She also said it was hard, because children naturally look at adults as authority figures who give help.

Mrs. Juliano decided that she would invite a police officer in to speak to them, and then they would do some role playing so the students could actually practice what to do if an unfamiliar adult tried to approach them.

Step 7—Arrive at Generalizations

Students' Generalizations
1. Sometimes children don't see danger.
2. Children trust people and animals.
3. Children usually look to grown-ups for help.

Step 8—Evaluate

The emphases in this model are on increasing the students' abilities to articulate their own views of a situation and increasing their abilities to see that same situation from the perspectives of others. To do this, they must begin to realize that often others literally have not seen or heard exactly what they have. In addition, because of views held previously, others may not interpret what they have seen or heard in the same way. These are complex ideas, even for adults, but they are the foundation for resolving conflicts in a constructive manner.

Summary of Steps in the Resolution of Conflict Model

1. *List all facts pertinent to the conflict:* These data should be written down and visible. The facts will form the basis for further deliberation. What happened? What did you see? What did you hear?

2. *Identify the reasons for the actions and feelings of the participants, and the reasons for those feelings:* Why did . . . do . . . ? How was . . . feeling? Why was . . . feeling that way?

3. *Propose solutions and hypothesize about their effects:* Ask students to think of solutions to the conflict and to articulate the effects on the persons involved.

4. *Decide on the best solution and hypothesize about consequences:* Students consider the proposed solutions and choose the one they think is best. They should give their reasons. How would that make everyone feel? Why would the people feel that way? Is it possible to be fair to everyone?

5. *Discuss similar situations:* How did the participants feel and why?

6. *Evaluate the decision and look for alternative solutions:* Students try to imagine the effects of the action chosen and they look for other solutions and their impact.

7. *Arrive at generalizations:* How might people in similar situations behave? Why would they behave that way?

8. *Evaluate:* Have the students improved in their ability to propose solutions that take everyone's feelings into account?

Courtesy: The most important goal in these discussions initially is courtesy. Students need to understand that what teachers value most is their being polite to one another. Students who are afraid of being ridiculed or misunderstood are not going to present their views; only when students trust one another will they share their ideas.

Listening: Students can listen attentively without having the same views or agreeing on most points. Disagreement is healthy. More thoughtful ideas emerge when students differ, and when they challenge one another, as long as they do so politely. This is only possible when students listen to one another—really listen—rather than preparing their own responses while appearing to listen. Instead of attacking a view that a student does not agree with, however, students should be encouraged to say "I understand that your point is . . . ; however . . ." They may also politely question "Why do you think that?" or "What would happen if that were done? How would the others feel?"

Participation: Participating without dominating is essential. If a student continues to dominate or to be rude or to belittle another student, ask him or her to sit out for one or more discussions, possibly keeping track of how many times participating students respond.

Views: Later, the thoughtfulness and originality of views will be given more weight.

EXERCISE 12.1

Mark true or false beside the following statements. You may disagree with our answers, and your reasons may be perfectly sound. These are judgment calls, not absolutes.

1. Teachers should fire questions rapidly to keep students from getting restless.
2. When a student has answered a question incorrectly, let him or her know right away.
3. A resolution proposing no action is incorrect.

Possible Answers to Exercise 12.1
1. False. Rapid discussion is frequently not thoughtful discussion. Encourage a slow, thoughtful pace. One way to do this is not to always call on students whose hands go up first.
2. False. Not in this model. You hope the ensuing conversation will serve to clarify the points of error. Even if it does not, this is not a right-or-wrong kind of investigation.
3. False. There may be valid reasons for taking no action. The reasons should be stated. ■

Basis for the Resolution of Conflict Model

Educators often believe that the speed with which a youngster goes through each intellectual stage is indicative of intelligence. Hilda Taba believed that the depth of each stage was more indicative of intelligence. Participating in inductive questioning, as in the resolution of conflict model, is one way of increasing the complexity and depth of youngsters' thought processes:

> The funded capital of human experience is more successfully transmitted through a goal seeking type of experience (inductive questioning) than through a formally organized passing on of information from the notes of the instructor to the notes of the student without passing through the mind of either.[6]

As we are inundated with more and more data today, there is a tendency to "cover" material quickly. Many of our standard tests make this a necessity. Frequently the lecture method and other methods of conveying material quickly do not engage the student intellectually or emotionally, and the learning is transitory. Learning that stays with the student occurs when the student interacts with others, when the student is verbalizing his or her own ideas, and when those ideas are reacted to, even challenged.

According to Taba, a genuine learning experience involves the emotions of the learner. We all have our private core, that arena where thoughts and feelings merge to dictate behavior. If learning is to be effective, it must have an impact on that inner world. "The fundamental point is that the quality of the inner subjective world, created by each individual and used by him to guide impulses into behavior, is the heart of the education process."[7] This is not to discount the importance of data. Each of these models is predicated upon and acts upon data. The data conveyed by the class in the ensuing Lincoln discussion became more meaningful to the students as they acted upon and fit that data into a larger picture.

Since the writings of Descartes, Western society has tended to view the intellectual realm and the emotional realm as quite separate, even mutually exclusive. This Cartesian view has created many stereotypes, such as the unemotional mathematician and the overemotional artist. One skeptic of this separation is Israel Scheffler, director of the Philosophy of Education Research Center at Harvard. In an article entitled "In Praise of Cognitive Emotions," Scheffler writes,

> Strongly entrenched, this opposition of cognition and emotion must nevertheless be challenged, for it distorts everything it touches: Mechanizing science, it sentimentalizes art, while portraying ethics and religion as twin swamps of feeling and unreasoned commitment. Education meanwhile—that is to say, the development of mind and attitudes in the young—is split into two grotesque parts—unfeeling knowledge and mindless arousal. My purpose here is to overcome the breach by outlining basic aspects of emotion in the cognitive process.[8]

It is always exciting when scientific findings begin to support gut instinct. In the introduction to his intriguing book, *Descartes' Error*, Dr. Antonio R. Damasio, a neurosurgeon, writes,

> Although I cannot tell for certain what sparked my interest in the neural underpinnings of reason, I do know when I became convinced that the traditional views on the

nature of rationality could not be correct. I had been advised early in life that sound decisions came from a cool head, that emotions and reason did not mix any more than oil and water. I had grown up accustomed to thinking that the mechanisms of reason existed in a separate province of the mind, where emotion should not be allowed to intrude, and when I thought of the brain behind that mind, I envisioned separate neural systems for reason and emotion.[9]

However, Dr. Damasio then gives examples of patients who had suffered brain damage. When the physical structure of their brains was repaired, these patients remained unable to make decisions, to behave in a socially appropriate manner, and to inculcate basic values into their lives. These capabilities had been present before the damage occurred. He states,

This is Descartes' error: the abyssal separation between body and mind, . . . the suggestion that reasoning, and moral judgment, and the suffering that comes from physical pain or emotional upheaval might exist separately from the body. Specifically: the separation of the most refined operations of mind from the structure and operation of a biological organism.[10]

Dr. Damasio adds,

The role outlined for feelings in the making of rationality has implications for some issues currently facing our society, education and violence among them. . . . Let me comment that educational systems might benefit from emphasizing unequivocal connections between current feelings and predicted future outcomes, and that children's overexposure to violence, in real life, newscasts, or through audio-visual fiction, downgrades the value of emotions and feelings in the acquisition and deployment of adaptive social behavior.[11]

Although a relationship between intellect and emotion is convincingly established in the book, the physical connection Dr. Damasio has witnessed does not mean that schools should become places where everything must be warm and fuzzy, where the student must receive positive feedback whether or not he or she deserves it, where confidence is built at the cost of academic stringency. The relationship between intellect and emotion is still a mystery, but we do know that a relationship exists. We know it scientifically, and we know it empirically in the classroom when students become curious, incurably curious, until the current puzzle is solved to their satisfaction. We know it because when students enjoy academic success, when they experience that "Aha!" sensation, they become excited, sometimes frantically excited. Although emotion can be a hindrance when one is trying to find out what has caused a fight, it can be a crucial ally in the quest for intellectual answers.

It has been our experience that students reach their deepest insights when they are most excited. Indeed, are not intense curiosity and fervent caring what drives intellectual pursuit through its often lonely and frustrating periods? When reason is employed in the classroom in ways that excite and stimulate students, students reach their deepest understandings. Two examples follow.

High School Scenario

The class is an advanced American history class taught by Mr. Moore. The class has just studied the Civil War. Mr. Moore is concerned that the students, sophisticated as they are, still view President Lincoln's behavior prior to the war as indecisive and weak and that they have little understanding of the man. To get beyond this superficial grasp, to get into the situation and the man, Mr. Moore has decided to use the part of the resolution of conflict model dealing with feelings. The class has used this model several times.

To introduce this strategy, Mr. Moore reads aloud the first stanza from Vachel Lindsay's poem "Abraham Lincoln Walks at Midnight":

> *It is portentous, and a thing of state*
> *That here at midnight, in our little town*
> *A mourning figure walks, and will not rest*
> *Near the old courthouse pacing up and down*[12]

Mr. Moore and the class have discussed the word *portentous;* Mr. Moore's questions to the class are "Why is President Lincoln pacing up and down? What is he feeling?"

In step 1, the students compile a database, which in this case is not taken from the poem but from their knowledge of the real conditions Lincoln was facing as he paced. You will notice that Mr. Moore will challenge the students about whether their contribution to the database is fact or inference. You may want to do this with classes that are used to the model. If the point is sound, Mr. Moore will write it on the chalkboard.

Step 1

MR. MOORE: What was the situation in this country that led up to the crisis President Lincoln was facing? Be as factual as possible.

SALLY: Going back a little, the Missouri Compromise, instead of helping, had increased the focus on the issue of states' rights and slavery.

JESS: By demanding that the South abolish slavery, Garrison had actually united the South. These feelings continued to intensify into an either/or frame of mind.

MR. MOORE: Is that a fact or an inference?

JESS: A fact. . . . On page 185 it states . . . (Mr. Moore wrote: Garrison's demands united South).

BEN: But the Compromise of 1850 had helped decrease tensions for a while.

MR. MOORE: Can you prove that?

BEN: (Finds a statement that tensions decreased, but it did not specifically state the cause. The class decided the relationship was obvious, that one could hardly conclude otherwise, so the statement stood.)

The class continued to compile a database, mentioning things such as the Kansas-Nebraska Act, the Dred Scott decision, Fort Sumter, and Lincoln's inability to trust those close to him. Those close to him had their own biases and were telling others that they had Lincoln's backing. He also knew that the iron workers in Pennsylvania and the wool growers in Ohio couldn't compete with England because of low tariffs supported by the South. He knew, too, of the suffering of the slaves.

BEN: He realized that instead of calming down, everyone seemed to be getting angrier.

JANE: And he didn't know what to do about Fort Sumter.

Mr. Moore decided it was time to move on to step 2.

Step 2

MR. MOORE: I think that is sufficient background. Why do you think President Lincoln was pacing up and down at midnight? What was he feeling as he paced, and why?

SHIRLEY: He was angry.

MR. MOORE: Why do you think he was angry, Shirley?

SHIRLEY: Because he had been deceived by his own secretary of state and others. They had substituted their own versions of Mr. Lincoln's views in critical messages, versions that would promote the actions they wanted.

ANNE: I think he felt betrayed.

MR. MOORE: Why did he feel betrayed, Anne?

ANNE: Because he felt he couldn't trust anyone. Remember he said, "If you can't trust your own Secretary of State, whom can you trust?"

BEN: Going back to what Shirley said, I don't think he felt angry. I think he felt indecisive and powerless.

MR. MOORE: Why do you think he felt indecisive and powerless rather than angry?

BEN: If you're angry you usually take action. If you're indecisive, you pace. Remember, the *New York Times* had called him indecisive. If he had been angry, the secretary of state and others would have been more frightened of him, less apt to cross him.

TED: But they implied he was indecisive because he was weak. I don't think his indecision came from weakness.

MR. MOORE: Can you explain what you mean, Ted?

TED: I'll have to think about that for a minute.

MR. MOORE: Take your time. Meanwhile, the rest of you think about this: Was Mr. Lincoln's apparent indecision caused by weakness or strength or something else? (Silence.)

TED: A weak man might have gone along with what all the vocal people wanted and defended Fort Sumter knowing that meant war. It took courage to wait. Lincoln's indecision stemmed from his wisdom and his feelings, not from fear. He saw the bind the South was in. He also saw that the new nation couldn't survive secession. He saw, too, how horrible a war would be. But he felt powerless to stop things and silence the hotheads.

JANE: Yes, the message he sent to Fort Sumter backs up what Ted is saying. He tried to give the Confederacy a way of saving face.

MR. MOORE: How, Jane?

JANE: By saying he was only sending provisions, not ammunition, to the fort. By doing that he was preserving the status quo, not being aggressive.

JERRY: I think he felt all those things: anger, sadness, frustration, indecision, powerlessness, betrayal, fear. He was driven by so many conflicting emotions he couldn't sleep. He had to pace.

(Because the class had discussed steps 3 and 4 at length earlier, Mr. Moore went right to step 5.)

Steps 5 and 6

MR. MOORE: I know you all have never been president of the United States, nor have you tried to stop a war, but have you or anyone you know ever been in an impossible situation where you have tried to prevent trouble and where nothing you could do seemed right? (Pause.)

SHIRLEY: Well, this didn't even happen to me, but when my uncle was called to go to Vietnam he was pretty frantic. He believed in being patriotic, and he believed in obeying orders, but he also couldn't understand why we were going. He had heard of people leaving the country, but he didn't think that was right either. He said it's terrible when you're in a situation where nothing seems right. That's the situation Lincoln was in. He wasn't carried away by the glamour of the war. He knew it would be a nightmare. But he couldn't stop it.

MR. MOORE: Do the rest of you see some comparisons between Lincoln's feelings and the feelings of people in similar situations?

SALLY: Yes, in a minor way. It's funny to think of the president of the United States being helpless.

PAUL: Couldn't Lincoln have gotten the leaders in the North and South to sit down and talk?

JANE: Sally, what did you mean about Lincoln's being helpless?

SALLY: I'm not sure exactly. It's as if Lincoln saw more than what was around him, like Congress and the Cabinet and armies and messages and betrayal.

TED: Yeah. He saw the big picture. I mean, he didn't like slavery, but he could understand how dependent the South was. He wasn't mad at anybody. He felt sorry for them all. It's sort of like Shirley's uncle. He just felt helpless.

MR. MOORE: Do you think Lincoln could have gotten the leaders together and talked?

SALLY: I don't think so. That's what I meant by the big picture. He knew so many forces had been set in motion—and everybody was so spread out—in the North, the South, and the territories—it would be hard to change the direction of events.

TED: Yeah—not just forces but emotions. People felt so strongly that they talked themselves into action.

JANE: They didn't really think about consequences. Very few people had his vision. That's why he paced.

Gradually the students had painted a picture of a man tortured and struggling, a specter who caused people to start from fear, not of him, but of a situation in which events were out of control and leading inexorably to what would be a horrible war. By trying to understand some of the feelings of the man, the students had come much closer to understanding Lincoln and the moment than if they had just stayed with the facts. They also obtained a glimpse of the loneliness and powerlessness of this man at the top.

These are only inferences; no one can know precisely what Lincoln was feeling. But actions stem from both thoughts and feelings, and Lincoln's actions appear to point to the students' conclusions. We can try to study a situation in all its complexities and then imagine what feelings those events would engender. History examines concepts and thoughts, but feelings also play a role in the intricate realm of cause and effect. They are more obscure and less easily documented, but they may play the larger role. To ignore them because they are elusive may distort our picture of the past more than any attempts to assess them, as long as we are careful to remember we are making assumptions.

Elementary School Scenario

Mrs. Jones had decided to try a resolution of conflict discussion with her third-grade class using Hans Christian Andersen's short story "The Ugly Duckling."[13] She read the story to her class up to the point where the mother duck had taken her ducklings to the big pond and the other birds had picked on the ugly duckling and made him miserable. The class then made a database on the chalkboard.

In step 2 she had asked questions such as: Why had the mother duck taken her ducklings to the big pond? How were the other ducks in the pond feeling before the mother duck arrived? Why? Did they want more ducks around? Why? Why not? How did the old matriarch of the ducks feel? Why? Why did the turkey cock single out the ugly duckling? How did picking on the ugly duckling make the turkey cock feel? Why? How did the mother duck feel? Why? How did the ugly duckling's brothers and sisters feel about him? Why? Sometimes one reason is sufficient; other times you may want to ask if there are other reasons.

We pick up this discussion in step 3, when the students talk about how this problem could have been solved:

MRS. JONES: What could each of these characters have done to make the situation less painful for the ugly duckling? (Pause.) What are some things the old queen could have done to make the ugly duckling feel better?

BILLY: If she had accepted him, the other ducks would have accepted him too.

MRS. JONES: How could she have done this?

ANNE: She could have praised him for being a strong swimmer or for being big.

MRS. JONES: Would this have changed the attitudes of the other ducks?

BILLY: Yes. They really liked the old queen and wanted to please her.

SARAH: Lots of times kids copy the way older people act.

MRS. JONES: So you think the other ducklings would have made friends with the ugly duckling if the queen duck had?

ANNE: Yeah! Even the mother. She tried to stick up for him at first, but then even she stopped.

MRS. JONES: And what about the ugly duckling? Were there things he could have done to make things easier for himself?

BILLY: If he had tried to impress the old queen she might have become his friend.

MRS. JONES: How could he have done that?

BILLY: He could have bowed elegantly. He could have sat up straight and proud.

CHAD: Maybe he could have found her an eel's head.

WHIT: Maybe he could have talked it out with her, told her how he felt and asked for her help.

MRS. JONES: What could he have said?

WHIT: Maybe he could have said that there are lots of different kinds of ducks, and maybe he was a special kind.

PETE: He should have painted himself brown.

MRS. JONES: Would looking more like the other ducks have helped?

BILLY: Yeah. Looking so different, his brothers and sisters were afraid he was making a bad impression for the family.

MRS. JONES: Why do you think we're uncomfortable when someone is different?

CHAD: Because you don't know what he might do.

WHIT: Yeah, you're not used to him.

PETE: He could have hit the other ducks.

ANNE: Ducks don't hit.

PETE: Well, he could have bitten them and flapped his wings. After all, he was bigger.

MRS. JONES: What do you think they would have done?

ANNE: Maybe they would have stayed away and been afraid of him.

EMILY: Maybe they would have been his friend because they were afraid not to.

WHIT: Maybe they would have bitten him back.

MRS. JONES: Do you think it takes more courage to bite him back or to not bite him back?

WHIT: Not to. It's like hitting on the playground. You have such an urge— such an urge to hit back, but you know you'll be in trouble.

In some conflicts, resolutions are possible when only one participant changes his or her behavior; however, often they are possible only when several participants change their behavior. This was the case here, and Mrs. Jones needed to encourage the students to be specific. Questions like "How could he have done that? What could he have said?" helped students do this.

Mrs. Jones used this discussion as a springboard to discuss how we treat people who are different. In step 5, she inserted a few questions such as: Had the students had experiences with someone different? How had they felt? Had they felt friendly? Competitive? Uneasy? Excited? Envious? Had they felt the new person might be a threat? Do people who are different, as the ugly duckling was, make us feel uncomfortable? Curious? Friendly? Smug? Why? How might these feelings affect our actions? When you feel comfortable with this model, you can adjust it slightly to perform specific tasks or to fit specific situations.

Summary

In Stephen Ambrose's account of the expedition of Lewis and Clark, *Undaunted Courage*, he described Thomas Jefferson's goals. One of these goals was to court the Indians Lewis and Clark encountered and to convince them that the mission was peaceful and that they wanted to trade. At one point, the expedition found itself near the territory of three Indian chiefs who did not get along with one another. Captains Lewis and Clark invited all three chiefs to join their campfire. Through sign language and interpreters, each chief presented his position. At the conclusion,

> the captains said they would proceed to Broken Arm's camp in the morning, and see how many horses and saddles they could collect. This was satisfactory to Twisted Hair and Cut Nose, who had calmed down considerably after being allowed to tell their sides of the story.[14]

Resolving conflicts is not a simple task, but frequently just being able to express one's perspective, being able to describe one's position and the reasons for it, and having others listen, really listen, has a very calming effect. Unfortunately, as Mr. Scheffler's quote indicated, instead of recognizing the role and the power of emotion—for good and for evil—our Western view has encouraged us to deny our emotions, thinking that denying them will contain them. Consequently, most of us have thereby failed to capitalize on the positive side of our emotions and failed to subdue the negative side.

There is a cycle in our lives in which thoughts and feelings dictate actions. These actions cause more thoughts and feelings that dictate further actions. Suddenly we are caught up in events dictated by an action taken long ago, often without sufficient consideration. In this complicated cycle that produces the momentum that directs our lives, exploring and examining feelings may be one key to breaking down barriers between people and allowing them to stand briefly, albeit hypothetically, in another person's shoes.

As our world becomes smaller and more crowded, it becomes more important to learn techniques for arriving at fair and amicable resolutions to conflicts. This model can help students communicate more effectively, resolve conflicts more equitably, and exert more control over the direction of their lives.

WEB RESOURCES

1. http://www.stark.k12.oh.us/Docs/units/conflict

A development team at Crenshaw Middle School in Canton, Ohio, developed this unit on resolving conflicts peacefully. In it, they addressed three questions: What is conflict resolution? Why is conflict necessary? What can be done to resolve a conflict?

2. http://eric-web.tc.columbia.edu/digests/dig97/html

A Directory of Anti-Bias Educational Resources and Services is the result of a survey intended to identify anti-bias projects conducted recently by the ERIC Clearinghouse on Urban Education. This ERIC digest describes the different approaches to bias reduction and violence prevention taken by these projects.

3. http://www.ed.gov/databases/ERIC_Digests/ed387456.html

This digest prepares teachers to handle conflict resolution and peer mediation, and to attempt to prevent violence in their classrooms.

4. http://www.clcrc.com/pages/conflict.html

This site asserts that conflicts can be valuable when they are handled constructively. Following a definition of conflict and a discussion of the potential benefits of constructive conflict, an approach to teaching conflict resolution is provided.

5. http://www.education-world.com/a_curr/curr170.shtml

This site offers easily accessible links to 10 web sites that provide a wide range of practical materials for supporting and instituting school conflict resolution programs.

6. http://www.thirteen.org/peaceful/resources.html

This site includes a listing of organizations and readings related to conflict resolution and violence prevention under such topics as "bias awareness," "media literacy," "academic controversy," and others.

N O T E S

1. Lewis Carroll, *The Annotated Alice* (New York: Bramhall House, 1960), 129–130.

2. Hilda Taba, *Hilda Taba Teaching Strategies Program*, Unit IV, Secondary Edition (Miami: Institute for Staff Development, 1971). Dr. Taba originally devised the resolution of conflict model. She referred to it as a strategy under the umbrella term *model*, which included all her strategies for thinking. We refer to each strategy as a model, because each is a step-by-step procedure that leads to specific learning outcomes. This model combines some of her steps.

3. Margaret J. Wheatley, *Leadership and the New Science: Learning about Organization from an Orderly Universe* (San Francisco: Berrett-Koehler, 1992).

4. Taba, 7. These steps have been changed slightly.

5. "Red Riding Hood," in *A Child's Book of Stories* (New York: Duffield & Co., 1986), 57–60.

6. Taba, 157–158.

7. Taba, 161.

8. Israel Scheffler, "In Praise of Cognitive Emotions," *Teachers College Record* 79, no. 2 (1977): 171.

9. Antonio R. Damasio, *Descartes' Error* (New York: G. P. Putman's Sons, 1994), xi.

10. Damasio, 249–250.

11. Damasio, 247.

12. Vachel Lindsay, "Abraham Lincoln Walks at Midnight," in *Collected Poems* (New York: Macmillan, 1923), 53.

13. "The Ugly Duckling," in *Andersen's Fairy Tales* (New York: Grosset & Dunlap, 1945), 70–83.

14. Stephen E. Ambrose, *Undaunted Courage* (New York: Simon and Schuster, 1996), 362.

13 The Values Development Model

Mining the Curriculum for Ethical and Social Values

Every teacher can recall incidents in teaching that, in retrospect, turned out to be watershed events. That term best described our experience a few years ago as we observed a teacher teaching a short story by Molly Picon to a group of level-four 10th graders. (In this particular school, primarily level ones go to college.) The story is entitled "I'll Give You Law!"[1] The main plot is simple: A boy and his grandmother find a very expensive pendant. The grandmother promptly turns their find over to the lost and found at the police station, where the officer at the desk explains to her that if no one claims the pendant and chain within 90 days, then by law the jewelry is hers to keep. Every day she goes to the station to admire her found treasure, and every day, to her relief, she learns that no one has claimed it. Finally, the day of her dreams arrives and the pendant belongs to her, to wear forever and to cherish as an heirloom for her grandson. Then comes the inevitable—another woman arrives at the door to retrieve the necklace, despite the police officer's protest that by law she now has no claim to it. "I'll give you law!" she yells. "That's my necklace and I want it back."

So that is the dilemma that arises on the next to last page. At this point, the teacher asked the students to stop and predict what the grandmother would do—would she give the pendant back or keep it, as by law she was entitled to do? What would they do if they were in the same situation? What the students got from the conversation that followed varied, undoubtedly. Of course, they had read enough stories to know that in the end the "foolish" grandmother would give the pendant back, and the teacher knew enough not to tell the students what they should say, but there was no way he could be truly neutral on the question either.

It was at that moment that every adult (and maybe some of the students) in the room realized that this story, like most stories, is about values. Issues of character come into play where dilemma exists—without temptation, there is no ethical or social issue. In the present case, the dilemma came down to a conflict between the precept "Treat others as you would want to be treated" and the contrary precept "Finders keepers, losers weepers." The lost and found pendant is now not the point at all; the plot has been transformed into a vehicle for exploring the character traits of the story's protagonist.

Stories and informational text alike create opportunities for readers to consider values that guide human action. These are issues of character that may be related to the real context of the readers' lives. As we reflect on the experience of Molly Picon's story with these readers, we realize that the whole curriculum of schooling is about the same thing. At a bedrock level, it has everything to do with how human beings shall conduct and comport themselves in relation to one another. In what follows, we shall elaborate that insight and explore what we take it to mean for teaching.

We assert at the outset that the debate over whether teachers should or should not discuss ethical and social values is an empty argument, fodder for bad letters to the editor from the fringes of political and religious fronts. The option not to teach values or to maintain a stance of neutrality in respect to values-laden issues is untenable. It can only say to children "It is up to you. Whatever choice you make is inconsequential, and tolerance demands that we accept all views and choices so long as they do not impinge on the rights of others or violate public policy." Nonsense. School is an instrument of society created precisely because society is formed on principles of sound moral behaviors. Furthermore, the values we do teach will lie not in what we choose to say about values but in what we choose to do, the positions we take on issues, and how we respond to what children say.

As to which values we will teach, that too is a red herring. Our culture, like all cultures, is founded on values that are the thread of our fabric—they are our way of being. They are in the Declaration of Independence, they are in the Constitution, and they are written into the code of every state. Society's values are the basis of legal arguments and decisions ranging from the Magna Carta to the sanction of sports heroes whose transgressions so often form headlines in our newspapers. Though many of these values are written into our laws, most are part of the cultural understandings and mores that guide ordinary civility and good citizenship. We do not mean to imply that these issues are easy to deal with but to suggest that teachers will deal with them, in school and out of school. When Thomas Jefferson wrote the famous words "We hold these truths to be self-evident; that all men are created equal; that they are endowed by their Creator with certain inalienable rights; that among these are life,

liberty, and the pursuit of happiness," he surely thought his toughest audience was the British Parliament. He could not have guessed how long it would take Americans to understand what he said or that some Americans would take umbrage with his claims. Perhaps the implications of this famous pronouncement are difficult precisely because Jefferson was addressing the values that would guide our lives as Americans, values with which we still wrestle.

The values development model is aimed at the specifics of a values-centered curriculum. Consider:

- There are values in the history taught in school (which is the reason that history is under constant revision).
- There are values in the sciences. (A generation ago, the word *ecology* was not in the index of high school science books.)
- There are values in the language arts. (Ever wonder why the people in stories are called "characters" or why character development is such an issue in teaching children to write?)
- There are values in the social studies. (The curricula of civics, sociology, and economics all seek the goals of shaping individual character and promoting civic responsibility.)
- There are values in mathematics. (Where better than in the context of mathematics could one teach the idea that an action on one side of an equation will have a predictable effect on the other side? Life, like mathematics, is a series of actions, choices, and consequences, and in no other subject taught in school are the two most common words *balance* and *equality*.)
- There are values in the fine arts. (In art and music, skills are only part of the curriculum; just as important is the appreciation for the arts that children develop.)
- There are values in every extracurricular endeavor nurtured and promoted in school. (Would it be naive to suggest that how children play the game matters most, that the satisfaction of giving their best in a fairly played contest really is the point of every game?)

The paradox is that most of the time these values are hidden or overlooked or ignored. Yes, there is inherent controversy in raising the issue of values, and it is not a topic often spoken about openly. But for the sake of the argument, we ask you to try on the idea that embedded in what you teach and how you teach are some very important values. These ethical and social precepts are basic to what you teach, so basic they serve as part of the reason you teach in the first place. Try that on—like trying on a new coat in a store. You do not have to buy it, just wear it for a while to see how it fits.

ACTIVITY 13.1

What are the values you can see embedded in what *you* teach (or what you love to study)? Think of your favorite thing to teach (or study), and then ask yourself what values derive from learning it. Think beyond the surface of fact to the deeper levels of meaning and implication. ■

Say, for example, you are a math teacher. You might be thinking "Well, I see how there are values in history, and maybe in science, but mathematics? I am not convinced." To which we would reply, "Why do you teach math? Is it really to prepare students for the next course in the sequence, and then for the next course after that, ad infinitum?" No, and we propose that in studying math and every other subject in school, students and teachers alike must stop to ask "Why are we doing this?" Answers will vary, but as one math teacher has said to us, math is worth studying for one reason above all others. It is elegant—aesthetically, logically, artistically elegant. It can be taught in ways that promote reverence for the aesthetic. And if it is taught without drawing students into an appreciation of its central value, without drawing them into a love of mathematical logic and precision, the subject will reduce to mere algorithm and rule. What is more artistically pleasing than a geometric figure or more perfect than a circle? What is more aesthetically balanced than a two-function graph or the golden section the Greeks incorporated into their architecture? What is more logical than a mathematical syllogism? If $x + y = 27$, and $x = 12$, what is the value of y? How do you know for certain, and is certain knowledge ever possible? (The answer in math is YES!)

The question remains of how teaching can be planned to accommodate the values on which it rests. If we do not plan to teach values, they will be left to chance, and anything so important cannot be chanced!

Steps in the Values Development Model

1. Identify the theme of what is to be taught.
2. Specify the "big question" in what is to be taught.
3. Select supplemental resources on the topic of study.
4. Explore interdisciplinary connections to the topic.
5. Teach the lesson in ways that entice students into caring about what they are learning.

Step 1—Identify the Theme of What Is to Be Taught

The idea of theme refers especially to a subject, an idea, a point of view, or a perception that is developed and expanded on in the process of studying. To identify the theme of study, ask questions like these: What is the basic text we will use to develop this theme? What are the specific skills and applications we are trying to teach? Assuming we are successful in teaching, what should students be able to do after they learn this that they cannot do now? Will knowing and being able to do this make them better citizens, help them to be more responsible or caring?

For a primary-grade lesson on the topic of community, you might decide that *community* is not just a title but a theme in its own right. After all, the word shares its root with words like *communication, communion,* and *communism* and with the ideas of *common interest* and *common good.* You might reasonably and rightfully conclude that many values of the curriculum lie in the study of community. Other lessons will not be so obvious. For example, why do we teach about invertebrates in science? Is it only because educated people ought to know the major animal classifications? More to the point, what could insects have to do with values? Think about theme. Is it possible that the point of teaching students about invertebrates is to help them gain respect for things they otherwise might think despicable? Could the theme be "respect for life"? It is not likely a textbook will say so, but the point of getting the theme out in the open is to bring relevance to the textbook, to make the topic relevant to the lives of the students.

ACTIVITY 13.2

Think again of that favorite topic of yours. Does it seem to have a theme that unites its parts? Make some notes to yourself as to what the theme might be. ■

Step 2—Specify the "Big Question" in What Is to Be Taught

Curiosity and inquisitiveness motivate human knowledge and so must motivate teaching. What "big" question drove people to understand each topic of the curriculum? For the lesson on community, the paradox might concern how a society like ours can achieve unity when we are so plural. On each U.S. coin, the Latin phrase *E Pluribus Unum* appears to answer this big question. Literally translated, the phrase means "from many, one." This could easily provide introduction to a lesson on community, bringing immediately to light the values undergirding the lesson.

For the lesson on invertebrates, one might begin with the information that there are over 1 million different kinds of animals in the world. Of these, 50,000 are vertebrates and 950,000, or 95 percent, are invertebrates. So the big question becomes "Why would we want to refer to a small portion of the world's animals as one thing, vertebrates, and to the other much larger portion as NOT that thing, or invertebrates?" The answer? In the words of one fifth-grade girl: "Because we are the one thing." That out of the mouth of a fifth grader! What could more perfectly set the stage for learning about the invertebrates than focusing on what we have in common with all living things?

Step 3—Select Supplemental Resources on the Topic of Study

The source of how students will live is generally not to be found in textbooks but in the literature of their study. In answering the question "Where is the value in what I teach?" look not to the textbook you teach from. It has been our experience that the textbook will say "what is so." The question the students will have is "So what?" The question that needs an answer is "What now?"

The manner in which textbooks treat important issues is nothing short of amazing. In fear of offending one or another special-interest group, committees that write textbooks more often than not create a neutralized survey. History textbooks, for example, because they fail to emphasize anything in particular, leave their readers to think of the events in the past as mere historical fact, not worth caring about.

Consider, for example, how one U.S. history book treats the events surrounding the Holocaust:

> *Germany is taken over by the Nazis.* Germany was another country where discontent brought change. At the end of World War I, the Germans set up a republic with a constitution, a president, and a congress. Unfortunately, many Germans disliked the new republic. They blamed it for signing the hated Treaty of Versailles. As you learned in Chapter 29, the Treaty of Versailles had held Germany responsible for starting World War I and had reduced that nation's power, wealth, and territory. In spite of these difficulties, the new German government might have succeeded if hard times had not hit Germany. In the years following the war many Germans could not find jobs and there was much poverty. During the worldwide depression of the early 1930s, conditions went from bad to worse.
>
> Taking advantage of widespread discontent, a dictator came to power in Germany in 1933. The German dictator was Adolf Hitler, and his followers were called Nazis. Hitler promised to make Germany a great nation again and to recover the land it had lost. To carry out his ambitions, Hitler began to rearm Germany and set its factories to making war materials.
>
> Under Hitler, Germany once more became a powerful country. But this gain was achieved at heavy cost. Under the Nazi government, people were no longer free. Anyone who disagreed with Hitler lived in fear of the Nazi secret police. The Nazis imprisoned, tortured, killed, or drove from the country anyone who dared speak out against them. They were especially cruel to Jews, whom they blamed for all of Germany's troubles. By the time World War II ended in 1945, the Nazis had killed some six million European Jews. This mass murder became known as the Holocaust.[2]

This selection, typical of textbook coverage, qualifies as a neutralized survey. It sets out by painting Germany as a victimized country whose citizens would naturally gravitate to a hero like Adolf Hitler, a leader who elevated his country once again to the status of a world power. "But this gain" is a phrase that makes the Holocaust almost an incidental event. It suggests that "stuff happens." Because the text fails to emphasize anything in particular, the reader is left to think of the events as mere historical fact, unworthy of caring about.

Too many textbooks are guilty of a fault that is sometimes called "mentioning," the awful tendency to say very little about very much. A lot has to be covered, and so the textbook must make mention of many facts. But the root of the word *cover* has the meaning "to conceal, or hide." The effect of textbook coverage results in the tendency to neutralize by objectification. Perhaps the reason so many people learn to despise what they are taught in school is for precisely the reason that the facts of the subjects taught in school tend to devalue human beings. Textbooks are what they are and perhaps must be, and we are not suggesting that anyone throw them out. They can only do what they do—survey objectively, without voice. There is too much to mention to allow time to explain.

If textbooks do not convey the values we might wish, the question remains, does literature? And does this literature really undergird the curriculum? To answer that question, look carefully at the informational books now available for young people. Eve Bunting has written well over a hundred books for children, among them a story of the Holocaust entitled *Terrible Things: An Allegory of the Holocaust*. The flyleaf summary captures the theme of this moving tale:

> The animals of the clearing were content. They shared the trees and the shade and the cool brown waters of the forest pond. But that was before the Terrible Things came.
>
> The Terrible Things first came for every creature with feathers and caught all the birds in their fearsome nets. Little Rabbit wondered what was wrong with feathers, but his fellow animals silenced him quickly. "Just mind your own business, Little Rabbit. We don't want them to get mad at us."
>
> As one creature after another must leave the clearing, Little Rabbit learns that the Terrible Things need no reason for their actions. He fears for his friends.[3]

In the end, Little Rabbit, too, must leave. He goes away to find someone whom he can tell what he has seen and only hopes maybe someone will listen. *Terrible Things* is a story about the responsibilities that members of a community bear to one another and a story about what the absence of caring can do to a community.

Actually, there are more than 20 stories of the Holocaust for children and young adults, the most famous of all being *The Diary of Anne Frank*. But are books like these merely about the events of 1937–1945 in Germany? Surely not. On the contrary, each is a way of saying there is no room in our small world for prejudices of any kind, one person or group against another. All these books are about justice and fair play, respect for the rights of others and responsibility. They are about the human family as community.

Do not think for a minute that all books about community need be somber. Read the hilarious *Araboolies of Liberty Street* by Sam Swoope. The houses of Liberty Street are all the same, the "little boxes" Pete Seeger warned of in his 1960s folk tune. That is, until the day the Araboolies came. Do they ever have a lesson in tolerance to teach their new neighbors! All the Araboolies know is how to have a good time, much to the great delight of all the children who just love the fact that these new occupants come in so many different colors and have so many strange pets. Of course, one stuffy neighbor wants them run out of town by the army, but in the end the tables are turned.

Or look at *Old Henry* by Joan Blos. Old Henry moves to town into a dilapidated old house, which suits him fine. But the neighbors think he should fix the place up a bit, mow the grass, and sweep the sidewalk. Old Henry would rather read his book, and so a great conflict arises in the neighborhood. The open-ended conclusion to the book is perfect for raising questions of how much we have the right to expect of one another because we live in the same community.

What about invertebrates? Don't textbooks generally do well enough with such a mundane topic? Before jumping to any such conclusion, look at Eric Carle's *The Very Quiet Cricket* or any of dozens of books about the marvelous lives of insects and spiders, the social structure of ant communities, and the language and divisions of labor of bees. Seen as examples of life itself, these wonderful creatures can help students gain perspective and respect for all creation, including human beings.

ACTIVITY 13.3

Back to your favorite topic: What resources other than commonly used textbooks could you use to teach it? The next time you visit your local public library, ask the children's librarian to help you find some children's books on the subject. (It does not matter if you are a high school teacher. Children's books can sometimes be exactly what you need to get your point across. And after all, the students you are teaching will one day soon need to know some good books to share with their own children.) ■

Step 4—Explore Interdisciplinary Connections to the Topic

Interdisciplinary teaching can foster the connections that life outside of school requires. One unfortunate aspect of learning in school relates to the tradition of curricular disintegration. Divisions of the curriculum are an administrative convenience, but they are artificially imposed on human knowledge. Yet there is another side to this story—everything taught in one subject area of school is reinforced somewhere else in a different subject. Furthermore, that reinforcement is constituted of the values that tie the curriculum together. There is more overlap between school subjects than uniqueness within subjects.

For example, the fundamental ideas of balance and equality in equations overlap the idea of balance and equilateral relationships in foreign affairs and the ideas of balance and equilibrium in an ecosystem. The concepts of longitude and latitude are completely reinforced by the concept of plotting data as the intersection of x and y axes and interpreting line graphs. All of these ideas bear a relationship to the bigger issue of how seemingly unrelated values can sometimes be understood only in relationship to one another.

In practical terms, the connected curriculum is created in instructional conversations in which teachers explore the web of information into which fits each topic or piece of information to be taught. For example, one fourth-grade team planned to teach addition, the regions of North America, biospheres, and stories about animals—all during a 2-week period. As they discussed how those pieces of content were connected, they chose *Diversity in Unity* as their unifying concept for the 2 weeks, a theme of value that knitted everything together. Another group of teachers decided that "change" was the value unifying what they had to teach in a few weeks. This was the concept they used to relate tenses in English, evolution in science, revolution in social studies, conversion of fractions and decimals in math, and the short story "The One-Eyed Cat" in reading.

Connecting the curriculum requires a conscious effort to recognize and build the connections that are the point of learning and for learning. In science, ecology could be a topic just as dramatic as the Holocaust. In elementary school, children read books like Chris Van Allsburg's *Just a Dream* and the perennial favorite *The Lorax* by Dr. Seuss. These children's books clearly deal with all of the values mentioned earlier, certainly in the sense that each generation does not merely inherit the earth from the past but borrows it from the future. Responsibility is part of the human condition. Considering that half the earth's rain forests have already been destroyed, that the current rate of destruction is 100 acres per minute, that 100 species of life are destroyed per day, Dr. Seuss was a visionary to write *The Lorax* over 20 years ago. Incidentally, we decided to check to see how current biology textbooks might treat a topic like destruction of trees for commercial gain. Read what one of them has to say about the destruction of rain forests. The science books seem very accurate regarding the dangers of the slash-and-burn policies of many countries (though they never use such words), but something is missing:

> Tropical rain forests are very fragile ecosystems. The soil is poor, and nutrients are easily washed away by the heavy tropical rains. Most nutrients are stored in the vegetation. The soil is not good for farming or for grazing animals, yet expanding human populations have cleared large areas of the forest at a rapid rate. After a short period of high productivity, fertility declines and the soil is quickly eroded. Once degraded, the tropical rain forest grows back very slowly or not at all. The tropical animal species are sometimes unable to recolonize the cleared areas. As this process continues, many species of plants and animals have become threatened with extinction.[4]

What an extraordinary use of the passive voice, with the effect of de-emphasizing the issue of human responsibility to other species of the planet! Without looking too far, we could find two children's picture books on rain forests: *Where the Forest Meets the Sea* by Jeannie Baker and *Rain Forest Secrets* by Arthur Dorros. These authors may not be as accurate on details, but they do get closer to the point.

Step 5—Teach the Lesson in Ways That Entice Students into Caring about What They Are Learning

We emphasize the use of good children's literature in teaching values-centered lessons because literature embodies a major part of the reason, explanation, suggestion, and model young people need in order to come to own the values of their culture. If you are wondering what the recipe is for teaching that literature, we hasten to say there is no recipe. The values live in you, not in your lesson plans, and they are not rules to live by as much as they are the topic of the conversation that defines teaching.

Having said that, we want to suggest a framework for planning and teaching anything. The framework is ARC—anticipation, realization, and consolidation. In the *anticipation* phase of teaching, share with students your thinking about the topic and your plan for teaching it. Let them know why you think it is worth their time to study this topic—what the values are that gave it a place in the curriculum of school. Draw out from students their ideas about the theme, engage them at once in the big question surrounding the topic, ask the students if they have read and studied the topic previously, and invite them to think about where they may have encountered the topic in other places in school. Explain with candor your conviction that caring about what you are learning is the first step toward successful learning.

In the *realization* phase of teaching, model for students the pursuit of curiosity by using multiple sources of information. Look at the textbook treatment of the topic. But look also at the way the topic is handled in a variety of other sources, searching always for evidence of the values perspective the author has taken on the topic. Different authors will take different slants on the same topic, and that is based on the values they see illustrated by the topic. The goal for students here is to make real what may before have been mere abstraction. As the values inherent in the topic come to life for the students, they will want to pursue it for themselves—because they are committed to understanding it.

In the *consolidation* phase of the lesson, work with students to draw together all they have learned and create products that illustrate their understanding. Let them share some of the ways in which their pursuit of the topic has yielded its results. Sometimes the most useful activity to conclude learning is to write about it—whether that writing takes the form of essay or story or poetry or song or choreography. Putting new information in a different form will often bring renewed, even unique clarity to it. The American physicist and astronomer James Van Allen once commented, "I am never as clear about any matter as when I have just finished writing about it."

Students will understand best what they care about most. There is no objective information, no value-free fact. Henri Poincaré, the famous mathematician, astronomer, and philosopher of science at the turn of the 20th century, reminded his readers that "science is built up with facts, as a house is with stones. But a collection of facts is no more a science than a heap of stones is a house." Students (and the educational community) need to understand that education is built up with facts, but to be in possession of facts is not to be educated. Too often, students miss the point of the facts they are asked to learn. Their grades in school reflect their knowledge of "what is so." Where is the conversation for "So what?" Who will ask "Now what?" Who will answer?

Summary of Steps in the Values Development Model

1. *Identify the theme of what is to be taught:* Ask yourself why what you are teaching must be taught, and try to move your answer past the issue of utility. Sure, it may be useful for students to know what they are taught, but how will knowing it affect the kind of persons they are becoming?

2. *Specify the "big question" in what is to be taught:* Most of the mundane facts, information, and ideas that are taught in school were at some point in history earthshaking answers to very important questions. Those questions have centered on humankind's relationship to nature, on relationships among people, and on spiritual concerns. Help students to formulate some of the questions before they begin to study some of the answers. Make sure they also understand that throughout time, people have struggled to get the questions right, and the struggle goes on even now.

3. *Select supplemental resources on the topic of study:* In any classroom, there is always a range of interests, abilities, intelligences, and ways of knowing. If everyone is to know the "same" thing, the widest possible access to that "thing" must be available. Make available to students as great a variety of sources as you can—children's literature, fiction and nonfiction books, Web addresses, films and recordings. All will help ensure opportunity for every learner to learn.

4. *Explore interdisciplinary connections to the topic:* The values in what we teach will often lie in connections that cross the disciplinary boundaries of school. If you teach in a teaming situation, be sure every team member knows all the major topics of every subject. If your teaching is isolated by a departmentalized schedule, raise the questions of connection with the students. You could ask, for instance, "What has the concept of a food web (in science) got to do with social policy (in civics) or with literature (the content of some of Thoreau's essays, for example) or with mathematics (the sheer numbers of organisms at the bottom of the web)?" Lead students to see that all human knowledge is connected, often by the values that make the knowledge important.

5. *Teach the lesson in ways that entice students into caring about what they are learning:* Memory of what is learned depends on caring, as we point out in the chapter on Models for Memory. Teaching well usually depends on the teacher's ability to help students to (1) connect what they are learning to what they already know, (2) get engaged with the process of learning, and (3) reflect on what they have learned. If you plan your lessons around activities that draw on prior knowledge, engage learners, and lead to reflection, you are almost guaranteed to improve the chance of meaningful learning.

Basis for the Values Development Model

The national organization called the Character Counts Coalition, made up of 27 culturally and politically diverse groups, has attempted to specify the values that might guide teaching. The coalition has concentrated its efforts on six core values—trustworthiness, respect, responsibility, fairness, caring, and citizenship. It has defined ethics "in terms of the moral duties and virtues that flow from six core ethical values." It is easy to imagine the thinking that prompted these choices—they undoubtedly stem from the idea of a society in which each individual fulfills his or her own potential and at the same time accepts responsibility for ensuring everyone's right to the same fulfillment. Literature particularly confronts the reader with precisely such issues, values that any literate American could define (the problem arises in their particular application):

Trustworthiness: Trustworthiness embraces four separate values: honesty, integrity, promise keeping, and loyalty.

Respect: This is the duty to honor each person's right to autonomy and self-determination, privacy, and dignity.

Responsibility: The idea of responsibility embodies three values: accountability, self-restraint, and pursuit of excellence.

Fairness: In deciding any course of action or behavior, one should take the interests of others—humans, animals, plants, the planet Earth—into account. This idea embraces equity, due process, openness, and consistency.

Caring: This is concern for the interests of others.

Citizenship: This involves recognition of the obligation of every citizen to contribute to the overall public good, to become involved in public affairs, and to do one's share.

Certainly another group might come up with a different list of specific values than the list created by this coalition, but surely there would be tremendous overlap among all such lists created within our culture. Furthermore, whether we are willing to call a piece of writing by the name *literature* depends in part on whether it does effectively convey or confront values of exactly this kind.

Concern over values development in schools has recently been renewed, spurred by despair over the September 11, 2001, attack on our country from outside its borders and also by dismay over the country's drug problem, rampant crime, disintegration of the family unit, and all manner of threat to the social fabric that defines our culture. Schools will never have within their power the ability to cure all of the ills and trials that confront society and threaten civilization. Nevertheless, parents, educators, and community leaders expect schools to be involved with educating young people about values and morals. Every teacher has a role to play in this, both incidentally and deliberately. This role is played out not just by what we say to our students but also by what we do in the face of conflict and by how we react to what young people say and the questions they ask.

Scenario

Mrs. Garrett had attended an in-service workshop on the values model, and she came away feeling quite confident that she could use the model in teaching her next reading lesson, which happened to be a lesson centered on the children's book *Little Bear's Friend.* "What a natural," she thought. "Issues of family, loyalty, friendship, and responsibility are what this delightful story is about." Her mind raced at once to all the stories of friendship that her second graders would love. The outline of the model almost fell into place by itself.

Mrs. Garrett knew, however, that on any given day, she had to teach more than just the stories and children's literature that formed the basis of her language arts program. She was looking for ways to bring the same sort of enthusiasm to science and social studies and (this was always a challenge) mathematics. "What," she asked herself, "could be gained in the nature of values from the study of the facts of arithmetic?" And then an idea began to form in her mind. The coming lesson in mathematics was on the topic of basic geometric shapes—squares and rectangles, circles and ovals, and various triangles. As she related it to us, her thinking about this lesson went something like this. We are quoting as nearly as we can:

Shapes. Not a hard topic to teach, in itself, but I had to wonder how I might use the outline of the values model to plan this lesson. Where are the values in shapes? I just couldn't see it.

Before giving up on an answer, I asked myself, "What do I want the students to know and be able to do, regarding the basic shapes?" Well, I wanted them to be able to identify the shapes, to distinguish them in the environment, and to have a rudimentary grasp on the defining characteristics of basic shapes, even if they don't use this language.

It occurred to me that the theme of this lesson might be "Integrity." You know, a thing is the thing it is, no matter, as long as it follows the rules. This is a hard idea to teach to young people, but, for example, triangles may be radically different from each other and yet still be triangles if they are enclosed figures with three straight sides. That's the triangle rule.

That took me to the big question, the paradox: How can a thing be both similar and different at the same time? To be called a certain shape, a figure has to be *true* (meaning accurately shaped). And yet, a shape can be true but vastly different from other shapes that are equally true. I knew I'd have to be careful not to get technical about this, but it dawned on me that I could use the ideas of similarity and difference to teach a lot of other things at the same time I was teaching shapes.

Next I paid a visit to the local public library. Our school library is okay, but I needed some books the kids might not have seen before. And did I find them! Tana Hoban has a whole series of books on shapes of all kinds, perfect for my class. A book by Ehlert called *Color Zoo* and one by McMillan called *Fire Engine Shapes* would help me place the idea of shapes in familiar contexts. I also figured we could do some shape poems, like a "diamonte," a poem in the shape of a diamond—two triangles stacked base to base. We could also do some circle poems, in which the lines of the poem start at the outside and work inward to form a series of concentric circles. That would make a nice language arts connection, I thought. We might do shape poems on some values issues, choosing different shapes to represent what it means to be fair, or kind, or honest.

This led me directly to other interdisciplinary connections. In science, we will later be looking at how like things go together—plants, animals, and minerals, basically. And then, different kinds of animals are grouped, of course, just like what we do with squares, circles, and triangles. The connection could be mentioned now and then used later when we get to that unit in science. I remember in college, in art class, we studied cubism. I thought I could show the kids some examples of these strange paintings. In many of Picasso's paintings, he relied on naturally occurring shapes, and I can get some art books from the library to show some examples. Maybe we'll try to do some of these in art ourselves. I figured I'd talk to the art teacher about it, first thing. Then the connection to geography came to me—a map of the United States is full of straight-edged figures. On the other hand, the whole of South America is shaped somewhat like a triangle, almost as if it was torn off of Africa. That thought reminded me of plate tectonics, and I thought the children might not have yet noticed the complementary shapes of the continents.

By now I was just full of ideas, and they would all tie together on this unusual theme of integrity—a thing is a thing, no matter what the variation or orientation, so long as it follows certain rules. Isn't that what integrity is all about? I probably won't even use the word, but I can talk to the children about the importance of consistency, and of being sure the image you project is the image you intend. Being courteous is something we practice all the time, for example, and not merely when the mood strikes us. That's where consistency comes in.

The only thing left was to plan my lesson. It would take a few days, of course, and I planned to start with asking the children to name the shapes they could think of and to give me some examples.

What they gave me was a list of plane and three-dimensional figures. I said to them, "Think of some shapes we see every day."

Susan said, "A circle."

Robert said, "A ball."

And then Melanie piped up, "House. House is a shape, isn't it?"

Now that took some thinking, but then I realized, they're talking about 3-D figures that are made up of combinations of plane figures. The end of a house is a square or rectangle with a triangle on top, for example—which I sketched on the chalkboard.

So I said, "A house has different faces, and depending on where you view it from, you see a different face." At that point I thought to ask the kids if they knew what "two-faced" means. They all agreed that it was a person who says one thing to your face and another thing behind your back. "Right," I said, "like when you look at anything from different sides, you see a different face. Same house, different view." But you know, I would not have thought to ask this if I had not been thinking about values, and specifically the value of integrity.

The math book was pretty good on this particular topic, but the library books were so lavishly illustrated! I read the children the book called *Shapes* by Reiss. Then I gave them an overnight assignment to look for all the examples of squares and rectangles, circles and ovals, and various triangles they could see around them—in nature and in the constructions people have put up. When they came back to class, they all got a chance to share, and we spent some time discussing problems they came across. For example, Robbie asked about the illusion of the train tracks coming together in the distance. "Is that a triangle?" he wondered. We decided that there are often differences between what your eyes tell you and what is actually so. (The issue of integrity arose again, this time a negative example! What you see is not always what's so.) I told them of an architectural curiosity of the National Cathedral in Washington, DC. The designers of this building did not want the nave of the church, surrounded by huge columns, to give the effect of seeming to narrow at the front. They actually wanted the opposite effect, so they placed the columns farther apart toward the front, just far enough to fool the eye into thinking the columns form the sides of a rectangle when they actually violate the rule of rectangles, that opposite sides are equal. (I drew this on the board to make the point, but still not everyone got it until I asked, "What would you have to do to the tracks of a railroad if you didn't want them to seem to come together?" They knew the answer—"Make the tracks go apart the farther they go.")

In order to be sure everyone was fully engaged in this lesson, I let the students cut and paste shapes from magazines into their own shape books. The directions were to put the various shapes of the same kind together—grouping the squares, circles, and triangles, at least, and going to finer distinctions if possible. It worked very well, actually. I think every student got the basic idea of how we decide a thing is a thing because it has the qualities of the "ideal" thing. I feel sure that there will be many other chances to discuss this precept, but for now I'm glad to see that this values model really does apply to subjects in which it might not at first be apparent. At the end of the three days of teaching this math lesson, I knew I had a bonus for my efforts. Not only do I think they know a lot more about the basic shapes, but they have a foundation for using the concept of an ideal, or type of thing, against which to judge the "trueness" of a token, a specific instance of a thing. That just has to be a good thing for them, but one I would have missed if I had not been thinking about the big question as I made my plans to teach my lesson on the basic shapes.

Look now at Table 13.1, a five-column chart of the lesson on shapes that we have described in this scenario. The chart actually provides a template for planning values-centered lessons. The first column lays out the theme of the lesson and specifies the basic text and skills to be taught. The second column specifies the dilemma and values to be incorporated into the lesson. The third column is a bibliography of resources—books and other resources you will want to use in teaching the lesson. The fourth column ensures the connections to other disciplines and topics of the curriculum. The fifth column is akin to a traditional lesson plan—plans for what to do to prepare students for their study, to guide the students in their study, and to bring closure to the study.

TABLE 13.1 Planning Values–Centered Lessons

TOPIC: Shapes

Theme: Integrity	The Big Question	Supplemental Resources	Interdisciplinary Connections	The Lesson Plan
I. Basic text: expository/narrative Grade-level math book	I. The paradox: Things can be different *and* the same at the same time.	I. Expository texts: *Shapes*, by Reiss *Round & Round & Round*, by Hoban *Color Zoo*, by Ehlert *Fire Engine Shapes*, by McMillan	*Science:* Classification *Math:* Integers (whole numbers) *Music:* Identify musical notes and other symbols	I. Anticipation: Brainstorm list of shapes, categorize as two- or three-dimensional Discuss how 3-D shapes are extensions of 2-D (concept of "face")
II. Specific skills and applications: Identifying shapes Recognizing shapes in environment Distinguishing different shapes Sorting by criterial attributes	II. Underlying values: True (meaning accurate) Variety (variations on a theme) Integrity (a thing *is* the thing it is)	II. Narrative selections: *A Fishy Shape Story*, by Joann and David Wylie "Concrete" poems Shape poems, e.g., "diamonte" III. Web sites: http://explorer.scrtec. org/explorerdb/ browse/dynamic/ Mathematics/index.html	*Reading/Language Arts:* Letter shapes *Art:* Cubism and basic elements design *Geography:* Physical features and shapes of landforms	II. Realization: Read in text and in library resources Look for shapes in the environment Create shapes poetry III. Consolidation: Share examples of shapes found in nature, in homes, in pictures, in magazines Read additional shape books Make shape books

A C T I V I T Y   1 3 . 4

Using a blank copy of the values lesson planning chart in Table 13.1 and thinking of a topic you may be teaching soon or would like to teach, fill in a draft plan and share it in conversation with a fellow teacher or your group. The chart will help you get firmly in your mind the values that might be brought into the conversation as you teach this topic. There is rarely a reason to be didactic with children, but by helping them see the values implication of almost everything they study, you'll help them to see connections that make the lesson much more meaningful. ▪

Summary

The curriculum of schools in every culture rests on what is valued in that culture. In U.S. schools, these values are often stated as responsibility, justice, fairness, citizenship, and the democratic principle. The content of schooling, or what a society chooses to teach its children, will reflect values such as these. One might accurately say that the point of schooling is not so much what students learn as it is what kind of people they become. When teachers plan for teaching that acknowledges the values that justify what they teach, their students will have a much greater chance of ultimately putting their knowledge to work in a manner that benefits others as well as themselves. Furthermore, because students can see the value in what they have learned, they will be more likely to understand and remember it.

W E B   R E S O U R C E S

1. **http://www.yahoo.com/education/theoryandmethods/charactereducation/**
   Yahoo.com provides a gateway to sites related to the important and sometimes controversial issues surrounding character and values in education. Several links on this page will lead you to resources for designing curricula, units, and lessons related to the values taught in schools.

2. **http://www.ethicsusa.com/**
   This is the web site of the National Character Education Center. From this home page, click on "Ethics Links" to discover dozens of web sites related to ethics and character education, preschool through college. You can also click on "Join" to join the Character Education Values in Action! Network. Benefits include a free newsletter and access to a discussion board devoted to issues in character education.

3. **http://www.charactercounts.org/**
   This is the home page of Character Counts!, a voluntary coalition that supports character education nationally. The six pillars of character identified by the coalition are respect, responsibility, trustworthiness, caring, fairness, and citizenship. A variety of resource materials are available through the web site. You can also enroll in training sessions and nominate a student for an American Youth Character Award.

4. http://www.cortland.edu/www.c4n5rs/
The State University of New York at Cortland is home to the Center for the Fourth and Fifth Rs, which refer to "respect" and "responsibility." The major effort of the center is to host an annual summer institute in character education. In addition, it circulates a newsletter online, along with articles related to character education nationwide.

5. http://www.communitiesofcharacter.org/
From the home page of Communities of Character, you can find information about numerous resources for parents, teachers, and students concerning character education and training.

6. http://www.nwrel.org/scpd/sirs/7/cu13.html
The Northwest Regional Educational Laboratory offers a review of studies focusing on that crucial part of moral education, the nurturing of empathy.

7. http://www.heartwoodethics.org/
The Heartwood Institute is a nonprofit educational organization devoted to promoting the understanding and practice of ethical values that are the foundation of community among all people, with particular emphasis on children and families. The institute's primary mission is to provide teachers with the resources they need to use literature at every grade level to spread the understanding and practice of seven ethical attributes: courage, loyalty, justice, respect, hope, honesty, and love. Get a quick overview of the institute by clicking on the "About" link on the home page.

NOTES

1. Molly Picon, "I'll Give You Law!" in *High Marks: Stories That Make Good Reading*, ed. Annette Sloan and Albert Capaccio (New York: Amsco School Publications, 1981), 41–46.

2. Howard B. Wilder, *This Is America's Story* (Boston: Houghton Mifflin, 1986), 653.

3. Eve Bunting, *Terrible Things: An Allegory of the Holocaust* (Philadelphia: Edward E. Elson, 1989).

4. Peter Alexander, *Biology: The Living World* (Englewood Cliffs, NJ: Prentice Hall, 1989), 773.

14 Cooperative Learning Models

Improving Student Achievement Using Small Groups

Early in their careers, most teachers discover the power and effectiveness of students teaching other students. For example, a high school teacher who is coordinator of an independent study program supervised three students preparing for the Advanced Placement European History test. She examined the sample history test and found that the first section tested overview knowledge. The second section required an in-depth essay but gave wide latitude in topic choice. The third section was document-based, testing the student's ability to think critically, to manage material, and to write clearly. "A good test," the teacher mused, "testing for in-depth knowledge as opposed to 'skimmer bug' knowledge."

Seeking a way to help these students benefit from one another in their study, the teacher called a member of the history department at a nearby college for assistance in planning the students' programs. "I know how specialized your department is," she said, "so you will probably laugh when I tell you I am proposing that a sophomore, junior, and senior study together and teach each other European history. To do this, I need the entire subject divided into nine broad topics, or questions. I also need suggested readings."

The professor was intrigued, provided the requested materials, and met with the students occasionally. Each student selected three of the broad questions for in-depth study and prepared to teach his or her peers. The students took their work seriously. Because the only knowledge they had on a particular topic came from their research or that of their peers, they checked on each other regularly. The students gained general knowledge of the subject as well as expertise in the three areas studied. The success of this approach was apparent the day of the test: The three students earned top scores! The teacher was struck by this almost untapped source of power in teaching, the students themselves.

The models presented in this chapter are based on the work of educators who had similar experiences with cooperative education. These models are effective not only with advanced students but for most students in almost all grade levels. Further, benefits go beyond academics, with improvements seen in socialization skills and building class unity. Researcher Robert Slavin says of cooperative learning:

> Of course, cooperative learning methods are not new. Teachers have used them for many years in the form of laboratory groups, project groups, discussion groups, and so on. However, recent research in the United States and other countries has created systematic and practical cooperative learning methods intended for use as the main element of classroom organization, has documented the effects of these methods, and has applied them to the teaching of a broad range of curricula. These methods are now being used extensively in every conceivable subject, at grade levels from kindergarten through college, and in all kinds of schools throughout the world.[1]

There is no doubt that the concept of cooperative learning is as old as formal education. Team sports, group science projects, student drama productions, and school newspapers are but a few of the cooperative activities found in most public schools. But occasions for cooperation are relatively rare during students' academic careers.

What social skills must we help students develop in conjunction with their knowledge base? Certainly we want to prepare students to work *independently*. Given the amount of time spent working independently at their desks, students appear to have ample practice to acquire this skill. Working *competitively* must be considered to be important. Students in traditional classrooms often compete for grades, the teacher's attention, and help with their work. Indeed, *competition* appears to take on more importance in schools than in other social settings.

Working *cooperatively*, however, may be the most critical social skill that students learn, when one considers the importance of cooperation in the workplace, in the family, and in leisure activities. If there were no other benefits, the importance of learning to collaborate would justify building a part of the school experience around cooperative learning activities.

Two prominent cooperative education advocates, David Johnson and Roger Johnson, compared traditional classrooms with cooperative classrooms (see Table 14.1).[2] Johnson and Johnson have identified the following five elements critical to successfully implementing cooperative learning:

- The first is what we call positive interdependence. The students really have to believe they are in it together, sink or swim. They have to care about one another's learning.
- Second is a lot of verbal, face-to-face interaction. Students have to explain, argue, elaborate, and tie in the material they learn today with what they had last week.
- The third element is individual accountability. It must be clear that every member of their group has to learn that there's no "hitch-hiking."
- The fourth element is social skills. Students need to be taught appropriate leadership, communication, trust building, and conflict resolution skills so that they can operate effectively.
- The fifth element is what we call group processing. Periodically the groups have to assess how well they are working together and how they could do better.[3]

TABLE 14.1   Comparison of Traditional and Cooperative Learning Groups

Traditional Learning Groups	Cooperative Learning Groups
Low interdependence. Members take responsibility only for self. Focus is on individual performance only.	High positive interdependence. Members are responsible for own and one another's learning. Focus is on joint performance.
Individual accountability only.	Both group and individual accountability. Members hold self and others accountable for high-quality work.
Assignments are discussed with little commitment to one another's learning.	Members promote one another's success. They do real work together and help and support one another's efforts to learn.
Teamwork skills are ignored. Leader is appointed to direct members' participation.	Teamwork skills are emphasized. Members are taught and expected to use social skills. All members share leadership responsibilities.
No group processing of the quality of its work. Individual accomplishments are rewarded.	Group processes quality of work and how effectively members are working together. Continuous improvement is emphasized.

Source: Reprinted from D. W. Johnson and R. T. Johnson, *Learning Together and Alone*, 5th ed. (Boston: Allyn and Bacon, 1999), 72.

Before beginning cooperative learning, inexperienced students may benefit from participating in simulations of effective group procedures. They can practice moving quietly into groups, alternating speakers, attending to the speaker, remaining in the group for the duration of the activity, and allowing all group members an opportunity to participate.

Speaking and listening skills deserve attention also. Jacqueline Rhoades and Margaret McCabe have noted that the four communication skills—reading, writing, speaking, and listening—get uneven treatment in most schools.[4] Reading and writing are the primary focus in most classrooms; outside school, speaking and listening are the important communication skills. In cooperative classrooms, speaking and listening acquire increased emphasis.

Initial speaking skills that must be taught include methods of getting the listener's attention by calling his or her name or saying a simple phrase such as "May I ask you a question?" Next, a skillful speaker makes eye contact and expresses his or her message in the first person. For example, the speaker may say "I think there are several permissible answers" rather than "They said the answer was (b)."

Effective speakers learn to state their thoughts clearly, concisely, and completely.[5] Giving adequate background information to put thoughts in context without losing the main point in detail is a skill requiring practice. For complex concepts, students should learn to rely on visual aids, notes, and outlines, following the examples of competent teachers. Periodic checks for understanding are exercised as well. Questions regarding the content or simply checking for comprehension ("Are you following this?") serve this purpose.

Listening skills include giving attention to the speaker, interrupting if the message is unclear, asking clarifying questions, and paraphrasing the speaker's points. Awareness of responses to nonverbal messages requires practice as well.

Constructive use of group meeting time can be encouraged in several ways. Fostering the use of problem-solving strategies may provide the means for resolving conflict as well as afford opportunities for applying strategies learned in school to real-life situations.

The same may be said for implementing strategies for critical thinking. Students have the opportunity to share the process employed in reaching conclusions by thinking out loud; that is, by verbalizing their thinking step by step as solutions to problems are sought. In short, cooperative learning groups provide an excellent chance for applying skills learned in content areas.

Two models presented in this chapter in detail are Jigsaw and role playing. Three additional models—Team Interview; Graffiti; and Think, Pair, Share—are presented in a less detailed format. These five cooperative learning models have been well researched and are widely used in classrooms. For purposes of illustration, examples or scenarios are used to explain the steps.

Model One: The Jigsaw Model

Steps in the Jigsaw Model

1. Introduce Jigsaw.
2. Assign heterogeneously grouped students to study teams.
3. Assemble expert groups to study material.
4. Experts teach their study teams.
5. Evaluate and provide team recognition.

Jigsaw is used when students are assigned narrative materials to read and learn. The original Jigsaw was developed by Elliot Aronson to increase students' interdependence.[6] Instead of providing each student with all materials to study independently, Aronson assigned students to teams and gave each team member one piece of information. To have all components of the lesson, students were forced to fit their individual pieces together as if they were working a jigsaw puzzle. The puzzle could not be completed unless each team member shared his or her piece.

Step 1—Introduce Jigsaw

Jigsaw may be introduced with an explanation similar to the following:

To help you learn the materials in our new unit, you will be studying with a small group of your classmates, which will be called your study team. There will be four members on your team, and each of you will be responsible for learning as much as you can about one topic that is important to your team. To help you learn, you will have opportunities to study with other classmates who are assigned the same topic. We call this your expert group. When you become an expert on your topic, you will teach your study team everything you have learned. You will be working for an individual grade and a team score.

Step 2—Assign Heterogeneously Grouped Students to Study Teams

Jigsaw is like other cooperative learning strategies in that students are assigned to heterogeneously grouped teams formed by the classroom teacher. By controlling team assignments, the teacher may ensure that teams are balanced in terms of ability, motivation, gender, ethnicity, and other factors deemed important. When students are allowed to choose teammates, friendships tend to determine team membership and many of the advantages of cooperative learning are lost.

To form study groups, the teacher ranks students according to ability and past performance on similar materials. In the example we will use to illustrate the Jigsaw model, the teacher decided to assign her 24 students to 6 teams of 4 students per team. To determine team membership, she began with Mary and numbered 6 students from 1 to 6 in order of ability, with 1 being the highest. The teacher reversed the order of numbering with each 6 students. Then she formed groups of students (study teams) by putting ones, twos, threes, fours, fives, and sixes together. Thus each group had one high achiever, two average achievers, and one low achiever. The procedure is illustrated in Table 14.2.

After the teacher assigns students to study teams, each team meets to get acquainted and select a team name. Each team then constructs a display chart for the bulletin board announcing its team name and membership. Team names and membership for this example appear in Table 14.3.

After the study teams are assembled and names are selected, the rules that govern behavior during team meetings are announced:

1. No student may leave his or her team area until all students have completed the assigned work.
2. Each team member is responsible for ascertaining that his or her teammates understand and can complete the assignment successfully.
3. If a student has difficulty in understanding any part of the assignment, all teammates are asked for assistance before the teacher is asked.

Next, the teacher introduced the new social studies unit for the fifth-grade class in this example entitled "The African American Experience." The focus of the unit is on the civil rights movement of the 1950s and 1960s. In preparation for Jigsaw, *Martin*

TABLE 14.2 Study Group Formation

Ability Level	Class List	Group Number
High ability	Mary	1
	Beth	2
	Jim	3
	Bob	4
	Arlene	5
	Jake	6
High average ability	Kathy	6
	Richard	5
	Billy	4
	Martha	3
	Joanne	2
	Jackson	1
Low average ability	Martin	1
	Simone	2
	Paul	3
	Sonny	4
	Laurie	5
	Wayne	6
Low ability	Dionne	6
	Taylor	5
	Sammie	4
	Gus	3
	David	2
	Sandra	1

TABLE 14.3 Study Teams

1 Warriors	2 Scholars	3 Moguls	4 Superstars	5 Winners	6 Tigers
Mary	Beth	Jim	Bob	Arlene	Jake
Jackson	Joanne	Martha	Billy	Richard	Kathy
Martin	Simone	Paul	Sonny	Laurie	Wayne
Sandra	David	Gus	Sammie	Taylor	Dionne

Luther King, Jr.: The Man Who Climbed the Mountain[7] was read to the students, and news videos from the era were viewed. Terms and phrases such as *civil rights*, *separate but equal*, *integrate*, *segregate*, and *discriminate* were also discussed. Study teams read the appropriate chapter in the textbook, with team members assisting one another in reading as necessary.

Step 3—Assemble Expert Groups to Study Material

After completing the reading, each student in a study team is assigned an expert topic. Mary, a member of the Warriors, received the expert sheet *Working against Discrimination*. Mary had the following four questions, provided by her teacher, to research and learn:

1. What was the subject of the 1954 Supreme Court decision, *Brown* v. *Board of Education of Topeka*? Why did the case go to the Supreme Court?
2. In what ways did segregation affect the lives of southern blacks and whites?
3. What protest strategies did opponents to segregation use? What were the results?
4. What roles did the federal government play in ending segregation? How were federal actions enforced?

Jackson, Martin, and Sandra were each given an expert sheet with a different set of questions pertaining to other topics discussed in the chapter. Jackson's topic was *The Contributions of Rosa Parks*, Martin's was *Participation of Other Minority Groups*, and Sandra's topic was *The Women's Movement*.

The same four expert topics were assigned to team members in the remaining study teams. All students with the same topic to research met as a group to devise the best possible answers to their questions. Mary, Beth, Martha, Sonny, Taylor, and Dionne researched *Working against Discrimination* together. When the experts had a clear understanding of their topic, they planned teaching strategies for presenting the information to their study team members.

Step 4—Experts Teach Their Study Teams

When all students master their expert topics, study teams are reassembled and the experts teach their topics in turn. Each expert is responsible for teaching his or her topic, checking for understanding, and assisting teammates in learning the material.

Step 5—Evaluate and Provide Team Recognition

On completion of Jigsaw, students are tested for the following reasons:

1. To identify what, if anything, must be retaught
2. To assign grades
3. To calculate team scores

TABLE 14.4   Improvement Points Scale

Quiz Score	Improvement Points
More than 10 points below base score	0
10 points below to base score	10
Base score to 10 points above base score	20
More than 10 points above base score	30
Perfect paper (regardless of base score)	30

Source: Adapted from R. E. Slavin, *Using Student Team Learning*, 3rd ed. (Baltimore: Johns Hopkins University, 1986).

Prior to beginning Jigsaw, each student's *base score* is established by a pretest. The base scores for the Warriors were:

Student	*Base Score*
Mary	89
Jackson	82
Martin	83
Sandra	73

Following testing after Jigsaw, teachers can use the scale shown in Table 14.4, developed by Slavin, to determine improvement points. These are figured by computing the difference between base scores and Jigsaw quiz results.

The team score is determined by adding the improvement points for each team member and averaging. Team recognition is based on the team improvement score. The Warrior's team improvement score was 20, as shown in Table 14.5. As promised,

TABLE 14.5   Warriors' Team Improvement Scoring

Student	Base Score	Jigsaw Score	Improvement	Improvement Score
Mary	89	94	5	20
Jackson	82	71	–11	0
Martin	83	100	17	30
Sandra	73	88	15	30
Total team improvement points			80	
Number of team members			4	
Team score			20	

the team with the highest improvement score was announced in the school newspaper and led the lunch line for one week.

Summary of Steps in the Jigsaw Model

1. *Introduce Jigsaw:* Explain the process to the class and explain that they will be working for both individual and team scores.

2. *Assign heterogeneously grouped students to study teams:* The teams are assembled and the rules for the process are explained. Background material is read.

3. *Assemble expert groups to study material:* The students from the teams meet with their expert groups and are provided material to be mastered.

4. *Experts teach their study teams:* Each expert is responsible for teaching his or her teammates the learned material.

5. *Evaluate and provide team recognition:* The scores are calculated and grades are assigned.

Model Two: The Role Playing Model

The purpose in role playing is to give the students an opportunity to work with others in determining how an individual or group might behave in response to a particular situation. Participants in role playing are provided an opportunity to consider how individuals may feel, think, or act when faced with a problem and to consider alternative possibilities.

In most versions of this model, role playing is used primarily as a means to promote classroom discussion. The use of role playing as a cooperative learning model also includes classroom discussion as a vital step, but in this approach the entire class is involved in preparing and presenting role plays through group activity.

It is important to structure the role playing experience so that it does not deteriorate into "clowning around" or "hamming it up." Stating the rules clearly and preparing the class for the exercise are essential.

Steps in the Role Playing Model

1. Choose an interesting situation.
2. Select the teams.
3. Assign the problem and explain the task.
4. Teams prepare the role play and select the players.
5. Assign tasks to the observers.
6. Teams present their role plays.
7. Teams return to their groups to discuss the role playing experience.

8. Class discussion.
9. Evaluate.

Step 1—Choose an Interesting Situation

Ideal for role playing are characters related to historical events such as French workers and aristocrats during the Revolution or Union and Confederate soldiers during the Civil War. Role playing is also an excellent model for exploring solutions to social problems. For instance, young children can role play possible solutions to the problem of a bully on the playground or the problems related to coming home to an empty house after school. Older students could explore such issues as drug abuse and violence.

Another effective role playing exercise is "What if?" For instance, What if the Axis powers had won World War II? What if Abraham Lincoln had lived to complete his presidency? What if the South had won the war? For students who require more structure or for the first time that role playing is used, the teacher may present the groups with possible scenarios. For instance, the teacher may say that each group is to prepare a role play around the situation of a Maryland family gathered for Thanksgiving just before the Civil War in which some of the family members are supporters of the South and others of the North. Or the teacher might present each group with a different scenario. For instance, group 1 could prepare a role play for the scenario just described, and group 2's scenario could involve soldiers meeting in a dense fog in which they could not see their uniforms. The soldiers are sharing their experiences and enjoying one another's company before realizing that they are on opposite sides of the conflict. Group 3 could develop the role play for a scenario in which two men meet after the war. They had fought on opposite sides and were once good friends.

As the class becomes more experienced, the teams should be able to develop their own scenarios, or the class as a whole could develop a number of scenarios from which each team could then select a particular one to develop into a role play.

Step 2—Select the Teams

If the role play is to include research, then having a cross section of academic abilities in each team will be essential. However, an additional factor to be considered in this model is the personalities of the students. Try to assign shy students to groups where they will be encouraged and avoid grouping several very assertive individuals together.

Role playing is an effective way to see students in a different perspective. Individuals who do not succeed as well academically may be successful in this activity.

Step 3—Assign the Problem and Explain the Task

Emphasize that this is a group presentation, not a personal performance. Students are to work together for an effective presentation. The team should select a captain who will be responsible for communicating with the remainder of the class.

Step 4—Teams Prepare the Role Play and Select the Players

The intent is not to write a script and memorize lines but to describe the characters and outline a possible course of action. Encourage the students to do research, if necessary, to clarify the characters or the events. Thus the students select the cast of characters and discuss how these characters are to respond to the situation. For instance, if there is a mother in the role play concerning the family before the Civil War, her personality will be described by the group. She might be very domineering or she might be a very sensitive individual given to fainting spells or she might be a very wise person who is able to help the family resolve some of its problems. Although there is no written dialogue, the group needs to develop the course of events in the role play. For instance, the family will be reconciled or they will part in anger.

For young children, the teacher will need to help identify the various characters and the possibilities for their actions. When the bully picks on a particular person, how will that person react, and how will the bully respond?

Step 5—Assign Tasks to the Observers

The majority of the class will be observers as each team is role playing. The teacher may distribute a checklist of points for the observers or assign specific tasks to various individuals such as observing one character in each of the role plays. A series of questions could be posted prior to the role playing activity that will form the basis for the classroom discussion following the activity, and the observers could be asked to take notes relating to those questions.

Step 6—Teams Present Their Role Plays

There should be a time limit of about 10 minutes for each team's presentation with a warning given at the 8-minute mark. Following each role play, the teacher may choose to lead a short discussion, or this may be deferred to the end of all the presentations. The teacher may wish to have the participants describe their feelings regarding the experience at this point.

Step 7—Teams Return to Their Groups to Discuss the Role Playing Experience

When all the teams have presented, the students return to their teams to discuss the experience and how their interpretation related to that of other teams. During this discussion, the team members are encouraged to discuss how they felt during the role play and what would make the experience more effective. If possible, the teams may be given an opportunity to reenact the role plays after this step. In any event, the team leader prepares a brief report of the issues discussed in the meeting to be shared with the class.

Step 8—Class Discussion

Each of the team leaders presents a brief summary of the points made in the team meeting. The teacher then leads a discussion regarding the role plays and encourages the students to generalize about the experience.

Step 9—Evaluate

The teacher may have students complete evaluation forms, or he or she may interview individual students regarding the experience. A videotaped record of this activity to be viewed by the teacher would also provide valuable information regarding the participation of the class.

Summary of the Steps in the Role Playing Model

1. *Choose an interesting situation:* Select a situation that provides a variety of possible outcomes and character interpretations.

2. *Select the teams:* Choose team members based on both academic and social characteristics.

3. *Assign the problem and explain the task:* Emphasize cooperation and communication in the process.

4. *Teams prepare the role play and select the players:* The teams determine the characters for the role play and the general direction of the action.

5. *Assign tasks to the observers:* Determine what the observers are to focus on during the activity.

6. *Teams present their role plays:* Set time limits and choose the method for follow-up.

7. *Teams return to their groups to discuss the role playing experience:* The team leader will prepare to report the results of this discussion to the class.

8. *Class discussion:* The teacher leads the group in reviewing the process.

9. *Evaluate:* A written or taped record of the process should be kept for future reference.

Additional Models

The cooperative learning strategies described thus far continue to be used effectively in all subject areas and at most grade levels. They represent, however, only two of the cooperative learning strategies that are developed with increasing frequency in classrooms across the United States. Spencer Kagan, founder and head of Resources for

Teachers, has described Jigsaw, along with more than 70 additional cooperative learning strategies, in his book *Cooperative Learning*.[8] Kagan's premise is that it is not enough for teachers to desire to use cooperative learning strategies; they must have a set of *structures*, or lesson designs, that are applicable with many content options. He acknowledges that cooperative learning classroom environments evolve only after students receive direct instruction in necessary socialization and communication skills. Team Interview; Graffiti; and Think, Pair, Share are three examples of models described by Kagan.

The Team Interview Model

Team Interview was developed by Jeanne Stone, a consultant for Resources for Teachers, and may be used, for example, as a getting-acquainted activity, a team-building activity, a method for checking reading comprehension, or a method for group book reports. As a getting-acquainted activity, these steps are followed.

Step 1—Assign Students to Teams

Students are assigned to teams of three, four, or five members. Students are asked to number themselves 1 to 3, 4, or 5, depending on team size.

Step 2—Instruct Team Members

Each team member stands in turn and is instructed that he or she will respond to questions from teammates for a specified amount of time, usually 60 to 90 seconds.

Step 3—Conduct Interviews

Team members ask the standing student (interviewee) questions about his or her background, family, likes, dislikes, interests, and so forth, in an effort to get to know their peer. Interviewees are instructed to answer the question asked *or*, if they prefer not to respond to the question as stated, the question they wish had been asked. For example, if the interviewee prefers not to state his or her age, he or she may respond by giving the name of a favorite pet.[9]

Step 4—Continue Interviews

The remaining team members are asked to stand in turn and answer questions until all team members have been questioned.

Step 5—Debrief

The teacher debriefs the teams with questions such as the following: "How did the mood of the team change from the first to the final interviewee?" "Did the level or nature of the questions change? If so, in what way?" "Are there additional questions that you want to ask the first or second interviewees now that you have had more experience?"

As a reading comprehension check, team members are assigned roles as characters in a story or book and are interviewed as those characters. For book reports, students may take the role of either a character in the book or the author. In a social studies class, students could become either historical characters or witnesses to well-known historical events. Using the latter strategy, students can write and perform a newscast based on the interview information.

The Graffiti Model

Graffiti is a cooperative learning structure in which students are asked to give written responses to questions posed by the teacher.[10] Graffiti is an excellent way in which to check for understanding, to evaluate instruction, or to do an informal needs assessment.

For the purpose of this example, assume that a class has been divided into four groups with five members in each group. The teacher announces that the topic for the day is a review of their Civil War unit in preparation for an upcoming test.

Step 1—Prepare Graffiti Questions

The teacher prepares four review questions for the unit and writes each question in large print on a separate sheet of paper, 3 feet by 5 feet or larger. Sample questions for a social studies unit on the Civil War might include:

1. Name a Confederate political leader and describe one of his contributions.
2. Name a Union political leader and describe one of his contributions.
3. Name a major battle and state its outcome.
4. List a major resource and its importance to the Union states.

Step 2—Distribute Materials

Colored markers are distributed to team members so that each team has a different colored marker. By doing this, each team can keep track of its own answers.

Step 3—Answer Questions

Each team is given a question, and the teams write their responses on one of the large sheets for a set amount of time, usually 3 to 5 minutes.

Step 4—Exchange Questions

At the end of the timed interval, question sheets are exchanged. The process continues until each team has had an opportunity to answer all four questions.

Step 5—Return to Original Question

Each team returns to its original question. Team members review all the answers on their graffiti sheet, arrange the answers in categories, and arrive at generalizations regarding the categories.

Step 6—Share Information

Each group is given the opportunity to share the information from its graffiti sheet with the full class.

Graffiti has been used extensively by one of us in developing in-service programs with school faculties by having teachers respond to such questions as:

1. How can we help the students in our school be successful academically?
2. What policies and practices are really working in our school?
3. In what areas do we know we need to improve?
4. How can we help our students to feel that they belong in their classes and the school?

Positive responses are reviewed periodically for reinforcement. The areas that teachers identify for improvement can become the basis for in-service training sessions.

Professors in methods classes in teacher preparation programs have used student responses to the following questions in planning pre-student-teaching classes:

1. What frightens you most about your upcoming student teaching experience?
2. What are your greatest strengths regarding what you have to offer children in your classes?
3. Why do you want to teach?
4. Recalling your own school days, what were the characteristics of teachers who you thought were good teachers?

Following student teaching, students are asked to evaluate the program by responding to such questions as:

1. What did you need to know that you did not know when you began student teaching?
2. In what areas did you feel most prepared?
3. What experiences in your college classes helped you most in student teaching?
4. What were your biggest surprises during student teaching?

Responses from the students have been used to modify curriculum and instruction so that each better matches student needs.

Understanding the difficulty in finding cooperative learning strategies for kindergarten and the primary grades, Lorna Curran has published a guide for applying structures for young students entitled *Cooperative Learning Lessons for Little Ones*.[11] She includes Round Table, Line-Ups, Corners, Formations, Partners, and cooperative projects in her guide. In addition to teaching signals, active listening skills, debriefing, and other socialization skills, she recommends using picture representations and extensive modeling to implement cooperative learning in primary classrooms.

The Think, Pair, Share Model

Think, Pair, Share is a simple technique with great benefits. It results in increased student participation and improved retention of information. Using the procedure, students learn from one another and try their ideas in a nonthreatening context before making their ideas more public. Learner confidence improves and all students, rather than the few who usually volunteer, are given a way to participate in class. The benefits for the teacher include increased time on task in the classroom and greater quality of students' contributions to class discussions. Students and teachers alike gain much clearer understandings of the expectation for attention and participation in classroom discussions. The model was first proposed by Frank Lyman of the University of Maryland.[12] There are four steps to Think, Pair, Share, with a time limit on each step signaled by the teacher. (A kitchen timer works well for this.)

Step 1—Teacher Poses a Question

Think, Pair, Share begins when the teacher poses a thought-provoking question for the entire class. This may be a straightforward question or a problem that the teacher presents to the class for solution. Examples include "What would have been the likely outcome if the United States had maintained its isolationist position and not entered the European theater of World War II?" and "What is symbolized by the apple in the story of Snow White?" Low-level, single correct answer questions are to be avoided in this model. Questions must pose problems or dilemmas that the students will be willing and able to think about.

Step 2—Students Think Individually

At a signal from the teacher, the students are given a limited amount of time to think of their own answer to the problematic question. The time should be decided by the teacher on the basis of students' knowledge, the nature of the question, and the demands of the schedule. It may be helpful, although it is not required, to have the students write their individual responses and solutions. The students should understand that although there may be no one right answer, it is important that everyone have some reasonable answer to the question. This step of the procedure automatically builds "wait time" into the classroom conversation.

Step 3—Each Student Discusses His or Her Answer with a Fellow Student

The end of the think step signals to the students the time to begin working with one other student to reach consensus on an answer to the question. Each student now has a chance to try out possibilities. Together, each pair of students can reformulate a common answer based on their collective insights to possible solutions to the problem. At times, the process can be taken one step farther by the teacher asking pairs of students to regroup into foursomes to further refine their thoughts before sharing with the group at large. These small group settings are less threatening to individual students than venturing forward before the whole group with an untried answer. The pair step in the model also promotes much more conversation among students about the issues raised by the question.

Step 4—Students Share Their Answers with the Whole Class

In this final step, individuals can present solutions individually or cooperatively to the class as a whole group. Where pairs of students have constructed displays of their answers, as in a chart or diagram, each member of the pair can take credit for the product of their thinking.

The final step of Think, Pair, Share has several benefits to all students. They see the same concepts expressed in several different ways as different individuals find unique expressions for answers to the question. Moreover, the concepts embedded in the answers are in the language of the learners rather than the language of textbook or teacher. And where students can draw or otherwise picture their thoughts, different learning modalities and preferences can come into play in the attempt to understand the ideas behind the answers.

The success and quality of Think, Pair, Share will depend on the quality of the question posed in step 1. If the question promotes genuine thought for students, genuine insights are sure to emerge in successive steps.

Pointers for Using Cooperative Learning Teams Effectively

It is recommended that study teams be changed at the beginning of each new unit or every 5 to 6 weeks. Changing teams will avoid establishing cliques and will allow many students to get to know and like one another as they study together. Further, if a team appears to be weak academically, students are not penalized over a long period.

In Jigsaw, students grow more sophisticated in identifying main ideas and important information for their expert sheets; thus, as students gain experience with the model, fewer guides may be given, encouraging students to become independent learners. References other than textbooks may be incorporated, along with interviews, films, videos, and original sources.

Role play provides an interesting and stimulating context for increasing the probability that information will be committed to long-term memory. In addition, using these strategies motivates students to review for quizzes and tests.

Basis for the Models

Much of the impetus for the current cooperative learning movement had its origins in the early 1970s when social scientists at the Center for Social Organization of Schools at the Johns Hopkins University were called on to help Baltimore public school teachers manage newly integrated classrooms. The teachers found that children from diverse ethnic groups tended to resegregate themselves in the classroom, lunchroom, and social settings. They sought ways to encourage students to get to know and accept one another. Shared learning activities were developed in which teams of learners could study together, tutor one another, and earn team rewards. When researchers evaluated team learning, they found that students' interaction increased and acceptance of minority students improved, as did the self-esteem of all students.

On another important variable—student achievement—improvement was also reported. Academic achievement gains have been found to occur with such consistency that increased achievement has become one of the principal positive outcomes of cooperative learning. In a summary of 99 studies, Slavin reported positive achievement gains for students in 64 percent of the studies.[13]

In essence, students' opportunities to learn increase to the extent that achievement is nearly inevitable. In traditional classes, most of the students' experience with content is limited to listening and taking notes. In cooperative classrooms, students listen, write, tell, paraphrase, read, illustrate, repeat, and interact. In short, increased modalities are involved so that students who are not aural learners or are poor note takers have many opportunities to explore materials. Students are actively involved with the subject matter rather than being passive receivers of information. Consequently, engaged time tends to increase in cooperative learning classes. The positive relationship between engaged time and student achievement is well documented.[14] Because they are working in small groups, students are less reluctant, generally, to ask clarifying questions and to receive corrective feedback.

More recently, a movement termed *constructivism*, based on cognitive psychology and the work of Jean Piaget, Jerome Bruner, L. S. Vygotsky, and others, has emphasized participation in collaborative group work as an important means through which learners construct their own knowledge. Students working in teams under the guidance of the teacher will, according to this view, "more easily discover and comprehend difficult concepts if they can talk with each other about the problems."[15]

Every teacher has had the experience of explaining a concept repeatedly, only to hear "I don't get it" from students; then a knowledgeable student explains and the concept is understood. At times, students find language to communicate when adults cannot. In the same vein, students are more likely to know and remember information they have taught. When students are responsible for teaching content, they have opportunities to learn during the preparation *and* presentation experiences and retention of the information increases.

In summary, academic achievement increases with the implementation of cooperative learning strategies because students have numerous opportunities to learn new materials. If deficiencies are noted, correction tends to be nonthreatening for students.

Scenario

In science class, Ms. Wright planned a unit on reptiles that combined the concept development and Jigsaw models. During the introduction, in which she used the concept development model, Ms. Wright asked students to tell her everything they knew about snakes. Their responses were listed on the chalkboard.

They're slimy	They lay eggs
They're cold-blooded	They are poison
They kill people	They eat rats
They live in nests	They live in water or deserts
They can be huge—20 feet long	Some are little, green snakes
Snakes have scales	They don't have legs
They hatch out of eggs	They can climb trees
People are afraid of them	They are mean and vicious
Some help by killing rodents	They use their tongues to smell
They eat animals whole	Some poison, but some squeeze
Some have rattles	They hiss
Forked tongues	Mothers leave eggs
On their own when born	Leathery eggs
Fast runners	Bury eggs in sand
Poison with their tongues	They live in holes

Next, Ms. Wright asked the children to list items that seemed to go together. They produced the following groups and labels:

Physical Characteristics	*Reproduction*
Slimy	Hatch out of eggs
Cold-blooded	Lay eggs
Poison	Bury eggs in sand

Not all are poison	Mothers leave eggs
Huge—20 feet long	On their own when born
Eat animals whole	Leathery eggs
Some have rattles	
Don't have legs	
Some little, green	
Use tongues to smell	

Defenses	*Habitat*
Poison	Live in nests
Some squeeze	Live in holes
Hiss	Live in desert
Mean and vicious	Live in water
Kill people	Climb trees
People are afraid of them	Born in sand
Fast runners	

The students were ready for Jigsaw! Each study team member was assigned one topic to study. On the Scholars team, for example, Beth was responsible for *Physical Characteristics;* Joanne was allotted *Reproduction;* Simone, *Defenses;* and David, *Habitat.* After receiving assignments, the expert teams assembled to copy the information generated during the concept formation exercise onto retrieval charts. For the following two class periods, team members researched their topics to correct misinformation and to add new details to the retrieval charts. Affirming that the new information was correct and complete, experts prepared to teach their study teams.

Ms. Wright used this procedure to direct the study of lizards, turtles and tortoises, alligators and crocodiles, and tuatara so that students could understand and make generalizations regarding reptiles.

ACTIVITY 14.1

Select a chapter from a content-area text. List four or five important subtopics presented and develop expert question sheets for each subtopic. Select an appropriate model of teaching that can be combined with Jigsaw to provide an introduction to the chapter. ▪

Summary

In traditional classes, most of the students' experience with content is limited to listening and taking notes. In cooperative classrooms, students listen, write, tell, paraphrase, read, illustrate, repeat, and interact. They are given multiple learning opportunities and generally show greater achievement gains than students in traditional classes. Students are actively involved with the subject matter rather than being passive receivers of information. Because they are working in small groups, even reticent students tend to enter discussions and ask clarifying questions.

WEB RESOURCES

1, http://www.ncrel.org/sdrs/areas/rpl_esys/collab.htm
The North Central Regional Educational Laboratory provides a thorough explanation of the collaborative classroom, including a section on challenges and conflicts.

2. http://www.ed.gov/databases/ERIC_Digests/ed370881.html
This ERIC Digest site describes essential elements of cooperative learning and contains an extensive listing of resources on this topic.

3. http://www.pgcps.pg.k12.md.us/~elc/learning1.html
An Electronic Learning Community guide to cooperative learning, this web site describes commonly used cooperative learning techniques, including several models that were not included in this chapter.

4. http://fga.freac.fsu.edu/academy/k1us.htm
At this web site you will find a series of cooperative learning lesson plans for teaching young children the concepts of global and spatial directions.

5. http://www.interactiveclassroom.com/articles_002.htm
The article "Using Multilevel Young Adult Literature in Middle School Social Studies" describes one teacher's approach to integrating literature in the social studies classroom. Included at the end of the article is an extensive, annotated list of readings that can be used in a Jigsaw exercise.

6. http://www.jigsaw.org./index.html
Visit the official web site of the Jigsaw classroom to read an overview of the Jigsaw technique, a history of the Jigsaw classroom, tips on implementation, and links to other sites on cooperative learning, school violence and its prevention, and the Jigsaw classroom.

7. http://www.asu.edu/
The Arizona State University web site contains an excellent series of cooperative learning web pages, including a description of an interactive lecture that can be accessed directly. From the home page, simply type "cooperative learning" in the "Search ASU" section at the top lefthand corner, and you will find hypertext links to a wealth of information on the topic.

8. http://naio.kcc.hawaii.edu/techprep/wwow/castle/default.html
This web site contains a lesson plan using Jigsaw to teach a science lesson on conventional farming, hydroponics, and organic farming.

NOTES

1. Robert Slavin, *Cooperative Learning*, 2nd ed. (Boston: Allyn and Bacon, 1995), 4.
2. D. W. Johnson and R. T. Johnson, *Circles of Learning* (Alexandria, VA: Association for Supervision and Curriculum Development, 1984), 8–10.
3. Ron Brandt, "On Cooperation in Schools: A Conversation with David and Roger Johnson," *Educational Leadership* 47 (November 1987): 14–25.

   4. Jacqueline Rhoades and Margaret E. McCabe, *Simple Cooperation in the Classroom* (Willits, CA: ITA Publications, 1986).

   5. Rhoades and McCabe, 25.

   6. Elliot Aronson, *The Jigsaw Classroom* (Beverly Hills, CA: Sage Publications, 1978).

   7. Gary Paulsen and Dan Theis, *Martin Luther King, Jr.: The Man Who Climbed the Mountain* (Milwaukee: Raintree, 1976).

   8. Spencer Kagan, *Cooperative Learning* (San Juan Capistrano, CA: Resources for Teachers, 1992).

   9. Kagan, 2.

   10. Barrie Bennett, *Cooperative Learning: Where Heart Meets Mind* (Toronto: Educational Connections, 1991), 210–211.

   11. Lorna Curran, *Cooperative Learning Lessons for Little Ones* (San Juan Capistrano, CA: Resources for Teachers, 1991).

   12. F. Lyman, "The Responsive Classroom Discussion," in *Mainstream Digest*, ed. A. S. Anderson (College Park: University of Maryland College of Education, 1981).

   13. Slavin, *Cooperative Learning*, 21.

   14. Thomas L. Good and Jere E. Brophy, *Looking in Classrooms*, 3rd ed. (New York: Harper and Row, 1984), 35.

   15. Robert E. Slavin, *Educational Psychology*, 6th ed. (Boston: Allyn and Bacon, 2000), 259.

15 Models for Memory

Techniques for Improving the Recall of Information

A second-grade teacher tells of a boy in her classroom who came to her after music class one day to whisper a secret. In a quavering voice, he said that Nancy, the girl sitting next to him, was a witch who used magic. On inquiring just why he had come to this conclusion, the boy said that Nancy could say a magic spell and always get the right answer when the music teacher asked the names of the notes on the chart. "She even says things under her breath about good boys. Maybe, she means me," he said, his eyes wide with fear. When the teacher explained to him that Nancy was recalling the notes by quietly saying the sentence, "Every Good Boy Does Fine," in which the first letter of each word is the name of a note on the lines of the staff, his face lit up with excitement. "Now, I can get the right answers, too," he said.

Like this boy, many children who do not know how to use mnemonics, the techniques for remembering information, think that there is some kind of magic in the process. Only in recent years have we realized that a good memory is not just a gift of nature. Some people are indeed born with exceptional memory abilities, but most acquire these abilities through discipline and hard work. The salesperson who remembers the names of all customers, the teacher who learns the names of all students following the first day of class, and the medical student who remembers the names of all the bones in the body are all participating in a process essential to success.

Even though recall is not the most significant learning process, it is basic to many other levels of knowledge. Some pieces of information require immediate access yet are difficult to recall without a memory aid. For instance, the acronym *Roy G. Biv* quickly gives access to the order of the colors in the spectrum: red, orange, yellow, green, blue, indigo, violet. "I before E, except after C, or when pronounced as A, as in *neighbor* and *weigh*" is a readily available spelling tool, and "Thirty days hath September, April, June, and November" is a calendar aid for the mind. Such mnemonics are essential for remembering what might otherwise be forgotten. The word *mnemonic* derives from the Greek word *mnemon*, meaning "mindful," from which we also get such words as *remind* and *reminiscent*. Ultimately, the word *mnemonic* is linked to Minerva, the goddess of memory.

In addition to mnemonics are many other aids to memory. When students master the techniques, they will have much greater success in finding what they need when they need it. Imagine never having the embarrassment of forgetting the name of a person to whom you were introduced only moments ago!

In this chapter, four basic memory models useful for recall of exactly that kind of information are described: the link model, the loci model, the memory through motion model, and the names and faces model. These four models, as well as some variations, were selected from a large number of possible models that are available for instruction in the classroom. These models can be used by the teacher to teach particular types of information, and for students they are important processes that can be used in retaining information.

Conditions That Affect Memory

It is important to consider some general conditions related to the memory process before considering specific memory models. For instance, physical and emotional states dramatically affect a person's ability to remember. A learner who is hungry or poorly nourished has great difficulty in remembering information. Likewise, lack of sleep and emotional upset hinder retention.

Less obvious are the attitudes that many people have regarding their ability to remember. Many people suffer from test anxiety and fall apart at the prospect of having to recall information under the pressure of an exam. Many individuals are extremely anxious about their ability to retain information in a variety of social situations, so anxious that their palms sweat and their hearts race at the prospect of having to introduce a group of people. Most people accept this anxiety as fate, believing that things like this do not happen to other people.

Many people also experience the frustration that comes in moments when essential facts cannot be recalled, such as during a meeting when a statistic crucial to the

discussion cannot be retrieved or when recommending a book to a friend and suddenly forgetting the title and the name of the author. These momentary feelings of frustration and inadequacy should help teachers bear in mind the constant feelings experienced by learners who lack skill in remembering.

In addition to the specific techniques described in this chapter, attitude and the ability to relax are important to memory. Instead of assuring oneself over and over that "I have a lousy memory," one can say "I *can* remember and I will." The ability to visualize oneself being confident and relaxed in social situations or when called upon to remember can be an effective memory tool.

When the body is tense, the mind cannot function. Exercise also helps the body to relax and the mind to function effectively. Before and during a test, many teachers have students stretch and breathe deeply to relax.

Memory and learning are almost always more effective in conditions of relatively high challenge and relatively low threat. This is what Geoffrey Caine and Renate Nummela Caine refer to as relaxed alertness, which they explain in the following way:

> An optimal state of mind for expanding natural knowledge combines the moderate to high challenge that is built into intrinsic motivation with low threat and a pervasive state of well-being. We call that a state of relaxed alertness. Ongoing relaxed alertness is the key to people's ability to access what they already know, think creatively, tolerate ambiguity, and delay gratification, all of which are essential for genuine expansion of knowledge.[1]

Paying careful attention to others in introductions and connecting their name to something about them is very helpful. Paying attention to lectures, taking well-organized notes, and clarifying information that is confusing are all aids to remembering. Also, repeating information orally or in writing and then periodically reviewing what has been learned assists in retaining information. Repetition and rehearsal are key ingredients to remembering.

The most important task in helping students develop a good memory is to convince them that having a good memory is possible. Remembering is not magic or a rare talent shared by only a privileged few; it is a gift available to all. The first step in improving their memories will be to provide students with some techniques they are likely to find successful. The memory models are exactly that.

Model One: The Link Model

The link system and the variations described are based on the process of association. By associating or linking already familiar information to new data, the new information can be retained and accessed more readily. This model is useful in committing to memory such items as grocery lists, assignments, the names of the presidents, the bones in the foot, and the planets in the solar system. This model is also effective as an aid to remembering key concepts such as those in the Bill of Rights or the Ten Commandments.

Steps in the Link Model

1. Select the items.
2. Organize the material.
3. Prepare the associations.
4. Explain the process and present the associations to the class.
5. Practice developing associations.
6. Evaluate.

Step 1—Select the Items

When first teaching this technique, you may find that any list of items is an appropriate teaching tool. Later, it is important to help students determine if the material is really worth committing to memory. For instance, it may be more efficient to write down a grocery list and take it to the store than to commit it to memory, but the names of the 13 colonies or the presidents of the United States could be useful items to retain in long-term memory.

Step 2—Organize the Material

Although the items can be learned in any order, it makes sense to group and categorize if possible. For instance, if remembering a grocery list, putting the items into categories such as vegetables, meats, and so forth, can facilitate the memory process. If remembering things that need to be done, such as assignments or appointments, organize by the days of the week or the times of the day.

For example, say that the items you have chosen are products grown in the Southeast:

peanuts, pork, sorghum, soybeans, apples, oysters, corn

Although it is not essential, alphabetizing the items helps, particularly in recalling the first word. In this list, there happens to be a word that begins with the first letter of the alphabet, *apple*, making the start of this memory task easy. Alphabetically, the list is as follows:

apples, corn, oysters, peanuts, pork, sorghum, soybeans

Step 3—Prepare the Associations

Before the class meets, form a strong visual word association between the first and the second item, then between the second and the third, the third and the fourth, and so on through the list. For instance, if the first word is *apple* and the link is to the next item *corn*, imagine an apple eating an ear of corn or an apple tree growing ears of corn. Next link *corn* to *oysters*. Imagine an ear of corn eating an oyster or an ear of corn riding on an oyster. Next associate *oysters* with *peanuts*. Imagine an *oyster* jumping out of a *peanut* shell or an *oyster* eating *peanuts*. The more ridiculous the association, often the more likely it is to be remembered.

Step 4—Explain the Process and Present the Associations to the Class

Explain the steps in the process and the reasons for developing memory skills to the class. Introduce the first four associations that were prepared in advance. Have the students work together as a class to form ridiculous associations for the remainder of the items on the list. At the end of this step, review the reasons for making these associations.

Step 5—Practice Developing Associations

As a group, practice recalling the list through the process of association. Present another list of words to the students and let them as a class or in small groups form the associations. The class as a whole can vote on the most effective associations to use.

In this step, it is important to emphasize that the more ridiculous the association, the more likely it is to be remembered. Also, it is helpful to make simple drawings of the associations to serve as an additional memory aid.

For homework, ask each student to create a set of associations to be used in memorizing a data list provided by the teacher. These associations are to be shared with all members of the class on the following day.

Next, review the lists in class. Practice going backward from the last item to the first. Make each list a little longer than the one before.

Step 6—Evaluate

Have the students use the information they memorized in a written assignment and on a short quiz. Discuss with the class how the process worked and when it was most effective. Discuss what images they retained and what seemed to be least memorable. Stress how funny and ridiculous images seem to be most easily remembered. Review the technique periodically and test for retention. Have the students keep a diary in which they track their ability to remember items.

Variations on the Link Model

Story/Link: Use a story to link the various items. For instance, a bright apple and an ear of corn get married. The oysters all clapped as the apple and ear of corn came down the aisle, but instead of throwing rice they threw peanuts. The pigs were supposed to play on their fiddles, but they all slipped and fell down in heavy sorghum molasses, so the soybeans had to toot on their whistles instead.

Item/Relationship: The item/relationship variation on the link model is helpful when remembering a group of items that have related functions attached; for instance, the names of the members of the president's Cabinet. Say that the secretary of labor is Henry Smith. The mental image to be created needs to link the function of his office, *labor*, and his name, *Smith*. One could visualize a man laboring as a blacksmith or a labor union leader carrying a blacksmith's hammer. Say that the secretary of commerce is named Franklin. The image could be of a person selling frankfurters or of people in a country grocery store gathered around a Franklin stove.

Main Idea: When memorizing a list such as the Bill of Rights, the learner must first determine the main idea of a particular passage and then isolate a word that will trigger the content of the main idea. For instance, in the Bill of Rights, the First Amendment guarantees religious freedom. The main idea is *religion*, so the number 1 must be attached to the image of religion. The image could be of one person alone praying or of the first person in line to enter a church.

Peg System: The peg system is a very useful technique that requires developing a permanent association with each number in a series and then using these number pegs to form associations with items on a list. For instance, the following are a series of links between the numbers 1 through 10 and word images:

One is gun.	Six is ticks.
Two is cue.	Seven is heaven.
Three is tree.	Eight is plate.
Four is shore.	Nine is pine.
Five is hive.	Ten is hen.

Any series of items to be remembered can be associated with these permanent peg words. For instance, in the example of the agricultural products of the Southeast, the peg word for one or gun would be associated with apple or a gun shooting apples (a modern William Tell); corn would be linked to cue or an ear of corn being used as a pool cue; and oysters would be linked to tree or a tree full of oysters. The same pegs are used whenever a list is to be remembered so that they become permanent memory pegs for the learner.

Key Word: The key word association technique was first described in 1975 by Richard Atkinson.[2] Although adaptable to many situations, it has been widely researched as a useful tool for learning foreign language vocabulary. The first step in this model is to select a key word for the foreign word to be learned. This key word will be a word already familiar to the learner. For instance, if the word to be learned is the French word for dog, or *chien*, the key word could be the similar sounding English word *shin*. The next step is to form a visual image between the key word and the English meaning, such as a dog biting a person on the shin.

The basic link model, together with the variations, associates items to be remembered with something already known and familiar, creating vivid mental pictures and one of the most effective ways known to increase memory.

Summary of Steps in the Link Model

1. *Select the items:* Choose items important enough to be committed to memory.

2. *Organize the material:* Put the material in some sort of order. This may entail outlining or alphabetizing.

3. *Prepare the associations:* Associations should be ridiculous and even humorous.

4. *Explain the process and present the associations to the class:* The students should first understand the steps and the importance of the process. Present to the class the associations that were prepared in advance.

5. *Practice developing associations:* Have students practice as a class, in small groups, and through homework assignments.

6. *Evaluate:* Determine the effectiveness and review and discuss the process.

EXERCISE 15.1

A teacher prepared the following associations for remembering a list of items that included *chair*, *policeman*, *orange*, and *canary*.

> A *chair* was sitting in a room full of *policemen*.
> A *policeman* was eating an *orange*.
> There was an *orange* feather on the *canary*.

How could this set of associations be improved?

Possible Answers to Exercise 15.1
1. The list should be alphabetized: *canary, chair, orange,* and *policeman.*
2. The associations need to be ridiculous. For example:

> A *canary* was sitting in a *chair*.
> A *chair* was jumping up and down on an *orange*.
> An *orange* was eating a *policeman*.

3. The items should be consistent in meaning. An orange is either a color or a fruit but not both. ■

Model Two: The Loci Model

One of the oldest systems for remembering important points in a sequence, such as the main ideas to be presented in a speech or to be recalled for an essay exam, is a system developed in ancient Rome called the loci or place system. *Loci* is the plural of *locus*, meaning a place or location.

Orators who were preparing to speak in the Forum without any notes would select a particular location with which they were very familiar, such as a room in a house or a path on which they walked. Within this place they selected a number of objects for reference. For instance, if they visualized themselves walking along a familiar path, the first object might be a large stone on which they sat to rest. The second could be a large tree, the third a stream that crossed the path, the fourth a hollow log, and so on. Each of these loci, or places, would be a way of locating the points of their speech.

The orators would then associate a point in their speech with each place. For instance, voting might be associated with the stone by thinking of the votes being carved in the stone. A point about the military might be associated with the trees by thinking about warriors hiding behind a tree on the path. The expression "In the first place, and the second place, and so on" comes from the practice of the ancient orators using particular places as memory cues for the main points of speeches.

Once a series of loci or places are identified, they can be used over and over to remember different points or ideas. It is important to select a location so familiar that it is permanently fixed in the mind. Then the new information to be remembered can be hooked to this familiar image.

Steps in the Loci Model

1. Select appropriate material.
2. Outline the material to be recalled.
3. Identify the location to serve as a reference.
4. Relate the items to the places within the location.
5. Practice.
6. Evaluate.

Step 1—Select Appropriate Material

Select a body of material for which the main ideas are to be recalled. This may be the main points of a speech, as part of a unit on public speaking. Or, it may be the main headings of a unit, such as the causes of the Civil War; different types of dinosaurs; or the plot of a novel in which the students need to recall main concepts for an essay exam.

Step 2—Outline the Material to Be Recalled

After the material has been studied and fully comprehended, have the students outline the material. They should identify the main heading for each part of the text and put the minor points under each major heading. For instance, in a unit on traditional literary genres, the outline may look like this:

   I. Poetry

    A. Ballads
    B. Odes
    C. Sonnets
    D. Free Verse

   II. Fiction

    A. Short Story
    B. Novel

   III. Nonfiction

    A. Biography
    B. Essays
    C. Travel

   IV. Drama

    A. Comedy
    B. Tragedy

Step 3—Identify the Location to Serve as a Reference

Have the students identify a very familiar part of the school, such as the classroom, the gym, the lunchroom, a walkway outside the building, a field, or a tennis court. Then locate significant objects within that area. For instance, if the classroom is chosen, one place of reference could be the chalkboard, a second the teacher's desk, a third the intercom speaker, and a fourth the light fixtures.

    If the baseball field is chosen, the first place could be the pitcher's mound, the second could be the batter's box, the third could be first base, and so on. Students who are expert in baseball will know that the positions in the game are numbered for purposes of recording play of the game, and so these loci will be perfect for them.

Step 4—Relate the Items to the Places within the Location

Connect the main points of the outline to the places in the location selected by the class. This could be done first as a whole group and then practiced in small groups. For instance, if the classroom is the chosen location, poetry could be associated with the chalkboard, fiction with the intercom, nonfiction with the teacher's desk, and drama with the light fixtures.

    An association is then formed between the place and the point to be remembered. For instance, one could visualize the board being filled with poetry or the poet writing on a piece of slate. In an association between fiction and the intercom, one might think of the morning announcements beginning "Once upon a time . . ."

Step 5—Practice

Have the students, in small groups, practice their ability to recall the main points of the material in order and take turns listing the items.

Assign a new piece of material that has been learned by the class. Have the students, working in groups, repeat the process of outlining the material, selecting the main points, and then assigning each point to a location. This time have each person prepare to present the ideas to the class.

Step 6—Evaluate

Discuss with the class the effectiveness of this technique. Determine those locations that were the most effective in recalling the main points. Determine what could be done to improve the process. Compare the results of an essay test given before this technique was presented with one given after, and have the students describe how they used the process.

Summary of Steps in the Loci Model

1. *Select appropriate material:* This model lends itself well to extensive material such as that to be recalled on an essay exam or when giving a speech.

2. *Outline the material to be recalled:* The students should at least be able to identify the main points or key words in the material to be remembered.

3. *Identify the location to serve as a reference:* The location should be a place very familiar to all participants.

4. *Relate the items to the places within the location:* Stress the possibility of using these places repeatedly once they have been identified.

5. *Practice:* Have students practice in small groups and through homework assignments. Assign a new topic and have students repeat the process.

6. *Evaluate:* Determine if students are using the technique and if it is improving their memory skills.

EXERCISE 15.2

Which of the following would be most appropriate for using the loci system?

A. Recalling where a series of items are stored
B. Organizing the main points of a debate

    C. Preparing for an essay exam
    D. All of the above

Answer to Exercise 15.2
The answer is D, all of the above. ■

Model Three: The Memory through Motion Model

Many people can recall being required to commit poems, essays, and literary passages to memory, and many can still remember the pain of standing before a class, unable to remember the next line of a Shakespearean sonnet or the Gettysburg Address. For some, the recitation of these pieces before a class of giggling peers was a nightmare that still produces feelings of anxiety. Because of this trauma, most such required memorization activities in school have been abandoned.

Yet often words that were learned so reluctantly return to provide comfort and inspiration when no book is available. Psalm 23 may be a great solace in times of anguish, and the inspiring words of the Declaration of Independence can make hearts soar at a parade. It will be sad if this generation of young people has no such resources available in their memories.

Our teachers did not intend to inflict injury upon us; they were trying to provide, through memorization, access to beautiful poems and ideas that would stay with us throughout our lives and which we could recall when needed. Many teachers would still like to provide this access to their students, but they realize how painful the process can be and thus avoid any memorization assignments. The memory through motion model provides every student the opportunity to memorize material without being singled out and embarrassed by failure to perform. In addition, it enables the teacher to work with the group to emphasize the rhythm and beauty of the language.

Memorizing text, particularly beautiful text, can be facilitated by linking the words to symbolic movement. This works particularly well when the passage to be memorized contains many powerful images. The process is a group process, and thus the agony of a painful and embarrassed forgetting is eliminated. As in many of the other models in this text, the students learn from one another during the process and are able to hear others speak the words with fluency and feeling.

Steps in the Memory through Motion Model

Steps 1 through 3 are completed by the teacher prior to instruction.

1. Select a passage.
2. Prepare a chart.
3. Select the key words and motions.
4. Introduce the material.

5. Present the motions to the class.
6. Have groups complete the motions for the remainder of the material.
7. Have groups present the motions.
8. Practice.
9. Evaluate.

Step 1—Select a Passage

The passage chosen should be worthy of being remembered and should contain powerful and moving images. This might be a poem, a portion of an essay, a speech, or the words to a song. These should be words that you can envision your students recalling years later and being inspired and moved by the memory.

Step 2—Prepare a Chart

Write the passage on a large chart or sheet of paper that has enough room for you to make notes or pictures. In some classrooms, printing the material on a roll of shelf paper or newsprint that can be wrapped around the room is appropriate. Other teachers use a flip chart or an overhead projector. Because you will want to refer to this material periodically, the chalkboard is not the best place for a permanent record.

Step 3—Select the Key Words and Motions

Before class, select some motions that will illustrate the key words in each line or phrase of the material to be remembered. For instance, if the words to "America the Beautiful" are to be remembered, the first movement could be slowly reaching the arms up toward the sky to signify "O beautiful for spacious *skies*." For the next line, "For amber *waves* of grain," the hands could move together to form a motion of waves. With "For purple *mountain* majesties," the hands could be raised with the tips of the fingers touching to form an upside-down V for a mountain peak. For "Above the *fruited* plain," one hand could be reaching up as though to pluck an apple.

Step 4—Introduce the Material

In class, introduce the material to be memorized by reading it aloud or playing a recording. It is assumed that the material to be learned will be a part of a unit being studied and will be taught within the context of a more general body of knowledge. Memory is enhanced by being related to other information and placed within a framework of related material.

Make certain that each student comprehends the material and understands the meaning of the words. Point out the key words that you have selected for each part. Misunderstandings are avoided if students fully comprehend the meaning of the words to be remembered. Before adding the movements, explain the process and the steps to follow in memorizing the material.

Step 5—Present the Motions to the Class

Have the students stand in a semicircle so that each can see you, the rest of the class, and the words on the chart. Prepare the students for the exercise by explaining that they will first create movements and then illustrate the main images or the key words in the piece. These movements do not need to be complicated or vigorous.

Now, by yourself or with a student who enjoys performing before the group, demonstrate the motions that you selected to accompany the passage and have the students perform these as they say the words together. Each time a new motion is introduced to the group, repeat all the material that precedes it.

Step 6—Have Groups Complete the
Motions for the Remainder of the Material

Have the students work in groups and assign each group a portion of the remaining material for which they are to develop an appropriate gesture. (If working with young children, complete the activity with them as a large group, going over and over the motions together.)

Move from group to group during this part of the activity. Be sure that the students have identified the key words in the passage assigned to their group and encourage them to use their imagination in creating the motions.

Step 7—Have Groups Present the Motions

Have each group stand and repeat the entire passage together from the beginning, including the motions for the groups that preceded them and the new motions that they developed for their part of the material. As each group goes through the material, point to the words of the text and encourage the group to speak the words with feeling.

Step 8—Practice

When all groups have presented, have the entire class stand again and repeat the passage together with the movements from beginning to end. Direct the students to practice the passage at home before a mirror until they are confident that they have committed it to memory. Then have them practice the material without the motions to see if they are able to recall the words only.

Step 9—Evaluate

Have the students write the passage from memory and then check to see if all have recalled the passage. If there are students who cannot write, have them say the passage to a partner without the movements. If possible, videotape the activity to determine how well the students are participating and if there is progress within the group.

Return to this material periodically and have the class share the process, including the movements.

Select another piece of material but do not prepare any movements in advance. Let the entire class or the class working within groups prepare the movements.

Variations on the Memory through Motion Model

Drawings—such as a pair of hands reaching toward the sky, waves, and mountains—can be added to the chart to help students recall the movements. This is particularly useful for young children or students who are poor readers. These visual cues need not be fancy drawings, just simple representations of the key words.

For individuals who are confined to wheelchairs or unable to stand, the movements can be done sitting or even lying down.

If the teacher or someone in the class knows sign language, the signs can be used to represent the key words.

Summary of Steps in the Memory through Motion Model

1. *Select a passage:* Choose material that is worthy to be remembered and that contains strong images.

2. *Prepare a chart:* Write the material to be memorized on an easy-to-read chart.

3. *Select the key words and motions:* These movements should be simple and graceful.

4. *Introduce the material:* Make certain that the students understand the meaning of the words.

5. *Present the motions to the class:* Demonstrate and have the class repeat the words and the movements.

6. *Have groups complete the motions for the remainder of the material:* Encourage the groups to identify the key words and select appropriate motions.

7. *Have groups present the motions:* Each group stands and repeats the entire selection including the new motions added by the group.

8. *Practice:* Have the entire class stand and repeat all the movements together with the words several times.

9. *Evaluate:* Determine if students can write the passage from memory or can repeat it to another student.

EXERCISE 15.3

Which of these selections would be appropriate for the memory through motion model?

A. The Declaration of Independence
B. The names of the presidents of the United States

C. Psalm 100

D. The main points in a debate

Possible Answers to Exercise 15.3

A and C would be most appropriate for this use because these are beautiful passages with strong verbal images. Memorizing lists is done more effectively through the link model, and the loci model is effective for remembering the main points in a debate. ■

Model Four: The Names and Faces Model

Learning to remember names and faces represents an important life skill because in the process we learn to pay careful attention to those around us. Teachers are particularly concerned about the ability to remember the names of the students in their class as quickly as possible, recognizing how essential this can be for the self-concept of learners and for their feelings of confidence and well-being.

There are a number of sources for the names and faces model. Kenneth Higbee, in his book *Your Memory: How It Works and How to Improve It*, clearly describes this process.[3] The steps as described by Higbee are as follows: (1) Make sure you have heard the name. (2) Make the name meaningful. (3) Focus on a distinctive feature of the person's appearance. (4) Associate the name with the distinctive feature. (5) Review the association.

The following are these steps expanded and adapted for use in a classroom environment. The technique of using pictures of people rather than having the students practice on one another is based on the knowledge that adolescents, in particular, can be cruel in regard to physical characteristics and that most of the students will already know the names of their classmates.

Steps in the Names and Faces Model

1. Select pictures of interesting faces.
2. Assign a picture to each student.
3. Students introduce their picture faces.
4. Students select distinctive features.
5. Students associate the name with the feature.
6. Review the names and practice.
7. Evaluate.

Step 1—Select Pictures of Interesting Faces

Select and then mount pictures of interesting faces on cardboard. You may assign fictitious names to these pictures, or you might choose actual historical characters unfamiliar to the students. Pictures of individuals to be studied during the year or of famous people in the news are also possibilities.

Step 2—Assign a Picture to Each Student

Divide the class into groups and assign each individual a picture to represent. The name that goes with the picture is printed on the back.

For younger children, or as an introductory exercise, you may want to put all the pictures in front of the room and conduct this exercise with the entire class.

Step 3—Students Introduce Their Picture Faces

Tell the class that they are to pay careful attention to the name of each "person" as he or she is introduced. Have each student in the group introduce his or her picture personality to the others. Suggest that others in the group ask to have the name repeated. Encourage the students to write the name down and to use the person's name during the conversation. For instance, they might say, "I am pleased to meet you, Thomas Jefferson." Later in the discussion, they could say to another person in the group, "Thomas Jefferson tells me that he is planning a trip soon." At the end of the period have them close by saying, "It was nice meeting you, Mr. Jefferson."

Step 4—Students Select Distinctive Features

Have students focus on a distinctive feature of the picture person's appearance. We are used to looking at others without really attending to their features. We tend to remember very beautiful or very unattractive faces, but we forget most of the others. Remind the students to note the color of the hair, the eyes, the shape of the nose, and the ears. Does the chin jut out or recede? Is there a cleft in the chin or a dimple in the cheek? Are the eyebrows bushy? Is the hairline receding? Have students pay careful attention and select some feature to relate to the name of the person.

Step 5—Students Associate the Name with the Feature

Students can associate the names with something distinctive about the person's appearance. For instance, Thomas Jefferson had bright red hair. One might recall a tomcat named Jeff with red fur.

The names to be remembered can also be associated with a familiar concept. Many names are already associated with concepts from everyday life such as colors (*Green, White, Brown*), occupations (*Baker, Cook, Farmer, Wright, Brewer*), places (*North, West, London*). If the name cannot be readily associated with a common concept, change it to something that sounds familiar. For instance, *Gunter* could be "gunned her"; *Estes* could be "Best S"; *Schwab* could be "She robs." When selecting the names for the class to practice, first select simple names that are easily associated with a mental image.

Some names are less complicated than others. For instance, Ms. Green who has dimples could have green grass growing out of her dimples, or Mr. Baker who has fat, red cheeks could be baking doughnuts in his cheeks. Have the class work in their groups to identify the physical characteristics and then the associations.

Once again, the more vivid and even ridiculous the image the more likely it is to be remembered. Higbee points out that many people fear they will remember the association rather than the name.[4] This is unlikely, however, because the processes of paying careful attention and focusing on the individual in steps 2 and 3 are likely to assure the retention of the appropriate name in the future.

Step 6—Review the Names and Practice

Review the names and practice the associations as often as possible. Have the students stand and introduce the names of all the picture people in their group and then explain to the class the techniques used to remember the names.

Step 7—Evaluate

Have the class practice remembering the names of the picture people in their group several times over a period of weeks. By having listened to the introductions and using the new technique, the students should be able to introduce picture people from the other groups. You can evaluate your own progress in remembering the names of students in the class by keeping a record of your improvement over time.

Summary of Steps in the Names and Faces Model

1. *Select pictures of interesting faces:* These can be interesting faces of strangers cut from magazines or the faces of famous individuals to be studied in the curriculum.

2. *Assign a picture to each student:* With younger children, the picture faces may be lined up in the front of the room and the class can complete the activity as a group.

3. *Students introduce their picture faces:* The listeners are encouraged to make the names meaningful by asking to have the names repeated and by writing the names.

4. *Students select distinctive features:* The class is urged to attend to interesting facial characteristics.

5. *Students associate the name with the feature:* The more ridiculous the association, the better it will be remembered.

6. *Review the names and practice:* Review and practice in the groups or for homework.

7. *Evaluate:* The exercise should be repeated periodically to determine retention.

Basis for the Memory Models

A good memory is an acquired skill. Popular opinion to the contrary, the quality of a person's memory is not determined at birth. Even very intelligent people do not automatically have good memories. Before the invention of the printing press, people had to learn a number of techniques for remembering important information. Only through memory could most information be passed from one generation to another. The retrieval of important material depended on the memory of individuals rather than on computers and elaborate filing systems. Tools for remembering were important to survival in the Middle Ages. For instance, monks committed to memory thousands of items by relating the items to locations within the cathedral.

Today, we tend to think of memory techniques as nonessential "extras" that are not really important to the average learner. Too often we think that good memories are gifts to the gifted. Good students, however, the ones who seem more intelligent, are more likely to learn and use memory aids. Their memories are like most other skills that people develop, more the result of practice and refinement than of any particular gift. If students who are less able are taught the use of these techniques, they become more able.

To understand why, we have only to look at how memory actually works. Edmund Bolles, in his book *Remembering and Forgetting*, suggests a sequence, or pattern, of how memories are formed. The pattern he describes seems justified by what we know about the brain and learning, and perhaps it should be carved in stone in every teachers' lounge, kindergarten through college. Think about what this implies for all teaching:

> People remember what they understand;
> They understand what they pay attention to;
> They pay attention to what they want.[5]

That last word is accurate but abrupt. It might be read as "value" or "love" or "care about." Whatever its interpretation, it is the first step in teaching. In many ways, teaching is the art of reminding and nurturing. In a sense, teaching has the qualities of a mnemonic, which is easiest to understand when we look at how remembering works and at what causes forgetting.

Memory does not reside in one area of the brain. Modern research on the brain points to a much more generalized brain activity than once was thought. Memories seem to involve the interaction of many different parts of the brain. Recall from memory involves the retrieval of material that was first learned and then "stored" in the brain, although the idea of storage is probably more figurative than literal. Some research indicates that there are permanent changes within the cells of the brain as new learning takes place. It is possible that "hooking" new learning onto prior knowledge may literally mean taking advantage of pathways or connections in the brain that have been established in previous learning experiences. New learning overlays old learning, and new memories replace old memories by lying on the same neural pathways.

Humans seem to have two separate processes for remembering things. The first is short-term memory in which we remember information for a brief period. This type of memory serves us well for recalling items and experiences we need to remember for only a short period and can then forget. Our minds would be a jumble of information if we had to remember everything that we experienced. Forgetting may well be as important as remembering!

Notice these features of short-term memory:

- Short-term memory lasts no more than 20 seconds unless renewed by rehearsal.
- Short-term memory is limited in capacity to about seven (plus or minus two) items at one time.
- The brain is very aware of (conscious of) what is in short-term memory.
- Short-term memory may be as short as 1 to 3 seconds.
- Short-term memory is encoded as interrelated bits, seven (plus or minus two) bits at a time.

The other memory the brain is capable of is called long-term memory. This is the memory toward which teachers hope to teach. Long-term memory is the focus of the instructional models in this text. It is this type of memory in which retrieval of what has been stored is most essential and frequently the most difficult. Contrast its features with short-term memory:

- Long-term memory lasts an indefinite time, perhaps from the onset of language to death.
- Long-term memory has illimited (perhaps unlimited) capacity.
- The brain is unaware of (unconscious of) what is in long-term memory.
- Long-term memory is timeless.
- Long-term memory is encoded as words, concepts, feelings, and so forth.

The goal in learning is to move information from short-term to long-term memory, whether by using memory aids or other means. Because most of what gets into short-term memory does not get transferred to more permanent, long-term memory, what can be said about preserving at least *some* memories? Figure 15.1 is an attempt to illustrate what we know in answer to that question. Notice first the two memory bottlenecks: the passage from sensory data (everything going on within reach of the learner) to short-term memory and the passage from short-term to long-term memory. The first crucial impediment to learning (or catalyst for learning) is attention and caring. Recall what Bolles had to say about this: Learners pay attention to what they care about. What they do not attend to or care about is quickly filtered from consciousness before it ever has a chance to get into short-term memory (sometimes called "working" memory) where maybe something else can occur. Notice also that, aside from the issue of low capacity, what does manage to get into the initial stage of memory is marked by consciousness and present time. Information in short-term memory is information the learner knows for certain that he or she knows, but it may or may not be information that will be retained. Most likely it will not be, unless something happens to make that possible.

Look now at the next bottleneck, the narrow passage from short-term to long-term memory. If information in short-term memory is elaborated on or made meaningful by connection to something in long-term memory, then it may move over into long-term memory. The determining factors for this event are relevance, meaning,

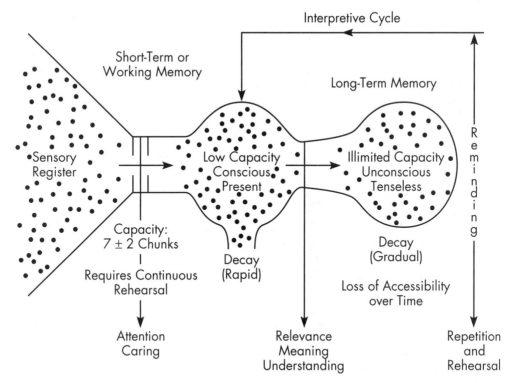

FIGURE 15.1 Information-Processing Model

Source: Adapted from R. N. Caine and G. Caine, *Making Connections: Teaching and the Human Brain* (Menlo Park, CA: Addison-Wesley, 1994), 43.

and understanding. Learners remember what they understand, and what they understand is what they find relevant and meaningful. It is this information that they are able to "store" in long-term memory, memory whose limits are unknown, memory that is unconscious and timeless.

Decay from long-term memory is very gradual, and what actually decays is accessibility. This is very important because when, as often happens, students seem not to know something they "should" know, they may only be having difficulty with accessing what they do indeed know. Thus the art of teaching is bringing to mind again information that was once relevant, meaningful, and understood. This reminding sets up an interpretive cycle in which what once was known is known again in the presence of new information in short-term memory from whence it enters long-term memory anew, elaborated and refined by learning. This cycle is the mechanism for learning. It is stimulated by teaching that continually brings back to mind what was previously learned and that can give relevance in the present to what is being learned.

Conditions for Memories

What are the conditions that facilitate memory for learners? As noted, long-term memory is the focus of all the instructional models in this text. The memory models in this chapter highlight a more pervasive concern with memory in which retrieval of what has been stored is the most essential and frequently the most difficult aim. This is the memory that depends on four essential conditions: comprehension, organization, repetition, and association.

Comprehension

Before information can successfully be committed to memory, it needs to be understood. This seems so obvious that it is easy to forget how often learners are asked to memorize something without understanding its meaning. For instance, many people completed algebra by memorizing the step-by-step procedures for solving certain problems, but they never really understood what such problems had to do with anything except getting the right answer. Do you remember the way to solve the problem of two trains simultaneously leaving Los Angeles and New York traveling at different speeds? This is not your everyday big problem. Today, very few adults retrieve this information from long-term memory because it had no meaning for them when they learned it.

Information is remembered more readily when the learner is interested in learning it and sees some reason and purpose for committing information to long-term memory. A good question to ask about any assignment that requires memorization is whether it is worth remembering. Would the learner be better served by instruction on where to retrieve the information in a library or from a computer network? Because memory does not grow stronger simply through the activity of memorizing, there is no reason for selecting trivial or unimportant material to be memorized.

Organization

Organizing information into a particular framework can be helpful in the processes of comprehending and retaining information. Alan Baddeley compares the organization of information stored in the mind to a vast library. "In order to be useful," he points out, "the books in a library must be organized and shelved in a systematic way, otherwise finding the appropriate book becomes so slow as to make the library unusable."[6] Alphabetizing is one simple way of ordering information. Another way is termed *chunking*, in which numbers or letters are combined in such a way as to make them more accessible. Most of us remember our social security numbers in chunks like 123-45-6789, and we remember phone numbers in chunks like 123-4567.

Outlining is an effective way to organize the main ideas in material, perhaps using a technique such as *webbing*, in which a main concept is surrounded like a web with related concepts. The concept development model in which students learn to group data into categories is an effective way of organizing information to be retained.

Rhyme and rhythm are forms of organization that are valuable tools to memory. For instance, consider the lines,

Twinkle, twinkle, little star,
How I wonder what you are!
Up above the world so high,
Like a diamond in the sky.

The rhyme and the pattern of accented and unaccented syllables provide a pattern. We recall nursery rhymes because of the rhythm and the rhyme as well as the vivid mental images that they convey.

Repetition

Repetition of material to be memorized is essential whether it is a name, a series of numbers, or concepts. This repetition needs to take place frequently during the learning of material and then periodically thereafter. In Figure 15.1, notice that repetition and rehearsal keep information in consciousness. "Use or lose" seems to be the rule for much of what is committed to memory. For instance, it was suggested in the names and faces model that the name of the person to whom one is being introduced be repeated immediately after the introduction, during the conversation, and when parting from that individual. The more often the repetition of the name takes place, the more likely retention will occur.

Association

It was stated earlier that to remember any new thing we must associate it with something that is already known or remembered. Harry Lorayne restates this by saying that "in order to remember any new thing, it must be associated, [often] in some ridiculous way, with something you already know or remember."[7]

Marilee Sprenger has identified five separate pathways or lanes that lead to the different areas of memory in the brain, which she calls the semantic, episodic, procedural, automatic, and emotional lanes. The semantic memory lane is connected to words and information. The episodic relates to location—where you were when something occurred. The procedural pathway is the "how-to" memory lane for activities such as driving a car or tying a shoe. The automatic, or stimulus-response, lane leads to the area where such things as the alphabet or the multiplication tables are stored. In the emotional lane are the powerful memories triggered by feelings. As Sprenger notes, "We can teach in ways that help students store information in most memory lanes, and we can assess students in ways that help them better retrieve information."[8]

Research on mnemonics generally indicates that the use of memory techniques improves the academic performance of students. For instance, in an experiment using the loci model, the group using the method improved in their recall over the group that did not. The authors asserted that "the spontaneous use of mnemonics, which is an effective learning strategy, was shown to be associated with academic performance."[9]

Mnemonic techniques can be taught to children of preschool and kindergarten age as well as to older children and adults. Michael Pressley and Janet MacFadyen conducted research in which preschool and kindergarten children were tested on their ability to recall interactive pictures of paired items. Those youngsters who were subject to mnemonic plus retrieval procedures "produced recall significantly greater than control performance at both age levels."[10]

Scenario

Hank Brown, an eighth-grade social studies teacher, is part of an instructional team that includes a language arts teacher, Grace Pearl, and a science teacher, Frank Johnson. He convinced his team members that memory skills would be an important addition to their curriculum and offered to design a plan in which the teaching of some of these skills would be incorporated into their units for the year.

The first part of the plan that Mr. Brown designed would occur in the science class. Here the students would be introduced to the link model when they were learning some of the chemical elements or the phyla in biology. Then he would pick up the model in social studies, using it to teach the students how to remember the amendments to the Constitution and the first 13 colonies. In language arts, they would use the technique to learn a list of the main characters in a play and lists of important vocabulary words.

All three teachers agreed that the peg model would be a good alternative to describe to the classes when they had mastered the association process in the link model. Many of the students would be intrigued by the possibility of developing a permanent set of memory pegs to associate with a list of items.

The memory through motion model would originate in the language arts classroom when the students were learning to memorize a poem. It would be reinforced in social studies for memorizing the first part of the Declaration of Independence. Mr. Johnson, the science teacher, decided to not use this model. "I can't imagine them moving gracefully to a recitation of the bones in the body," he said. Then he laughed and added, "Of course, there is that old song 'Them Bones, Them Bones.' Maybe I could give that a try."

The loci model was to be introduced in the social studies unit on debate. Mr. Brown would teach the students to locate the main points of their presentation with specific places in a familiar location. This model would be reinforced in language arts in a unit on public speaking, and the students would be encouraged to use the same places they had used in social studies to form a permanent framework for remembering a series of ideas. With regard to science, Mr. Johnson said, "I have them write an essay on water conservation for their final exam. I will remind them to use this technique when they are studying for their examination."

Throughout the year, the teachers discussed with the students the reasons for developing memory skills and ways to improve the techniques. A sample of the students were tested and interviewed at the beginning of the year and at the end to determine the effectiveness of the various procedures. Summarizing the experience, Mr. Brown said:

I know that there are models for memory in math, and I have come up with techniques for using key words to associate with foreign language vocabulary and improving reading skills. This summer we should suggest to the other teachers that memory models would be helpful in many subject areas.

ACTIVITY 15.1

Select a unit that you plan to teach and identify the information that should be a part of the long-term memory of the learners. Consider which of the memory models described in this chapter would be most appropriate to include in your instructional design to teach this information. ■

Summary

Mnemonic techniques can be used in the classroom to help learners acquire information, and the specific techniques can be taught to students for their use as effective learning skills. Some of the techniques are appropriate for remembering lists and random data, others are more effective in recalling main points or the sequence of information, and still others depend on visual cues or physical motion to help the learner recall the material. These techniques are all based on the premises that a good memory can be developed and that all learners can profit from instruction on these techniques.

WEB RESOURCES

1. **http://www.sccu.edu/faculty/ddegelman/amoebaweb/**
   This is the site you needed in those psychology courses you took in college. On the main page, you will see a link to "Memory," which takes you to more information on memory than you could have believed existed. Of course, you will want to check out "Memory Techniques and Mnemonics" as well as "Memory Strategies," and its subcategory on mnemonic devices. The first of these is a thorough elaboration of all that you have just read in this chapter, but more than we had the space to mention. You will notice also that the main page of AmoebaWeb has links to other sites of interest to you as a teacher—for example, "Intelligence," "Language," and "Learning."

NOTES

1. R. N. Caine and G. Caine, *Making Connections: Teaching and the Human Brain* (Menlo Park, CA: Addison-Wesley, 1994), 143.

2. R. C. Atkinson, "Mnemotechnics in Second Language Learning," *American Psychologist* 52 (1982): 821–828.

3. Kenneth L. Higbee, *Your Memory: How It Works and How to Improve It*, 2nd ed. (New York: Paragon House, 1988), 194.

4. Higbee, 198–199.

5. E. M. Bolles, *Remembering and Forgetting: An Inquiry into the Nature of Memory* (New York: Walker and Co., 1988), 23.

6. Alan D. Baddeley, *The Psychology of Memory* (New York: Basic Books, 1976), 285.

7. Harry Lorayne, *Super Memory, Super Student* (Boston: Little, Brown, 1990), 15.

8. Marilee Sprenger, "Memory Lane Is a Two-Way Street," *Educational Leadership* (November 1998): 66.

9. Robert F. Carlson, J. Peter Kincaid, Sara Lance, and Thomas Hodgson, "Spontaneous Use of Mnemonics and Grade Point Average," *Journal of Psychology* 92 (1976): 117.

10. Michael Pressley and Janet MacFadyen, "Mnemonic Mediator Retrieval at Testing by Preschool and Kindergarten Children," *Child Development* 54 (1983): 478.

Matching Objectives to Instruction

A Models Approach

In Part Two, we surveyed a selection of models for teaching, ranging from direct instruction to the models for memory. Throughout we have tried to emphasize that models are akin to blueprints or patterns, sets of plans that describe but do not rigidly define approaches to teaching. All plans are subject to interpretation, modification, and adjustment, and models of instruction are no different. Every model must be seen as a flexible plan, subject to constant adaptation within the limits of its intended purpose.

Furthermore, models of instruction cannot be adopted in disregard of what will be taught and to whom the teaching will be directed. One does not merely say "I think I'll use model X today. Now what is it I need to teach?" If anything, the opposite should be the case: After considering the subject matter and the particular class to be taught, the teacher then selects a model of instruction that best combines the two variables. The instructional models discussed are best seen as approaches to teaching that must be selected with judgment.

Although Part Two does not present an exhaustive list of models, it covers the range of types. We hope that our descriptions and explanations have left every reader confident that he or she can make judicious choices of models for teaching and that doing so will have a positive effect on instructional outcomes.

Putting It All Together

Matching Objectives
to Instructional Models

An essential activity of the professional instructor, as emphasized in the preface to this book, is the process of designing or structuring (the root of *instruct*) that which is to be taught. We have emphasized the process of setting goals and objectives and designing the units and lessons.

In Part Three, we describe the integration of planning, instruction, evaluation, and management that takes place in an effective classroom environment. Each teacher, however, must develop his or her own way of achieving this integration. There is no one way to approach the process of putting it all together in the classroom. But every good teacher attends to certain essential components of this process: (1) planning, (2) instruction, (3) evaluation, and (4) classroom management.

In Parts One and Two, we discussed the first three components. In Part Three, we describe how teachers in classrooms use the ideas presented in Parts One and Two, and we give some general suggestions for managing the classroom. Of the four chapters in this section, Chapter 16 is a case study of a kindergarten class plan, Chapter 17 is a middle school case study, and Chapter 18 is a high school case study. Evident in these three examples are individual approaches to instructional planning, which use some of the processes and strategies described earlier. The teachers in these examples do not arrive at their plans by the same route nor do they incorporate exactly the same instructional steps in their individual plans. All the teachers do, however, attend to the needs of their students, and they systematically determine objectives and match those objectives to instruction.

Chapter 19 describes techniques for dealing with classroom management. Most of the material presented in this last chapter is drawn from our personal experience; we have attempted, however, to connect this experience with research regarding effective classroom practice.

It is our belief that teachers are essentially instructional experts, not therapists or counselors. Like all good managers, they must have very keen interpersonal skills and be able to think quickly on their feet. Anyone responsible for managing groups of people and for the welfare of individuals under their direction should have the personality and skills to manage the group and to give direction. But we should not ask of teachers what we do not ask of other professionals. Teachers should not be expected to prescribe and treat seriously disturbed individuals without help from other professionals, such as psychologists, social workers, and guidance counselors, nor should they be expected to teach in life-threatening situations.

Having said this, it is our belief that many students who are considered to be serious discipline problems and are sent out of the classroom, often labeled as hyperactive or emotionally disturbed, are in fact suffering because of the way they are being taught. Youngsters who are bored, whose learning style is different from the teaching style, or who are asked to learn material that is too difficult or too easy can become discipline problems. Too often, teachers diagnose instructional problems as emotional, physical, or mental problems, thus failing to meet the challenge of finding an instructional solution. In this part of the text we reemphasize the need for careful instructional planning and design and for creating a classroom environment in which students can and will learn.

CHAPTER

16 A Kindergarten Case Study

Gloria Abbott, kindergarten teacher at Central Elementary School, relaxed one warm summer afternoon with a pad and a pencil and wrote down some thoughts on her chosen profession, on the role of education, and on what she wants for her students. She realized that some rethinking of her approach to teaching would help her to begin the new school year with a renewed energy and commitment. Miss Abbott made these notes:

> I went into teaching because I enjoy being with children and because I think that teaching is the most important profession. It has always seemed to me to have the greatest potential to make the most lasting positive difference to the largest number of people. The fate of our democracy, our very way of life, depends on the political and economic participation of all its citizens. But despite these lofty ideals and aspirations, my frustration is that I may not be able to do my part. Although I want all the students to learn, I know that many of them leave my classroom without the skills they need to succeed at the next level. Some of the children are bored because they already know what I am trying to teach. Others are frustrated because they have difficulty in learning what I am teaching.
>
> What I love most are the times when I read to the children and we talk about the characters and the story. Some of the so-called slower children have the best insights. I want them all to love ideas and to exercise their imaginations in creative use of language. I also want these students to gain respect for one another; too often I see that some children are left out of activities and ignored by the rest. I want the students to work together and to learn to cooperate with one another in the classroom. Most of all, I want them to leave kindergarten with more curiosity about learning than when they walked into school in September.

In reading what she had written, Miss Abbott circled the key words and phrases that indicated her primary concerns for the children in her classroom. Then she wrote the following goals:

1. The children will develop the skills necessary to succeed in first grade.
2. Those who have attained a certain skill level will not be bored while others are still learning those skills.
3. The children will be introduced to ideas and language that will stimulate their imaginations.

4. The students will develop confidence in their abilities to learn.

5. The students will appreciate one another and learn to work cooperatively.

"Fine," she thought to herself. "Now, how do I make this happen?"

The first step was to find out as much as possible about the children who would be coming next fall, a habit she had neglected in recent years. The school is located in a small southern city, in a neighborhood close to a university. Some of her students are the children of university faculty and others are the sons and daughters of the hourly employees, such as secretaries who run the offices, janitors who clean the buildings, and cooks who prepare the meals. Most of the children of the faculty are white; many of the children of the support staff are black. Some of the children have traveled around the world; some have never been out of the city.

Frequently, she had walked around the neighborhoods where students in her class lived. There were some streets where maids were carefully sweeping the porches and gardeners were mowing the verdant lawns. On other streets, houses stood on lots where no grass grew in the hard-packed dirt in front of sagging stoops.

She knew that regardless of the neighborhood, some children would suffer from abuse and neglect and others would be nurtured and cared for. She realized how important it was for her to bring together these children from different neighborhoods and family environments and to provide a classroom atmosphere where all could succeed. Could she make each child feel important, safe, and competent with her and with one another? Could each of them feel that school was a place of happiness where they were glad to be? Could she feel that way as well?

Readiness tests had been given to each child when he or she had enrolled in the system. Miss Abbott spent the next day going through the results. One of the children who would be in her classroom could have entered the second grade on the basis of the tests. More than one third of the children, however, were more than 1 year below the norm. Over half the children would be eligible for the after-school child-care program because of working parents. Most of the children showed some potential for problems in their readiness to learn. In the past, she would have focused on the number of children with potential learning problems and wished that they were in some other class. This time, she told herself that these children must be a part of the challenge of teaching. In the planning process, she would attend to their special needs.

The old school building was not air-conditioned, so she would again have to get the children outdoors as much as possible during the early fall months. These ventures must be tied to learning, however, and not just for cooling off. There was no money in the school budget for trips, so when they went outside it would need to be in the neighborhood of the school or on the playground. Also, if she were going to move the group around, they would need to understand the rules and to cooperate with her and with one another.

She thought about the subject matter the students needed to learn and recalled a chart prepared by the school system that listed the important skills children should master in kindergarten. One skill relating to hand/eye coordination would be developed by teaching the children to stay inside the lines as they colored with large crayons.

The word *line* caused her to remember that during the first weeks of school the students would learn to line up before leaving the room and stay in line as they moved through the halls. This was important when she took the children on walking trips in the neighborhood. On the playground they were to develop gross motor skills by bouncing a ball across a line.

As she reviewed the skills chart, it occurred to her that the concept of *line* arose frequently and might be an excellent focus for the first unit; she could introduce a number of ideas about lines that could be expanded upon throughout the year. For instance, the concept of *lines* can represent a drawing within, as well as an acceptance of, limits. Lines are used to form boundaries and to represent infinity. Two ends of a curved line can be joined to form a circle. Straight lines can be assembled to form a square. Miss Abbott smiled as she realized that in her enthusiasm she could go off in many directions at once. There was a limit to what she could include in one unit and how much these children could absorb. "Keep in mind how many times the same concept has to be experienced before it can be understood," she reminded herself. It was time to order her own thoughts in developing the unit on lines.

Miss Abbott's Plan

Typically, Miss Abbott planned a unit to last for 2 to 6 weeks, depending on the time of year and the content to be covered. Miss Abbott usually divided each unit into four to six lessons, with each lesson lasting 3 to 5 days. There was an organizing theme for each unit (for example, the unit on community helpers that every kindergarten teacher taught) and an organizing subtheme or idea for each lesson (e.g., nurses and doctors, police and fire officers). The unit objectives were explained to the students at the beginning of the unit; lesson objectives were explained at the beginning of each week and cumulatively reviewed each day in oral and written form. A space on the chalkboard was reserved solely for this purpose; if the students were to learn to read, they needed to see important information in print, and this was one way to effect that. And she had always thought it important to keep the kindergartners informed about what led to what in their study.

Her experience had taught her much about teaching. In the past, Miss Abbott had often developed daily lesson plans that were unrelated to one another and were not part of any design. Over the years, she became convinced that students did better when they could see connections in what they were learning each day. Unit planning helped her to decide what to include and in what order.

She decided that the general objectives for this first unit on lines would be as follows:

■ Students will feel a part of the group and be enthusiastic about the learning process (an affective objective).
■ Students will understand the meaning of the concept *line* (a cognitive objective).
■ Students will line up when asked to do so, within 30 seconds, without intimidation (a psychomotor, cognitive, and affective objective).

- Students will increase hand/eye coordination as evidenced by the ability to stay inside the lines when coloring (a psychomotor objective).
- Students will be able to distinguish between a straight line and a curved line (a cognitive objective).
- Students will be able to identify a circle (a cognitive objective).
- Students will be able to identify a square (a cognitive objective).

Then she preliminarily organized the content for the unit in the following arrangement:

Learning about Lines

Straight lines	Lines that curve
Lines of people/Lines on a page	Faces and flowers
Squares	Circles

As she moved parts around and decided what the children could learn and what would be appropriate, she realized that there was probably more content here than she could cover in one unit. Why not limit this introductory unit to 2 weeks and reserve major study of the concepts of geometric shapes—the square and the circle—for a separate, but related, unit to follow? There would then be less chance of confusion at the critical stage when the young learners would need to be clear on the fundamental notion of *line* as distinct from two- and three-dimensional shapes. Besides, by separating this first unit into two related units, she could do more with the second part on geometric shapes.

Thus the initial unit on lines would be planned in anticipation of a follow-up unit. Now her diagram of the content included squares and circles, but these would each be the focus of a future unit of study. In other words, she could make lines the organizing concept of the unit and that would tie several units of study together. Her revised diagram looked like this:

Learning about Lines

Squares	Circles
Lines that are straight	Lines that are curved
Soldiers in a parade/Lines in a book	Faces and flowers
Angles and sides	Inside and outside of lines

As she prepared the first lesson in the unit on lines for the opening day of school, Miss Abbott was plagued again by second thoughts. After all, this was a difficult concept and these were very young children. Yet, she thought, they hear this word *line* all the time. Adults are always talking to them about lines: "Wait in line to get on the bus," "Make a beeline for bed," and "Draw a line." Even so, she wondered how to make this abstract concept more concrete.

It occurred to her that the children might need to have a line to hold in their hands to touch and to feel. The kind of line that would be the most familiar to them would be a fishing line, but nylon fishing line might cut. The line she needed would have to be something strong that would not break and still would not hurt the children's hands. She visualized bright lines of yarn extending out the door of the classroom on the first morning to draw in the children. Now she felt more confident about planning the details for the unit on lines. She calculated that each lesson in the unit would occupy less than an hour each day.

Unit: Lines That Draw Us Together

Teaching time: Ten days, 1 hour or less per day.
Unit objectives: The students will do the following:

1. Feel at home and wanted in the classroom (affective).
2. Define the concept line (cognitive).
3. Describe inside and outside the line (cognitive).
4. Form a line in an orderly and expeditious manner (psychomotor, cognitive, and affective).
5. Discriminate between lines and nonlines (cognitive).

Opening Activity—Drawing in the Students

Objective: The children will feel welcome and wanted in the classroom.

Just outside the classroom will be a table. Lines of yarn will extend from the classroom and will be draped across the table. Attached at the end of each line will be a cardboard fish with a child's name on it. A parent volunteer will stand at the door, and as the children arrive they will line up. One at a time, the children will come forward, and the volunteer will give each child the string with his or her name on it and call out the name. The teacher will pull in the yarn and welcome each child. When all the children are assembled in the room, and throughout the first week, stories emphasizing lines will be read aloud to the class (e.g., *The Line Up Book* by Marisabina Russo and *Lines and Shapes* by Solvig Russell).

Estimated time: Day One of unit; 30 minutes.

Materials: 12-foot lengths of heavy, brightly colored yarn; cardboard name tags in the shape of fish; and appropriate books.

Evaluation: Ask the parent volunteer to observe the children's reactions, particularly those children who display fear or frustration with the activity. Make notes following the activity.

Lesson One: Practicing the "Line-Up"

Instructional model: Direct instruction.

Estimated time: On appropriate occasions each day of first 2 weeks, 2 to 7 minutes (or faster) per occasion, depending on skill level.

Objective: The children will form a line in an orderly and expeditious manner.

Rationale for choice of model: "People moving" is one of the fundamental routines that teachers must establish at the beginning of each year. Going to lunch, to recess, to other classrooms, to the bathroom are all part of the typical day of the elementary student and his or her teacher. Precisely because lining up to move is such a basic routine, direct instruction is most suitable for its mastery. Sometimes the model is called the training model, a terminology we have rejected as having a negative connotation, although it does get the point across. Kindergarten-age children do have to be trained to get in line with minimum confusion; in a week of short practice sessions, the students will be so accustomed to lining up on command that the procedure will be second nature to them. Such behavioral habits lend themselves perfectly to a direct instruction approach.

Application of the model: Lines will be taped to the floor with a place for each child marked on each line. Each child will practice taking his or her place on the different lines, on command, as appropriate to the purpose of the line-up. The children will be called to their places: by name at first, then by rows, and then by boys/girls. As each student takes a place on the line, he or she will establish a direction and a path from desk to line, depending on where the line-up is and how it is arranged. Short practice periods each day will establish the necessary behavioral patterns.

Evaluation: The activity of lining up will be timed repeatedly and a daily record will be kept of the increasing efficiency of the class in taking their places on the line.

Lesson Two: Defining a Line

Instructional model: Concept attainment.

Estimated time: Day Two of unit; 20 minutes.

Objective: The children will develop an initial definition for the concept *line*.

Rationale for choice of model: A concept is a general idea derived from encounters with specific instances. Before this lesson and the lessons and units that will build on it can proceed, it is crucial that students have a working definition of lines. There will be many opportunities for them to refine their concept of line in the lessons and learning activities to follow. The intent of this concept attainment activity is to establish the general idea of line so that students have the groundwork on which to build successively sophisticated understandings. For example, these children eventually will learn that although two points define a line, every line extends in two directions to infinity. An infinite number of lines in a plane define that plane, which is also infinite in its single dimension. But these and many other very sophisticated concepts will be built on the initial understanding of what a line is and is not. Thus the choice of concept attainment as the instructional model to introduce the general idea of line is appropriate.

Application of the model: The children will sit in a circle on the floor. They will then be presented with a number of positive and negative examples of the concept.

Positive Examples

A clothesline

A fishing line

A line drawn on the board
A line taped to the floor
The cracks between the ceiling tiles and between the floor tiles
A picture of the crosswalk on the back-to-school safety poster

Negative Examples
A bowl
A fork
A shoe
A picture of a fish

Evaluation: A variety of items like those used in the lesson will be placed on a table. At different times of the day, ask each child individually to select something that can be used as a line or to represent a line, and ask the child to explain the selection. Those children who did not understand the concept can receive individual attention at this stage.

Lesson Three: Refining the Concept of Line

Instructional model: Concept development.
Estimated time: Day Three of unit; 30 minutes.
Objective: The children will discriminate between those items that are lines and those that are not.
Rationale for choice of model: Having acquired the basic idea of line, the students will now need practice in applying their idea to a variety of circumstances. It is not enough to know, conceptually, what a line is unless the learners can categorize things they encounter as lines or not lines. Although this skill was alluded to in the previous day's lesson, the question now is: Can the children think with their new ideas? The development of concepts rests only superficially on definition. To think *with* definitions, the learners will need practice in categorization. Categorization is the essence of concept development; thus that is this lesson's model of choice.
Application of the model: Pictures of different items will be selected and prepared for the flannel board; some items will be lines and some will not. Of the lines, some will be curved and some will be straight. The group will decide which items can be grouped together and will talk about what these items all have in common and why they are alike in some way.
Materials: Pictures of lines and pictures of other items; a flannel board and material to prepare the pictures.
Evaluation: A parent volunteer will observe the group and note those children who are not participating or who do not seem to understand the concept of line well enough to apply it to the task of discrimination. In addition, students will be asked to look for lines on their way to and from school, and they will discuss the examples they find in class.

Activity: The Line Game

Objective: The children will describe staying inside and outside of a line.

Description of activity: Two lines will be drawn on the playground. The students will line up just outside the lines, on each side, to begin the hokey pokey song. The first time they will practice just "I put my body in, I put my body out" and so on. The emphasis will be on going inside and outside the line as they dance, in preparation for learning to color inside the line. The related concepts of inside and outside, however, will not be stressed at first. The activity will be repeated several days for fun and then used as an organizer in teaching students about "staying inside the line" (e.g., "When we do the hokey pokey on the playground, what do we say we are doing with the line?").

Evaluation: See if the children can follow the directions. Make a clipboard list of those children who cannot remember the words or who have coordination problems.

Notes on Lessons One, Two, and Three

The following is an anecdotal record of what happened when Miss Abbott taught her unit on lines.

The opening activity went very well except for the awkward moment when several of the children arrived at the same time and the lines got tangled. Miss Abbott decided that the next time she used this activity she would use soft clothesline rope.

Preparing the concept attainment lesson had taken more time than Miss Abbott had anticipated. Her first task was to define for herself the meaning of *line*. She wrote down that a line was something that had a beginning and an end and was connected. Then she realized that she could not tell what was the beginning and what was the end and just what was it that connected the two. The definition of a line was not as simple as she had thought. The dictionary had 30 different definitions of the word, but the root of the word was from the Latin *linea* for "linen thread." The definition she finally settled on was two ends connected by something that looks like a string or a rope.

After each child had been seated in a circle on the floor, Miss Abbott held up the word *line* and said, "This is a word we are going to learn all about today. This word is *line*."

Tommy said, "I can read that word."

Miss Abbott remembered the high test results for Tommy. "Good, Tommy," she said and continued. "Look at the line you followed into the room today. Tell me what it looks like."

The children said that it was made of yarn, that it went from one place to the other, and that you could follow it. "Let's look at another line and see if it is like the line you followed."

This time she held up a clothesline. "Is this one made of yarn?"

"No," came a chorus of answers.

"Then a line doesn't have to be made out of yarn. How is this line like the one you followed?"

"Well, it has two ends like a snake. But it doesn't have a head and a tail," said one of the children. Several of the children began to talk about snakes and Miss Abbott had to bring them back.

"Tommy, point to the two ends of the line you followed in and to the two ends of the clothesline. That's right, Tommy. Now, everybody find the two ends of your line. Can we say that a line has two ends? What is between the two ends?" Miss Abbott asked as she held up the line of yarn and the clothesline. The children were puzzled and several began to creep away from the group. Miss Abbott realized that for most of them this was too hard, but Tommy came to the rescue.

"Something that's skinny and bends," he said. This response caught the attention of the children and they got back in the circle.

Miss Abbott held up a fishing line. "Does this have two ends?"

"Yes," they chorused. "And you can catch fish on it," one of the little boys said.

"Are the two ends connected by something that is—can I use the word *thin*, Tommy?—that is thin and can bend?"

Shanice said that she liked the word *skinny*, and so did the rest of the class. Miss Abbott decided that for the time being she would accept their word.

Next she pointed to a line that had been taped to the floor. "This is a line, too," she said. "Does it have two ends?"

"Yes," they chorused.

"Is it skinny?"

"Yeeess!" They were really into the action now.

"But," she asked, "will this line bend?"

Tommy did not want to lose his definition. "You could draw another line that would be bent," he said.

"Yes, Tommy, you are right. But this line will not bend. So, in your definition, a line doesn't have to bend. Tommy, you hold up the clothesline. Shanice, you hold up the fishing line, and all of you look at your yarn lines. What can we see that is the same about them all?"

"Well, they have two ends, and they have a skinny thing in between and they are floppy," said Maria.

"Don't forget the line taped to the floor," said Miss Abbott. "Is that line floppy?"

Maria liked the word *floppy*, but she agreed that the line taped to the floor was not. "Our lines have two ends with something skinny in between."

Miss Abbott thought about how "skinny" seemed to please the children. It had not occurred to her when she planned the lesson, but it was a word that seemed to fit. She held up a cup. "Is this a line?" she asked.

"No," they said in unison. "Because it doesn't have two ends and it isn't skinny."

"It isn't floppy either," said Maria, attempting to get her word back in.

Tommy said, "It doesn't have to be floppy, stupid."

Miss Abbott put her hand on Tommy's shoulder and said, "No one in this class is stupid. We all work together." She made a mental note to think through why

Tommy needed to say what he did and to plan for a lesson soon using the exploration of feelings model through which they could discuss name calling.

Miss Abbott held up a long piece of string. "Is this a line?" she asked.

"Well, it has two ends with something skinny between. Yes."

A fork got a quick rejection, as did a plate and a hat.

The next day they had lesson three, using the concept development model, in which she asked the children to put together all the things that were lines and those things that were not. So far, so good, she thought. And then she realized that she was really excited about what was happening in the class. Exciting and stimulating were two words that had been missing from her classroom for some time.

Epilogue

As the weeks progressed, Miss Abbott became more enthusiastic about the abilities of all her students. Tommy, who was often the catalyst for ideas and a source of information, gradually developed a respect for the rights and abilities of the other students. As concepts grew one upon the other, the children responded to the logic behind what they were being asked to learn. One memorable moment came during the lesson on squares when they were discussing the relationship between lines and squares. Shanice said, "You know, Miss Abbott, skinny isn't a very good word to describe a line." And all the class agreed.

In the months that followed, Miss Abbott introduced the related concepts of circle and square building on the concept definition of a line as two ends connected by something that looks like a string or rope. A clothesline was used to show how simple geometric figures could be formed from a line.

ACTIVITY 16.1

Regardless of the age of students you teach or plan to teach, develop lessons that will fit into the unit described in this chapter for kindergarten youngsters. If you do not wish to use *line*, try *square* or *circle*, or choose a concept of particular interest to you. Select a concept, however, that will be challenging to young minds and then challenge yourself to design lessons appropriate for the kindergarten classroom. Use as many of the instructional models as are appropriate in your lesson plans. ■

Summary

Knowledge of the background and abilities of the students in a class is essential to planning, if that knowledge is coupled with a determination to see each child's needs as a welcome challenge. Young children can be presented with content that is challenging and interesting to them as long as appropriate instructional techniques are used.

CHAPTER

17 A Middle School Case Study

The interdisciplinary teaching team for the seventh grade at Mumford Middle School had a problem. Some of the teachers on the team, which covered the subjects of math, social studies, language arts, and science, were concerned that the students were fixed in their opinions. As Alice Brown, the science teacher, said one morning in frustration, "Narrow-minded, that's what they are! These kids just won't entertain a new thought about a fact or idea in the courses they take or about each other. Sometimes teaching them feels more like plowing rock than planting seeds."

So began a conversation that would extend over several days and result in one of the most exciting teaching experiences any of these teachers had known. Like many teachers, the team had fallen into a rut, but they were about to find a way out of it.

Sam Lopez, the math teacher, who was a native of the small midwestern farming community in which the school was located, came to the defense of the local community. "This may not be cosmopolitan Madison Avenue, Alice, but in place of refinement, there is good, solid common sense in this community and in these kids. Their behavior is generally very good, and you know it is. They do what they are told and what their parents expect them to do."

"Yes," replied Alice, "but they also think the way they are told, and they can be cruel to those who are different in any way. In science, it is very important to be willing to look at ideas with an open and inquiring mind."

Mary Teague, the social studies teacher, took her usual role of conciliator. "I appreciate that they are dependable and that they are motivated to do well. I, too, however, am concerned that we challenge their intellects and encourage them to play with ideas instead of being so concerned that they get a good grade."

Henry Martin, the English and language arts teacher and the usual bemused observer, said, "If we decide to challenge their intellects, we'd better be sure that the school board doesn't decide to challenge us. Those board members may not be very enthusiastic about the kids playing around with ideas."

"I'm not thinking of turning them into radical revolutionaries," said Alice. "I just want them to have some perspective, a point of view broader than that shared by the members of this community."

"Sounds radical enough to me," Henry rejoined. "Oh, well, it might break the boredom for a while."

Alice ignored the cynicism. "It just so happens that lately I've been thinking of a unit of study based on the concept of *perspective*. My hope is that I can get our students to consider the various ways in which a problem may be approached, whether it is a problem in science or in any other subject."

"It's funny you should mention the word *perspective* this morning, Alice," said Sam. "I have been working on a unit in geometry, where perspective is all-important. My thought was that because the kids are fascinated with the design capabilities of computers, I might introduce them to linear perspective in a way that would teach them both about a new design program we have and about lines in three-dimensional space."

Alice responded with renewed enthusiasm, momentarily forgetting her frustration with the students. "You know, understanding the use of perspective marked the Renaissance. It literally changed forever the way we would describe and know the universe. I have always wanted to know more about the mathematical principles involved in the great paradigm shift of the Renaissance. I'd also like to teach the impact of perspective on our understanding of the physical world, particularly in regard to mapmaking. Could we plan this unit together?" she asked Sam.

"The concept of perspective certainly fits into the unit I am preparing to teach on the westward movement," Mary interjected. "I've been trying to think how to get across the idea that historians have their own perspectives that influence the way in which they recount events. No doubt, any historical perspective differs from that of the people who were involved in the events of history. Think how much difference it makes if one looks at the westward movement from the perspective of a settler or from the perspective of a Native American. I've heard it said that those who win the wars win the right to write the histories."

"You know, we haven't taught an interdisciplinary unit in a long time. Why don't we design a unit with a focus on the concept *perspective?*" said Alice, her excitement evident to all.

Henry abandoned his role of detached observer and enthusiastically joined in. "I have been planning a unit in literature on point of view, but perspective is really the basis for understanding the meaning of point of view. As I recall, the viewpoint—or point of view—is the point where parallel lines converge in a painting to convey a sense of depth." Turning to Alice, he said, "It was the Renaissance painters who rediscovered this technique from Greek writings and who were able to create perspective in their painting just as the mapmakers learned to do. Perspective is a much better concept to use for the focus of my unit. And I can choose material that will fit into your time frame of the westward movement," he continued, as he turned toward Mary. "That way we can look at historical perspective through the eyes of fictional characters as well as the historian."

As usual, the other team members were astonished at the wealth of information Henry could bring to a discussion when he chose. Everyone was ready, without actually putting the matter to any sort of vote, to try an interdisciplinary unit based on the concept of *perspective.*

The four team members shared a common planning time and were able to schedule the students for blocks of time each day. The rooms in which they taught were traditional classrooms except for one movable wall that allowed them to create a larger classroom for special purposes. In the past, their attempts at team teaching had been only partially successful, but this time they seemed to have ignited one another's interest.

At the next team meeting, Mary suggested that they brainstorm objectives for the unit. "For instance," she said, "I want the students to compare and contrast the perspectives of various groups regarding the westward movement. I want them to evaluate the perspective of the historian who is writing as well as to identify other possible perspectives of those who were involved in the events."

"I am concerned that they be able to define the term *perspective* in a general sense and then to see how perspective relates to writing," said Henry. "In their writing, I want them to use various perspectives to describe an event as well as develop more dynamic ways to describe how others feel and act."

"I want them to be able to accept the possibility that there are various ways to look at the same phenomenon," said Alice, "and I want them to recognize and value the importance of looking beyond and questioning what appears to be obvious. I also want them to use the scientific approach in solving problems that require inquiry, particularly problems in which perspective affects how we interpret the physical world."

"I want them to use parallel lines and viewpoint to create perspective in simple designs with the use of the computer," said Sam. "Some of these kids are way ahead of me already on the computer, and I am really going to have to do my homework to keep up. That's part of the great fun we have teaching in a field that is developing faster than any of us can imagine, let alone keep up with. But in all the excitement of computers, I want the students to develop respect for the capabilities of this tool in describing three-dimensional phenomena on a two-dimensional screen."

Henry rolled his eyes as he sensed just how enthusiastic everyone was becoming, but he did so very slightly, not wishing to offend as much as to poke a little fun. But Alice wasn't going to let the seriousness of the moment pass. "And all of us are concerned that the students develop more understanding for others and increase their willingness to consider another point of view in solving problems in human relations," she said.

"We have our objectives for the unit right in front of us," said Mary. "There is *so much* content that we could incorporate into this unit! I think we should each bring to our next meeting an outline of the most important concepts that need to be covered in each discipline."

When they met again, each of them had diagrammed the main concepts that they thought should be included in the unit on *perspective*. (See Table 17.1.)

It was obvious that *viewpoint*, so important in creating perspective, had become an essential concept as it applied to understanding events and ideas relating to perspective. The teachers then realized that the meaning of *viewpoint* was one that the art teacher, Mrs. Fisk, could best explain to the students. She agreed that a discussion on the point at which parallel lines converge in a painting, or in a design, to create the illusion of space would serve as an excellent advance organizer for the study of perspective. It was exciting to think that a fundamental concept of the art curriculum would be the focal point for study in many different disciplines simultaneously. This single concept would bring everything together, just as it had during the Renaissance!

TABLE 17.1   Main Concepts for an Interdisciplinary Unit on Perspective

Geometry	Earth Science	Literature	History
The viewpoint	The viewpoint	Point of view	Point of view
Geometry	Exploration/Mapmaking	Characters	Participants
Parallel	Scientific method/Inquiry	Plot	Events
Point, line		Narrator	Historian
plane			

After their discussion with Mrs. Fisk, she agreed to do the keynote lesson twice—each time in the double classroom with two of the teachers and their classes present. The advance organizer for this lesson is shown in Table 17.2.

The Mumford Plan

When designing the unit, the team members decided to emphasize the geometry and earth science portions during the first part of the unit, followed by the literature and history sections. The art teacher's introductory lesson would extend across two days, at which time the main concepts related to perspective would be introduced. *Viewpoint*, or physical point of view, would be tied to visual perspective and to ideas and attitudes.

Mrs. Fisk planned to teach the definition of *viewpoint* by using the concept attainment model, allowing the definition to serve as an organizer and point of reference for all the team teachers throughout the unit. Her idea was to spend one day helping the students to capture elementary perspective in their own drawings. The

TABLE 17.2   Perspective: Advance Organizer—Viewpoint

Art	Geometry/Science	History/Literature
Space	Design	Plot/Events
Distance	Point, line, plane	Character
Relative position	Parallel	Narrator
	Convergent	
	Scientific method	

next day she would bring in prints of pre-Renaissance and Renaissance art to use as positive and negative examples of perspective in art. A collection of M. C. Escher's pen-and-ink drawings, in which the mathematician/artist plays with perspective in a variety of ways, would serve as material for a culminating reinforcement activity. She would close with a brief lesson on how the students could achieve such play and deliberate ambiguity in their own drawings.

Following this lesson, all the teachers would explain the plans for the unit as it pertained to their classes, provide an outline of assignments and activities, and answer any questions the students might have about the unit. A test of the students' understanding of the content to be covered, to provide valuable information to the teachers regarding any changes or modification that might need to be made in the unit's design, would be given at this point. The test was particularly important to Sam in setting up the teams for instruction in computer skills.

The geometry and science lessons would be taught for approximately 3 weeks. After the students had a basic introduction to computer-aided design (CAD), they would learn to create simple three-dimensional designs with the use of the computer. Sam decided that a form of the Jigsaw model used in conjunction with direct instruction would be an excellent way to teach the principles of CAD. Students would first work through a tutorial on the basics of computer design individually. Then, pairs of students would be given elementary problems to solve with immediate feedback on their success. Next, teams of students with a range of abilities related to the computer would be formed, making it possible for students with more advanced computer skills to work with those with less skill. Each team would be charged with solving a different problem set while acquiring a different set of computer skills associated with computer-aided design. Individual team members would be expert in a particular aspect of design, and they would have the responsibility of teaching other students in their study group.

Following the computer lessons, the science teacher would introduce the relationship of perspective to an understanding of the physical world, particularly in recording what is observed through the design of maps. Alice would present puzzling but relatively common problem situations involving perspective. The students would solve these problems with an inquiry approach using the Suchman model. For instance, one problem would be to describe the appearance of a ship on the horizon and explain why it seems to grow larger as it draws near. Another problem would be to explain why the moon seems to be very large on the horizon but appears to grow smaller as it rises in the sky. The third and most difficult problem the students would be asked to solve by inquiry would be that of how to transfer the surface of a sphere (like a globe of Earth) onto a flat surface without distorting the relative sizes of land masses.

With these introductions to the concept of *perspective* as a foundation, Mary and Henry would work with the students toward an understanding of the way in which individuals interpret events in literature and in history, stressing that interpretation often depends on the individual's point of view. They decided that concept development, direct instruction, and Jigsaw models would be effective in meeting their objectives. (This part of the unit is described in more detail in the next section.)

The concluding lesson in the unit would be to discuss how an understanding of perspective applies in human relations. Using the exploration of feelings/resolution of conflict model, each teacher would lead groups of students in applying what they had learned regarding perspective to the exploration of feelings and the possible resolution of conflict in a particular situation.

To illustrate how the models approach to teaching would work in this unit, we present the detailed lesson design from the portion that focused on the concept of *perspective* in history and literature, which is described in Table 17.3.

TABLE 17.3   Perspective in History and Literature, Middle School Plan

Lesson	Time	Objectives	Models and Activities	Materials
1. Point of view (4 days)	4 hours	1. Generalize that a variety of points of view can exist on a given subject.	Concept development	Series of quotations
		2. Relate meaning of *point of view* and *perspective* in art, science, and math to attitudes and beliefs.		
		3. Define *bias* and *preconceptions.*	Vocabulary acquisition	Dictionaries
2. Perceptions (3 days)	3 hours	The students will describe how preconceptions and experience offset perception.	Direct instruction	Filmstrip from AA
			Role play	Overhead projector
3. Relating perceptions to perspective (3 days)	3 hours	1. Relate the concept of *perspective* to literature and history by recognizing how individuals perceive events.	Jigsaw	Readings for Jigsaw groups
		2. Identify various perspectives in writing.	Classroom discussion	Quotations for class discussion

Unit: Perspective—It All Depends on Where You Were When

Teaching time: 2 weeks.
Objectives: The students will do the following:

1. Compare the meaning of perspective in geometry and science to the use of the concept in literature and history.
2. Relate the concept *perspective* to literature and history by recognizing how individuals perceive both real and fictional events.
3. Identify various perspectives in a situation, explain the point of view of each participant, and explain how the point of view determines the perspective.
4. Describe how previous experiences and preconceptions affect the perception of events.
5. Be willing to describe a perspective other than their own in relation to a situation.

Advance organizer: Relate the meaning of *viewpoint* as it has been discussed in art, geometry, and science to the application of the term in literature, history, and human relations. Introduce the idea that it is the point of view that determines perspective.

Lesson One: Toward a Perspective on Point of View

Instructional models: Concept development and vocabulary acquisition.
Estimated time: 2 hours.
Objectives: The students will do the following:

1. Generalize that a variety of *points of view* can exist on a single subject.
2. Relate the meaning of *point of view* and *perspective* in art, science, and math to attitudes and beliefs.
3. Define *bias* and *preconceptions* and relate these terms to their own experience.

Rationale for choice of models: It has been said that there are three kinds of thinkers: those who think that what they think is the only way to think, those who think others who think like they do are the best thinkers, and those who can think in several ways about the same thing. The psychologist Jean Piaget termed the first thinker *egocentric*, the second thinker *concrete*, the last and best thinker *formal*. But Piaget's great contribution to psychology was in proving that the child learns from experience by constructing a model of how the world is. Concept development will provide the students the opportunity to see that different points of view (of possibly equal validity) can be held by reasonable thinkers on the same topic. As they have the chance to discriminate between different points of view on a similar topic, they will see that each thinker is at once a concrete thinker, who sees the world through one set of eyes, and a formal thinker, who can recognize the reasonableness of alternative views of the same facts and ideas. Vocabulary acquisition will provide a definition for the terms *bias* and *preconceptions.*

Application of the models: After the students have clearly identified the terms, they will be given a series of quotations representing points of view that are both alike and different in various ways. For instance, some will represent the same bias, some will be about the same event, some will be spoken by the same person. The students will be asked to group and categorize these quotations and then to explain the reason for their decisions. The students will work in pairs and then come together as a large group to discuss their decisions and the reasons for their decisions.

Evaluation: At the conclusion of this model, the students will discuss what they learned earlier in the unit during the math and science portions and how that material relates to the new learning of this lesson. This discussion will also serve as a midpoint evaluation of the students' progress.

Lesson Two: Perception—It Depends on Where You Are Coming From

Instructional models: Direct instruction and role play.

Estimated time: 3 hours.

Objective: The students will describe how preconceptions and experience affect the perception of an event.

Rationale for choice of model: Instruction will be both indirect and direct in that the teachers will set up a circumstance that gives rise to questions that will be answered by direct instruction followed by a role play that will provide the material for a class discussion. (As this example demonstrates, direct instruction does not equal passive learning.) Basically, the questions the teachers will pose and the activities in which the students will engage center on the issue of perception: what one is predisposed to see and what one sees. But predisposition is always governed by three factors, and those factors are the point of this instruction. By setting up a series of experiences for the students whereby they see that the relation between where they are (figuratively and literally) and what they are observing determines what they see, the stage is set for presenting the three factors that define "where the observer is coming from."

Application of the models: The lesson will begin with the reading of a description of a house. The description includes the setting of the house; the number of windows, doors, and rooms; the present furnishings and decorations; where the occupants keep their valuables; and so on. Half the class will be asked to read the account as if they were a professional burglar, and the other half will read the account as if they were a prospective buyer of the house. (Because directions to the students will be written, rather than given orally, each half of the class will be unaware of the alternative perspective taken by the other half.) Following a silent reading of the passage, students will retell what they recall. (Research has shown that readers will focus their attention on the aspects of the information that bear on their interest.[1]) This initial experience will provide dramatic proof that the same experience for different people is a different experience. When perception is different, experience is different.

Next the teachers will have one group of students role play an armed robbery and have the observers write what they perceive to have happened. A second group will then enact the robbery after having been given additional information by the teacher. The observers will be asked to reevaluate their original perspectives based on perceptions they now have and with different information. This activity can be continued until all groups have an opportunity to participate in the role play. Following the role plays will be a discussion of the effect of the change of perspective on their reactions.

Using this activity as an organizer, the teachers will present the three factors that influence the perspective of those who witness events:

1. The viewpoint of the perceiver
2. Previous experience of the observer
3. Preconceptions

After these have been explained, with many examples, students will be questioned and will be asked to give examples themselves to check for understanding. More guided practice will occur when students view a filmstrip of an accident and then identify the various perspectives of the witnesses as these relate to point of view, possible previous experiences, and preconceptions. For independent practice, the students will be given an assignment to describe an event depicted on a television sitcom from the point of view, previous experience, and preconceptions of the different characters involved. They will then be asked to retell the event using another point of view, experience, and preconception.

Evaluation: Students will be given a worksheet to take home that will ask them to answer specific questions relating to the television program. Those students who choose to write their own essay may do so, but those who have more difficulty in writing may follow the format of the worksheet. These worksheets and essays will be evaluated to determine if the class understood the assignment.

Lesson Three: Relating Perception and Perspective

Instructional models: Jigsaw and classroom discussion.
Estimated time: 3 hours class time plus outside work in preparation.
Objectives: The students will do the following:

1. Relate the concept of *perspective* to literature and history by recognizing how individuals, both real and fictional, perceive events from their particular points of view.
2. Identify various perspectives in a writing, explain the point of view of each author, and explain how perception determines perspective.

Rationale for choice of models: Jigsaw is both an instructional model and an instructional activity, with the great virtues of accommodating a wide range of student abilities in a single classroom and allowing for great efficiency of effort on the part of the group. In this instance, the students can collectively read many selections and thus encounter many historical and fictional perspectives and points of view. By cooperating in their learning and sharing in their understandings, they will cover much ground quickly, reading, literally, hundreds of pages of material and experiencing the same ideas through many different eyes. Jigsaw thus allows each learner to come to the insights of many different learners merely by sharing his or her own insights.

The classroom discussion model is an effective way to conduct the discussion following Jigsaw. The teacher can select appropriate factual, interpretive, and evaluative questions related to the research conducted in the Jigsaw process.

Application of the models: The students will be assigned to teams of four, with a range of ability in each group. Each individual in the team will be given a reading assignment related to the westward movement; assignments will be selected to match the reading abilities of different team members. The teams will be given different sets of readings: some short stories, some selections from novels, some from original source documents, and some from textbook chapters on the westward expansion. The students have 3 days to study the material and will be directed to discuss their selections with members of a study group who have been assigned readings similar to their own. They are to identify the perspective of the author and of the major characters or persons in the story or essay and then to explain this perspective to the other members of their team. Following team discussions, the class as a whole will discuss the selections and the various perspectives presented in the material using the classroom discussion model.

Evaluation: The class discussion will be audio- or videotaped for the teachers to review and determine if the students have reached the objectives of the lesson.

Epilogue

At the end of the actual unit of study, the interdisciplinary teaching team had dinner together to discuss and evaluate their experience in teaching the unit. Although some activities had been unsuccessful, everyone wholeheartedly agreed that the unit had been a great success. The evaluations of how well the students had met the cognitive objectives indicated a high rate of success, and attitudinal surveys, designed to ensure anonymity, indicated that most of the students had enjoyed the unit and had an increased awareness of different perspectives.

The team remembered the final discussions with particular pleasure. The students had been presented with a situation that involved a person from another country with an entirely different culture enrolling at the school. The discussion centered on the various problems the student would encounter and how that individual's perspective would differ from that of others. The teachers had taped and compared the various discussions. All agreed that the students had gained insights into how others might feel about a particular situation. The teachers had also learned that these young people had the capacity to deal with complicated ideas and to respond to material that challenged their preconceptions. "My perception is that these really are a great bunch of kids," said Henry. And to that, there was agreement all around.

ACTIVITY 17.1

Regardless of the age of the students you teach or plan to teach, become a part of this interdisciplinary team. Design lessons that can be used in this unit or in a unit that focuses on an interdisciplinary study of another concept. ■

Summary

Cooperative planning by teachers across disciplines can provide a rewarding professional experience. In addition, such cooperation enriches the learning experience for students, particularly young adolescents, who enjoy seeing the way in which a concept threads meaning through a variety of disciplines, increasing the understanding of each.

NOTE

1. E. T. Goetz, D. L. Schallert, R. E. Reynolds, and D. I. Radin, "Reading in Perspective: What Real Cops and Pretend Burglars Look for in a Story," *Journal of Educational Psychology* 75 (1983): 500–510.

CHAPTER

18 A High School Case Study

As the pungent scent of Rudy's Dry Cleaners greeted Jake Samuels, an unfamiliar voice said, "Hi, Mr. Samuels."

"Hi," responded Mr. Samuels, trying to place the friendly face.

"I'm Chris Pezzoli. I go to Madison High School. May I help you?"

"My cleaning, please," Mr. Samuels answered, as he handed Chris the laundry ticket, still curious about where he had seen this young man. He was just a face in a sea of faces in the halls at Madison.

"Yes, sir. Coming right up." Chris started the line of clothes moving around. As Mr. Samuels's suit appeared, Chris handed it to him, saying, "I always wanted to have you for English, but I'm in a general class. I've heard what a good teacher you are, but you teach only the advanced classes." He hesitated, feeling a little embarrassed at his own boldness.

"Thanks for the vote of confidence. I'm sorry I'm not teaching you, Chris. I'd like to."

"So long." Chris shrugged and smiled. "See you around."

As he left the cleaners, Mr. Samuels thought about Chris. He thought about his own schedule. Now that he was chairperson of the department, he taught only three classes; and Chris was right, they were all top-track classes. The encounter reminded him, though, that he missed the general classes he used to teach. Those students struck a special chord for him, possibly because his was the last English class they might take. He remembered how he always wanted to give it all to them—everything he loved about English—served up on a silver platter so invitingly that they would surely seek more.

He began to think aloud. "Instead we water it down, trying to make it more palatable. But there's a contradiction in that. Shouldn't it be just the reverse? Shouldn't we enrich the content of classes for general students?"

As he turned onto Madison Avenue he was deep in thought. Sure, there had been problems when he taught general education and remedial classes. His teaching style of lecture and discussion did not work for students who had difficulty taking notes or paying attention for long periods. But he had learned so much in the past few years as department chairperson, observing other teachers and attending workshops and in-service sessions on instructional strategies. He had learned to use a variety of instructional models in his advanced classes, and he was certain that these would work well with all students. The idea he was contemplating would give him an opportunity to put his theory to the test. He wanted to try it.

At 4 o'clock the following Monday afternoon, Mr. Samuels poked his head into the classroom next to his. His colleague, Ms. O'Brien, was correcting papers.

"Liz, do you have a minute?"

"Sure, come on in. I'm always too drained to get anything accomplished this time of day. Good to see you, Jake. How do you manage to look so chipper at the end of a long day?"

"Thanks, I don't always feel chipper. It's just a facade I put on. I need to talk to you, though. I met a student of yours the other day, Chris Pezzoli. Tell me about him."

"Well, Chris is a very nice young man, imaginative and hard working, very likable. He's in my fourth-period class. I see his parents around town now and again. His dad was laid off when the woolen mill closed. He does odd jobs, forced self-employment, he calls it, but he hasn't been able to pick up anything steady. Chris's mother works, but they really need what Chris brings in from his job at a dry cleaner's. I know he's going to work there full time after graduation. I'm trying to talk him into taking community college courses at night, but I think it's futile. Of course, if his dad does find something steady. . . ." Her words trailed off without much hope in her voice.

Mr. Samuels interrupted, "I've been thinking about these kids in the general classes and about how much I miss teaching them. I had an idea. How would you like to try switching classes fourth period for about 4 weeks as a kind of experiment? I have some ideas I'd like to try with the kids. I thought I'd try to teach them *Macbeth*." After a pause, he grinned. "Think I'm crazy? You'd be teaching the poetry of the romantics, not one of my favorite units, but just your cup of tea, I know."

Ms. O'Brien looked at him for a minute as his suggestion took shape in her mind. "Do I think you're crazy? Yes. Do I think it's a good idea? It just might be an excellent idea. I'd love to see how they would respond, . . . and I'd love to have a crack at your kids. Nineteenth-century poetry is my first love."

Mr. Samuels's Plan

That night Mr. Samuels put aside the papers he was planning to grade. He thought about Chris and the large, probably slightly jaded group he would face. But the challenge of it was energizing; he was more excited than he had been for some time. He began making notes on what he wanted to accomplish.

First, he wanted them to enjoy the play. He pondered a minute, then crossed out *enjoy* and replaced it with an overworked word he seldom used in such a context, *love*. Yes, he wanted them to *love* this play, maybe the finest piece of literature ever written. He starred that goal. It would guide everything he did those 4 weeks. Next, he wanted them to appreciate how shrewd Shakespeare was and how relevant his thinking remains today.

Mr. Samuels wanted them to examine the concept *ambition* and how it can be a constructive force in moderation and a dangerous force in excess. To do this they must understand the complexity of Macbeth's and Lady Macbeth's characters. If seen as all bad, the students would miss a great deal of the play's wisdom. He wanted them to grasp the power of suggestion and of what it could mean to plant an idea in an all-too-fertile mind. Further, he wanted them to be stirred by the beauty, subtlety, and bawdiness of the language. He hoped to draw them into this Elizabethan world, much as Shakespeare had drawn his audiences into his plays.

Where did these goals come from? Mr. Samuels was an expert teacher with years of experience, and because of that he was willing to rely intuitively on his judgment as a teacher, his expertise in *Macbeth*, his convictions about these students' needs, and his knowledge of his community's expectations. Thus with some confidence he translated his vaguely defined goals into a specific list.

The students would do the following:

1. *Love* the play.
2. Gain confidence in their own intellects by partially mastering very difficult material.
3. Appreciate the power and relevance of Shakespeare's work.
4. Grasp some of the complexities related to the concept *ambition*.
5. Understand the complexity of the characters in *Macbeth*.
6. Recognize the effect of the power of suggestion.
7. Become attuned to the richness of iambic pentameter.
8. Become acquainted with the major distinguishing characteristics of Elizabethan England.

In the not-so-distant past, he might have stopped his general planning at this point and begun to think in terms of daily lessons. He had recently realized, however, that he needed to be far more precise in his planning. This meant listing specific student needs after researching the students' backgrounds. It meant selecting specific objectives and models that would help him reach those objectives. It also meant devising means of evaluating how well he had achieved those objectives. It sounded complicated, but it was becoming second nature and saved time and effort in the end. Most of all, it increased his sense of satisfaction.

During the next week he gathered a lot of data: He talked to Ms. O'Brien; he reviewed records and test scores; he casually and unobtrusively observed the class he was to teach; and he carefully reread the play and outlined the content for essential concepts. He remembered Chris's shrug. It had been eloquent; it had said, "We don't deserve the best."

Mr. Samuels believed that the students needed to be given challenging material, and implicit in his choice of *Macbeth* was the statement "You can do it; I will not teach down to you." But that in turn implied a commitment to give the students the support they needed to become independent. Although the thought seemed almost contradictory, it implied that he must not fail them or allow them to fail themselves. He knew they would not, but if the unit were to build their confidence, they would first have to commit themselves to the challenge, to like what they were doing well enough not to fail in it. He listed what the students would need:

1. To be presented with challenging material
2. To know that someone thought they could grasp difficult material
3. To be taken seriously and have their opinions sought and valued
4. To gain confidence in their own abilities
5. To talk about important issues and real feelings
6. To gain a sense of accomplishment because they had mastered difficult material successfully

Based on the combination of goals and needs that he had listed, Mr. Samuels wrote general objectives for the unit on *Macbeth* and considered how he might evaluate the unit's success. After all, if he could not demonstrate to himself that the students had learned and profited from this unit, then he should stay with the advanced classes. Mr. Samuels wrote his objectives, including methods to evaluate each objective.

1. Students will *love* the play *Macbeth* and be interested in learning more. This will be evaluated by using a pre- and postunit questionnaire in which the students can check their reactions without fear of being identified.

2. Students can relate themes in the play to their daily lives. This will be evaluated in skits developed by the students to place scenes from *Macbeth* in contemporary settings.

3. Students will demonstrate appreciation for the elegance of iambic pentameter and for how sound can augment meaning and humor. This will be evaluated by having them present a piece of their favorite music and explain how beat and lyrics work together.

4. Students will analyze the main characters and identify the elements in those characters that create complexity. A writing assignment will be used to evaluate this objective. Pictures could also be used to illustrate these elements; these pictures could be drawn or created as a collage of pictures cut from magazines. (He knew that in the past he had sometimes failed to realize that a student had understood a concept that had been taught but that the student had been unable to express the concept in written terms. The student could, however, sometimes express that concept if given another medium. Writing would not be neglected, but he wanted to be sure that he measured what he was teaching and not just the students' reading and writing skills.)

5. Students will demonstrate familiarity with Elizabethan England by teaching some aspects of that society to small groups (here using a cooperative learning model). Evaluation will be based on the students' performance in this activity.

6. Students will exhibit understanding of the power of suggestion and the idea of a self-fulfilling prophecy by giving examples from their daily lives. This will be evaluated through discussions and brief, taped oral presentations.

With these objectives in mind, he contemplated the possible models he would use to achieve them, in what sequence he would use them, and how much time he would allot for each part of the unit plan.

1. He would start with a concept attainment lesson on classics . . . no, he would use the term *best-sellers*, because that had more drawing power and was much more appropriate. Shakespeare, after all, was very conscious of box-office appeal. (Later, they would talk about the distinction between a classic and a best-seller and about how some works of art are both.) He would use positive examples of best-sellers, such as the Bible, *Gone with the Wind* (the movie), and Beatles music. His negative examples would consist of a lesser-known short story from their text, a poem he had written, a record called *Comin' Home* that a friend had cut, a favorite painting by a little-known artist from his hometown. Once they could define the concept of best-seller, he would ask what elements they would include if they were trying to write a play that would be a best-seller. He would make a list of their ideas (he predicted that they would mention things like suspense, violence, and a little romance), and then as a group they would try to derive a set of standards of excellence from this list.

Later they would apply their standards to *Macbeth*, considered in the time of its first appearance in the Globe Theatre. How many of the same standards did Shakespeare seem to apply? What standards did he employ that they did not? What ingredients did they think of that Shakespeare did not cover (for example, the medium of delivery)? How would the passage of 350 years alter the standards of literature? These questions and others that arose would cast a new light on the play for these young readers.

2. Next, he would use direct instruction with lectures, monologues, filmstrips, and artwork to give them background information on Shakespeare's life and times. He would emphasize the tricks Shakespeare used to capture the attention of the audience in the opening scenes. He would show the ghost in the opening scene of *Hamlet* and the fight in the opening scene of *Romeo and Juliet* and would make the students guess what ploy would be used to open *Macbeth*.

3. He would also use a cooperative learning model, Jigsaw, for background information. He would divide the class into five groups. The groups would research in preparation for teaching one another, in a variety of ways, about Elizabethan daily life (food, fashion, sports, sanitation, etc.), government, art and architecture, social class structure, education, and agriculture and industry.

4. He would open the play with the movie version of the first two acts of *Macbeth*, allowing the students to track the play in their books as they watched it. With a basic understanding of the plot firmly established, they would read act 3 together, dramatizing various scenes and speeches and closely examining words, connotations, and concepts.

5. He would have the students perform the concept development model on the word *ambition*.

6. If the reading of act 3 went well, they would read act 4 together rather than view the film. He would use cooperative learning again for act 5. In groups, they would role play various possible scenarios to present to the class.

7. While they were working on their scenes, he would interject a lesson on Lady Macbeth using the synectics model. This would be a powerful and effective tool for showing them the contradictions and opposing forces within a character.

8. When they had finished the play, he would use the exploration of feelings model in a discussion. To gain a more sympathetic view of the main characters, they would look at events through the eyes of the characters and try to assess their feelings.

9. Finally, he would build on these insights by using an inquiry model to explore how the tragedy came about. At the beginning of the play, Macbeth is not such a villain. He had many good qualities, but in a very brief time he had caused the downfall of most of his country's leadership. How had this happened? Was so much violence plausible? This was the puzzle he hoped to get them to consider. He suspected that they would see the cause of the tragedy purely in terms of too much ambition, and he wanted them to look further, to delve into other causes. To understand the answer to the questions posed, they would have to go outside the play and inquire about conditions in 11th-century Scotland. What about the isolation of life then, near the height of the Dark Ages? Perhaps it is easier to plot against someone you seldom see. It was a violent time, with frequent attacks from unknown sources, and a street-gang mentality had developed in response to the constant threat against the territory. Macbeth had gained his reputation by warring successfully. Mr. Samuels wanted the students to search for these explanations themselves; he did not want to spoon-feed them.

Mr. Samuels charted the sequence of lessons within the unit that he had developed (see Table 18.1). He felt that one detailed lesson—using concept development and classroom discussion—held an important key for understanding the play. Initially, he had focused solely in this lesson on the concept *ambition*, but the more he thought about this, the more he felt two primary concepts—*ambition* and *the power of suggestion*—were inextricably woven in the play. This lesson is described in the next section.

TABLE 18.1   *Macbeth*—A Study in Ambition Turned to Avarice

The Stage of Anticipation (Before the Play)	The Stage of Realization (During the Play)	The Stage of Contemplation (After the Play)
Concept attainment on best-sellers (1 day)	Synectics on Lady Macbeth (2 days)	Exploration of feelings of characters (1–2 days)
Direct instruction on background (1 day)	Concept development and classroom discussion on ambition/ power of suggestion (5+ days)	Suchman inquiry (1 day)
Jigsaw— research and student presentations on background (4 days)		
	Role plays of scenarios for act 5 (3 days)	

Unit: *Macbeth*—A Study in Ambition Turned to Avarice

Sample Lesson Five: Ambition and the Power of Suggestion

Teaching time: 6 to 8 days, on approximately the following schedule:

Monday and Tuesday: Concept development lesson on the witches, culminating with a paragraph by each student on one group of items in concept development lesson. The group's label will be the topic sentence, and the categorized items will be the supporting evidence.

Wednesday: Classroom discussion of the dual concepts of ambition and power of suggestion in *Macbeth*.

Thursday: Classroom discussion to continue, with emphasis on contemporary examples.

Friday: Students to find expression (e.g., a formal paper, collage, tape recording, drawing, or dialogue) for the single idea from the discussion that they found most interesting.

Monday: Students share their work in groups of three to get feedback, reactions, and suggestions.

Tuesday: Students share their final products with the class.

Lesson objectives: The students will do the following:

1. Express in one of several artistic media their comprehension of the meaning of the word *ambition* in its best sense.

2. State orally their understanding of the danger of a trait possessed in excess.

3. Demonstrate in writing how the concept of ambition relates to their daily lives.

4. Infer from discussions about the causes of Macbeth's and Lady Macbeth's ambition.

5. Describe in writing the power of suggestion by using examples from their daily lives.

6. Give examples of the connection between the two concepts.

7. Hypothesize orally about what form the witches might take in contemporary life.

Instructional Models: Concept Development and Classroom Discussion.   *Rationale for choice of models:* The students in this class will be likely to see things in rather concrete terms and to cast things in black and white. By verbalizing all the impressions they have of the witches in this play, they should see collectively what they may not see individually—namely, that the witches are symbolic of the fate that plays in every person's life. The students also need to see that the witches are Shakespeare's ploy for speaking directly to his audience about what is going on in Macbeth's mind and how strong the power of suggestion is. The classroom discussion model will extend the ideas generated by the class in the concept development activity. In addition, the discussion model will provide factual, interpretive, and evaluative questions regarding the *power of suggestion* and *ambition.*

Application of the Concept Development Model.   In effect, these two sophisticated concepts, the power of suggestion leading to unbridled ambition, will be approached through the witches.

Specific learning activities will have the students do the following:

1. List everything they remember about the witches (including inferences about their purpose).
2. Group these details.
3. Label these groups, showing their understanding and agreement on the reason for connecting the items.
4. Rethink these connections and new ones by forming new groups.[1]
5. Demonstrate their grasp of the witches' role by synthesizing the items and forming generalizations.

The following questions will direct this concept development lesson. (The parenthetic instructions are reminders Mr. Samuels made to himself.)

1. What specific things does the word *witches* bring to mind in the play *Macbeth?* Or, name everything you can think of that is connected with the witches. (Do not stop until you have a comprehensive list.)
2. Look carefully at this list. Are there items that belong together or that are alike in some way?

3. Why do you think *cauldron* and *smoke* go together? (Do not label the group until the students have agreed on the reason for the grouping.)
4. Look at the original list again. Are there other groups we could put together? (Move slowly here. Give them time to rethink. List groups.)
5. Looking over the entire chalkboard, what can we say in general about witches?

Evaluation of the concept development model: The students will express their enriched understanding of the witches' role by developing one of the groups into a paragraph in which the label becomes the topic sentence and the items become supporting evidence.

Application of the Classroom Discussion Model.   A follow-up discussion to the concept development activity.

Estimated time: 2 days.

First Cluster: Role of the Witches.   The discussion will begin with a few factual questions. The majority of questions will be interpretive. The basic question with which this cluster will begin and end is *Would Macbeth have killed Duncan if he had never heard the witches' prophecies?*

1. Where were the witches seen?
2. Under what conditions were the witches seen?
3. What did the witches look like? (Discuss the implication of beards.)
4. What did the witches do?
5. Were there limits to their powers?
6. What could be the meaning of "Fair is foul and foul is fair"?
7. Is there a logical way they could have obtained their information?
8. Why do you think they appeared three times?
9. Do we have anything like the witches in our lives? (One class called them the voices of ambition within us, another the voices of temptation, another the voices of family or friends who want us to do things that are wrong.)
10. What does Banquo mean when he says, "The instruments of darkness tell us truth"?

Second Cluster: The Power of Suggestion and Ambition.   In this section, most of the questions will be evaluative. The purposes will be to build on the ideas generated by exploring the witches' role and to help the students connect these to ambition both in the play and in their own lives. Some sample questions follow. The basic question for this cluster is *What forces shape our goals in life?*

1. Was Lady Macbeth ambitious? In what sense? What form did her ambition take?
2. Are the concepts of ambition and the power of suggestion related in the play? If so, in what way?

3. Have you seen examples of the power of suggestion in your own lives (e.g., horoscopes, fortune tellers, tarot cards, advertising)?
4. Have you seen examples of ambition in the classroom? On the athletic field? In your family? With your friends? In politics?

Mr. Samuels always prepared more questions than he could use. He gauged when to move on to the next question by the content and caliber of the discussion. He moved very slowly so as to give several students time to respond to each question.

Evaluation of the classroom discussion model: The discussions would give Mr. Samuels an excellent idea of how well the students were grasping these concepts. But their knowledge would be taken one step further. They needed practice in writing, because this was a weak area, and it was necessary to know how well each student had grasped these sophisticated concepts. He would ask them to do two of the following:

1. Represent through pictures modern versions of the witches.
2. Choose one of the concepts, and in a one-page paper, give an example of how that concept has affected you in your daily life.
3. Write a one- to two-page paper on your goals in life and what forces have shaped them.

The students were to write a first draft of their papers, share them with small groups of students to get *positive* suggestions, and then write a final draft.

Epilogue

When the 4 weeks ended, Mr. Samuels was pleased with the outcome of his experiment. By and large the students had responded to his vote of confidence in their ability, and as he had suspected, they had been capable of talking about far more sophisticated ideas than they had been able to get on paper. He was disappointed that they had not been able to read more of the text together. As he had anticipated, it had been very difficult for them, and they had gotten discouraged and a bit defensive. The reading would have gone much better if they had seen the entire movie version first so that they would have known what to expect.

The instructional models had allowed the students to be active participants in the learning process. As a result, they had fidgeted less than normally and had seemed to take pride in participating. One highlight of the unit had been the synectics lesson. The following is an abbreviated description of that lesson.

Step 1: Students worked in groups of three to discuss Lady Macbeth and to brainstorm ideas and impressions of her. As follow-up, each student wrote a short paragraph about her. From these paragraphs, the students compiled a list of their strongest specific descriptive words: *shrill, shrew, iceberg, obsessed, conspirator, vixen, acid-tongued, murderous, two-faced, treacherous, sly, wily, conniving.*

Step 2: The students were asked to look at what they had written, to see if those words suggested an animal or a machine. Here are some examples of their answers:

tiger (stalks its prey secretly)
spider (lures its prey within its clutches)
stiletto (looks delicate, is deadly)

Step 3: Next, the students were asked to pick one item from the list, to pretend they were that object, and to describe how that object felt. They picked the stiletto. Here are some of the feelings individual students described:

I feel *dainty:* I am slender, small, tapering, fancy, swift (and deadly).
I feel *proud:* I am slim and fancy and quite beautiful.
I feel *sly:* I can be easily hidden and I fly quickly, silently.
I feel *powerful:* I can hurt enemies before they even know it.
I feel *sneaky:* I can be concealed and used on someone unsuspecting.
I feel *lonely:* I have no friends; I sit alone in my case.
I feel *imprisoned:* I am kept covered and hidden.
I feel *helpless:* I have no control over when and how I am used.
I feel *deadly:* I am small and quiet but razor sharp.

Step 4: The students then were asked to look at their list of feelings and pick out words that seemed to contradict or fight with each other. They picked

proud and *sneaky*
dainty and *powerful*
imprisoned and *powerful*
dainty and *deadly*

Step 5: The class chose *imprisoned* and *powerful* to pursue. They were asked to name things that are both imprisoned and powerful. They named the following:

Nuclear power
A submarine captain
A boxer against the ropes
A wounded bear
A gladiator performing for an emperor
A tiger in a cage

Step 6: Returning to the subject of Lady Macbeth, Mr. Samuels asked the students to choose one of these images and compare it to her. Most chose "a gladiator performing for an emperor." They described her as powerful and deadly, but a puppet of her ambition as a gladiator is a puppet of his emperor.

ACTIVITY 18.1

Consider a general or average class. Design a lesson for teaching a topic that will be challenging to these students but that is generally considered to be reserved for advanced students. Plan specific steps for using at least two different instructional models. ■

Summary

Teaching strategies that work for advanced classes are generally effective in average and remedial classes. The combination of careful planning and instructional variety allows students to become engaged in learning challenging material that is often withheld because it is thought too difficult. Students who may not go on to college have a particular need to encounter such content in primary and secondary school, for if not here, they may never have the chance.

The teachers described in this chapter and the two preceding are all individuals with different backgrounds, interests, and teaching experiences. Like those of you reading this text, they have a variety of concerns and they approach instruction in different ways. They all share, however, a respect for their profession and a desire to improve, to find better ways to reach students, and to be successful in the classroom. They are all seeking answers.

None of these professionals is willing to follow prescriptive formulas in a mindless fashion, but all attend to essential concerns in their planning. The focus of these teachers is on the learners. They give careful thought to the outcome of instruction and assume the responsibility of evaluating to determine if what was taught was also learned.

It is our hope that these chapters raise more questions than answers in the minds of our readers. We believe that teaching is an adventure for life and that no day is like another. No one can tell you exactly how to teach. We have suggested directions; you must chart the course.

NOTE

1. Hilda Taba, *Hilda Taba Teaching Strategies Program*, Unit I, Secondary Edition (Miami: Institute for Staff Development, 1971).

CHAPTER

19 The Wisdom of Practice

Creating a Positive Learning Environment

The difference between the expert and the novice in any profession is something more than years of service. There are professionals with 20-year service pins that should read "one year's service 20 times." Teaching is not exempt from this paradox. Some teachers are novices forever, and some are experts when they put their foot in the door. But what are the differences between ordinary and expert teachers? Are gifted teachers born with their gifts, or can those gifts be learned? By examining the nature of expertise, the first question can be answered. It will then be apparent that the second question is moot: These gifts are not really gifts at all. What are seen as gifts in others are actually the result of deliberative, reflective efforts to become expert. The expert will always relish the challenge and delight in the work of confronting a new circumstance or problem, armed with knowledge gained from previous experience.[1] To paraphrase Thomas Edison, successful teaching is usually one part inspiration, nine parts perspiration. It also helps to be reminded that *expert* and *experience* share the same origin in language; both are close linguistic relatives of the word *peril*.

One big difference between the expert and the novice teacher is that the expert has a greater repertoire of instructional strategies to fall back on when things do not go exactly as expected. The corollary to this difference between novice and expert is that the expert knows how to arrange matters in advance so as to improve the chances of success. It is the expert teachers, or those who are called gifted, who most often beat the odds of failure. How does this happen? What does the expert teacher know that all good teachers should know?

Before we try to answer that question, remember that there is no formula for becoming a good teacher. Models of instruction are not formulas such as "one part oxygen plus two parts hydrogen equals water." Rather, models of instruction are more akin to recipes that have to be adapted to the needs and tastes of the cook and to the available ingredients. Teaching, like cooking, is a deliberative activity in the sense that through conscious reflection or deliberation the process can always be improved. Its quality and its outcome always depend on the judgment of the teacher. Part of that judgment centers on the students and their changing needs, and part centers on the process of teaching.

To say that there is no formula for good teaching is not to deny that an accumulated wisdom about the practice of teaching does exist. Judgments are always grounded in knowledge, and the expert knows things the novice does not. Fortunately, there is a large body of recorded experience and research on effective schools and instructional practices that provides the basis for many generalizations about teaching. In this chapter, we share some of those generalizations under the rubric "The Wisdom of Practice." The basis of these generalizations lies in a corpus of research and in our own experience and that of countless other teachers whom we have asked, "What makes you a good teacher?" But research and the experience of others are never quite enough to define someone else's choices. We invite you to test each generalization in your own practice.

One of the world's experts on expertise in teaching, David Berliner, has pointed out that "two large domains of knowledge must be readily accessed [by the expert teacher]. Those two domains of knowledge [are] subject matter knowledge and knowledge of organization and management of classrooms."[2] It was of particular interest to us, then, to note that of the 25 different characteristics and behaviors one group of teachers mentioned in answer to our question ("What makes you a good teacher?"), only one teacher mentioned knowledge of subject matter. That gave us pause at first; certainly teachers must be expert in the content they wish to teach. When we stopped to reflect, though, we realized that good teachers likely take knowledge of their subject matter as a given, a necessary but not sufficient condition for good teaching. In other words, most teachers would probably say that knowing what you are trying to teach is essential to good teaching, but knowing how to teach it is what distinguishes good teachers from mere content experts. Perhaps the real earmark of expertise in teaching lies in understanding how to blend two different domains of knowledge—knowledge of what to teach and knowledge of how to teach—in a way that compromises neither domain. We have condensed that understanding into 11 insights that good teachers have.

Good Teachers Are in Charge of Their Classrooms

We have asked students of elementary and high school age the same question: "What changes would you make in the instruction you have received thus far in school?" We prefaced the question by explaining that the administration had asked us to make recommendations on how to improve instruction in the school, but that we did not feel capable of framing those recommendations without trying to see the present instructional program from the eyes of those learners who had experienced it.

In general, the learners had only three things to say, although they said them in many different ways. Notice that in every case, their proposed changes were under the teacher's control.

- I'd like teachers to stick to the point.
- I'd like a classroom in which kids didn't get away with fooling around.
- I'd like to know that whatever I'm to be tested on, I have been taught.

Whether teaching 6-year-old or 60-year-old students, the teacher is the person in charge of the classroom, and everyone will feel better if that is clearly established from the start. The teacher is not a buddy or a chum, but neither is the teacher a warden or a tyrant. The teacher is the professional responsible for keeping the class focused on what is being taught, for maintaining discipline in a fair and consistent manner, and for ensuring the reliability and validity of evaluation.[3] Although much of that responsibility can and should be shared with learners, the teacher must retain the right of ultimate authority in the interest of the safety and physical, emotional, personal, and intellectual well-being of the students.

The teacher's bearing, voice, appearance, and approach to the class should emphasize professionalism and careful preparation for the job. We all are reassured when we feel that persons responsible in controlled situations know what they are doing and will do it responsibly. Students of all ages depend on their teachers for that reassurance. To gain insight into what that would look like at the opening of a class period, where the tone for the day is set, consider this conclusion from a comparison of experienced, effective teachers with inexperienced, ineffective teachers:

> If you had to prescribe to a junior high school teacher an apparently effective method for opening a class period, the scenario would be as follows: Develop a routine opening that features 1) visual scanning (a brief glance at the room that announces the class is about to commence), 2) a quick call to order in a business-like tone of voice, 3) a method of roll taking that is time efficient, and 4) an opening verbal sequence that includes behavioral and academic expectations, anticipates areas of confusion in explanations, and calls for questions before signaling the beginning of the first activity.[4]

Crisp, businesslike, and to the point describe a classroom under a teacher's control. Research on classroom management quite clearly shows that good teachers establish a system of control as soon as possible in organizing each new class of students. "The effective teacher at the beginning of the year has an objective of setting up an efficient and smoothly running classroom where instruction, not management, is the major thrust."[5] Expert teachers agree that the first few days of school are critical in establishing and practicing instructional and managerial routines for the smooth operation of the classroom. A substantial line of research supports this insight.[6]

To make these routines automatic, good teachers tell their students what they expect, they demonstrate it for the students, they guide the students in practicing expected moves, and they accept no less than mastery execution of the routines necessary for successful learning and instruction. It is important to note that demonstration and guidance aimed at correct routine are more effective than later correction of errors in routine. An ounce of prevention is the watchword in classroom management.

Good Teachers Create a Pleasant Physical Environment for Learning

In the landmark study *A Place Called School*, John Goodlad paints the picture of the typical American school and classroom. He calls the place "aesthetically drab and emotionally flat."[7] But adequate work space and a pleasant environment for learning are undoubtedly associated with student motivation, behavior, and achievement.[8] There is perhaps little the individual teacher can do to create an attractive school building, but the tone of the individual classroom is very often under the control of the teacher and the students who share the room. Effective teachers tend to be managers who plan environments that enhance learning. Teachers can do many things to create a pleasant setting for students to learn, including working on four aspects of the classroom that do affect learning: displays, physical environment, announcements, and seating.

Displays

Insofar as possible, the classroom should be an attractive, inviting place to be. Colors and design can make the environment of a room more interesting and more exciting. Displays of students' artistic efforts—mobiles, dioramas, models, diagrams, and charts—give ownership of the class to the students. Bulletin boards and visual display areas can be used to reinforce the essential concepts of a lesson or unit. For example, you can devote one section of your bulletin board to a display of words and concepts being encountered in the current unit of study. Arrange the words, with the help of the students, to reflect the relationships among the concepts you are teaching. Leave the words in place even when students are writing exercises and being tested on the material; this will provide easy access to the words and concepts you are teaching.

On another section of the bulletin board, or on a reserved section of the chalkboard, place a "trivia" question related to the lesson of the day. In a geography class, sample questions could include the following, each related to a topic of study:[9]

Related to ecology: "What continent holds most of the world's fresh water?"

Related to history: "When Napoleon was defeated at Waterloo on June 18, 1815, what country was he in?"

Related to study of the various states: "What is Alaska's state motto?" (Answers are given in the Notes section.)[10]

Put students' work up for all to see, in a manner that reinforces all the students and not just a few. Pictures of class members and examples of student hobbies or collections can make the classroom reflect positively on individual students and groups.

At the beginning of the year, perhaps as an introduction to the process of history, ask each student to bring to class some object of future memorabilia by which archaeologists a thousand years hence will know of the student's family, interests, hobbies, or style of living. Display these items with a picture of the student and a brief biographical sketch.

Climate Control

Although it is not absolutely essential to provide bulletin boards and displays, it is essential to attend to lighting, air, and temperature. Many excellent lessons have been ruined because the temperature in the classroom was too hot or too cold for students to concentrate.

If the room in which you teach is too crowded, if it is too hot or too cold, or if the air is stale, try to find another space. Talk with the principal about the physical conditions that are creating a problem. As an instructional specialist, you will be the person most aware of the effects of the physical environment on the learners.

Announcements

A problem frequently mentioned by teachers is the intrusive presence of the sound system in their classrooms. If classes are continually interrupted by announcements or by students being called to the office, try to work out a plan for improving the situation. Administrators usually respond better to a plan than to a complaint.

One teacher developed a plan in which each week a different student sat by the door and received any messages sent to the room by the office. If the message was for another student, the message was handed to the student and that student quietly left the classroom. If the message was for the teacher, it was placed on the teacher's desk.

Seating

Few classrooms today have seats permanently fixed in one spot, but many teachers behave as though the chairs were immovable objects. The uniformity of seating arrangement in high school classrooms is part of the "deep structure" of schooling. Walk into any American high school and you can expect to see the same arrangement in most classrooms. Form follows function, and so the seats are arranged for lecture. Almost all students in all American schools sit in classrooms facing the front of the room. They have done so since colonial times when people believed that children were like little animals in need of taming.[11]

Seating arrangements can do a great deal to enhance the success of instruction, and it is essential to plan for the orderly rearrangement of seating as the class activities change. Unless the class is very crowded or particularly difficult to manage, row seating in which most of the students are looking at the back of the person in front of them is undesirable. Circles and semicircles are generally more effective for sharing information and discussion. Clusters of two, three, or four desks create a setting for small-group, cooperative work among students.

Students need instruction in how to change seating patterns in the classroom efficiently. For instance, if after a presentation the students are to work in small groups, it is necessary to explain carefully in advance how the seats will be arranged and where each group is to be located. Classrooms can also be set up in such a way that individual and group work can go on at the same time. Plan in advance for the type of seating arrangement you will need so that sound and sight disturbances can be minimized. Procedures for furniture arrangement should be routine.

Good Teachers Manage Human Relations Effectively

Some believe that teachers are in classrooms just to teach and that control of disruptive behavior should be the responsibility of the parent or administrators, not the teacher. Although it is certainly true that addressing violent and threatening behavior should not be the sole responsibility of the teacher, most discipline problems in the classroom need to be negotiated and resolved by the teacher and the student. Otherwise, when the student returns to class, the problem will return as well.

The problem of discipline is a human relations problem, and as the responsible adult in the situation, the teacher is the expert who must set up circumstances to resolve conflicts that will inevitably arise. (See Chapter 12 for guidelines in conflict resolution.) James Batesky boils classroom discipline down to 12 tips that we summarize with only slight modification:

1. Let students know they are successful.
2. Have five or six short rules.
3. Do not threaten students.
4. Communicate to students directly what is expected of them, but listen carefully and respectfully to the students' requests.
5. Correct behavior problems quickly, before they escalate.
6. Give I-messages, such as "I am concerned about what I see here." Do not be afraid to tell students what you want.
7. Do not overreact or display cruelty.

8. Have a planned discipline strategy.
9. If confrontation proves necessary, conduct it one-on-one with the students involved, rather than before the entire class.
10. Use a variety of teaching styles, methods, and models to prevent boredom, increase student involvement, and improve learning.
11. Insist on your right to teach and the right of all students to learn.
12. Make the best possible use of the facilities.[12]

Thomas Lasley has suggested four generalizations about classroom and behavior management that he finds justified by research. According to his extensive review of the literature on the issue of classroom management, the effective teacher does the following:

1. Develops and implements a workable set of classroom rules.
2. Structures and monitors the classroom in a manner that minimizes disruptive behavior.
3. Clearly defines and quickly and consistently responds to inappropriate behavior.
4. Couches the response to inappropriate behavior in a tone that does not denigrate the students to whom the response is directed.[13]

Good Teachers Engage Learners in the Process of Their Own Learning

Eleanor Duckworth tells her undergraduate classes in education that there are two important principles they must always keep in mind as they teach.[14] First, she says, always put learners in as direct contact as possible with whatever you want them to learn. That is usually the purpose of field trips and other hands-on activities in schools. But there are many ways that students can be given direct contact with their learning. They can model the formation and movements of the solar system. They can keep diaries of their observations of animals that share their community. They can construct models, engage in mock and simulated experiences, and conduct interviews.

Second, and this is related to the first principle, Duckworth admonishes her teachers-to-be to provide frequent opportunities for learners to explain what they understand, both to the teacher and to other students. Anytime teachers are tempted to tell students something they want them to know, they should start by asking the students to explain what they already know.

We agree that these guidelines are critical to a beginning teacher's instructional effectiveness. We know that learners will learn more in proportion to how engaged they are with what they are trying to learn. This is the *law of meaningful engagement*, although it is a law violated all too often.

Renate Nummela Caine and Geoffrey Caine, in a book mentioned in Chapter 15, have described the features of a learning environment organized for brain-compatible learning. At the top of their list is orchestrated immersion, followed by relaxed alertness and active processing.[15] *Orchestrated immersion* centers on how students are exposed to content. When every sense, every emotion, and every movement are related to the information being studied, "wholeness and interconnectedness cannot be avoided [and] students are obliged to employ their [whole minds] in the exploration of content."[16] *Relaxed alertness* is the combination of high challenge and low threat. As the Caines note, "An optimal state of mind for expanding natural knowledge combines the moderate to high challenge that is built into intrinsic motivation with low threat and a pervasive sense of well-being. We call that a state of relaxed alertness."[17] *Active processing* is "the consolidation and internalization of information by the learner in a way that is both personally meaningful and conceptually coherent."[18] These three ingredients of successful learning experiences are similar to what we have referred to as meaningful engagement.

Not all students have the same time for learning in school, and sadly, the students who need the most time to learn may be given the least. For example, Michael Brady and Philip Gunter found that the times of engagement vary from 90 percent to 4 percent of class time for different students in different classes throughout the day.[19] Benjamin Bloom has suggested that the academically lowest 10 percent of students might need five to six times the amount of time to learn the same thing as the academically highest 10 percent.[20] Our experience tells us that providing direct contact with what is to be learned and giving students frequent opportunities to explain what they know are corollaries to the law of meaningful engagement. Implicit in these principles is that teaching is more akin to drawing out than to putting in.

None of this is meant to suggest that, in the context of the instructional models we have advocated, teachers should not provide learners with information or sources for that information. On the contrary, good information presented in a variety of forms is essential to learning. But models of instruction are powerful when they serve not as rules for teaching and learning but as signposts to understanding.

The learner's understanding and insight must be the goal of instruction. One of the great paradoxes of education, which few laypersons but every good teacher will sooner or later discover, is that understanding cannot be given to the learner directly any more than a parent can teach a child to tie her shoes by merely telling her how. Give her a shoe to practice on (or, better, let her practice on her own shoe), and have her explain to you or to another person what she is doing as she practices. If that advice is good for learning to tie shoes, how much better is it for learning all the complicated things students are expected to know in school?

Good Teachers Teach Up

They Recognize the Pygmalion Effect

In Greek mythology, Pygmalion is the king of Cyprus who carved and then fell in love with a statue of a woman whom the goddess Aphrodite later gave life. The Pygmalion theme repeats itself often in Western literature, in stories and verse. Bernard Shaw made Henry Higgins, aristocrat whose hobby is phonetics, and Eliza

Doolittle, Cockney flower-seller, immortal. Hollywood loves this romantic, fairy tale theme, centered on the power of education (particularly, language) to elevate one's social class.

Maybe love does not conquer all, but it is a powerful ingredient of education, or so the Pygmalion story would imply. It is best not to forget, too, that in each version of the story, the sculptor has much to learn from his creation. That important lesson is expressed by Eliza near the end of Shaw's play, where she is trying to explain to her friend and benefactor Colonel Pickering how she was transformed from flower girl to lady of refinement. Liza is sitting on a couch next to Pickering, casually engaged in needlework as she speaks:

LIZA: [to Pickering, taking no apparent notice of Higgins, and working away deftly] Will you drop me altogether now that the experiment is over, Colonel Pickering?

PICKERING: Oh, dont. You mustnt think of it as an experiment. It shocks me, somehow.

LIZA: Oh, I'm only a squashed cabbage leaf—[which Higgins had called her moments before].

PICKERING: [impulsively] No.

LIZA: [continuing quietly]—but I owe so much to you that I should be very unhappy if you forgot me.

PICKERING: It's very kind of you to say so, Miss Doolittle.

LIZA: It's not because you paid for my dresses. I know you are generous to everybody with money. But it was from you that I learnt really nice manners; and that is what makes one a lady, isnt it? You see it was so very difficult for me with the example of Professor Higgins always before me. I was brought up to be just like him, unable to control myself, and using bad language on the slightest provocation. And I should never have known that ladies didnt behave like that if you hadnt been there.

HIGGINS: Well!!

PICKERING: Oh, thats only his way, you know. He doesnt mean it.

LIZA: Oh, *I* didnt mean it either, when I was a flower girl. It was only my way. But you see I did it; and thats what makes the difference after all.

PICKERING: No doubt. Still, he taught you to speak; and I couldnt have done that, you know.

LIZA: [trivially] Of course: that is his profession.

HIGGINS: Damnation!

LIZA: [continuing] It was just like learning to dance in the fashionable way: there was nothing more than that in it. But do you know what began my real education?

PICKERING: What?

LIZA: [*stopping her work for a moment*] Your calling me Miss Doolittle that day when I first came to Wimpole Street. That was the beginning of self-respect for me. [*She resumes her stitching.*] And there were a hundred little things you never noticed, because they came naturally to you. Things about standing up and taking off your hat and opening doors—

PICKERING: Oh, that was nothing.

LIZA: Yes: things that shewed you thought and felt about me as if I were something better than a scullery-maid; though of course I know you would have been just the same to a scullery-maid if she had been let into the drawing room. You never took off your boots in the drawing room when I was there.

PICKERING: You mustnt mind that. Higgins takes off his boots all over the place.

LIZA: I know. I am not blaming him. It is his way, isnt it? But it made such a difference to me that you didnt do it. You see, really and truly, apart from the things anyone can pick up (the dressing and the proper way of speaking, and so on), the difference between a lady and a flower girl is not how she behaves, but how she's treated. I shall always be a flower girl to Professor Higgins, because he always treats me as a flower girl, and always will; but I know I can be a lady to you, because you always treat me as a lady, and always will.[21]

From that speech we get the expression *the Pygmalion effect*. The Pygmalion effect in schools was made famous by Robert Rosenthal and Lenore Jacobson in the late 1960s.[22] Essentially, their research asserts that a teacher's expectation that the student *will* do well can have a positive effect on the academic success of that student. The opposite of the Pygmalion effect in schools, that teachers treat high- and low-achieving students differently to the detriment of the low-achieving student, has also been brought to light by research.[23] Thomas Good lists several ways in which teachers most often discriminate in their treatment of the high and low achievers.[24]

- By seating low-achieving students farther away from the teacher than other students
- By paying less attention to low-achieving students than to other students
- By calling on low-achieving students less frequently than other students to answer questions
- By giving low-achieving students less time to answer questions when they are called on than other students
- By not providing cues or asking follow-up questions to help low-achieving students answer questions
- By criticizing low-achieving students more frequently than other students for incorrect answers
- By giving low-achieving students less praise than other students for correct or marginal responses
- By giving low-achieving students less feedback and less detail in the feedback they are given than other students

- By interrupting the performance of low-achieving students more often than that of the high-achieving students
- By demanding less effort and less work from low-achieving students than from high-achieving students

A first-grade teacher said to one of us, "All of my students think they are good readers." We know why: Their teacher makes them feel that way. But how do teachers do that, honestly, without glossing over problems or saying things that are not really true? After all, it would be a mistake to hold the same expectation for all students. How do teachers achieve the *optimum* expectation for each student? There is no easy answer to that question, but some behaviors such as those described in the following sections will help teachers encourage *all* students to reach their full potential.

They Capitalize on What Students Know

Teachers should find something in what students already know to establish a basis for new understandings. Students often feel as if they know nothing of what is taught in school and could not care less because it all seems so irrelevant. But good teachers help learners see that they already know much about what they are trying to learn, and they impress on students that *what they already know is the single most important factor influencing what they will learn.* Learners are crucially important to their own learning, and teaching should make them feel that way.

Gordon Wells calls children "meaning makers."[25] He draws an irresistible analogy in discussing how adults must communicate with children, saying that it is very like playing ball with a young child:

> What the adult has to do for this game to be successful is, first, to ensure that the child is ready, with arms cupped, to catch the ball. Then the ball must be thrown gently and accurately so that it lands squarely in the child's arms. When it is the child's turn to throw, the adult must be prepared to run wherever it goes and bring it back to where the child really intended it to go. Such is the collaboration required in [teaching], the adult doing a great deal of supportive work to enable the ball to be kept in play.[26]

Wells was talking about conversation with children. We think that the analogy is perfect for the requirements of teaching and so we substituted the word *teaching* for *conversation*, which also reminds us that teaching is very like a conversation.

They Celebrate Differences among Students

An old adage says "None of us is as smart as all of us." That statement is also true in a classroom. If teachers make it clear that what each one knows or learns is of value to everyone, then they make it safe for everyone to share whatever they know and thus to value their own understanding, no matter how meager. Half of this concept is polite behavior—respect—and the other half is intellectual honesty: No one knows everything about anything, not even the teacher, and that is acceptable. Simply put, two heads are always better than one.

They Realize That There Is More Than One Right Answer to Important Questions

Every teacher's manual includes suggestions about what to say to students and what to expect them to say in return. The manuals for teaching reading to elementary school students often go as far as to put what the teacher is to say in one color print and what the students are to say in another color print. But a lesson script can only be an approximation. In fact, the one certain truth found in all teacher's manuals is that answers will vary. Part of the art of teaching lies in knowing how to take advantage of the variance.

They Recognize Achievement and Minimize the Importance of Error

Remember learning to drive a car? If you were lucky, the person teaching you kept affirming that you could do it and praising you for all you were doing right. When difficulties arose, your instructor concentrated on helping you focus on what to do rather than berating you for your shortcomings. But if you were unlucky, the person teaching you continually harped on everything you were doing wrong. The effect of this was to shake your confidence, whether or not that was the intent. The first rule of assertive discipline is to emphasize the positive,[27] and one might take that rule as the key to successful teaching.

Research in human relations indicates that "there should be five times as many positive moments as negative"[28] in successful relationships. However, George Prince and colleagues write, "In our observation of classrooms, the ratio of one discount to five validations is almost never maintained. All the correcting, punishing and complaining with relatively rare validations means that we are bringing out something less than the best in our children."[29]

Good Teachers Are Good Learners

They Serve as a Model for Learning

Although we are tempted to say that the teacher should be the best learner in the class, we know how stiff the competition for that honor will always be. Also, we would not want to set it up as a competition. Yet the teacher must be an eager learner and be willing to share the process of learning with other learners, the class. Good teachers learn from their own study and share that study with their students. Frequently, even daily, they bring a new idea to class from something they have read or seen. They are scholars, and they share the process and the product of their scholarship. Teachers learn from their students, both about teaching and about the content they are studying together. Having the chance to teach someone else is one of the best ways to learn, and it is always a favor to both the learner and the teacher to reverse their roles from time to time. Teachers learn from teaching, and not just about their teaching but about their students and what they are studying.

It is a serious mistake for any teacher to project the image of the person who knows it all and is here to tell everyone. First, such an attitude conveys an erroneous impression of the nature of knowledge, as if it were a once and for all matter. It has been said that the half-life of human knowledge in any field is about 6 years, and even that duration is slipping.[30] This does not mean that everything we know has to be replaced every 5 years because it is no longer true. But, the knowledge humans possess is expanding so rapidly that the infrastructure of knowledge has to be continually adapted to accommodate new insights and understandings. Thus teachers, like their students, are faced with needing to learn constantly just to keep abreast. The exciting result for the teacher who realizes this is that there is always a ready audience with which to share new insights and understandings. By contrast, a know-all, tell-all attitude treats knowledge as a fixed entity, excluding learners from the process of learning and dooming them to focus on the acquisition of information that may be obsolete even before their school days have passed. The more appropriate image of teacher as learner invites students to join with others (the teacher included) in the joy and thrill of coming to know. The long-term effect is that students will learn well, learn more, and be learners for life.

They Recognize the Importance of Professional Knowledge

There are professional organizations for every branch and subject of teaching and for the field of education in general. A major function of these groups is to provide a comprehensive literature to assist teachers and administrators in their mission to educate. This literature consists mainly of professional journals, books, audio- and videotapes, and research and technical reports available on microfiche, laser disk, and the World Wide Web. Each professional organization also acts as host for regional, state, national, and international meetings and forums in which teachers share and discuss common problems and ideas. Taken together, these sources form the basis of postgraduate professional study in education.

We mentioned earlier that the half-life of human knowledge is about 6 years. This is as true in education as it is in the sciences, as the sheer volume of what we know about what we teach and how to teach it increases exponentially. (It is probably no coincidence that most school systems adopt new textbooks every 5 years.) The teacher who does not continue to study the education profession may soon be as outmoded as yesterday's newspaper. The antidote is continuous staff development, available to virtually all teachers.

Judith Little identifies four factors that encourage teachers to pursue their professional development:[31]

1. Mutuality, respect, and collaboration among teachers
2. Multiple administrative mechanisms for cooperative planning among teachers
3. Opportunities for continuous learning by teachers, opportunities that are problem-centered, involve experiential application, and are properly sequenced
4. Mutually conducted evaluation of program effectiveness

They Act as Researchers

In addition to attempting to keep abreast of the professional literature (as any professional must), teachers are in a position to be their own directors of research and development.[32] It is no exaggeration to say that the observed result of every teaching experience forms the basis for refinements and improvements in teaching. A simplified model of the action research we have in mind, called the IPO model, is shown in Figure 19.1.

If the observed outcome of the teaching and learning process (what the teacher and students do) is what was expected, then the input and the process must have been appropriate. But if there is any discrepancy between the expected outcome and the observed outcome, the discrepancy is to be explained by a shortcoming in the input, the process, or both. The IPO model applies to virtually all teaching situations where the teacher has some degree of control over input (what to teach and what tools to use) and process (how to teach) and can make appropriate changes in either or both factors. Using the IPO model makes the teacher a student of his or her own experience.

Good Teachers Develop Instructional Objectives with Learners

They Vest Students with an Interest in Learning

The quality of instruction in a classroom will be determined largely by whether the students have a vested interest in the instruction and in their own learning. In other

---

Input
(all that goes into a lesson or unit)
is the basis of
Process
(all that occurs in the teaching and learning process),
which leads to
Outcome
(all that results from the process)

FIGURE 19.1 IPO: Input, Process, Outcome

words, they have to care about what happens in the class and be willing to cooperate to reach shared objectives. Instructional objectives, from the point of view of the learners, are learning objectives. Whether the objectives are achieved will depend on the learners' willingness to adopt the teacher's instructional objectives as their own learning objectives.

We are not advocating that teachers plan their instruction based on what students are willing to say they want to learn, even though that can often be taken into account. We do advocate that teachers share the process of their own planning for instruction with their students. One way to do this is to initiate a unit of study with an exploration of what the students have already studied on the topic, followed by a listing of what else they think they want to know. Many studies of effective instructional practices make clear that teaching that builds on what learners already know leads to higher achievement.[33]

They Develop Guides to Planning Instruction

Plan instruction by asking students to create a hypothetical outline of a (hypothetical) chapter they are going to read. Then check to see that the chapter (or the resources available) does indeed address the topic as anticipated; if there are any shortcomings, involve the students in deciding how to augment the available information. Plan instruction by providing the students with many different means and sources to learn the same thing and to accomplish the same objectives. Plan instruction by giving learners opportunities to help one another achieve shared objectives. Think of planning as engaging students in the design process for their own learning.

Good Teachers Find Out
Why a Plan Is Not Working

L. W. Anderson has summarized the major conclusions to be drawn from the vast body of literature on effective teaching.[34] Effective teachers, he suggests,

- Know their students.
- Assign appropriate tasks to their students.
- Orient their students to the learning task.
- Monitor the learning progress of their students.
- Relate teaching and testing, testing what they teach.
- Promote student involvement and engagement in the learning process.
- Provide continuity for their students so that learning tasks and objectives build on one another.
- Correct student errors and misunderstandings.

If these effective teaching behaviors are to be a reality, it is important that the teacher be aware of options. If one approach or technique is not working with a class, analyze the problem and redesign the instructional plan. For instance, some classes are not ready for group work. Many times, teachers will attempt a group activity and, when chaos develops, decide that they will never try it again. Students must be prepared for group activities, and the procedures for setting up those activities must be carefully planned and directed. The models described in the chapter on cooperative learning are only a few of many effective group-process models. With some instructional models, the students may need more preparation time. Perhaps certain steps in the model have not been adequately explained. Or, sometimes the instructional plan is too ambitious, the content to be covered is too extensive, or the students do not have the necessary readiness and predisposition for learning. Evaluate the situation and consider what options you have to correct the difficulty. Treat problems as challenges rather than frustrations.

Good Teachers Strive to Make Their Teaching Interesting

The relationship between interest and curiosity is no accident; learners are interested in learning those things about which they feel the greatest curiosity. Therefore, if teachers can pique the curiosity of learners, they will make what they teach interesting to learners. For example, if the topic of study is the Civil War, rather than rely on a textbook presentation of the major events of that great conflict, the instruction could draw on the vast literature that focuses on it, such as the short stories of Ambrose Bierce; the children's novel *Across Five Aprils*, by Irene Hunt; excerpts from the diaries of slaves contained in *To Be a Slave*, by Julius Lester; and selections from Kenneth Burns's PBS documentary, *The Civil War*. For every major topic of the curriculum, there is a vast literature to use in teaching. The effect is to open windows on scholarship for young learners.

Curiosity must be nurtured if it is to flourish. John Dewey once remarked that "curiosity is not an accidental isolated possession; it is a necessary consequence of the fact that an experience is a moving, changing thing, involving all kinds of connections with other things."[35] The key to curiosity rests in the idea of connections. Teaching in ways that make information interesting to learners helps them see the connections between what they are learning and what they know, between what they are learning in school and the world, and between the same information in different disciplines.

One writer asserts:

> No two brains are exactly alike; thus, no enriched environment will completely satisfy any two people for an extended period. Challenge and interactivity are essential. Passive observation is not enough. "Tell me and I forget. Show me and I remember. Let me do it and I understand," says the ancient Chinese proverb. . . . With our new understanding of the brain, we are in an excellent position to make it possible for people to become better learners.[36]

Good Teachers Give Learners Access to Information and Opportunity to Practice

Research on effective schools unequivocally supports the idea that learning is likely to occur when learners have access to information and the opportunity to practice using that information.[37] But what kind of information and practice are appropriate? Most obviously, students need whatever information is necessary to accomplish the learning objective at hand: accurate information presented in a palatable form. And students need practice in applying or recalling the new information as a means of solving problems that require it. In the case of a learning objective that called for students to compare and contrast the causes of the French and Indian War with the causes of the War of 1812, the students would need information about these two wars and guidance and feedback on their attempts to make appropriate comparisons and contrasts.

The information needed by students is more than facts, data, and algorithms, however. Paraphrasing from a research report by Robert Yinger, we can identify these other kinds of information as (1) knowledge of what to do with information gained and how to use it in practice, (2) knowledge of when the information will apply and how to apply it, and (3) knowledge of whether the uses of the information have been successful.[38]

Likewise, the practice students need is not solely of those behaviors implicit in the specific learning objective they have been given. In addition to learners applying or recalling information, D. N. Perkins and Gabriel Salomon state that learners need practice in "low-road" and "high-road" transfer.[39]

When teachers introduce a literary classic with reference to the related experiences of their students, they are creating conditions for low-road transfer. When teachers point out parallels between the elements of content, such as the points of comparison between the civil rights movement in the United States and the breakdown of apartheid in South Africa, they are facilitating high-road transfer.

Low-road transfer is direct application of information to contexts and problems like those in which the information was first encountered. For example, students might practice applying the Pythagorean theorem by calculating the diagonals of their classroom and of a football field. High-road transfer is indirect application of information to contexts and problems unlike those in which the information was first encountered. For example, students might compare the events and political alignments of the French and Indian War with the alignments of loyalties in the play *Romeo and Juliet*. It is always important to keep in mind that long-term, meaningful learning depends on the access students have to good information and the opportunity to transfer and apply that information in ways that make it both meaningful and memorable.

Good Teachers Teach for Two Kinds of Knowledge

It is impossible for students to learn in school all they would ever need to know in their lives. They must, therefore, learn how to learn. In every course of study in school, students are given access to a portion of the accumulated knowledge and wisdom of humankind: the facts, ideas, algorithms, events, and implications of history, literature, science, math, health, and so on. But such "knowing that" will not stand the learner in good stead in the future if he or she does not also acquire a complementary kind of knowledge: the skills of reading, writing, study, and thinking necessary for continued growth and life-long scholarship, or "knowing how."

Thus teaching in the classroom we envision would give students access to information to be learned and to a conscious knowledge of how to learn it. In this classroom, the teacher creates an environment in which students are responsible for knowing and for knowing how they know, for taking control of the processes of their own learning and thinking. The intended result is an improvement of the learning and thinking necessary for participation in the discipline under study. We would want teachers at all grade levels and in all content areas to believe that the most important thing they have to teach students is the process of learning. This thought reminds us of the old expression "Give a man a fish, and he'll eat for a day; teach a man to fish, and he'll eat for a lifetime." Consider the analogy: "Teach students only the information you want them to have and they'll pass the test tomorrow; teach students how to learn, and they'll pass the test for the rest of their lives."

Summary

There is more to managing a classroom of learners than just containing the students. In fact, the need for most of that kind of management is preempted when the teacher takes control of the learning in the classroom and in effect turns the responsibility for learning over to the learners. Good teachers manage their instruction with that objective in mind. They are able to do so because they operate out of a knowledge base and because intuition feeds their good judgment. In this chapter and throughout this book, we have shared the idea that there are always options the good teacher can consider, even though most of the time good teaching, like any skilled performance, looks completely spontaneous. We hope that our suggestions will become part of your instructional repertoire.

WEB RESOURCES

   1. **http://www.teachersfirst.com/new-tch.shtml**
   At this site new teachers will find the support and ideas they need to "survive" those first few years, including the U.S. Department of Education's *Survival Guide for New Teachers*. Be sure to see the "classroom resources" and "professional resources" links on the main page.

   2. **http://www.nea.org/helpfrom/growing/works4me/library.html**
   The National Education Association maintains this "Works4Me" site, an archive of its weekly e-mail messages containing classroom tips and a place where teachers share ideas with other teachers. The teaching techniques and management ideas make a visit to this site a must for all teachers.

3. http://www.teachers.net/

Teachers Net advertises itself as the ultimate teacher's resource. This lively looking site is filled with resources, including chatrooms, live events, columns, lesson plans, and useful articles. The site is regularly updated and is divided into easy-to-navigate categories, most of which have substantial numbers of web page listings. Don't miss the "Lesson Plans" category.

4. http://school.discovery.com/

This site is backed by the extensive resources of the Discovery Channel. Arguably the most important feature of the site is "Kathy Schrock's Guide for Educators," which lists Schrock's Web picks on everything from Aesop's Fables online to a zoology Internet resource guide! Find this guide by clicking on "For Teachers" on the home page and then on "Best Web Links."

5. http://www.eduhound.com/mainpage.cfm

"We tracked it down so you don't have to" is the subtitle of EduHound: Everything for Education K12. This web page offers a prescreened directory of over 20,000 links organized into over 50 categories. Click on a topic, and you will find hundreds of lesson plans and links to resources useful in every imaginable teaching situation.

6. http://www.learnersonline.com/

There is little doubt that teachers everywhere will increasingly use the Web as a tool for teaching. The major bottleneck to that reality is that teachers nowhere have the time it takes to comb the Web for the many resources they might use. This site, Learners Online, Inc., capitalizes on the extensive educational Internet resources. You are instructed to "bring along your browser and a curious mind." (There is a subscription fee for taking fullest advantage of this resource.)

7. http://www.hcc.hawaii.edu/intranet/committees/FacDevCom/guidebk/teachtip/teachtip.htm

Prepared by Honolulu Community College, this is an index of tools and ideas for excellence in teaching practice. Find ideas about every concern in education, from dealing with stress to preparing better lesson plans.

8. http://www.ed.gov/

Every year the federal government spends millions of dollars to improve educational opportunities for all children in the United States. At this site you will find links to much of the work the money funds, making all of it freely and quickly available to the classroom teacher and administrator. Teachers should not pass up the information, resources, and opportunities that are offered here.

NOTES

1. Robert Glaser, "The Nature of Expertise," Occasional Paper No. 107, National Center for Research in Vocational Education, Ohio State University, 1985.

2. David C. Berliner, "In Pursuit of the Expert Pedagogue," *Educational Researcher* 15, no. 7 (1986): 9.

3. J. S. Kounin, *Discipline and Group Management in Classrooms* (New York: Holt, Rinehart and Winston, 1970).

4. D. M. Brooks and G. Hawke, "Effective and Ineffective Session-Opening Teacher Activity and Task Structures" (paper presented at the annual meeting of the American Educational Research Association, Chicago, April 1985).

5. G. Leinhardt, C. Weidman, and K. M. Hammond, "Introduction and Integration of Classroom Routines by Expert Teachers," *Curriculum Inquiry* 17 (1987): 137.

6. E. T. Emmer and C. M. Evertson, *Effective Management at the Beginning of the School Year in Junior High Classes*, Report No. 6107 (Austin: Research and Development Center for Teacher Education, University of Texas at Austin, 1980); D. L. Duke, ed., *Helping Teachers Manage Classrooms* (Alexandria, VA: Association for Supervision and Curriculum Development, 1982).

7. J. L. Goodlad, *A Place Called School: Prospects for the Future* (New York: McGraw-Hill, 1984).

8. F. D. Susi, "The Physical Environment of Art Classrooms: A Basis for Effective Discipline," *Art Education* 42 (1989): 37–43; M. Rutter, B. Maughan, P. Mortimore, J. Ouston, and A. Smith, *Fifteen Thousand Hours: Secondary Schools and Their Effects on Children* (Cambridge, MA: Harvard University Press, 1979).

9. J. F. Marran, "Try Trivia for Openers," *Social Education* 58 (1988): 390–391.

10. Antarctica holds most of the world's freshwater, in the form of ice. Napoleon was defeated at Waterloo, Belgium. Alaska's state motto is "North to the future."

11. B. B. Tye, "The Deep Structure of Schooling," *Phi Delta Kappan* 69 (1987): 281–284.

12. J. A. Batesky, "Twelve Tips for Better Discipline," *Contemporary Education* 57 (1986): 98–99.

13. T. J. Lasley, "Research Perspectives on Classroom Management," *Journal of Teacher Education* 32, no. 2 (1981): 14–17.

14. E. Duckworth, "Teaching as Research," *Harvard Educational Review* 56 (1986): 481–495.

15. R. N. Caine and G. Caine, *Making Connections: Teaching and the Human Brain* (Menlo Park, CA: Addison-Wesley, 1994).

16. Caine and Caine, 115.

17. Caine and Caine, 143.

18. Caine and Caine, 156.

19. M. P. Brady and P. L. Gunter, *Integrating Moderately and Severely Handicapped Learners: Strategies That Work* (Springfield, IL: Charles C Thomas, 1985).

20. B. S. Bloom, *Human Characteristics and School Learning* (New York: McGraw-Hill, 1976).

21. B. Shaw, *Pygmalion* (New York: Penguin Books, 1913/1951), 97–98. Reprinted with permission of the Society of Authors on behalf of the Bernard Shaw Estate.

22. R. Rosenthal and L. Jacobson, *Pygmalion in the Classroom: Teacher Expectation and Pupils' Intellectual Development* (New York: Holt, Rinehart and Winston, 1968).

23. J. E. Brophy and T. L. Good, "Teacher Expectations: Beyond the Pygmalion Effect," *Phi Delta Kappan* 54 (1972): 276–278.

24. T. L. Good, "Teacher Expectations and Student Perceptions: A Decade of Research," *Educational Leadership* 38 (1981): 415–422.

25. G. Wells, *The Meaning Makers* (Portsmouth, NH: Heinemann Educational Books, 1986).

26. Wells, 50.

27. L. Canter, *Assertive Discipline: A Take-Charge Approach for Today's Educator* (Seal Beach, CA: Canter and Associates, 1976).

28. J. Gottman and N. Silver, *Why Marriages Succeed or Fail* (New York: Simon and Schuster, 1994).

29. G. Prince, W. Weaver, and K. Logan-Prince, "Liberating Creativity and Learning," in *Creative Education: Educating a Nation of Innovators*, ed. Vincent Nolan (London: Synectics Education Initiative, 2000), 14.

30. J. McTigue and J. Schollenberger, "Why Teach Thinking: A Statement of Rationale," in *Developing Minds: A Resource Book for Teaching*, ed. A. L. Costa (Alexandria, VA: Association for Supervision and Curriculum Development, 1985).

31. J. Little, *School Success and Staff Development: The Role of Staff Development in Urban Desegregated Schools*, Final report of the National Institute of Education (Boulder, CO: Center for Action Research, 1981).

32. C. M. Santa, "Changing Content Instruction through Action Research," *Reading Teacher* 40 (1987): 434–438.

33. L. M. Anderson, *Student Responses to Classroom Instruction* (East Lansing: Institute for Research on Teaching, Michigan State University, 1981).

34. L. W. Anderson, *Teachers, Teaching, and Educational Effectiveness* (Columbia: University of South Carolina, College of Education, 1982).

35. J. Dewey, *Democracy and Education* (New York: Free Press, 1916), 209.

36. John Abbott, "To Be Intelligent," *Educational Leadership* 54 (March 1997): 8.

37. C. Fisher, R. Marliave, and N. Filby, "Improving Teaching by Increasing Academic Learning Time," *Educational Leadership* 37 (October 1979): 52–54.

38. R. J. Yinger, "Learning the Language of Practice," *Curriculum Inquiry* 17 (1987): 293–318.

39. D. N. Perkins and G. Salomon, "Teaching for Transfer," *Educational Leadership* 46 (September 1988): 22–32.

Putting It All Together

Matching Objectives to Instructional Models

In Part Three, we exemplified the principles and practices advocated in Parts One and Two. Our examples came from various grade levels. We then presented a more general list of attitudes and practices that make a good teacher. Every teacher wishes to improve in the science and the art of instructional practice, and the case studies presented here, set against our general suggestions for creating a positive learning environment, are intended to assist in that improvement.

In our presentation of these three case studies, we intentionally varied the manner in which the steps were followed, precisely because there is no one prescribed formula to reach a successful instructional plan. One might rigidly follow a set of prescribed procedures and, without a spirit of creativity and enthusiasm, have a very negative teaching experience.

Our intentions through this book have been to suggest procedures for planning, selecting, and utilizing instructional models and to describe behaviors for interacting with learners in the classroom. In our many years of experience working with teachers and prospective teachers, we have found that the spirit of adventure, the intellectual excitement, and the creative innovations that they bring to the task are what make any set of procedures work in the classroom.

INDEX

PAUL TOURNIER'S
MEDICINE
OF THE
WHOLE PERSON

PAUL TOURNIER'S
MEDICINE
OF THE
WHOLE PERSON

39 essays
honoring the founder of
a school of medical practice
dedicated to treating each patient
as a human being

WORD BOOKS, PUBLISHER, WACO, TEXAS

PAUL TOURNIER'S
MEDICINE OF THE WHOLE PERSON

First Printing—April 1973
Second Printing—August 1973

Copyright © 1973 by Word, Incorporated
Waco, Texas 76703

Library of Congress catalog card number: 73-76259
Printed in the United States of America

*Lovingly dedicated
to Paul Tournier
on the occasion of his
seventy-fifth birthday*

Contents